MEMORIOUS DISCOURSE

MEMORIOUS DISCOURSE

Reprise and Representation
in Postmodernism

Christian Moraru

Madison • Teaneck
Fairleigh Dickinson University Press

Associated University Presses
2010 Eastpark Boulevard
Cranbury, NJ 08512

The paper used in this publication meets the requirements of the American National Standard for Permanence of Paper for Printed Library Materials Z39.48-1984.

Library of Congress Cataloging-in-Publication Data

Moraru, Christian
  Memorious discourse : reprise and representation in postmodernism / Christian Moraru.
    p.   cm.
  Includes bibliographical references (p.   ) and index.
  ISBN 0-8386-4086-9 (alk. paper)
    1. Postmodernism (Literature)   2. Memory in literature.   I. Title.
PN98.P67M67   2005
809'.9113—dc22   2005010155

PRINTED IN THE UNITED STATES OF AMERICA

The "reality" of "actuality"—however individual, irreducible, stubborn, painful or tragic it may be—only reaches us through fictional devices. The only way to analyse it is through a work of resistance, of vigilant counter-interpretation.

—Jacques Derrida, "Deconstruction and Actuality"

The world is memory.

—Kathy Acker, *Don Quixote, Which Was a Dream*

The work was all the more dangerous for not being new.

—Don DeLillo, *Cosmopolis*

Contents

Preface

THIS BOOK HAS AN INTERESTING BIOGRAPHY (WELL, WHICH DOES NOT?).
For a while, *Memorious Discourse* competed for my time with my previous monograph on postmodernism, *Rewriting: Postmodern Narrative
and Cultural Critique in the Age of Cloning*, and has been until recently
vying for my stamina and writing hours with another project of comparable scope. No doubt, there were "setbacks" in this contest as
Rewriting and other things came out ahead of *Memorious Discourse*.
But the latter has managed to hang in there and convince its author
that the issues it raises remain of vital importance.

Postmodernism, I have come to see more and more clearly as a
result of the thinking (and thinking over) that went into the book, is
anything but ahistorical, a culture without memory or dispassionate
exercise in political apathy. In fact, the opposite seems to be true, at
least if we read carefully—yes, "closely"—the writers and theorists
convoked below. As I keep insisting, the postmodern fundamentally
rests upon a complex "engagement" with the world, upon a relational pathos that renders postmodernism's texts, tunes, and art objects deeply "dialogic," as we used to say back in the Bakhtinian
eighties. In postmodern discourse, I listen, to recall Roland Barthes,
for the "rustle of language," but also for the murmur of culture and
history and the frissons of politics, albeit indirectly, intertextually,
by way of other texts and visions. These representations are *reprised*,
"remembered" and thus reenacted but not without alteration, as
postmodernism spins its own stories, *memoriously*.

Over the years, a number of friends and colleagues have encouraged
me to pursue this notion systematically, and here I cannot but recognize just a few. Once more, Matei Calinescu has been helpful in
more ways than I can name. I also want to thank the following individuals and institutions: Brian Richardson, David Herman, Paul Maltby, Marjorie Perloff, Jeffrey R. Di Leo, and my colleague, Kelley
Griffith (for calling my attention to Nicole Mones's first novel); Dr.
Harry Keyishian, Director of Fairleigh Dickinson University Press,
for his constant, patient guidance; Raymie E. McKerrow, reader at

FDU, who has offered detailed and apt criticism of the original manuscript; Denise Baker and James Evans, former English Department Heads at University of North Carolina, Greensboro; also from UNCG, I received a 2004 Summer Excellence Fellowship and a 2002–2003 Research Excellence Award; the UNCG College of Arts and Sciences Dean's Merit Awards for Research and Publication for 2002 and 2004 made a difference, too. It was a great honor to be the recipient of all these UNCG stipends and awards. Along the same lines, it gives me pleasure to acknowledge the assistance extended by the University of North Carolina Chapel Hill Center for Slavic, Eurasian, and East European Studies, whose fellow I have been since 1999. I thank the Center's Director, Dr. Robert Jenkins, for his generosity.

Like the other projects with which this book has been in "competition" since 1998, when UNCG became my academic home, *Memorious Discourse* reflects my teaching closely. Thus, I continue to be indebted to my students, especially to the graduate students from my spring 2002–fall 2004 postmodern literature and theory seminars, Studies in Contemporary and Postmodern American Literature, Studies in Contemporary Literary and Cultural Theory, Modern Literary Theory, and American Prose after 1900. Finally, my thanks go to my family—my wife, Camelia, my daughter, Maria, and my sister-in-law, Liliana—for bearing with me all these years.

While this book does not reproduce previously published articles properly speaking, some of its chapter sections rework or expand texts or portions of texts that initially came out as follows: 1995. "Time, Writing, and Ecstasy in *Speak, Memory*: Dramatizing the Proustian Project." *Nabokov Studies* 2:173–90; 1997a. "Consuming Narratives: Don DeLillo and 'Lethal' Reading." *The Journal of Narrative Technique* 27 (2):190–206; 1997c. " 'Zonal' Ethics: *Gravity's Rainbow*, Dislodged Subjects, and Infernal Technology." *Canadian Review of Comparative Literature* 24 (2):263–81; 2000a. " 'Vile Scripts.' Games of Double-Crossing in Nabokov's 'The Assistant Producer.' " In *Vladimir Nabokov's Short Stories*, ed. Steven G. Kellman and Irvin Malin, 173–87. Amsterdam: Rodopi; 2001. "Intertextual Bodies: Three Steps on the Ladder of Posthumanity." *Intertexts* 5 (1):46–60; 2001. "The Theater of Genre: David Antin, Narrativity, and Selfhood." *Review of Contemporary Fiction* 21 (1):82–94. I should also mention three short pieces from *Names*, parts of which have been worked over and into chapter 2: 1996. "Reading the Onomastic Text: 'The Politics of the Proper Name' in Toni Morrison's *Song of Solomon*." *Names* 44 (3):189–204; 1997b. Review of *On the Name* by Jacques Derrida.

Names 45 (1):67–72; 2000b. "'We Embraced Each Other by Our Names': Lévinas, Derrida, and the Ethics of Naming." *Names* 48 (1):49–58. I am grateful for the editors' permission to use all these materials. Likewise, I thank David Antin for allowing me to quote substantially from his works, especially from *talking at the boundaries* and *what it means to be avant-garde*. Finally, Rodney Graham has been kind enough to let me reproduce a photo image of his "Rheinmetall/ Victoria 8, 2003" installation series on the dust jacket of the book.

A last note, on translations: whenever I do not indicate otherwise, all translations are mine.

MEMORIOUS
DISCOURSE

Prologue: Postmodern Representation: Cultural Politics after "Originality"

> In any instance of at least written language, there is no such thing as a delivered presence, but a *re-presence*, or a representation.
> —Edward Said, *Orientalism*

"Origination" and "Reprise": Two Contending Paradigms of Representation

Casting aside the high esteem for rules and the "masters" who applied them, the moderns make originality the utmost gauge of artistic accomplishments, rendering it synonymous to creativity. And if to author involves representing the world, or *a* world, if to create means creating representations even after the vocabulary of romantic criticism switched to "expression," then in modernism authoring amounts to putting out *original* representations, presupposes the ability to literally *originate* them. According to the authorship paradigm revolving around originality and because, within this framework, the author holds the imaginative monopoly of representation, the latter originates in the author, and, vice versa, the author originates it, designates representation's origin, originating site, or "source." Built into this privileged position, deriving, that is, from the ideology of authorship as origination, are cultural, economic, and legal entitlements, which the modern author does not hesitate to claim. As Michel Foucault reminds us in his widely quoted essay "What Is an Author?," the rise of the modern notion of authorship goes hand in hand with the setting up of "a system of ownership and strict copyright rules" toward the end of the eighteenth century (1993, 124–25). At that turning point in Western cultural history, property and the proprietor-author as origin(ating) genius became the linchpin of romantic aesthetics, which thus found itself in an awkward position, both at loggerheads with, and akin to, early capitalism.

Today, in "late" capitalism's postmodernity more than ever be-

15

fore, Foucault's archeology of authorship, authorial origin, and property can provide us with the tools to think through the plethora of depropriations/appropriations at play in literature, painting, architecture, film, video, fashion, design, or advertising. Many contemporary authors forsake the modern idea of authorship rooted in the author as representation's *primum movens*—or "ultima Thule" perhaps, discourse's ultimate origin. This author is dead, Barthes announced in a famous poststructuralist obituary (2000, 149). Since authors do not "own" (147) language nor any linguistic constructs such as literary representations, since it is language that speaks through them and not the other way around, authors cannot be the origins of representations. Consequently, representations of life in a certain work and generally that work itself cannot be traced "theologically" to an originating "Author-God." In actuality, the work—the text, rather—is a "tissue of quotations drawn from the innumerable centres of culture." Downgraded to "scriptor," the Author is that "instance" that assembles these quotes, weaves them into his or her *textum* (tissue), ripping off, as it were, the "immense dictionary" (149) of culture and tradition, other authors and their texts. This process is hardly "original." Or, it foregrounds ever-receding origins because what the scriptor does to his or her precursors, to the textual archive generally, these precursors have done to theirs, and so on, ad infinitum.

As I will show at length, with postmodern authors or scriptors, representation-as-repetition challenges representation-as-origination. They set forth the alternate model of an *esthétique du recyclage*, a whole aesthetics of recycling, as Guy Scarpetta asserts in *L'Artifice* (1988, 121) and *L'Impureté* (1985, 73, 381). Anything but "neoclassical" or humbly imitative, driven by a complex cultural-aesthetic agenda, this model plays upon discriminate and polemical "repetition," upon a critical *reprise*, to borrow—or *reprise*, in my turn—a term from music and adapt it to underscore the strategic difference toward which postmodernism's repetitive acts are frequently geared. Built into this difference is a paradoxical yet real possibility: while romantic-modernist "invention" may on closer inspection come off less radical and innovative, more repetitive aesthetically and ideologically than usually thought, postmodernism's self-acknowledged *reprises* ever so often *surprise* us with their powerful, unorthodox deviations from the "model," with their unexpected plot twists, media mixes, and other deflections, inflections, and irreverent revisions, both textual and contextual, sociocultural.

Yet it is with the romantics and their modernist heirs that we officially live in a "culture of originals," or presumed originals, rather, as Mahler, Duchamp, Joyce, Pound, Eliot, Valéry, and Thomas Mann teach us. Postmodernism acknowledges, instead, that "there is very little pure invention in culture," as Stephen Greenblatt insists (2000, 504). So the logic of postmodern representation speaks to a "culture of the copy" to quote the title of Hillel Schwartz's 1996 book, where copy does not mean copy of "nature," untainted mimesis. For, Greenblatt also observes, there is no mimesis without cultural and textual exchange. That is to say, all representations cannot but incorporate previous efforts to interpret, imagine, and otherwise capture the world. But this is, I contend, primarily a postmodern realization, a belief that postmodern authors act on. In the "culture of the copy" thus understood, aggressive, if "inventive," "original" reproduction/appropriation of originals actually uncovers the reprise camouflaged in every origin, shows à la Foucault that "[o]rigin, for man, is much more the way in which man in general, any man, articulates himself upon the already-begun of labour, life, and language" (1994, 330). Again, this is a more recent, postmodern view of origination and historicity. Shared by many writers and artists of our time, this is also the reason they often attempt to deflate the "modern myth that authorship consists in an individual act of origination" (Woodmansee 1994, 21).

But how significant is this attack? Which are its practical gains? In "Appropriation and the Loss of Authenticity," a chapter in her book on the American art of the past decades, Eleanor Heartney concludes that "[w]ith the eighties, we have finally reached the stage where the very notion of artistic originality is suspect" (1997, 11). Nor does she find the "tactic" of cultural appropriation bespeaking this suspicion truly meaningful (12), which explains why she calls postmodern appropriation an "empty game" (15) and blames it for the shortage of "authenticity" in our culture.

I beg to differ. Postmodern representation, representation that "appropriates," represents life quite "naturally," after all, albeit through representations of life, according to John Barth (1984, 72). I would only add here, and argue more substantially later on, that in appropriating previous representations, representation often operates critically. Granted, it will always be a controversial, Janus-faced notion, as Judith Butler acknowledges in *Gender Trouble*. No doubt, representation illustrates and activates the *normative* function of language, trades in and upon conventional, socially palatable, cliché-type descriptions, which are as many already negotiated mimetic agreements. Representation tends to enforce such agreements rather than question them. At the same time, it disputes them. As I contend, it frequently turns against them, their premises, and against its own shoring up (reprise) of these premises. For representation, particularly *as* postmodern representation, habitually represents either more or less than it intends or is presumed to represent. It is not "exhaustion" that postmodern literature often conveys, but "replenishment" (Barth 1984, 206), a novel sense of originality and authenticity, literary, cultural, as well as political. Let me clarify this briefly, also with help from Foucault.

In "The Political Technology of Individuals," a piece from the 1988 anthology, *Technologies of the Self,* Foucault confesses that his struggle to rethink the genealogy of identity speaks to a broader attempt at "showing how we have indirectly constituted ourselves through the exclusion" (146) of others. Now, it seems to me that he builds his authorship paradigm along similar lines. He demonstrates that modern authorship is just another *institution that operates through mechanisms of exclusion.* The great excluded—secluded, ignored, swept under the rug, "institutionalized" metaphorically speaking—is that which unsettles the modern myths of creativity, originality, authenticity, novelty, and artistic prop(ri)erty; it is the textual trace, the pre-text, the inter-text, that which has been borrowed, "pinched," and appropriated from others wittingly or unwittingly, hence, the textual otherness subversively inscribed into the majesty of self-begotten, "original" sameness. Make no mistake: intertextuality is not just another hat for "influence." With influence, modernism can cope by simply turning its back to such a slavishly mimetic call. In effect, the modern genius comes along to deflect or "sublimate" influences like a latter-day alchemist. But the text as intertext is a far more troublesome affair. If a text is indeed a *textum,* a *fabricated* "tissue" of texts, idioms, languages—let alone "topoi," as classical aesthetics already allowed—then that genius, the one who "authenticates," "originates," "authors," and "authorizes," proves a fiction. The final product, the text as intertext and re-textualization, no longer refers back to an ultimate, univocal, unified source. The work as intertext de-authorizes itself and its author as supreme, stand-alone authority of the text and its meaning.

Critics such as Mikhail M. Bakhtin, Julia Kristeva, Jacques Derrida, Barthes, and Wolfgang Iser stress the literary-linguistic intertextuality of authorship, replace the author as origin or presence *behind* the text with a "posthumanist" model that views the author, the text's originating site and womb of meaning, as either semiotic play or reading effect, both textual categories, neither traceable to a pre-textual source. Along similar lines, Foucault and Foucauldians like Edward Said and Greenblatt, New Historians, and cultural critics set greater store on the social intertextuality or construction of the author. We have noticed, modern and, inside modernity, modernist worshipping of invention, originality, and the new *plays down* such construction. Reacting to modernist aesthetics, postmodernism provides for an acknowledgment of the *reprised*—for a spectacular return of the *repressed*, for a textual and cultural *revenant* and its haunting ontology, or, "hauntology," as Derrida writes in *Specters of Marx* (1994, 6). Postmodern critics and artists *play up*, systematically uncover, as I demonstrate in *Memorious Discourse*, the fictionality, the "constructedness" of creativity, authorship, and subjectivity largely speaking. To do so, they set off appropriation, deliberate borrowing, theft, piracy, recirculation, and remake as prime, self-conscious, often ironic *modi operandi*. Of course, such manufacturing protocols of reprise are by no means unprecedented. But, first, the protocols of authorship have never been more insistently formulated, shown off in the very body of the authored work than in postmodernism. Second, the flaunting of the constructedness of the work and its author may—and ordinarily does—serve a greater goal. Cultural appropriation can be a political move, a multiply revisionary undertaking, as I have argued in *Rewriting*.

Rewriting has a precise focus, literally spelled out in its title: acts of re-writing, of narrative repetition that rework former texts for ideologically critical purposes. *Memorius Discourse* backtracks a little to ascertain that the larger issue at stake here is representation. In other words, what I tackle in this new book is postmodern representation seized—in theory and practice—in its full, thorny complexity. On the one hand, postmodern representation re-presents, recovers— and thereby operates—intertextually, retrieving texts from our textual archive. As I stress across the following chapters, whatever "happens" in a postmodern text is hardly straight-out "reflection" of some preexistent, "natural," "bare," or "genuine" occurrence safely outside textuality, styles, conventions, regimens of discourse, culture. It follows that, on the other hand, postmodern representation does not "represent," if we take, as many have, representation and mimesis to be synonymous and, further, if we understand mimesis in the imitative-specular sense uncomplicated by the post-Aristotelian tradition.[1] It is the non-Platonic tradition of mimesis, however, in which twice-removed-from-the Ideas discourse, representation of a representation, does not merely and helplessly reflect empirical objects, that has enabled critics like Jerry A. Varsava to ascribe mimetic value to postmodern fiction (1990, ix–xi, 7–40). As Varsava insists, "Postmodern fiction is a *representation* of th[e] questioning of the values and preoccupations of our epoch; in this lies its mimesis, its mimetic function" (182). A case in point, Gilbert Sorrentino's 1979 bookish tour-de-force, *Mulligan Stew*, accommodates, in Varsava's view, both intertextuality and mimesis.

I would take a further step and propose that social mimesis in postmodernism obtains *through* intertextuality. Plato charged art with second-degree representation (imitation), which implied a multiple liability: aesthetic, moral, political, and ontological. Saliently anti-Platonic, generally antimetaphysical, postmodernism renders the liability an asset and defining platform, suggesting that Plato's analysis of mimesis, and both idealistic and realistic aesthetic doctrines do not reach deep enough, fail to take into account the *third-degree* representation at play in discourse. What this line of thought does not recognize, the postmoderns offer and I reiterate throughout the book, is that, to represent "real" things and situations, representation must work its way through, first engage with, literary and cultural texts, stylistic codes, and representation models—in brief, other representations. Plato posited, outside and before mimesis, an origin, center, or model for artists' mimetic activities; the postmoderns make no bones about sharing Derrida's belief that there is no such center prior, external to, or above structures and structuring, textuality, representation—no representable object that has not been fashioned by representation already.

Richard Powers's 2000 novel, *Plowing the Dark*, devotes some smart pages to this anti-Platonic rebuttal. The book tears into the "second-degree" argument explicitly by suggesting that Plato's cave should be replaced in our critical imaginary by the Lascaux cave (2000, 41). In the *Republic*'s metaphysical-aesthetic allegory, the shapes on the wall are, or are thought to be, things, images of the Ideas. Read through Powers's Lascaux, these shapes appear for what they are, namely, images of things, images of images of the Ideas. For what we see on the walls of the Lascaux cave is not images of the Ideas—a particular, living bison is an *eidolon* of the "Idea" of Bison, Plato would say—but indeed images of images of the Ideas. These pictures represent representations, are *re-presentations* of bisons, "cop[ies] of cop[ies]," therefore constitute "a debasement of the debasement of the Forms" (40). In fact, the software engineers in Powers's novel add another re-presentational layer to the Lascaux image model. Instead of using realistic pictures, video, and film footage to carry through their virtual reality project, they hire Adie, a painter capable to mimic, to draw—quite literally—upon the "pantheon" of pictorial styles (41). So the impressionist, surrealist, or, say, Rousseau le Douanier-like images she would "create" or re-create, rather, images of older artistic images, would be even farther removed from what Adie's "paintings" depict, or, they would re-present first and foremost in order to "just" represent something or somebody; they would paint previous paintings and pictorial styles. Nor would this be a shortcoming. The engineers understand that perfect ("uncanny") imitation of a particular thing entails, if not requires, "perfect parody" (41), collage, tapping into artistic-cultural memory, into the history of that thing's representation. With them and other postmoderns like them, appropriation, modification, and cross-graining of available images and techniques become the techniques of a new originality—postmodern originality, now determined, and acknowledged, as masterful, if "differential," "original" reprise, as deft *ars combinatoria*.

POSTMODERNISM THE MEMORIOUS: A CRITICAL METAPHOR

In this book, I define postmodernism as *memorious discourse*. Encapsulating postmodernism's distinctive relatedness, the formula calls attention to the postmodern representation chain, that is, foregrounds postmodern representation as reprise, as representation of other representations, in brief, as re-presentation in the non-Platonic sense specified above. When describing an object, narrating an event, or "reproducing" a social mechanism à la Varsava, postmodernism re-collects, remembers *and* gathers together (collagelike or otherwise), summons before its readership textual and nontextual, always past representations of other objects, events, and social structures—and, we shall see before long, this intertextual remembrance of things literary takes up striking forms even in self-acknowledgedly autobiographical works that do purport to record somebody's "real life" rather than fictions (intertexts). Barthes concludes that "*writing* can no longer designate an operation of recording, notation, representation, 'depiction'" (2000, 149). Yet what if postmodernism bestows upon "recording" or "representing" a memorious meaning? If we entertained this possibility, as I am, we could seize upon representation in postmodernism as a case of prodigious, "compulsive" cultural recollection.

Borges's fictions, in particular "Funes el memorioso"—"Funes the Memorious," from whose title I have borrowed mine[2]—furnish good illustrations of such a memory disorder, as well as the unifying figure of my book, the critical metaphor that I "appropriate" in my turn loosely to approach postmodern theory and fiction. In fact, disorder may not be the right word here since Funes's memory retrieves a thoroughly integrated, systematic, and infinite world.

Taking to a Kabbalistic extreme Marcel Proust's spontaneous memory, one present fact or detail involuntarily leads in Funes's endlessly relational universe to a "thing (in the) past," and that to another, and so on. Remembrance reaches deeper and deeper and concurrently branches off, in an equally ceaseless search for an ever-elusive origin or original memory:

> With one quick look, you and I perceive three wineglasses on a table; Funes perceived every grape that had been pressed into the wine and all the stalks and tendrils of its vineyard. He knew the forms of the clouds in the southern sky on the morning of April 30, 1882, and he could compare them in his memory with the veins in the marbled binding of a book he had seen only once, or with the feathers of spray lifted by an oar on the Río Negro on the eve of the Battle of Quebracho. Nor were those memories simple—every visual image was linked to muscular sensations, thermal sensations, and so on. He was able to reconstruct every dream, every daydream he had ever had. Two or three times he had reconstructed an entire day; he had never once erred or faltered, but each reconstruction has itself taken an entire day. (Borges 1998, 135)

As we learn in this passage, an image catches Funes's eye, and he actually sees (represents) it by comparing, and thus linking, it to a preceding image or representation, and so on. His perception, his ability to represent, categorize, and understand things, is memorious, works as associative remembrance, by "quoting" other, antecedent representations, through which he takes the surrounding world in. Thus, similar to the infinite books or libraries Borges dreams up in "The Book of Sand," "The Library of Babel," "The Total Library," and elsewhere as "countertrope[s] for Plato's myth of the cave" (O'Sullivan 1990, 114), Funes's sprawling memory provides me with a trope of postmodern discourse as *representation that operates digressively, and conspicuously so, through other representations,* picture that latches onto other pictures to bring its object to life. It is through this metaphor that I try to capture the relational, or, better still, interrelational nature of postmodern representation, its quintessential intertextuality. This is representation, language generally, that, in saying itself, says the other, as it were, re-cites other words, speaks other idioms, *the already- and the elsewhere-spoken and written.*

Funes could own, like Angela Carter's Desiderio in *The Infernal Desire Machines of Doctor Hoffman:* "I remember everything" (1994, 11). But, Milan Kundera writes in *Ignorance,* one of his most memorious books, "If someone could retain in his memory everything he had experienced, if he could at any time call up any fragment of his past, he would be nothing like human beings: neither his loves nor his friendship would resemble ours" (2000, 123). Nor is Funes everyman; his "total recall" is undoubtedly a superhuman feat. It surely is impossible to capture in writing the absolute "memoriousness" of language, the simultaneous co-presence of all representations in whatever I may be representing right now on paper, in my poem or short story. For one thing, this is because, as Borges himself points out in "The Aleph" à la Lessing, "language is *successive*" (1998, 283), runs through a string of present moments that pass and become past as soon as they have been completed. When we speak—refer to, represent—we cannot but speak about the past, refer to, and represent something no longer with us, in the ahead-pressing (ex-pressive) present of vocal or written expression. We could adapt a Saussurean-Jakobsonian terminology to suggest that postmodern representation works "syntagmatically," by incorporating surrounding representations, and "paradigmatically," by rolling prior representations into itself. Occasionally, and for the sake of the discussion, I may accept this distinction in *Memorious Discourse.* Otherwise, the syntagmatic and the paradigmatic sequences of representations no longer stand apart—or they do, but only theoretically—if "present" representations turn into past representations as soon as the "poetic function" of my unfolding sonnet, tale, or other kind of representation considers, taps, combines, and incorporates them (Jakobson 2000, 38). For all representations recuperated by my text, be those the images of trees and cars I am seeing through my window, are already past with respect to what I am putting on paper this very moment. Indeed, even "surrounding," "contemporary" representations "age out" instantly, get sucked into our cultural history and memory as I turn to them. Consequently, my text, my image is bound to always "come after."

Postmodernism, I submit, assumes this belatedness by acknowledging the past as its own, and by retrieving it. It goes without saying, this memorious retrieval is not absolute. Unlike the imaginary Aleph and no matter how closely it may emulate the Aleph's capaciousness, a "real" postmodern text is only potentially—theoretically, as I say below—the "point" (Borges 1998, 280), the textual unit that contains all points, all texts, all representations ever produced. Postmodern discourse recovers and absorbs with sufficient, reasonable obviousness a limited number of prior discourses. So infinitely memorious representation remains a utopia, outside the reach of human representation. Unlike Funes's, our memory itself is also an expert if unforgiving editor, steadily blue-penciling its own manuscript, discarding whole chapters of our lives into forgetfulness's waste bin.

Still, Funes's exceptional case helps me make my own. And I make it by recognizing, accordingly, that postmodernism is not absolutely memorious, or it is so just in theory. In practice, its critics are usually satisfied, as I am in the chapters ahead, if they can uncover at least one prior representation or text to which a novel or a play refers back in order to set itself up as a novel, play, or other literary representation. What this means is that I take up the Borgesian metaphor with a grain of salt: for reasons that have to do with analysis, I rein in the ever-receding play of this trope. In other words, the critical metaphor unifying my project is—must be—a "soft" version of Borges's image.

A feature of discourse generally, as I pointed out earlier, the inherently memorious texture, the intertextuality of representation, becomes dominant and distinctive in postmodernism, its unmistakable signature. In effect, in postmodernism intertextuality and representation virtually overlap, similarly to what happens in Powers and not unlike Funes's narrative "reconstruction." Narratologists such as Tzvetan Todorov and Gérard Genette would tell us that Borges's "artifice" documents a rare case of "duration," where the narrated event and the event's narration span the same amount of time. But we do know that most storytellers narrate selectively. Closely related to the better-known "ficcion" "Pierre Menard, Author of the *Quixote*," Borges's later memorious parable, "Shakespeare's Memory," stresses precisely this aspect:

> De Quincey says that our brain is a palimpsest. Every new text covers the previous one, and is in its turn covered by the text that follows—but all-powerful Memory is able to exhume any impression, no matter how momentary it might have been, if given sufficient stimulus. To judge by the will [Shakespeare] left, there had been not a single book in Shakespeare's house, not even the Bible, and yet everyone is familiar with the books he so often repaired to: Chaucer, Gower, Spenser, Christopher Marlowe, Holingshed's *Chronicle*, Florio's Montaigne, North's Plutarch. I possessed, at least potentially, the memory that had been Shakespeare's; the reading (which is to say the rereading) of those volumes would, then, be the stimulus I sought. . . . The man who acquires an encyclopedia does not thereby acquire every line, every paragraph, every page, every illustration; he acquires the *possibility* of becoming familiar with one and another of those things. (1998, 512)

Postmodern representation turns this possibility into practice— again, if not into an achieved utopia of cultural memory's *musée imaginaire*, then into a characteristic project. Postmodern authors, I demonstrate, are memorious writers who remember (texts) in order to—or because they—represent (the world). We shall see especially in chapters 4 and 5, it is in this sense only that whatever postmodernism presents is bound to be, one way or another, a re-presentation. As in Nietzsche's rhetorical analogy from "On Truth and Lying in an Extra-Moral Sense," the re-presentation side—the one bearing inscriptions of former acts of presentation—wears out progressively (1989, 250) and becomes less and less readable. It never wears away completely, though. It just calls for increasingly sustained acts of reading liable to discern, and resuscitate, representation's memory—its intertextual otherness, or, originality, its cultural indebtedness.

My book makes clear that this genealogy of representation—a cross section or X-ray of sorts—involves two notions seemingly at odds. Theorized by poststructuralism, the first one has been adopted widely in postmodern debates. The second speaks more accurately to the profound nature of postmodernism, at least to postmodernism as I see it. Thus, on the one side, postmodern theorists and to some extent writers themselves have intimated that theirs is mission impossible: they set out to speak the unspeakable, write the unreadable, represent the unrepresentable. It would seem that they always fall short, ever testing, bumping against the limits of representation and never quite breaking through. Critics have deplored the negative phenomenology of lack, absence, surface, simulation, and failure supposedly undergirding and dooming postmodern representation. On the other side, the same critics have been thrown by the latter's cultural "abundance" and "thickness," by its constructedness, by what in representation itself appears to be too much, "excessive" socially and politically as our time's postmodern writing goes to show that fiction, the way we imagine us and the world around us, does bear upon how we live, and vice versa. Thus, literary intertextuality and wider cultural intertextuality, the archival memory of the past and the evolving imagination of the present on the brink of becoming past and this past's recollection team up to foster postmodern, memorious discourse.

On closer inspection, this "lack-surplus," "un(der)representation-overrepresentation" contradiction looks less unequivocal. For at play here is a *productive* lack, a lack that, according to Derrida, must be "supplemented" and thus cannot but result in semiotic "overabundance" (1979, 423), in representational excess. Consequently, the unrepresentable should be understood throughout this book as promising a nonimitative and pluralist space of play, a field monopolized by no single, ultimate, stable, or pure representation.

Underpinning postmodern discourse, the unrepresentable does not undercut it. On the contrary, we see especially in chapter 5, the unrepresentable affords this discourse, *presents* or *offers* it as a domain where a host of representations, along with their memorious genealogies, cross and hence multiple interpretations can occur, can be *presented*. In the terminology of possible-worlds fictional semantics, the unrepresentable repeals the one-world model of dogmatic mimetic doctrine to bring forth *possibilities*: ontological possibilities, possibilities of being, of projecting "nonactualized possible states of affairs" or fictional world*s* (Doležel 1998, x, 16), and possibilities of making sense of these worlds. It follows that the unrepresentable is not some nonreferential, antirepresentational dead end but the opposite: that which makes representation—representation*s*—and our own representations or readings thereof ultimately possible. Preempting mimetic closure, deflecting mimesis in the narrow sense that posits the mirroring of one world by a single "suitable" image—Aristotelian *homoiosis* or medieval *adaequatio* rejected by Heidegger in "The Origin of the Work of Art" (1975, 36)—the unrepresentable opens the postmodern up to the intricate, the "abysmally" elusive and allusive, the intertextually labyrinthine.

Thus, in my memorious version and in response to the still authoritative aesthetics of reflection, on the one hand, and most critics of postmodernism, on the other, the postmodern takes in the world and its memory, becomes socially and politically relevant: not primarily as one-on-one correspondence, as a mirror and therefore stagnant, idle image of the world, but as an apparatus, a discourse machine into which writers feed other discourses or images of that world, break them down, and reconstruct them critically. Drawing upon Kristeva's militant intertextuality, Philippe Sollers has underscored that "the value of a text depends on how effectively it absorbs and destroys other texts" (1968, 75). I subscribe to his view. Deeply intertextual and therefore textually and culturally transformative, postmodern representation often works as critique.

This also indicates that *Memorious Discourse* has been written against the dogma that deems all postmodernism socially inconsequential and politically impotent. As the book will show, the logic of relatedness embedded in the memorious model of the postmodern work as net-work aims at correcting, sometimes directly, sometimes less so, the otherwise obdurate suspicions surrounding postmodernism and its alleged social and political lameness. The "ahistoricity," "short memory" charge is also countered by my reading, and valuation, of the postmodern's memoriousness, by a definition of the postmodern discourse as access to culture's treasure chest where personal and collective representations lie and await their reprise. Neither the lack of political interest in the present nor the ignorance of the past holds much water if this discourse proves tied into both the past and the present by its memorious ramifications and imbrications, whose wider, ideological implications also become apparent. With an analogy made popular by the recent movie identically titled, my book points to the memorious *matrix* underneath the postmodern text, the cultural-textual plurality out of which this text grows and to which it speaks—and even talks back. To recall Lacan, other discourses, options, values, representations, and various textual and nontextual ideological ramifications are there in my text's "signifying chain," hanging from various links, "suspended 'vertically'" (2000, 69) from them as it were, lying ensconced, almost invisibly inscribed in the body of the text, so they would have to be brought to light, excavated through a memorious kind of analysis. This invisible, compressed verticality of the past is flattened into a discourse whose otherwise actual thickness—literary and cultural memory, historical moorings in the past no less then sociopolitical plugs into the present—*Memorious Discourse* sets out to measure.

This does not mean that I will focus only, or primarily, on "political" writers and critics. Nor will I draw principally from authors of memoirs, autobiographies—from patent "memorialists." A person named Funes makes easier for us to understand how memoriousness works, but he is, as I have emphasized, a most unusual individual. Here memory is not necessarily *somebody*'s—an author's —recollection of past experiences. It is not personal reminiscence, although this can be involved, too, as we shall see in chapter 1. What I am driving at is, more broadly, a kind of generic memory of discourse, which, to personify this discourse, "remembers" other texts and discourses, existing images of the very thing it represents, *in order to* carry out this thing's very representation. What I illuminate is the "transpersonal," memorious constitution of relevant postmodern texts, autobiographical or not, and, warranted by this constitution, their connections with the neighboring world beyond the literary, beyond the aesthetic.

SCOPE, STRUCTURE, STRATEGY

To gauge the scope of memorious discourse, I turn repeatedly to postmodern, poststructuralist, and cultural critics, philosophers, and writers who have best formulated its problems and quandaries: Vladimir Nabokov, Thomas Pynchon, Don DeLillo, Philip Roth, Joseph McElroy, William Gibson, Mark Leyner, Paul Auster, David Antin, Kathy Acker, Toni Morrison, and Eva Hoffman; Emmanuel Lévinas, Jean-François Lyotard, Jean Baudrillard, Philippe Lacoue-Labarthe, Jean-Luc Nancy, Paul de Man, Foucault, and Derrida, among others. They supply various angles and vantage points from which I engage with the contemporary conundrums of representation. I listen—sometimes at length—to what they tell each other and to how they retell what others have told them, in hopes to shed light on the notions and practices that interest me here. I pay attention to the direct and indirect dialogue of theory and literature in the spacious arena of postmodernism. Therein, I come upon alliances, junctures when the postmodern appears to validate this or that hypothesis about representation and related issues, but also upon more equivocal moments that corroborate postmodern representation's unruliness, its refusal to rehearse—while re-calling—anything, including chic theories. Joining in the conversation myself, I read postmodern narrative "with" a certain theory, with a particular understanding of culture, discourse, representation, textuality, identity, and other concepts and paradigms that have gone into the poststructuralist-culturalist memorious model; conversely, I put the model to the test of postmodern narrative.

That is to say, I develop my argument no less memoriously. I assume its derivation, its deliberate, tactical *dérive* ("drift" and "detour" in French) through others' texts, through other fictional and theoretical representations, which I read, re-presenting them closely and critically, and writing "in their margins," as it were. If true to, and truly about, its topic, this book on the memorious postmodern should not have—and could not have—evaded the circumlocutory route of re-presentation. This is certainly a formal matter, a matter of poetics, implies a recognition of how postmodern literature and culture "are made." But it is also an ethical issue because, I argue, my critical approach is warranted, in fact called for, by the intimate structure, by the very "nature" of postmodern discourse.

Specifically, this book identifies five areas in recent Continental and American theory and fiction where, it seems to me, the discursive apparatus, workings, and individualizing problems of postmodern representation come to light and lend themselves to rethinking through the Borgesian-inspired critical metaphor: (1) the postmodern memoir and "personal" literature broadly, and their rowdy habit of lying astride boundaries such as textual/intertextual, fictional/nonfictional, critical (essayistic)/autobiographical, original/derivative, poetic/narrative, and so on; (2) the use of names, or, postmodernism's onomastic discourse; (3) the rise of "posthumanity" and the ethical and philosophical questions swirling around the "subject" in the posthuman era; (4) the sticky issue of "reality" and the controversial social and political bearings of postmodern ontology; and (5) the recent comeback of the sublime problematic and the new challenges it mounts to representation, reading, and literacy.

Thus, chapter 1 offers up the hypothesis of postmodern memory, where recollection, representation of the past, proves to be another name for intertextual re-presentation, to wit, for the re-enactment of the literary past—others' past as recorded in their own autobiographical texts. A less typical case of postmodern memory and loosely related to the *postmodern memoir* is the apocryphal memoir, an openly fictional narrative published under a name different from its subject (typically a historical figure). Among prominent twentieth-century examples one usually lists Robert Graves's 1934 *I, Claudius*, Hermann Broch's 1945 *Der Tod des Vergil* (The Death of Vergil), Marguerite Yourcenar's 1951 *Mémoires d'Hadrien* (Memoirs of Hadrien), David Malouf's 1978 *An Imaginary Life*, which, like Broch's book, focuses on a Roman poet's twilight years (Ovid in Malouf), and Paul Guth's 1979 *Moi, Joséphine, impératrice* (I, Josephine, Empress), published in the "Mémoires imaginaires" (Imaginary Memoirs) series of the Parisian press Albin Michel.

Ann Armstrong Scarboro mentions Guth's work in her afterword to the English translation of Maryse Condé's 1986 novel, *Moi, Tituba, sorcière . . . noire de Salem* (I, Tituba, Black Witch of Salem) (Scarboro 1994, 221–22). An ingenious fictional revision of *The Scarlet Letter*,[3] Condé's novel both echoes Guth's title and borrows his device (Scarboro 1994, 221), as much as it does with other similar intertextual tactics and moments, from Alex Haley's *Roots* to Arthur Miller's *Crucible* (Scarboro 1994, 222). Daring and jocular, intertextuality plays a central role—including a politically central role—in the overall architecture of the book. This is the critic's main argument for *Tituba*'s postmodernity (224) but not the only one, or the strongest, I think. Intertextuality and ontology games are the two sides of the same coin, and this is, I maintain across all chapters, emblematically postmodern: as we learn in the novel's last lines, Tituba narrates her story quite literally from beyond her grave, after her execution. It is her ghost, or spirit, that tells the story. But this does not make the latter ghostwritten in the more common sense, in which works composed by somebody else are published under the deceased author's name either as an "authentic," posthumously discovered work, or as if its dead author kept writing *d'outre-tombe*, "from beyond the tomb." I allude here to Chateaubriand's famous title, but otherwise his *Mémoires* are fairly traditional, a pseudo-, or, half-pretend apocryphal memoir whose classification—and classical poetics—is complicated mainly by the author's death in 1848, when his autobiography starts coming out.

A life story that follows both in earnest and tongue-in-cheek autobiographical and storytelling formats such as Chateaubriand's and Guth's, *I, Tituba* remains visibly novelistic. Overt, self-acknowledged intertextuality (Scarboro 1994, 212) does not alter fundamentally the book's genre. Nor does it affect the way we read it, for we notice that generic divisions still hold, and so do mimetic conventions. After all, this is a book *about* Tituba as a finally exonerated protagonist of the infamous Salem witch trials, and *about* resistance to Caribbean slavery. This constitutes a first-person novel that does not signal that it might want to be *something else*, such as a true memoir, and *somebody else*'s disguised memoir to that, in spite of the literary appropriations the book performs. What haunts it is Tituba's own, posthumous voice. The novel is the theater of her return, a "Chemical Theatre" à la Peter Ackroyd's neo-Victorian, memoriously Dickensian *English Music* (1992, 2, 313, 380), in which the fundamental spectrality of postmodernism takes center stage,[4] becomes an *apparition* and *apparent*, discernible. In short, while undeniably memorious, postmodern, *I, Tituba* gives us less trouble than its relative, the postmodern memoir, or, as I call it, the *postmemoir*.[5]

With works like Nabokov's *Speak, Memory*, Auster's *Hand to Mouth*, or Norman Manea's *Hooligan's Return*, which openly claim to be autobiographies, memoirs, personal chronicles, something more disturbing happens, turning autobiography's mimetic convention upside down. As chapter 1 shows, autobiography—writing of the self, writing of the *writing self*—supplies Nabokov with a genre framework inside which what is remembered, reread, and even rewritten is Marcel Proust's autobiographical fiction (another instance of self-writing) as much as Nabokov's own life. This life is fictionalized, and in chapter 4 we will see how this notion also shapes Nabokov's short fiction. But here, interestingly enough, fictionality grows out of an easily identifiable preexistent text, Proust's *À la recherche du temps perdu*, so the self obtaining "in writing," textually, is considerably "borrowed," *intertextual*, and marked as such. Both the "true" self portrayed in *Speak, Memory* and the memoir altogether are to a significant extent fictions, "inventions," or, even better, "constructions" and bricolage effects, appropriations of *another* writer's inventions. Recently, Michael Marr has used the word "cryptomnesia" to suggest that even Nabokov's "mock memoir" *Lolita* stems

from an unintentional resuscitation of a "memory representation of
. . . other person's work," where the "other work" is a 1916 short
story called "Lolita," by Heinz von Lichberg (Caldwell 2004, 11).
While composing his own *Lolita*, the argument goes, Nabokov "remembered" inadvertently von Lichberg's work, which he forgot he
had ever read. With a harsher word, unpremeditated plagiarism is
the result of this curious dynamic of intertextual remembrance and
forgetfulness. However, the jury is still out on whether Nabokov did
find inspiration in the German writer's "Lolita" at all.[6] His novel
does show off its memorious, re-presentational structure, but in relation to other works, abundantly referenced and alluded to in the
text.

Unlike *Speak, Memory* and definitely unlike *Lolita*, Azar Nafisi's
2003 "memoir in books," *Reading Lolita in Tehran*, reprises both
Nabokovian texts alongside others to tell Nafisi's amazing life story.
If Pia Pera's *Lo's Diary* and Lee Siegel's *Love in a Dead Language*,
which I discuss in the epilogue, are memorious novels, Nafisi's work
is a memorious memoir where the line between critical representation (of Nabokov and other writers) and autobiographical representation is practically impossible to draw. I must stress, though, not all
memoirs are memorious even in postmodern times of epidemic
genre confusion and unrivaled transgeneric crossings. My book does
not urge us to discard the distinction between "memorial" and
"memorious," for not any act of memory is memorious (intertextual)—not any engagement with the past is a substantial engagement with (the) past('s) texts. It is in postmodernism that it
becomes saliently so. More often than not, remembrance has not
been an intertextual affair, and autobiography has focused, as I
point out above, chiefly on the writing self, has been "original" writing *about* that self. Most classical and modern memoirs possess and
act on very mimetic, referential ambitions, and so does even Ger-
trude Stein's *Autobiography of Alice B. Toklas*, where Stein recounts
her life while pretending to narrate somebody else's. Critics from
Philippe Lejeune to Paul John Eakin have insisted that underwriting
the autobiographical genre is usually a "pact" between the author
and the reader, vouching for the "referentiality" of the narrated
events, reassuring us that the text tells the life story of the person
identified as the text's author. In other words, "in order for there to
be autobiography (and personal literature generally), the *author*, the
narrator, and the *protagonist* must be identical" (Lejeune 1989, 5).
But the memoir's memorious substance, in my book's sense, fore-
closes this identity. Nabokov breaks the pact, not least the "contract
of reading" (Lejeune 1989, 28) tied into it, since his fictionalized

autobiography entails a rewriting of Proust's autobiographical fiction.

Forerunner of the more spectacular genre transgressions of the sixties and seventies, *Speak, Memory* threatens to wipe out an important formal and ontological distinction underlying much of modern literature and scholarship: fiction versus nonfiction or autobiography—autobiography as a nonfictional genre, to be more precise. In this view, I find it telling that recent attempts to reinforce the "distinction of fiction" so as to stave off further "destabilization of the borderline between fiction and nonfiction" (Ryan 1997, 165), in our case between fiction and autobiography, also build a case against postmodernism. Revealingly entitled *The Distinction of Fiction*, Dorrit Cohn's book reacts to contemporary developments in narrative and historiographical scholarship that give up inherited oppositions and categories. As she explains, "The 'distinction' that my title attributes to fiction is to be understood in two senses of the word:. *uniqueness* and *differentiation*." Intent upon proving that "fictional narrative is unique in its potential for crafting a self-enclosed universe ruled by formal patterns that are ruled out in all other orders of discourse" (1999, vii), she responds to Hayden White's "literariness of historical writing" (White 1999, ix). One of her purposes, Cohn declares in *The Distinction of Fiction*, is to show that the division between fiction and history "remains with us even (and perhaps especially) in the face of certain postmodern practices that have pretended to efface generic borderlines" (vii). Grounding her argument in the "overridingly distinctive nature of fictionality" (viii), she means to correct what Hans Veihinger called in *Die Philosophie des Als Ob* "the chaotic and perverse linguistic usage" of the term "fiction" (qtd. in Cohn 1999, 1).

I will grant "anti-panfictionalists" like Cohn or Marie-Laure Ryan that postmodern writers do give in to this sort of "perversion." As a matter of fact, they thrive on it. What is more, postmodern critics have theorized it. They have insisted that, especially in the wake of the de Manian critique of empiric reference, one cannot avoid anymore "the recognition that direct or phenomenal reference to the world means, paradoxically, the production of fiction" (Caruth, 1995, 94). Similarly, John Johnston has averred that "in a culture in which events are created or usurped in advance by their mass-media simulations, contemporary writers can no longer rely upon strategies defined by a stable opposition between the fictional and the real" (1998, 12). Yet, unlike Johnston, White, Peter Brooks, and others, Cohn recommends that we maintain "the distinction between fictional and nonfictional narrative" (1999, 54, 39), in other words, between narratives that *must* refer to the real world and those that *can but need not* (15). Cohn's examples, virtually all of them modernist, serve her well. But again, not unlike Ryan,[7] Cohn barely touches on the postmodern "transgressions" (29) of the above-mentioned genre borders. And, notably, her own analysis of genre ambiguity in Proust's novel—the ultimate modernist text—leaves us torn between the "horns of the generic dilemma" (78).

Nabokov sensed this dilemma and exploited it. And so have, even more systematically and openly, postmoderns like Eva Hoffman and David Antin, on whose works the first chapter's second and third part, respectively, focus. Thus, I move from *Speak, Memory* on to Hoffman's 1989 memoir *Lost in Translation: A Life in a New Language* because her work's ties to Nabokov are conspicuously memorious but also, and more importantly, because some of the issues briefly touched by Nabokov are here unpacked methodically, with theoretical acumen *and* in vigorous dialogue with older autobiographical representations. We shall see, if Nabokov "translated" Proust into (or as) his own memoir metaphorically speaking, Hoffman undertakes this kind of translation quite literally, more extensively, and more self-consciously. As she translates her native Polish identity into Americanness and Polish words into English to understand and express her new life, she also translates previous texts where such identity formation questions have been tackled. Therefore, her memoir is memorious. In it, personal recollection works as and through a re-collection of a whole Babel of voices and texts. This determines *Lost in Translation* as an intertextual reprise formally attuned to the new Babel of the global age, an aspect to which I come back in the epilogue, also in relation to the theme of translation as a vehicle of memorious exchanges under globalization.

The opening chapter's last section examines the narrative and, more broadly, textual-cultural production of selfhood in David Antin and the issue of generic boundaries—and boundaries in general—foregrounded by this production. Setting off sumptuous flashbacks, the latter deploys a unique model of narrativity at the crossroads of traditional genre divisions such as poetry and prose, fiction and nonfiction, criticism and literature. I use "production" in a representational as well as performative sense—both at work in the German *Vorstellung*, "representation"—because David Antin's "theater of genre" conjures up the unexpected, the unimaginable, the unrepresentable. Outside the cycle of Nabokovian intertexuality—his texts do not summon Nabokov—David Antin is even more firmly dedicated to sorting out the "trouble with postmodern representation" by further troubling it, by pushing the envelope of genre and testing the formal confines within which representation has traditionally occurred. Thus, his "boundary" talk probes the limits of what can be said and in what fashion, not least the limits of saying itself, in sum, a whole aesthetics, ontology, and politics of liminality, another pivotal concern in *Memorious Discourse*.

Chapters 2, 4, and 5 deal with these questions more directly, rendering the dialogue and interplay of poststructuralist-cultural theory and postmodern fiction increasingly evident. The second chapter examines onomastic representation and its multiply intertextual bearings upon the postmodern self. While students of literature and theory have raised onomastic issues, as far as I know there has been no sustained treatment of names in postmodern scholarship. Nor can this chapter alone fill the gap, but I do hope it paves the way to a more systematic debate along the lines of my book's broader argument. The first part of this chapter, " 'We embraced each other by our names': The Name, the Other, and the Politics of Onomastic Intertextuality," purports to clarify the relations among naming, identity, identification, representation, and the "problem of the other" in Lévinas and Derrida. As I suggest, contemporary philosophers of naming make a case for the name's memorious structure. Names are, they tell us, social glue, fundamentally relational because as they name us they relate us to other names and to the people bearing those names. My name represents me as it re-presents others, links me up to them. "In my name," the other names himself or herself, and an important responsibility stems from realizing that names, too, are intertexts, inter-onomastic constructs.

Chapter 2's second part, " 'Nom de Nom': The Unnameable and the Unspeakable," demonstrates that onomastic representation, its limits, and intertextuality also preoccupy major writers such as De-Lillo and Auster. DeLillo is literally fascinated by names, so much so that he devotes to the topic his 1989 novel, *The Names*. But this section of *Memorious Discourse* zeroes in primarily on *Ratner's Star*, an earlier, underread book. I insist here on the memorious structure of the world, characters, and their names. Drawing from Foucault and others, I scan the "horizontal" layout of DeLillo's fictional universe. I find this universe to be a *syntactic* one, organized around intertextual acts that occur on its skiddy surface at the expense of its archeological dimension, of its *semantic* depth, which, while still enigmatic, no longer ensconces meaning. Or, to put it otherwise, DeLillo suspects that meaning is relational, too, a matter of syntax, ties, collisions, and collusions: a posthermeneutic, intertextual value. This suspicion plays out in his characters' names, which boast no semantic "transcendence." All we can do is try to read them like texts alongside other texts. While pointing both to the limitations and mystery of naming, DeLillo resorts to the name as "performative" representation, "discursive construction" of the named self (Laclau 1989, ix–xv) to work out a personal understanding of what recent critics have called "posthumanist" subjectivity, or, the "post-human."

This chapter's last segment explores women's onomastic discourse. I focus here on Acker and Morrison and their memorious emphasis on the literary-cultural "engendering of names" and on the related, "storied" origin of names. I look, that is, for the stories names tell, for how they tell the memorious stories of their origins, seeking to show how those stories cannot be understood without recourse to the older stories and tales that they are enmeshed with and have "originated" them. Pursuing the memory of onomastic representation in Acker's and Morrison's novels and essays, I bring to the fore a politics of naming, "unnaming," and renaming that gets its meanings and strength from gender- and race-specific contexts and traditions.

Picking up where the DeLillo discussion left off, chapter 3, "Remembering the Posthuman: Intimations of Heterogeneity," carries on this inquiry and expands it through readings of narratives by Pynchon, Roth, McElroy, Leyner, DeLillo, and Gibson. The first section employs the "analytic of the subject" Derrida sketches out in his interview " 'Eating Well' " (1992) and in the conference on "nuclear criticism," "No Apocalypse, Not Now (Full Speed Ahead, Seven Missiles, Seven Missives)" (1984), to set up a framework for revisiting Pynchon's *Gravity's Rainbow* as a posthumanity narrative. The novel strikes me as one of the most ambitiously memorious in the postmodern canon. What Borges suggests within a few pages Pynchon does in 760, and what he does amounts essentially to limning out an apocalyptic intertextuality, a panorama of a linkage-saturated world where "everything is connected."[8] The connections may have been set up and maintained by humans, yet the human subject is no longer this world's center and origin. What we face here is a post-anthropocentric move, a leap beyond the human. I try to account for this maneuver by pondering the dehumanizing/posthumanizing role of technology, a morally ambiguous process that Pynchon both critiques and builds on. This process involves, first, a hyperbolic, deliberate augmentation of the human subject's constructedness or techno-cultural becoming, with which poststructuralist models of multiple, decentered, flowing subjectivity help us come to terms. Second, Pynchon shows that this technology-induced crisis of the

subject uncovers what the latter has never been: "original," pure
and purely rational, immaterial, uncontaminated, disembodied rationality, safely in charge. But on the ground of this postmodern and
poststructuralist realization, the posthuman subject and its agency
may not be impossible to refigure after all. *Le technologique,* as Pynchon writes, hints at the demise of the human, more exactly, the
humanist subject. Memoriously engineered *post*humans may be able
to *live* with, if not off, the consequences of this death.

  This is, in brief, the fundamentally postmodern *double bind* of Pynchon, DeLillo, Powers, Jonathan Franzen, Rushdie, or Acker: they
speak the idioms, mimic the styles, and take in the ampler "system"
that they live in but whose cultural grammar, obsessions, reflexes,
voices, and libidinal energies they harness to a critique of that system. Their texts represent, point up the vaster representational ensemble they themselves are also part of—languages, lifestyles,
histories, ideologies, mores. Yet this representation does not muzzle
dissent because neither the authors nor their works are fully determined or contained by the whole. In other words, the writers and
their texts are entwined with culture's memorious network, which
their books acknowledge, indeed, represent critically, in a discourse
itself memorious. *Memorious discourse speaks the language of what it
speaks against.* It does it from within, setting a critical tone and opening up a tentative, fluctuant enclave of resistance, a sort of "intramu-
ral" *outside inside* the represented world and against the belief put
forth by a hero in DeLillo's *Cosmopolis,* who opines that "there is no
outside [anymore]," (2003a, 90). For, indeed, this quotation reflects, as we shall note later on, the position of some of DeLillo's
characters from *Cosmopolis* and other books, not necessarily the author's. Like the texts we write, he implies, we are positioned within
social and historical intertextuality, and shrugging off our cultural
construction hardly helps. But this construction—another "grand,"
totalizing theoretical narrative after all—is neither absolute nor definitive, hence it cannot be above critical *re*-construction. In fact, it
provides the postmodern writer with the very tools for its own overhaul, which would impact the structures around us. This is how postmodern discourse turns the tables on the postmodern world it
represents. This is how the postmodern author rebuts the charge of
cultural-political complacency and "incorporation." We shall see in
chapter 5, DeLillo's *Mao II* calls Beckett the last writer society cannot
"incorporate." But the truth is, Pynchon, DeLillo, and others like
them mark off a lopsided, eccentric, and fluid space where the lin-
guistic-cultural interplay of the part and the whole can be exploited
strategically against the totalist pressure of the system.

In Roth's *The Breast,* McElroy's *Plus,* and Leyner's *Et Tu, Babe,* the representation of posthuman evolution is even more patently memorious. It is, to be more precise, a many-sided literary metamorphosis as Roth's David Kepesh metamorphoses Kafka's Gregor Samsa, and McElroy restages Beckettian situations in science fiction settings. The chapter closes with a look at DeLillo's *White Noise* and Gibson's *Neuromancer.* I unravel there—again with help from Derrida—a particular fictional "hologrammatology," or, postmodern discourse as hologramlike writing where narrative representation "reflects" a world of reflections, simulacra, effects, and "fallout," and in doing so speaks critically of, and to, a culture oversaturated with "uncritical," media-shaped images. No doubt, as Brian McHale contends in *Postmodernist Fiction,* this raises ontological issues, and DeLillo's and Gibson's texts do make for ideal opportunities to think about a postmodern ontology and its posthuman ramifications. Earlier, I mentioned Derrida's "hauntological" play. It certainly bears reiterating here, with the proviso that the ghostliness, the spectral iconology of DeLillo, Gibson, Bruce Sterling, and others like them, stems primarily from the media: the latter are no longer the message; the media are the *mediums.*

Chapters 4 and 5 scrutinize this postmodern ontology more closely. To my mind, McHale rightly insists that if *the* "postmodern question" is, "Which world is this?," then, what we must ask next is, "What is to be done in it?" (1987, 10). These two chapters, and virtually the whole book for that matter, make a case for a certain politics of the postmodern worldview—for a way of reading and assessing postmodernism's politics in some of postmodernism's most defining "documents," I should say. No doubt, this is not the *only* way to go about it. But it may have become clear by now that *Memorious Discourse* rebuts the charges of ahistoricism, cultural obliviousness, political indifference, and overall "superficiality" leveled against postmodernism. This is not—not in my reading—an irresponsible art of forgetfulness. As a matter of fact, my "memorious" thesis argues the contrary. Elsewhere, I took issue with Fredric Jameson's (mis)use of Baudrillard in the former's case against the putatively depthless and powerless postmodern. This time around and still against prevailing orthodoxies, I look deeper into simulation theory for it seems to me that a certain ethical position, political stance or critique (*Kritik*) may be rescued—also critically—from the ontological model of Baudrillard and Lyotard (chapter 4), let alone from the works of Lacoue-Labarthe, Nancy, de Man, and, again, Lyotard (chapter 5). True, the model is not without its problems. Nor do I wish to throw the baby out with the bathwater. The ontological description or representation of the world typically involves in such critics and philosophers self-reflective recourse to the notions of representation and the representable, reading and the readable, and their poststructuralist/postmodern opposites, the unrepresentable and the unreadable.

By no means identical—in fact, quite distinct on several accounts—poststructuralism and postmodernism benefit in my book mutually, from an alliance whose building block is re-presentation, intertextuality broadly conceived, and, in relation to it, fictional discourse as cultural politics. As far as I am concerned, this alliance is a salient feature of the "postmodern condition." "Negative," essentially deconstructive and poststructuralist concepts such as the unrepresentable, the unnameable, the unspeakable, the unreadable, and the like lay the groundwork, "make room," as I suggest above and will discuss in chapter 5 in greater detail, for postmodern representation no less than for its culturally and politically perceptive interpretation. Memorious discourse springs from what seemingly rules out its own possibility, from the apparent cancellation of referentiality and by the same token of ontological and social pertinence. But it is this radical critique of representation's premises that ultimately enables representation and its critical function in postmodernism.

In stressing this critique I submit the hypothesis of a pragmatic, action and "reality"-oriented strain in poststructuralism and postmodernism. Giles Gunn (2001, 39–41) is among those who have made a similar attempt; here, I take a different road. This leads us through "high theory'"'s discourse on postmodern representation, which discourse, I believe, carries significant political potential. Finally, I go back to Nabokov, in the fourth chapter, and again to DeLillo, in the fifth. Unlike in many respects and responding to distinct cultural environments, Nabokov and DeLillo are both keen on the "society of the spectacle" and on how it stages "reality," "identity," and so on. Obviously more critical than Nabokov, DeLillo is particularly sensitive to this process, as my analysis of consumption and the scene of reading in his novels indicates. In *White Noise, Libra, Mao II, Underworld, Cosmopolis,* and elsewhere, DeLillo draws an arresting picture of what I dub "postmodern literacy," in which writing and reading imply our a priori, memorious inscription as subjects into various public and private texts and scenarios, hence the possibility of our own "deciphering" and "screening" as textual fragments thereof. More emphatically than other sections of my book, the latter half of chapter 5 underscores the politics of reading, writing, and other protocols of representation. Turning to Nabokov for the last time and to a Nabokovian like Lee Siegel, the epilogue revisits these protocols against the backdrop of postmodern culture's global phase to pinpoint the imperfect, uneasy isomorphism of memorious discourse and our "network society."

1

Time, Representation, and
Postmodern Memory

In the post–world war II history of representation that still awaits its Auerbach, Nabokov's work forebodes an impending paradigm shift. Alongside Beckett, Borges, and Joyce before them, the Russian-American writer had a unique insight into a future culture and its fictions. Texts like *Lolita* notwithstanding, this culture is not Nabokov's—not yet. Nor is the aristocrat-artistocrat Nabokov its best suited spokesperson. But many of its basic premises are here: acutely cosmopolitan, cross- if not multicultural outlook and identity politics where sex, gender, and ethnic fables take center stage; heterogenous, "high-brow"-cum-"low-brow" texture; linguistic prowess, jocular-ironic style, and self-conscious narrative sophistication; encyclopedic and mock-encyclopedic intertextuality, to name just a few. In varying combinations, we come upon them throughout contemporary literature. They mark, in fact, an entire post-Nabokovian strain running—to give only American examples—from the earlier generation of Updike, Pynchon, Barth, Sorrentino, Sukenick, Gass, Gaddis, Barthelme, and Robert Coover to Auster, Steven Millhauser, Lee Siegel, and the Fiction Collective/avant-pop group (Leyner, Curtis White, Harold Jaffe, Steve Katz, David Foster Wallace, and other "infinitely jesting" young writers). Nabokov is the belated modernist who gave us a foretaste of the postmodern. So the inquiry into memorious discourse might as well begin with him and his ambiguous, modernist/postmodern purview.

To come to terms with this ambiguity, critics have usually examined Nabokov's novels. I suggest that we look at his "revisited autobiography," *Speak, Memory,* instead, particularly at the interface of representation and intertextuality shaping it. For his memoir stands out as an eloquent document of that late modernism about to "tip over" or take a postmodern turn, which occurs with authors like Nabokov and texts such as *Lolita, Pale Fire, Pnin, The Gift,* and *Ada* in the late fifties and sixties. The turn is not complete at that time even though Nabokov's own early works, not to mention Joyce's, Beckett's, and others', had sown its seeds decades ago. *The Gift*, for instance, published in 1963, revises a text Nabokov had done in Russian back in 1937. Likewise, *Speak, Memory* itself revamps a 1951 book, *Conclusive Evidence*. But, in doing so, the 1966 memoir reworks much more in the process. It is on this textual and intertextual operation that I want to concentrate to better understand Nabokov's own "turn" to a mode of representing and remembering—of his own life, of his own texts, and by the same movement of texts by others—that in the sixties is becoming so typical of postmodernism.

MEMOIR AND REPRISE: READING NABOKOV READING PROUST

> . . . esthetically, ecstatically. . . .
> —Vladimir Nabokov, *Ada or Ardor: A Family Chronicle*

To bring to light this textual-intertextual dynamic, I focus on *Speak, Memory*'s reply to its seldom acknowledged narrative alter-ego,[1] Marcel Proust's *Remembrance of Things Past*. *Speak, Memory* dwells upon Proust's aesthetic memory motif, especially upon the interplay of time, timelessness, and writing in the *Recherche*'s last part, *Time Regained*. Calling back his past and thus composing his autobiography, representing his life, Nabokov concomitantly re-presents—recalls, rereads, rewrites—the quintessentially modernist attempt to represent time and bid its return, Proust's novel. Oversaturated culturally, Nabokovian recollection is recollection and textual collection at the same time, both memorial and memorious. Proust-reading is part and parcel of the "originating," writing process. Generally speaking, this constitutes, I submit, a postmodern process, as memory retrieves the narrator's childhood against the backdrop of the Proustian vision of "aesthetic time." Autobiographical representation, we shall notice immediately, involves an intertextual "deviation," a provocative interpellation of Proust's model of time as an aesthetic category. In the following, I review the key moments of such a conversation in *Speak, Memory*, insisting on those when Nabokov draws from the Proustian economy of time and writing to flesh out his own dialectic of temporality and aesthetics. I will therefore listen for that Bakhtinian double voice of discourse that makes up the memoir's memorious substance: Proust's voice translated, assimilated into, or ventriloquized by Nabokov's. To better gauge the scope of this dialogism, a brief discussion of the Proustian themes of time, memory, and writing should be in order.

Proust's bouts with the "considerable difficulties" arising from the temporality of the work of art[2]—trials that his narrator is "ready to undertake" (1982, 3:903)—presage many of Nabokov's reflections in *Speak, Memory*. In both writers, concrete, bodily sensations open onto a transcendent horizon; the controversial Proustian Platonism surfaces in Nabokov's experiencing of "raw" reality in his pursuit of the "supersensible." This Proustian "ontological leap" entails a kind of Hegelian *Aufhebung*,[3] with contingent time both medium and substance of recalled impressions, writing's *primum movens*. But writing ultimately sets in train the "absolute time"[4] where the "essence of things" comes forth and, we shall see below, allows the Nabokovian narrator a glimpse into higher truths. As Proust confesses, this induces a "felicity" whose "cause"

> I began to divine as I compared these diverse happy impressions, diverse yet with this in common, that I experienced them at the present moment and at the same time in a context of a distant moment, so that the past was made to encroach upon the present and I was made to doubt whether I was in the one or the other. The truth surely was that that being within me which had enjoyed these impressions had enjoyed them because they had in them something that was common to a day long past and to the present, because in some way they were extra-temporal, and this being made its appearance only when, through one of these identifications of the present with the past, it was likely to find itself in the one and only medium in which it could exist and enjoy the essence of things, that is to say: outside time. (3:904)

The passage uncovers the fundamentally Proustian dialectic of time and timelessness. As we learn, Proust's impressions "distill" the concrete "moments," purveying a new sense of time,[5] a different ontology altogether. "Nourished . . . by the essence of things" (3:905), this "extra-temporal being" does not merely bring about an "escape from the present" (3:904). It has "the power to perform that task which had always defeated the efforts of my memory and my intellect, the power to make me rediscover days that were long past, the Time that was Lost." Writing works scattered feelings and sensations over in its aesthetic "still," extracting "pure," extra-temporal meanings out of "impure," temporal references with the "miracle of an analogy" as a catalyst. The resulting precipitate phenomenologically "isolate[s], . . . immobilize[s]—for a moment brief as a flash of lighting what normally it never apprehends: a fragment of time in pure state" (3:905).[6] Proustian narrative thereby rolls, as it were, the same phenomenal Nabokovian magic "carpet" and its complex temporality, past, present, and future, all into one, layer upon layer, so that an identic, invariant "pattern" (Nabokov 1966, 139) shows through its "discrete" memories and impressions.

It becomes tempting, along these lines, to approach Proust's associationism as a narrative phenomenological reduction. The discursive logic of Proustian associations evokes another emblematically modernist paradigm, Husserlian *epoché*. For the buildup of successive temporal strata brings about eventually a spectacular bracketing off of time itself, "time in the pure state," or, as Nabokov will see it, "timelessness." By placing time between parentheses, by "limiting" time phenomenologically—and paradoxically—while time unfolds, writing "frees" the author from the temporal order (Proust 1982, 3:906) or, according to *Speak, Memory*, from the "prison of time" (20).[7] Blending a host of resurrections of past moments, writing extricates the writer from Time (Proust 1982, 3:908), propelling him in an ecstatic "extemporalité,"[8] which Nabokov limns ever so often. An overview, rereading, as well as final part of *Remembrance, Time Regained* clearly defines Proust's novel as laying out an aesthetics of ecstasy achieved by writing mechanisms that set up a specific relation with time. Characteristically, *Time Regained* comprises many such self-reflective, "metaretrospective" fragments, that is, analyses, rehearsals, and even retrospections of previous retrospections:

> Always, when these resurrections took place, the distant scene engendered around the common sensation had for a moment grappled, like a wrestler, with the present scene. Always the present scene had come off victorious, and always the vanquished one had appeared to me the more beautiful of the two, so beautiful that I had remained in a state of ecstasy on the uneven paving-stones or before the cup of tea, endeavoring to prolong or to reproduce the momentary appearances of the Combray or the Balbec or the Venice which invaded only to be driven back, which rose up only at once to abandon me in the midst of the new scene which somehow, nevertheless, the past had been able to permeate. (3:908)

We recognize in this passage earlier moments such as the madeleine episode and the paving stones of the Guermantes courtyard and St. Mark's. This magical "presentification of the past" engenders a "state of ecstasy," the ultimate outcome of remembrance in Proust: a flight from time by a paradoxical immersion in it. What we have here is the novel's poetics laid bare by the novel itself. A narrative poetics it is, but also a poetics of ecstasy, since the narrator ultimately strives for the "contemplation of the essence of things." The "immobilization" of this superior reality takes place in writing

(3:909) *and in its time* since it is only there that the writing subject can "escape" from chronology.[9]

Proust rejects mimetic realism, and Nabokov will take this rejection to another level in his fictionalized memoir and, as we shall observe in chapter 4, in his fiction generally. Realistic representation may well be memory's utmost accomplishment, only this recollection holds the subject captive in empirical time. As for the famous involuntary memory, although superior to the mechanical, voluntary type (Proust 1982, 3:906), it is just a first step in the long-winded process taking the narrator into a superior, extra-temporal world. The deliberate recollection of certain facts provides an initial impulse, casting him into a realm to which only remembrance can take us. Important as it may be, this is a moment that writing builds on, and integrates into, a more profound interpretation of things past. Indeed, what writing accomplishes is not just a transcription of recollections, but their hermeneutic. Retrieving that past, in other words, does not mean a recovery of its bygone body, the usual and utopian task of realist memoirs.[10] Proust aspires to capture the past's essence, to "read" its nature enshrined in temporal, palpable objects, in sensations unexpectedly felt in the present. His writing is a hermeneutic apparatus that reworks the raw materials supplied by memory, "interpret[ing] the given sensations as signs"[11] to extract their "spiritual equivalent" (3:912). This is Proust's "method," simply put. Yet it is not simple at all. As the narrator suspects, this "method" lies behind the "creation" of a "work of art." Retrieval of the past, followed by its "reading"—which tells the Proustian narrator what that past actually meant and means—is complete only in and through writing, in and through "creation," the creation of the *Recherche*, that is.

Artistic creativity in Proust's text rests, then, upon a two-story concept of writing featuring, first, a recollecting-hermeneutical layer and, second, a layer that, for lack of a better word, I will call productive: reading and writing of the past, both fused into one "creative" gesture. On the first, remembrance-interpretation level, writing grasps and peruses time, searching for trans-temporal meanings of time-bound events and objects; on the second, it *presents* its temporal representations to the external reader of the *Recherche* as an object to be read, interpreted, *represented* in its turn. In other words, writing deciphers time, reads into and beyond time's contingent body, and in the same movement enciphers its revelations in rich, sensuous, and by the same token temporal imagery. This is how writing interlocks two distinct semiotic operations: one oriented toward the mysterious signs etched in the "diegetic" past of the narrated story (*histoire*), the other toward the future, toward its virtual audience. Proustian writing decodes this *histoire* and instantly encodes, as *récit* (narration), its ecstatic discoveries, rewrites the stuff memory has just turned up and read, struggled to comprehend, in short, represented. *Time Regained* in particular illuminates the workings of writing as reading and rewriting. At this point, the *Recherche*'s text treats the narrator's dormant, deepest reminiscences as a "magical scrawl" consisting of "written truths" (3:913) to be dislodged from their perceptible, temporal wraps. If these reminiscences are "authentic," they are so insofar as they resurface involuntarily in the narrator's mind. In revisiting them, the narrator does search for the "trueness of the past," as he says, deliberately. Previous experiences—fragments of past, "contingent time"—set on him without warning, and he wrestles with their meaning. He endeavors to read them, to make sense of time, but then purposefully blurs the sense he has just made, scrambles his revelations.

The metaphor of the book is central to the Proustian definition of writing as reading and, conversely, reading as writing (3:913–14). The "laborious deciphering" of the "inner book of unknown symbols," the technique of "reading backwards" (3:932), if rigorously employed, leads to subjective "revelations" and "visions" (3:931) enabling us to "emerge from ourselves," that is, from our temporal-existential selves (3:932). The Book "suppresses the mighty dimension of Time which is the dimension in which life is lived" (3:1087), by embodying a "sort of three-dimensional psychology" and thus instituting the co-presence of all temporal strata. This co-presence converts the time in which we live our lives into a revelatory temporality of writing, a temporality that alleviates the painful perception of passing time—proof of our mortality. In light of this metamorphosis, Georges Poulet's point on memory's "supernatural role" (1956, 297), on "time regained as time transcended" (320), could help us come to grips with the function of writing in Proust and in modernism in general: the "fallen nature'"s "highway of salvation" leads inevitably t(hr)o(ugh) writing. Writing overcomes the "time of precariousness," Heideggerian lack and crisis, setting up as it does an absolute, ecstatic Time inside, and by means of, an aesthetic world. In other words, Proust's temporal, or, more precisely, trans-temporal aesthetics is also an "ecstatics." The writer is not a mere "secular antitemporalist," like so many other authors of the postromantic age (Douglas Kellogg Wood 1982, 17), but a mystic, an *aesthetic* mystic seeking to transcend time and space through a fundamental insight or "illumination." And I find it telling that Nabokov himself will use the word in relation to autobiography and its

engagement with time: "[T]he illumination is then completed," he
avers, "when the narrator realizes that a work of art is our only
means of thus recapturing the past, and to this end he dedicates
himself" (1980, 249).

Critics have pointed out that, taking place in and through writing,
the Proustian "rediscovery" of time past and its transtemporal "essence" is also the discovery of writing because Marcel becomes a
writer, masters *memory-driven writing*. A late modern about to cross
over into postmodernism, Nabokov writes an autobiography where
writing-driven memory reigns supreme, a *memorious memoir* that "recalls" the Proustian intertext by playing upon its mutual implication
of time and writing. From this vantage point, the memoir can be
read as a critical essay of sorts: where Marcel interprets his own past,
Balzac and other intertexts notwithstanding, Nabokov's narrator interprets Proust besides his own past. *Speak, Memory* is not just a gloss
on the *Recherche*'s model of "ecstetic"—ecstatic and aesthetic—time,
but also narration that filters its story through the famed model,
writing of one's life through somebody else's life-writing: *representation that re-presents*. Despite the notable differences between Proust's
more fictional, autobiographical novel and the Nabokovian less—or
less acknowledged—imaginary, "novelized" memoir,[12] *Speak, Memory* can be read as a dialogue with Proust's aesthetic treatment of
time, more precisely, as a rewriting of the *Recherche*'s temporal-
aesthetic discourse. This rewriting entails repetition no less than
variation, an homage to the "tutor" model but also a revision of the
model.

Both as a process and as a metafictional topic, writing holds in
Speak, Memory a redemptive role, not unlike in the *Recherche*. It deploys itself in time, feeds on it, on the character's/narrator's past,
whose ghost writing summons. But writing also aims at breaking out
of time or a certain time-bound reality by paradoxically giving temporality a central place in textual production.[13] Proust's characteristic interplay of aesthetics and ontology underwrites quite literally the
Nabokovian relationship between time and writing,[14] and this becomes apparent first and foremost in Nabokov's treatment of the
Proustian subject of literary apprenticeship—the aforementioned
authorial "coming-of-age" of Marcel, his discovery of writing. The
subject is part and parcel of the Bildungsroman—or Künstlerroman,
rather—embedded in *Speak, Memory*. To some extent, the Proustian
revelation of writing completes, rounds off the experiencing of the
world and brings about a climactic moment. It is noteworthy that
Nabokov links up writing and time from the outset: structured by

time, writing is also a rejoinder to it, bears upon it. The young protagonist's first poem, whose birth *Speak, Memory* relates in detail, is a
case in point for it slowly yet triumphantly coalesces as the beginning writer's ticket out the temporal prison house. The poem is a
scansion of the temporal flow while its verses are also scanned, ar-
rayed by this flow. Nonetheless, the poem—literature generally—
can, in the author's view, help us step across our temporal
boundaries:

> A moment later my first poem began. What touched it off? I think I
> know. Without any wind blowing, the sheer weight of a raindrop, shining
> in parasitic luxury on a cordate leaf, caused its tip to dip, and what
> looked like a globule of quicksilver performed a sudden glissando down
> the center vein, and then, having shed its bright load, the relieved leaf
> unbent. Tip, leaf, dip, relief—the instant it all took to happen seemed
> to me not so much a fraction of time as a fissure in it, a missed heartbeat,
> which was refunded at once by a patter of rhymes: I say "patter" inten-
> tionally, for when a gust of wind did come, the trees would briskly start
> to drip all together in as crude an imitation of the recent downpour as
> the stanza I was already muttering resembled the shock of wonder I have
> experienced when for a moment heart and leaf had been one. (Nabokov
> 1966, 217)

This is the moment—the momentum—of the first writerly event, un-
leashed as in Proust by a "certain intense human emotion" set off
in its turn by a natural phenomenon.[15] At this point, the narrator's
view of poetry seems expressive as well as mimetic. Expression and
mimesis both belong with, and refer to, historical time. They represent history, and whatever they fashion nests by and large within it.
However, the poem's rhythm does not primarily mirror the passing
of time, in contrast to Lessing's succession versus simultaneity opposition taken up by Borges, as we saw in the prologue. The poem
makes a "crack" in time, instead, opens up a gap. Writing, including
this preliminary stage of mental elaboration, does not cover a
"fraction of time." On the contrary—and unlike the Proustian cele-
bration of continuous temporality as a means to surpass time itself—
Nabokovian (re)writing "fractures" time, breaks up its contingent
continuity and contingency altogether.[16] It effects, in brief, an ontological breakthrough aesthetically. The poem deploys temporal references, objects, and the "patter of rhymes" to bring forth its own
prosodic *pattern*, which projects its author in an absolute space and
timeless time, in Proust's "extra-temporality." Here, subject and object merge: "for a moment heart and leaf" become "one." In a confession from *Strong Opinions*, Nabokov comes back to this very
Proustian notion of the "essence of time"—to the metaphysical

"surroundings" of the "essence of things," as he puts it—when he talks about an immersion into "empirical" duration. Referring to the protagonist of his probably most time-fascinated novel, *Ada*,[17] he alludes to the above-mentioned Proustian rhetoric ("rhythm") of temporality. In doing so, he rewrites not only certain passages of the *Recherche* and *Ada*, but also the longer fragment of *Speak, Memory* reproduced earlier (217):

> He [Van Veen of *Ada*] and I in that book attempt to examine the *essence of time*, not its lapse. Van mentions the possibility of being "an amateur of Time, an epicure of duration," of being able to delight sensually in the texture of time, "in its stuff and spread, in the fall of its folds, in the very impalpability of its grayish gaze, in the coolness of its continuum." He also is aware that "Time is a fluid medium for the culture of metaphors."
>
> Time, though akin to rhythm, is not simply rhythm, which would imply motion—and Time does not move. Van's greatest discovery is his perception of Time as the dim hollow between two rhythmic beats, not the beats themselves, which only embar Time. In this sense human life is not a pulsating heart but the missed heartbeat. (1973, 185–86)[18]

Time's folding/unfolding dialectic also shapes Nabokov's magic-carpet metaphor, a Proustian figure to which I will come back. For now, let me note that "the rhetoric of time," time's tropological texture organizing writing itself, also bears the memorious imprint of Proustian aestheticism. Following, like many modernists, in Proust's footsteps, Nabokov believes that "human life" *is* literature (1973, 186) because we only begin to live, to be truly, when we become "one" with a "superior" reality, and we enter this reality by forcing a break in the time of perception, which is exactly what the Nabokovian poem suggests. Indeed, it is, as we recall, Proust's most intimate conviction that "real life . . . is literature" (1982, 3:931). In this sense, representation now takes on a non-Platonic meaning: far from doing merely empirical, trivially mimetic work, representation is the pendulum ever swinging between two ontological poles: "Perceptual Time" and "Pure Time," "Time free of content and context," to use a typical Proustian-Nabokovian formula (Nabokov 1973, 186).

To be sure, the privileged moment of revelatory writing vanishes as suddenly as it came. A "dogged composition" follows suit, deprived of the prodigious quality of the "initial inspiration" ("the bright fissure had closed"), a composition that evokes the Proustian limits of voluntary memory while still signifying a unique, aesthetic tie to time and space. The "composer" (writer) sees his work as a "phenomenon of orientation rather than of art, thus comparable to stripes of paint on a roadside rock or to a pillared heap of stones marking a mountain trail" (Nabokov 1966, 217). So, poetry is a "positional" (218) phenomenon related to, and covering, space, that is to say, different places across a material geography, sites that the poet retrieves simultaneously, in an atemporal time and nonspatial space of his own making:

> But then, in a sense, all poetry is positional: to try to express one's position in regard to the universe embraced by consciousness, is an immemorial urge. The arms of consciousness reach out and grope, and the longer they are the better. Tentacles, not wings, are Apollo's natural members. Vivian Bloodmark, a philosophical friend of mine, in later years, used to say that while the scientist sees everything that happens in one point of space, the poet feels everything that happens in one point of time. Lost in thought, he taps his knee with his wandlike pencil, and, at the same instant a car (New York license plate) passes along the road, a child bangs the screen door of a neighboring porch, an old man yawns in a misty Turkestan orchard, a granule of cinder-gray sand is rolled by the wind of Venus, a Docteur Jacques Hirsch in Grenoble puts on his reading glasses, and trillions of other such trifles occur—all forming an instantaneous and transparent organism of events, of which the poet (sitting in his lawn chair, at Ithaca, N.Y.) is the nucleus. (218)

In Borges, Funes's memory slips back, farther and farther into the past while skidding off the track of this past into other "pasts" infinitely to uncover the absolute historicity behind things present—a "diachronic" cosmos. No less memorious, Nabokov's narrator believes the imagination takes in the world through what he calls "cosmic synchronization." Notably, this represents Nabokov's own view because the "philosophical friend" is Nabokov himself ("Vivian Bloodmark" is an anagram of the author's name). In Nabokov, and before him, in Proust, "cosmic synchronization" designates an author's true task. To fulfill it, one must, first, cancel the present's "ontological supremacy" so that the past can become a source of a "robust reality [that] makes a ghost of the present" (77). We may remember that Proust remarks that

> so complete are these resurrections of the past during the second that they last, that they not only oblige our eyes to cease to see the room which is near them in order to look instead at the railway bordered with trees or the rising tide, they even force our nostrils to breathe the air of places which are in fact a great distance away, and our will to choose between the various projects which those distant places suggest to us, they force our whole self to believe that it is surrounded by these places

or at least to waver doubtfully between them and the places where we
now are, in a dazed uncertainty such as we feel sometimes when an inde-
scribably beautiful vision presents itself to us at the moment of our falling asleep. (1982, 3:908)

Nicely anticipated in this passage, Nabokovian synchronization suggests interesting parallels to poetry theories springing up in the
wake of Russian formalism, especially in French structuralism and
phenomenology-inspired aesthetics. Nabokov's belief that a poet
must be able to think of "several things at a time" brings to mind a
host of models of poetic language from Roman Jakobson's to Jean
Cohen's and Michael Riffaterre's. More generally, and more importantly in view of my discussion of late modern and postmodern representation and its memorious relation to the Proustian spectacle of
time and remembrance, Speak, Memory shows that the link between
time and writing applies to all literature, including prose fiction. As
Vladimir E. Alexandrov argues in Nabokov's Otherworld, "cosmic synchronization" is not only an obsessive theme, present in different
forms in many other Nabokovian texts, but also a dominant narrative pattern in Speak, Memory.[19] And before long, this "referential-
agglutination" model, the juxtaposition of multiple, befuddlingly
heterogenous, spatial and temporal references with an ironic-playful
twist will influence postmoderns such as Barth, Pynchon, Sorrentino, and Georges Perec.

In Nabokov and Proust alike, memory plays a textual, creative
role.[20] But this is a special kind of memory because otherwise both
writers feel that writing and common recollection set up distinct relationships to time. In Speak, Memory, empirical remembrance reas-
serts our captivity in the "spherical . . . prison of time," a place
"without exits" (1966, 20). In fact, "the dawning of the sense of
time" (21) heralds the "awakening of [our] consciousness." By contrast, affirming our freedom, writing breaks down temporal boundaries. In Nabokov's view, writing aims at displacing our time-bound
condition through artistic creation.[21] Instituting timelessness, writing occasions an ecstatic experience, which is not unlike the Proustian quasi mysticism of "time in the pure state" (1982, 3:905). "I
confess," Nabokov's narrator tell us, "I do not believe in time. I like
to fold my magic carpet, after use, in such a way as to superimpose
one part of the pattern upon another. Let visitors trip. And the high-
est enjoyment of timelessness—in a landscape selected at random—is when I stand among rare butterflies and their food plants.
This is ecstasy, and behind ecstasy is something else, which is hard
to explain. It is like a momentary vacuum into which rushes all that

I love. A sense of oneness with sun and stone. A thrill of gratitude to whom it may concern—to the contrapuntal genius of human fate or to tender ghosts humoring a lucky mortal" (1966, 139).

We have already come across this strong feeling of cosmic participation in the description, drawn in identical terms, of Nabokov's first writing experience. The magic carpet enables the same survey of empiric reality, the same travel in time and space that takes us into "timelessness," into the realm of the aesthetic, that is. Butterflies are symbolic messengers of this ecstatic world, abundantly showing off an "artistic perfection usually associated with man-wrought things" (124). "I discovered in nature the nonutilitarian delights that I sought in art" (125), Nabokov writes apropos of the "mimetic subtlety" of certain lepidoptera. Fruit of the aesthetics of transcendent time, ecstasy triggers a fulgurant revelation of "oneness" similar to the illumination experienced through writing, "when for a moment heart and leaf had been one" (217). A poetic image or the glimpse of a butterfly in midair sets us free, like in Proust, "from the contingencies of time" and yields the pure essence of temporality "within a metaphor" (1982, 3:925). Time has its own rhetoric, which points at a world beyond material routine, as we have seen repeatedly; vice versa, the rhetoric of the text, a certain metaphor or rhythm, breaks through time, opening a window into the timeless hypostasis of being.

Basic textual mechanism and metatextual theme, Nabokovian memory does not simply spark recollection. It also analyzes the past. We have noticed, Proustian memory does this, too, through the textual metaphors of reading and the book. Nabokov employs, instead, the tropes of seeing and perspective, and the image of an "iconic" past. Proust's narrator *reads* his life; Nabokov's *watches* it rather, like a movie. Representing the past as a sequence of art(ificial) images (photos, slides, frames, etc.), Nabokov's memory model parts company with Proust's here. Time, but also life, reality, somebody's biography are a motion picture, a visual text already in place presenting us with a strange, hard-to-grasp fiction. More than Proust's psychological intimation of the past, Nabokov's visualization of time foregrounds a somewhat postmodern perception of life-become-fiction as it goes on, and consequently a "disenchanted" memory that senses the fictional quality of any (auto)biography, of any time, of anything that happens in time and would have to be narrated in it. True, the "reading scene," reading as such, is enormously important in Nabokov's works. *Speak, Memory* itself values it, in terms as Proustian as strikingly Borgesian—the narrator "imagin[es] paradise as a place where a sleepless neighbor reads an endless book by the light of an eternal candle" (1966, 110).

At least in this text, however, the visual metaphor holds sway. The past is, as in Proust, a "hermeneutic object"[22] to be viewed and reviewed by the discriminating, reading eye, but Proust's "text" of lapsed time is now Nabokov's "stereoscopic dreamland" (1966, 99), "fancy's rear-vision mirror" (100), "the screen upside down" of "pictures" (157) that decompose and recompose time aesthetically. Nabokov depicts memory as a scanning gaze, lens, or camera. Photos, slides, microscopes and telescopes, pictures in fast succession articulate, encapsulate, or frame "lost time" and simultaneously zoom in on it, betraying the narrator's essentially cinematic perspective on life. The "magic lantern"[23] uncovers, more substantially than in Proust, a transformation of the retrieved (remembered) object, a reconstruction of lapsed time in the very process of its recovery. Like Proust's, Nabokov's text refers to a "magic lantern," but it also works as one. "The images of [the narrator's] tutors appear within memory's luminous disc as so many magic-lantern projections," we discover right before the "magic-lantern sequence" (155). Past, if real, acquaintances are now movie characters, silhouettes on the magic-lantern slides.[24] Remembrance plays the tape of time, breaks up the motion picture continuum into pieces that the narrator (re)-views one by one like a spectator watching "through a tremulous prism" (155) the silent show of his life—"succession of fade-ins and fade-outs" (171).

This is another postmodern symptom. But the "condition" is not very serious. Again, not yet. Nabokov's "vision" is still modernist, aesthetic if not aestheticist, and, as Eva Hoffman maintains below, ahistorical. A case in point, *Speak, Memory* "disdains . . . to give the Russian Revolution more than a passing mention" (Hoffman 1990, 197). Driven by Proustian "extra-temporal" proclivities, Nabokov instantiates instead, in Paul Maltby's terminology, the modernist "visionary moment," the "flash of insight" that, in locating truth outside history (2002, 1–3), epitomizes modernism's mystical-transcendent epistemology. On the other hand, the rewriting of the *Recherche* alters the Proustian matrix along the lines of a novel, fairly consistent poetics of heterogeneity. This poetics involves, we have noted, recollection as fictionalization of the past, and intertextuality, which inlays literary memory into the memoir, memoriously; agglutination and sundry, metonymic juxtaposition of objects and facts; the Lacanian subject split, through the cinematic gaze, between the viewer (spectator) and the viewed (dramatis persona); and the movie trope itself, as opposed to the prevailingly textual metaphors in Proust. All these are likely to "aggravate" Nabokov's late modern condition and eventually bring on a postmodern one by way of more radical shifts in narrative representation. Nabokov sets the stage for these changes by narrowing the divides between fiction and nonfiction, invention and reminiscence, the novel and the memoir, representation as autobiographical textualization—the writing of the self—and re-presentation as the intertextualization—recuperation, appropriation, rewriting—of others and their texts. After Nabokov, full-fledged postmoderns like David Antin thrive on this sort of "genre trouble," as we shall see in the last section of this chapter. Furthermore, postmoderns such as Hoffman ascertain that boundaries and categories grow increasingly fluid inside no less than outside texts, in the fast globalizing world. To her memoir I turn now given its overtly memorious ties to Nabokov's.

POSTMEMOIR: EVA HOFFMAN, MODERN AMERICAN AUTOBIOGRAPHY, OR, THE POSTMODERN AND THE GLOBAL

> I'm a quantum particle trying to locate myself in a swirl of atoms.
> —Eva Hoffman, *Lost in Translation*

> Found in translation . . .
> —Clifford Geertz, *Local Knowledge*

> [F]ound in translation rather than lost in it.
> —Giles Gunn, *Beyond Solidarity*

Hoffman's *Lost in Translation* has been likened to Sartre's *Les Mots* (*The Words*), Saul Bellow's *Herzog*, Maxine Hong Kingston's *The Woman Warrior*, and Lore Segal's *Other People's Houses*,[25] which goes to show once more how tenuous the fiction/nonfiction distinction is getting these days. Danuta Zadworna Fjellestad also observes "that although the title of Hoffman's book uncannily echoes Isaac Bashevis Singer's autobiographical *Lost in America*, he is never mentioned in *Lost in Translation*. Yet another echo is that of John Barth's classic postmodern text, *Lost in the Funhouse*" (1995, 145). Further, Robert Frost's "famous definition of poetry, a quality obliterated by the utter incompatibility of language" is an additional possible allusion (Kellman 1998, 157), although, where poetry is concerned, James Merrill's well-known poem "Lost in Translation" would probably pop to mind first. Hoffman points to neither Frost nor Merrill, and on this account one might argue that in her 1998 bestseller *Lost in Translation* Nicole Mones pays Hoffman in Hoffman's own coin, for she gives the Polish-American author no credit for a text resembling Mones's painstakingly researched and glaringly intertextual novel.

Hoffman does acknowledge Nabokov's novels and especially *Speak, Memory.* "I wish I could breathe a Nabokovian air," she writes in a reference to his autobiography (1990, 197), admitting to her envy of his "Olympian freedom" (197), of the "aristocratic privilege" presumably enabling him to rise above the "confining categories" that otherwise remind her of what she is: "a Jew, an immigrant, half-Pole, half-American" (198). Bestowing upon his characters "the graced amorality of aesthetic objects" (198), Nabokov is a notable presence in *Lost in Translation* yet not necessarily a model. Nor are other fellow Poles and Central-East Europeans like Czeslaw Milosz and Milan Kundera for that matter. Bilingual "experts of mourning" (Hoffman 1990, 116) and exiled champions of "true memory," they are Hoffman's kindred spirits. By and large, they must take a back seat to Mary Antin and Henry Adams, though. Mary Antin's 1912 autobiography, *The Promised Land,* and Adams's 1918 personal memoir-cum-cultural history, *The Education of Henry Adams,* are not only *Lost in Translation*'s true precursors but also partners of intertextual dialogue. More notably still, I argue later in this section, through this memorious extension of the memoir, through a critical re-presentation of Mary Antin, Adams, and their modern narratives of selfhood and history, Hoffman represents herself. They help her come to terms with her own self, with the languages braiding it, and the global age—the new Babel—as an arena for this process.

To a substantial degree, Hoffman's is a story of lost home: teenage Eva and her family leave anti-Semitic Poland at the height of the Cold War to start afresh in Canada. After a few years in Vancouver, Eva goes off to college and then on to graduate school in the U.S., settling eventually in New York City. Her adjustment to North America takes place primarily in language and in translation, in the clash of English and Polish, with her native language a foreordained filter of experience, perception, and self-perception. Thus, she takes her new life in through Polish, summing up this process as "triangulation," or, inner translation. Indeed, for quite a while Eva triangulates. She absorbs American culture and English and, conversely, attempts to represent (make sense or use of) them through what they are not—Polish and Polish Jewishness—that is, through other, alien representations, words, and customs.

In his essay on "Assimilation in Recent American Jewish Autobiographies," Mark Krupnick calls *The Promised Land* a "paradigm" for the "conventional immigrant autobiography" where "the movement is from the narrowness and hardship of the Eastern European shtetl to the freedom and wonders of America. The pattern story, which," he notes, "is very self-conscious in Antin, is the biblical Exodus, with czarist Russia as Egypt and America as 'the promised land'" (1993, 457). No doubt, Mary Antin rarely loses sight of this trajectory. As she reminisces, Boston's Dover Street public library

> is where I liked to remind myself of Polotzk, the better to bring out the wonder of my life. That I who was born in the prison of Pale should roam at will in the land of freedom was a marvel that it did me good to realize. That I who was brought up to my teens almost without a book should be set down in the midst of all the books that were ever written was a miracle as great as any on record. That an outcast should become a privileged citizen, that a beggar should dwell in a palace—this was a *romance* more thrilling than poet[s] ever sung. Surely I was rocked in an *enchanted cradle.* (1946, 342–43; emphasis added)

From the Russian "Egypt" (7) to the "Promised Land" and its palacelike, free libraries; from ignorance to literacy and opportunity: this is, no question about it, a story of biblical ordeals and deliverance, but also a romance of sorts, a romance of Americanization patterned on a typically modern narrative of progress, self-improvement, and enlightenment. Above, Mary Antin uses the word romance advisedly to foreground both the exceptionality of the story whose heroine she is, and the fictionalizing, magnifying glass through which she reads her "greenhorn" experience. Nor is her account necessarily naive, and her 1914 militant book *They Who Knock at Our Gates* bears out an awareness of a darker story underneath *The Promised Land*'s romance with America. Her paean to American culture is every bit as legitimate—or unwarranted—as Hoffman's Edenic rendition of Stalinist Poland. In both, narrative "construction" holds sway. In Mary Antin, it smooths out the present in response to a horrendous past. In Hoffman, and not without her suspicion,[26] it is the other way around: the same narrative logic conjures up a prelapsarian, early childhood in fantasmatic reaction to her teenage immigrant frustrations. Hence, the immigration and acculturation story inescapably idealizes ("utopianizes") its content. The memoir's *fabula*, as the Russian formalists would call it, gets literally fabled, mythical, in the *hic* of Boston (Mary Antin) or the Edenic *nunc* of Cracow (Hoffman 1990, 5). Mary Antin's is a romance with the present, its culture, and language; especially during her Canadian years, Hoffman romances the past while composing an almost symmetric antiromance of the present and its cultural-linguistic environs. If Mary Antin's is a nicely progressing, essentially modernist, rational romance of identity formation and reformation, a story of unhampered assimilation and painless cultural rebirth, Hoffman spins out, in memorious if polemical conversation with *The Promised Land*, a discontinuous and angst-ridden counterstory. The intertextual rejoinder is so overt that *Lost in Translation* has been called a "revision" of Mary Antin's autobiography (Kellman 1998, 149). Beginning with the opening pictures in the two books— Mashke (later Mary) and her older sister Fetchke in Mary Antin, Ewa (afterwards Eva) and her younger sister Alinka, in Hoffman— conspicuous parallels, borrowings, and winks abound, so much so that "[s]ome episodes in Hoffman's book seem to be direct rewriting of passages in Antin's memoir" (Fjellestad 1995, 145).

This is certainly peculiar, that is to say, unexpectedly memorious. Emulating as it might a model stylistically, autobiography normally does not imitate, let alone rewrite, "content." Underwriting the genre is usually a "pact" between the author and the reader, which vouches for the "referentiality" of the narrated events, reassuring us that the text tells the life story of the person identified as the text's author. In other words, "in order for there to be autobiography (and personal literature generally), the author, the narrator, and the protagonist must be identical" (Lejeune 1989, 5). If this is the rule—and by the same token the usual expectation of readers—then Hoffman breaks it for she writes her life story while rewriting Mary Antin's. *Lost in Translation* sets the stage for the autobiographical convention yet declines to apply it, openly substituting intertextuality, literary reference, for autobiographical referentiality. Granted, Hoffman is not "lying" about her life.[27] Representing her own life through Mary Antin's—more significantly still, through Mary Antin's textualized life, through her text ultimately—Hoffman composes a postmodern memoir, or, what I would call "postmemoir": a *Speak, Memory* for postmodernity where the paradoxes of representation play out with surprisingly memorious vengeance.

Marianne Hirsch uses a similar term, "postmemory," to explain how Holocaust survivors' children relate to their parents' traumatic experiences. "Postmemory," she specifies, "characterizes the experience of those who grow up dominated by narratives that preceded their birth, whose own belated stories are displaced by the stories of the previous generation, shaped by traumatic events that they can neither understand nor re-create." The stories make such a powerful impact on the children "as to constitute memories in their own right" (1993, 8). Hirsch does not refer to Hoffman explicitly, but the observations do apply to her. *Lost in Translation* is, to be sure, a prime document of belatedness in the sense defined by Hirsch, as the book's first part demonstrates, but also, I would stress, in Harold Bloom's sense, which postulates a certain predecessor whom the "ephebe" revisits. In Hoffman, the "anxiety of influence" shows through in the self-acknowledged "envy" of precursors such as Nabokov or "New York intellectuals, like Alfred Kazin or Norman Podhoretz, who had the slight leg up of being born here, and who were therefore quick to understand where they wanted to travel, the parabolas of their ambitions" (1990, 160). But what Hoffman rememorates, à la Funes, what she reads, rereads, and rewrites throughout her own story is chiefly Adams's and Mary Antin's, and for good reason.

Both Mary Antin and Hoffman, to begin with, are Polish Jews (Polotzk lies in Russian Poland). Both leave their homeland at thirteen, wind up in Boston sooner or later, and move up the social ladder à la Horatio Alger's heroes, to whom Mary Antin refers (1946, 257) and whose "desperado drive" Hoffman identifies in "many immigrant Horatio Algers [who] overshoot themselves so unexpectedly as they move on their speed-up trajectories through several strata of society all the way to the top" (1990, 157). In both cases, the romance of Americanization is equally a romance of social Darwinism, an American dream twice come true against multiple odds—against the odds of language first and foremost.

But English factors into this narrative of transformation and ascent quite ambiguously, "pharmacologically." That is, it plays out like Plato's *pharmakon*, in Derrida's reading a perfect metaphor for written language and writing in general: it is at once "benefic" and "malefic" (Derrida 1972a, 78), hurts and disintegrates as much as it "heals" and nourishes its speaker or writer. Mary and Eva struggle with English yet somehow manage to make their handicap into a tool of social achievement early on, win school speech contests, publish poems and essays. English hinders and eases their self-fashioning simultaneously. Anything but docile, it has a life of its own, a curious autonomy that Mary Antin vaguely suspects while Hoffman, a Harvard English PhD, theorizes at length with poststructuralist acumen and against the backdrop of a growingly globalized Babel.

Consequently, language and its bearings upon the immigrant subject also set off the differences between Mary Antin and Hoffman. They both "make it" at last—and in English—but to Mary Antin's romance with the idiom Hoffman replies with a more complicated affair. Mary Antin's model inheres in the typically modernist self whose sundry, sequential makeup is suspected but disciplined by rational-teleological rites of self-determination and American self-invention. As she says in a passage whose memory resounds throughout *Lost in Translation*, "We are not born all at once, but by bits. The body first, and the spirit later; and the birth and growth of the spirit, in those who are attentive to their own inner life, are slow and exceedingly painful. Our mothers are racked with the pains of our physical birth; we ourselves suffer the longer pains of our spiritual growth. Our souls are scarred with the struggles of successive births, and the process is recorded also by the wrinkles of our brains, by the lines of our faces. Look at me, and you will see that I have been born many times" (1946, 87). But, she insists elsewhere, "I was Jew enough to have an aptitude for language in general" (206) and master even the "dreadful English *th*" (207). The dreadful *th*, whose own plight at the hands of New York's Mary Antins Henry Roth chronicles so touchingly in *Call It Sleep*, is part and parcel of a "bewilderingly strange, unimaginably complex" America (Mary Antin 1946, 181). Yet this strangeness, hitherto "delightfully unexplored," can be subdued. It does not pose a real threat. Nor does English for that matter, "love" at first sight and promise of "immortality" (207–8). "I love language too much to maul its beats," Hoffman declares (1990, 118), but only to echo Mary Antin's effusions: "I must love the English language!" (1946, 208). And still: "I love my beautiful city spreading all about me. I love the world. I love my place in the world" (300). "Mine is the whole majestic past, and mine is the shining future" (364) is the "emancipated immigrant"'s (356) closing sentence.

Mary Antin's rational, autonomous self-making falls in, actually, with the modern definition of the self. But, notably enough, this definition is about to get out of sync with America. Part and parcel of "modernization," migration and crosscultural contact intensify a great deal in the turn-of-the-century U.S., bring on further cultural developments and, on the latter's heels, a true sea change in the arts and sciences conceptualizing the self. Centered around a character itself "centered" or easily "re-centerable" around a new, putatively fissureless cultural-linguistic core, Mary Antin's narrative of plenitude gives way to different stories and truths. Obviously, both Mary Antin's and Hoffman's autobiographies cover, for the most part, their schooling years. But more is at stake here than pedagogy, unless we understand education broadly, as formation beyond the stage of formal instruction, in which case *The Promised Land* and *Lost in Translation* could very well be titled *The Education of Mary Antin* and *The Education of Eva Hoffman*, respectively.[28]

The aforementioned shift occurs across the humanities, betokening a radical turn in how we seize the human and its moorings in history, culture, and language. Mary Antin's account bodies forth an early modern, largely eighteenth-century model of identity that is becoming historically implausible when *The Promised Land* comes out. But its vulnerability to critique is not clear right away. The trans-ethnic-transcultural displacements of the self do not mesh with, and hence are not thought through in relation to, the global flow of people, values, and languages. Heroines of otherwise profoundly unsettling dramas like Mary Antin do not suspect that the former paradigm of selfhood has been, or is about to be, superseded, as long as a common, Euro-American narrative of advancement, learning, and eventual resettlement turns out by and large able to accommodate the "translation" from czarist Russia to the land of opportunity: the cultural codes are different but not invariably incompatible; there is a soothing, unifying "deep structure" underneath societies and languages that offsets the "surface" fractures and asymmetries. This is, in fact, a translation in space that does not require, to Mary Antin's mind, the kind of cultural translation and metamorphosis that we witness in Hoffman. It is the post–Cold War era's fast accelerating global mutations that afford Hoffman a critical insight where Mary Antin's pre–World War I purview remains limited. It bears reiterating that here the limits have to do with an otherwise ineluctable fictionalizing of the present of experience. But they are also buttressed—and this is where Hoffman's memorious critique comes in—by another fiction, namely, Mary Antin's modern understanding of the self. Further fictionalizing that experience, this representation of the self channels Mary Antin's own representation of her "greenhorn" self.

If Mary Antin's narrative model is the Exodus, Hoffman's is Paradise Lost (Krupnick 1993, 458), featuring a familiar "tryptic": "Paradise," "Exile," and "The New World." More markedly than in Mary Antin, her autobiography is a biography of language—*Lost in Translation*'s "underlying story," as Hoffman calls it,[29] which reproduces loosely the book's tripartite structure. This story's first two chapters tell of a native Eden of being and language, of after-the-Fall trials through naturally wanting, "fallible" translation, and stemming from this, of an inner rift, identity "loss" or crisis brought on, and showing, through Eva's second language. Not only does English in fine dethrone Polish. It also inflicts a semiotic wound on the language's body—and equally on the speaker's self—by splitting the signifier-signified unit down the middle and blowing away the "aura" around words. "[M]ostly," a teenage Eva feels, "the problem is that the signifier has become severed from the signified. The words I learn don't stand for things in the same unquestioned way they did in my native tongue. 'River' in Polish was a vital sound, energized with the essence of riverhood, of my rivers, of my being immersed in rivers. 'River' in English is cold—a word without an aura. It has no accumulated associations for me, and it does not give off the radiating haze of connotation. It does not evoke" (1990, 106). Or, as she says elsewhere, "You can't transport human meanings whole from one culture to another any more than you can transliterate a text" (175).

Critics have turned to a host of linguists to untangle this and other similar passages. But a basic Saussurean vocabulary would suffice, I think. What has been severed is the umbilical cord that, we instinctively assume, links up the two sides of the linguistic sign. In *Mimologiques. Voyage en Cratylie,* Genette calls this assumption "semantic fallacy" (1976, 328) and finds some of its deepest roots in Plato's philosophy of names (*onomata*) expounded in the *Cratylus.* Since we will come back to the dialogue in the next chapter, here I will rehearse just one side of the Cratylian debate: words mirror formally the "essences" of the objects they designate, in which case "there is a reason" the Polish word for "river" sounds the way it does. Thus, the word, as a sign, is "motivated." The signifier is the phonetic shadow or echo of the signified, and "naturally" so. For one thing, this mimetic principle backs up our belief in accurate, "exact" representation of what we "have to say." For another, it reinforces self-representation, our perception of our own identity by reassuring us that we can actually express ourselves and our selves, more basically, that we do have a self to express. The Platonic myth of language warrants, in its turn, a certain myth of "originating," immutable self.

Fallacious as it may be, this pre-Babel fiction shores up our sense of wholeness, our well-being and simply our being ultimately. For it is essential that we see ourselves as "whole." This is how we reflect the presumed unity of the world, which shows in, and is ascertained by, the Cratylian unity of the signifier and the signified. "Poland," "Polish," and "Ewa" are "construction sites" for this multiple unity. In the transition, and unsuccessful triangulation, from Polish to, and into, English, this fiction falls apart, blocking Eva's communication with others and, more damagingly perhaps, with herself. In the Canadian world and in "English," English words cannot represent ("evoke") Eva's Polish past because they "have not penetrated to those layers of my psyche from which a private conversation could proceed." Vice versa, Polish does not apply to her "new experiences," hence "in a short time, has atrophied, shriveled from sheer uselessness" (1990, 107). Hoffman lays bare another connection here: between language and a certain personal rather than metaphysical "feeling from which it springs" (107), between a word and whatever it makes us think of when we first learn the language and take in the world it maps. At the same time, she paraphrases Mary Antin, who tells us that "Particular words remain associated with important occasions in the learner's mind," so much so that the history of her "English vocabulary" is also "an account of my comings and goings, my mistakes and my triumphs, during the years of my initiation" (1946, 210).

This quasi-Proustian tie is anything but fictional. This immemorial memory, this sense of language that gives us a sense of identity, creates us as we acquire and use our native language. We are our own linguistic work-in-progress. We are language. But this memory that we never lose also gets in the way, in the way of triangulation, encumbers it (Hoffman 1990, 107) and thwarts re-construction—in another language and culture—while making us aware of how much gets "lost in translation." Through language, it soaks up everything—through either Polish or English, as the case may be—and it is language, too, that hampers this screening, forestalling, in other words, its own use as mere vehicle or window onto a nonlinguistic reality. The idiom declines to be treated like a transparent medium or representation instrument. Displacing Eva's former mythical Cratylism, this "structuralist"—or poststructuralist, rather—realization casts light on an "immanent," self-sufficient linguistic system operating in, yet independent of, a "disenchanted" world. "I am becoming," she intimates, "a living avatar of structuralist wisdom; I cannot help knowing that words are just themselves. But," she adds, "it's a terrible knowledge, without any of the consolations that wisdom usually brings. It does not mean that I'm free to play with words at my wont; anyway, words in their naked state are surely among the least satisfactory play objects. No, this radical disjoining between word and thing is a desiccating alchemy, draining the world not only of significance but of its colors, striations, nuances—its very existence. It is the loss of a living connection" (107). Surfacing in the harrowing asymmetry of English and Polish, in the resistance of things American to triangulation to Polish and, conversely, in the refusal of Polish memories to body forth in English words, the springing apart of the signifier and the signified threatens the very existence of language and the self's existence altogether. "I'm not filled with language anymore," Hoffman owns, "and I have only a memory of fullness to anguish me with the knowledge that, in this dark and empty space, I don't really exist" (108).

This is an interstitial space, for sure: not a nonlinguistic terrain per se, but a domain of language contest. Therein the self learns how to secure an identity, how to *be* not in *a* language but *through* language*s*, for Polish has "becom[e] a dead language, the language of the untranslatable past" (120), while English is too shaky, fresh, "impersonal" (121), and incompletely assimilated to reclaim the former sense of self, the original fullness of being. Nor will English ever drain Eva entirely of "Polish" and the unforgettable memories her native language preserves. True, English is "not the language of the self"—not yet—not the "private" or "aural" (118) language of jokes and humor, irony and wit, secrecy and eroticism that Polish and, partly, Yiddish used to be. But it is "the language of the present." On this account, it is the only one she can turn to in her diary, the language of written expression. By comparison, writing in Polish "would be a little like resorting to Latin or ancient Greek" (121). Eva may take up an "impersonal" idiom, but journal writing, the "act" in which she plies her newly acquired English, is "most private" (121). As such, writing bids fair to be the occasion of a breakthrough, marking, quite literally, the place where the self may be rebuilt:

> The diary is about me and not about me at all. But on one level, it allows me to make the first jump. I learn English through writing, and, in turn, writing gives me a written self. Refracted through the double distance of English and writing, this self—my English self—becomes oddly objective; more than anything, it perceives. It exists more easily in the abstract sphere of thoughts and observations than in the world. For a while, this impersonal self, this cultural negative capability, becomes the truest thing about me. When I write, I have a real existence that is proper to the activity of writing—an existence that takes place midway between me and the sphere of artifice, art, pure language. This language is beginning to invent another me. (121)

Eva discovers something "odd," though: she cannot say—better still, write—"I" in English. She steers clear of the "schizophrenic 'she'" yet feels drawn "to the double, the Siamese-twin 'you'" (121). Without doubt, this is a rhetorical issue with deeply existential ramifications—or roots, rather. For the rhetorical and the existential are one in Hoffman. Better still, they become so through autobiographical writing. But, echoing her own dilemmas as it does, her "discovery" nonetheless reworks the opening passage in the introduction to *The Promised Land*, where Mary Antin raises the same questions. Unlike Hoffman, she concludes that "I could speak in the third person and not feel that I was masquerading. I can analyze my subject, I can reveal everything; for *she* and not *I*, is my real heroine. My life I have still to live; her life ended when mine began" (1946, x). Polotzk *was* a chapter, and Boston *is* another one, part of the present life; she no longer is what she was: "I was born, I have lived, and I have been made over." Her previous life has ended, so it is time to write her life story: "I am just as much out of the way as if I were dead, for I am absolutely other than the person whose story I have to tell." As for living in the same body, or, as she puts it, "physical continuity," this is just an accident and, truth be told, "no disadvantage" (x). The body is no nightmarish memento. She cannot ignore all the "uprooting," the "pang" of immigration. Still, she wants to forget, to "be of to-day" because "it is painful to be consciously of the two worlds" (xiv).

Yet Mary Antin cannot forget: "I can never forget, for I bear the scars" (xiv). But does this failure of forgetfulness lead to "schizophrenia," as Hoffman might suspect? Not at all. Mary Antin's teleological narrative marshals this sequentiality of the self without problems. In Hoffman, though, this is *the* problem. The Polish-English, past-present, I-You split replicates the multiple predicament of representation: the linguistic (semiotic), cultural, and, with a Derridean term, "subjectile" laceration that triangulation proves unable heal. One more time, the realization of this predicament gets its force not only from personal experience—from memory in the common sense—but also from her reading experience, from the memorious exchange with Mary Antin. The eerie resemblance of her story to Mary Antin's strikes Hoffman, but there is "another side to [Mary Antin's] story" (Hoffman 1990, 163), which comes to light in the passages from the introduction. As I have suggested—and as Hoffman confirms—a "creature of he[r] time" (162), Mary Antin "was not encouraged to expand . . . the other story behind the story of triumphant progress" (163). Hoffman is right: America provided Mary Antin with "certain categories"—what above I call representations—"within which to see herself—a belief in self-improvement, in perfectibility of the species, in moral uplift—and those categories led her to foreground certain parts of her own experience, and to throw whole chunks of it into the barely visible background" (163–64).

Hoffman's own America, her world generally no longer make her "feel the benefits of the self-assured ego, the sturdy energy of forward movement and the excitement of being swept into a great national purpose." She comes to the U.S., as we say these days, "after the subject," after the Enlightenment subject underwriting Mary Antin's Franklinian story, which stage in modernity is, unsurprisingly, also transnational. If Canada marked the onset of a cultural binarism where "Ewa" had in part to give way and adjust to "Eva," the U.S. breaks up the binary into a dazing "multiplicity" (164). In Houston, she reports, "I step into a culture that splinters, fragments, and re-forms itself as if it were a jigsaw puzzle dancing in a quantum space. If I want to assimilate into my generation, my time, I have to assimilate the multiple perspectives and their constant shifting." "Who, among my peers," Eva asks,

> is sure of purposes, meanings, national goals? We slip between definitions with such acrobatic ease that straight narrative becomes impossible. I cannot conceive of my story as one of simple progress, or simple woe. Any confidently thrusting story line would be a sentimentality, an excess, an exaggeration, and untruth. Perhaps it is my intolerance of those, my cherishing of uncertainty as the only truth that is, after all, the best measure of my assimilation; perhaps it is in my misfittings that I fit in. Perhaps a successful immigrant is an exaggerated version of the native. From now on, I'll be made, like a mosaic, of fragments—and my consciousness of them. It is only in that observing consciousness that I remain, after all, an immigrant. (164)

These are the last lines of part 2, "Exile," and befittingly so, for, in a way, Eva's exile ends here. At last, she is taking in its pervasiveness, the uncertainty, the unsteady perspectives, the semiotic maze, the surrounding conglomerate of selves and her own fragmented self.

The same cultural phenomenology of multiplicity intrigues Hoffman in *The Education of Henry Adams*. So different from Mary Antin's, Adams's autobiography gives Hoffman mixed feelings, too, which mark her response to his inconsistent representation of the modern self in its individual and collective form. In this regard, Hoffman is in distinguished company. In his 1961 novel *V*, Thomas Pynchon famously draws from this representation to work out a postmodern model of history. By and large, Hoffman goes down the same memorious path, reprising and disputing Adams's modernism concurrently. As Ira B. Nadel has observed, the *Education* shares some of the defining features of modernist style with works by Joyce, Conrad, Forster, or Picasso, which also appeared in 1918 (1999, xxvii). Making it "equal to these other manifestations of modernity," its "play with narrative, language, and time, and its efforts to define the present by reassembling the past while glimpsing the future" (xxvii–xxviii) have certainly aroused her interest. But in *Mont-Saint-Michel and Chartres*, published privately in 1904 while he was at work on the *Education*, and especially in the latter's last ten chapters, Adams develops a modern theory of history and identity that Hoffman finds at once enticing and debatable.

The romance of being, the story of its blissful, harmonious becoming, may commence, as Mary Antin intimates above, in an "enchanted cradle" but is borne out by her academic success. Adams also thinks that "From cradle to grave this problem of running order though chaos, direction through space, discipline through freedom, unity through multiplicity, has also been, and must always be, the task of education," of society generally (1999, 16). This is, in effect, the primary focus of his self-conscious *Education*, which expounds the interplay of "unity" and "multiplicity" throughout. Especially following the "Dynamo and the Virgin" chapter, he limns a multifarious modernity dispersed by centrifugal ("dynamic") forces, a restless and many-sided world that imparts its structure—or lack thereof—to the modern psyche. Recent history is living proof, he offers, that "the multiplicity of unity had steadily increased, was increasing, and threatened to increase beyond reason" (332). Where the "ontologist" and the "theologist" may be at a loss, the Darwinian scientist—the biologist, the geologist—recognizes that the world has become more and more complex, disjointed, plural, so much unlike the centripetal, unified universe symbolized and held together by the Virgin and, more broadly, by Catholicism.

We stumble here upon an eminent dilemma of modern thought. For one thing, Adams has a keen eye for the symptoms of modernity, first and foremost for the entropic proliferation of nonhuman, impersonal, technology-derived "forces." "Forces"—like Adams, I use the plural advisedly—is the keynote in his "dynamic" account of modernity. (We will remember that *dunamis* means "force" in ancient Greek). They are omnipresent and anarchic, and their ever-chaotic tussle marks natural evolution (395), politics (352), history (395), education, not least human personality (361–62). They take center stage more aggressively in recent modernity to spawn unbridled multiplicity. "The child born in 1900," Adams concludes, "would, then, be born into a new world which would not be a unity but a multiple" (382). His book's full title should be, accordingly, "The Education of Henry Adams: a Study of Twentieth-Century Multiplicity" (363). For another thing, chapters 24 and 28 tone down this extreme judgment. A different voice makes itself heard here, definitely more temperate-rational, more humanistic in its faith in science, in the human mind's overall capacity to assimilate the contradictory world and settle its contradictions by wrapping them around the cogito. This is the same voice that has all along reported the quickened "dynamic" of modernity, an account in which one can invariably hear a muffled caveat. For all in all, centrifugal forces—unlike centripetal force—threaten Adams and his world. He supplies us with the "dynamic formula of history" (405) yet does not seem quite comfortable with it. Adams calls himself an "anarchist," but also a "Christian" and a "conservative"; nor does he hide his misgivings about this unlikely "scheme" (340). His allegiances and beliefs are deployed symmetrically along the One/Many, centripetal/centrifugal, rational-humanist-Christian/irrational-impersonal axis, but on closer inspection this axis turns out to be a rhetorically camouflaged hierarchy.

In "A Dynamic Theory of History" and "A Law of Acceleration," Adams shuttles back and forth between two ontologies, epistemologies, and views of the self. Still, step by step, a gravitational center emerges in the dazzling field of forces; "history," he declares, "is not obliged to decide . . . whether ultimate energy is one or many" (405), yet a personal decision or conclusion begins to form. Natural reactions to the modern "stupendous acceleration" of "supersensual forces" (405), wonder and shock come first. We stand baffled before modernity's "dynamic" show, but so did "a priest of Isis before the Cross of Christ" (405). Christianity, in other words, supplies a rational model for domesticating the modern world of "out-of-control," inhuman ("supersensual"), and inhumanly mobile forces, and deep down Adams nourishes the hope that history will repeat itself by reactivating that model. After all, "religion, philosophy, and science seem to go hand in hand" (406). "In the early stages of progress," he observes, "the forces to be assimilated were simple and easy to absorb, but, as the mind of man enlarged its range, it enlarged the field of complexity, and must continue to do so, even into chaos, until the reservoirs of sensuous or supersensuous energies are exhausted, or cease to affect him, or until he succumbs to their excess" (406). The "movement from unity into multiplicity" picks up speed between 1200 and 1900 (414), but by "experiment" and methodic "testing," some "mechanical formula of acceleration" (406) may very well be within the reach of the human mind, in which case the mind itself would be able not only to *react* to external developments "successfully" but also to "jump," to get ahead of the ontological-epistemological game. In consequence, Adams's model is prevailingly rational-humanist.

It is interesting to see how Hoffman's deconstructive reprise of this model heads in a direction opposite to her anatomy of Mary Antin's narrative. Re-presenting the latter critically, the postmodern author brings out in bold, as we have learned, the "trace of the other story" underneath Mary Antin's "story of triumphant progress" (Hoffman 1990, 163) and rational refashioning of the self. Hoffman's antiromance of selfhood unearths fragmentation, failure, frustration, and the flimsiness of the "center" in a "dynamic" landscape of the psyche best illustrated by the immigrant subject. Conversely, her critical re-presentation of Adams uncovers an unacknowledged yet active and reassuring core of values, cultural codes, and moorings that are not only "American" but also Eurocentric, as Adams's considerations on the "backward" rush of "forces" in Asia and Africa show (1999, 405). Revealingly enough, Hoffman turns to the cradle trope to articulate her suspicion. On one level, a fellow Bostonian and Harvard student, plagued by deep-seated "incredulity," "sense of failure" (1990, 160), and the internalized specter of the "Many," Adams resembles her. Perfectly contemporary to Mary Antin's, Adams's America, Hoffman notices, is anything but "a launching pad for individual ambition" (159) and cannot be so because Adams's sense of history and identity seems at odds with it. On a deeper level, though, "It doesn't matter." In a passage that recycles specific language from the *Education*, Hoffman contends that

> [I]n Henry Adams, for all the tortuous involutions of the psyche, I encounter a sense of belonging and of natural inheritance. And this, it turns out, from my displacement, is what I long for—the comfort that comes from being *cradled* by continuity, the freedom from insignificance. The more I come to know about America, the more I have the dizzying sensation that I'm a quantum particle trying to locate myself in a swirl of atoms. How much time and energy I'll have to spend just claiming an ordinary place for myself! And how much more figuring what that place might be, where on earth I might find a stable spot that feels like it's mine, and from which I can calmly observe the world. "There are no such places anymore," my fellow student informs me. "This is a society in which you are who you think you are. Nobody gives you your identity here, you have to reinvent yourself every day." (160; emphasis added)

"Invent myself I must," Hoffman resolves, but the available "identity options" perplex her; she stands nearly "paralyzed by choice." Even more than Kazin and Podhoretz, Adams did have—did inherit—a sense of "stable spot" or perspective. And this is, simply put, Hoffman's objection: in reality, he did occupy such a "central" position—by social background, a most privileged one—while arguing its theoretical incongruity with the modern world. No less than Mary Antin, Adams makes Hoffman aware of her manifold "belatedness" as an immigrant, as a self without "manifest" purpose or part in the national drama, and as an "ephebe" writer. Mary Antin and, in spite of his rhetoric, Adams speak to and from a *center.* "But I have come," Hoffman retorts, "to a different America, and instead of a central ethos, I have been given the blessings and terrors of multiplicity" (164).

Multiplicity terrifies because it obstructs identity remaking and identity altogether. Social life, not least the life of the psyche, hinges, she supposes, on a modicum of consistency, but this becomes a daunting proposition without a guiding "ethos." "In a splintered society," she wonders, "what does one assimilate to? Perhaps," she answers, to "the very splintering itself" (197). Be that as it may, at Rice Eva pines for "direction," even if it arrives from the outside. She wants to "live within language and to be held"—"cradled"— "within the frame of culture." But she finds herself out of sync with the sixties America, which, to the contrary, is scrambling "to break our of the constraints of both language and culture" (194). The anachronistic fiction of this tutelar exteriority of culture delays self-remaking. The cultural norm, or principle, would have to be determined individually, and there is no single social recipe, of course, but lots of them since America is "made up of so many sub-Americas" (202). Hence, officially less "American" than her American-born friends, the mosaic self Eva acquires on American soil bespeaks a more profound Americanness, upon which she will draw to deal with the trauma of cultural metamorphosis.

"Trauma" may overstate Eva's condition but is not completely out of place. A traumatic symptom, the "undoing of the self" results in "a radical disruption of memory, a severing of the past from the present and, typically, an inability to envision a future" (Brison 1993, 39). But the undone self can remake itself as it tells his or her story, whose job is to reconnect the past and the present. In Hoffman, this reconnection occurs as recollection—a recollection of traumatic experiences, as memorious autobiography that "remembers" past texts (Mary Antin and Adams) as much as the self's past. Self-(re)making is the postmodern effect of narrative representation *and* re-presentation. In constructing a story, Hoffman reconstructs herself, but, once more, it is important to keep in mind that the textual reconstruction takes place intertextually. It is through others and their texts that Eva overcomes the psychopathology of cultural hyphenation, her "neurosis." But how does memorious healing occur exactly? Which are its stages?

For a while, Eva thinks she can handle the "two-forked creature that we all are" (Hoffman 1990, 271). But she soon realizes that she was living "in denial," so she decides to see a "shrink." Not only do her psychiatric appointments initiate her into another routine of Americana; the "therapy" she undergoes is also "partly translation therapy, the talking cure a second-language cure" (271). "English" commences the "repair" of the divided self by throwing a bridge between the past and the present, between the past self and the present self as it points up a "way of explaining myself to myself." Little by little, "it becomes a process of translating backward" (271): "The way to jump over my Great Divide is to crawl backward over it in English. It's only when I retell my whole story, back to the beginning, and from the beginning onward, in one language, that I can reconcile the voices within me with each other." Finally, the person telling and listening to the stories "begins to emerge" (272). It is only now that English closes the gap and the "healing" can begin; it is only now that Eva "crack[s] the last barrier between [her]self and language" (186). English finally "works" because it is no longer exterior to her, which makes "triangulation" to Polish superfluous. She comes, at last, to "embody" her new language. She ontologizes it by stepping across the inner "divide" between being and speaking (or writing), herself and English. "The language," she discloses, "starts speaking itself to me from my cells" (243), without displacing Polish while sharing its status and "unconscious" (243) underpinnings.

This is another breakthrough, which opens the third and last chapter of the story of language and becoming in *Lost in Translation*. In hindsight, though, the entire memoir plays a therapeutic role, as a narrative—and an autobiographical one at that—and more broadly as a textual and linguistic domain where the subject can indeed form, "be in," as Hoffman insists ever so often. In a book aptly titled *Autobiography: The Self Made Text*, James Goodwin posits that "discourse"—unlike "narrative," which focuses "objectively" on the "facts themselves" without any reference to the narrator—"is the linguistic means of existence for individual subjectivity" (17). But, like many narratologists, the critic grants that the distinction does not operate absolutely. It does not make much sense particularly in autobiography, where discourse and narrative cooperate closely in the "textual making" of the self. *Lost in Translation* is certainly a case in point: in it, narrative, as story and retrospection, has "discursive effects," institutes a subjectivity. Janet Varner Gunn calls this process "presencing": the autobiographical text "presences" (1982, 17) its writing subject.

I would recommend caution here. Heavily memorious and fictional, "utopian" in the aforementioned sense, Hoffman's text hardly abides by Lejeune's "autobiographical pact." Hence, the "presence" arising in *Lost in Translation* is a construct, a discursive-narrative outcome. Trading upon Lejeune's work, Paul John Eakin takes aim at the poststructuralist critique of the subject and linguistic referentiality to propose that "construction" (fictionality) and reference can coexist (1992, 31). *Lost in Translation* manages, however, to build a self, but this self is not necessarily "referential."[30] Nor is it the "unified 'I'" Kristeva, the *Tel Quel* group, and Lacan before them, take issue with. Hoffman's self has never been a presence unto itself, not even in mythic Cracow, and the text does not "unify" it either. If there ever was any "imaginary plenitude" to that "natural" stage of being, that fiction gets further "divided," as Kristeva theorizes—or "self-divided," according to Derrida—once the speaking or writing "I" submits to "the order of discourse."[31] We shall see below, this evolving, both (re)constructed and deconstructed, spoken and unspeakable "presence" remains plural, although not traumatically splintered anymore; it is composite yet animated by an energy that takes in, and responds vigorously to, a world no longer like Mary Antin's and Adams's.

No wonder critics have called this subject and the form in which it appears before us poststructuralist and postmodern. "The New World" part flaunts the self's cultural heterogeneity and multifaceted "production": linguistic (in and through English), narrative (in and through the autobiographical story), and discursive (in and through a text that bears all the marks of the self coalescing in its space.)[32] But the poststructuralist-postmodern subject is also psychoanalytic. Self-narration entails retrospection, through which the self and its past are revisited, retold, in other words, made over, but also understood and by the same token "got over." "To some extent," Hoffman observes, "one has to rewrite the past in order to understand it" (1990, 242)—to repeat (replay) it in order to comprehend it and thus *not* repeat (reenact) it (278). And she does just that, rewriting her past and other past writings to shake off the traumatic un-truth, the burdensome fictions impeding her becoming, her "healing." For, looking back on her childhood and adolescence, Eva sees ("reads") both Cracow and Vancouver as disproportionate accounts of events, as "stories" whose impact was nonetheless real. A "radical," traumatic "discontinuity," "emigration . . . makes such reviews and rereadings difficult," and leads to either "nostalgia," now denounced as an "ineffectual relationship to the past," or "alienation," "an ineffectual relationship to the present" (242). So construed, as a narrative problem, trauma can be "treated" accordingly. The "right"—self-conscious—"storytelling" perspective marks the triumph over it.

Two faces of the same coin, narrative and psychological "correction" allow, together, for an existential and cultural readjustment of the narrating self. But the ramifications of this realignment reach beyond this self due to the double bind, memorial (personal) and memorious (intertextual), of rewriting in Hoffman. That is, to rewrite her own past and translate it into a language whose compatibility with the present would cure her split self, she rewrites the collective past, translates the already-written past of Mary Antin's and Adams's stories into her present and present text, *Lost in Translation*. It is in this sense that the latter "presences," or, in line with the whole argument of my book, *re-presences*. Like in other postmoderns, de-construction through rewriting is here a necessary—and necessarily postmodern—preamble to self-understanding. Furthermore, in coming to terms with herself, Hoffman comes to grips with *her* America as already represented, already written by Mary Antin and Adams. She rewrites them, and at the same time chronicles America's self-rewriting over the past century. As a result, a new homology emerges here. Eva resembles the new America; in turn, America reflects the changes of globalization. The private, writing self and the collective self are finally alike, "on the same page" in all senses. No doubt, we are facing here a new paradox. At last, Eva feels "American," but her "Americanness" is not Mary Antin's or Adams's anymore. It no longer extends the fictive embrace ("cradling") of a seeming cultural monolith to millions of seemingly monolithic selves. It has gone past the torturous dyad ("Polish" vs. "American") of Eva's first years in North America and generally past modernity's binary logic into globality.[33] Indeed, this is the America of the global age, where the subject recognizes in the surrounding, pluricentric, and multilingual new Babel an uncannily accommodating home.

Cracow and Vancouver were both biblical, if antagonistic fictions: the Eden and the Fall, respectively. *Lost in Translation* comes out in 1989, in the middle of another, if secular Fall. Marking (and prompting) unequivocally the onset of the global age, this geopolitical event brings into question, for better or worse, all the schisms, binaries, and boundaries of modernity. Murky, disorienting, decentered, a cacophonic "buzz" (272) of voices and cultural tunes, this world responds, and corresponds, to Eva's new self. In it, she acquires a "new assurance," feels she can "handle" it "as if the globe were a large toy to play with" (251). Mary Antin's cry of triumph crowned a narrative of rationally accomplished self-betterment. Hoffman's signals something else: the healing over—but *not* the closing up—of the psychological, linguistic, and cultural split, the "curing," through global awareness, of an entire localist neurosis, of a whole cultural psychosis or location, dislocation, and relocation. Eva understands that her inner "split," "gap," and other schizoid attributes of her self have generalized and become a given in global society, that there is no "split" or "gap," but a whole world of "splits," "gaps," and "splintered" subjects, outside and against any individual aberration or pathology of being.

In this sense, healing the self—and self-healing in Hoffman's autobiography—involves coming to the realization that the rest of the world is more and more like the self, that this plural self is becoming the norm and therefore normal. It does not mean "turning" back to the point of "origin" prior to the "Fall" or "filling" the inner "gap" between the "prelapsarian" and "postlapsarian" worlds and selves. For "there is no returning to the point of origin, no regaining of childhood unity. Experience creates style, and style, in turn, creates a new woman. Polish is no longer the one, true language against which others live their secondary life" (273). Therefore, Eva "no longer triangulate[s] to Polish as to an authentic criterion, no longer refer[s] back to it as to a point of origin" (272). Accordingly, "Polish insights cannot be regained in their purity; there is something I know in English too. The wholeness of childhood truths is intermingled with the divisiveness of adult doubt. When I speak Polish now, it is infiltrated, permeated, and inflected by the English in my head." So "each language modifies the other, crossbreeds with it, fertilizes it. Each language makes the other relative. Like everybody, I am the sum of my languages—the language of my family and childhood, and education and friendship, and love, and the larger, changing world—though perhaps I tend to be more aware than most of the fractures between them, and of the building blocks. The fissures sometimes cause me pain, but in a way, they're how I know that I'm alive" (273)

No center, no origin and original "unity"; whence no *nostos*—instead, the superfluity of nostalgia; no Adamic language and value system whole onto itself and grounded in a privileged locality. This is Hoffman's exilic consciousness and implicit cosmopolitan credo. Following Freud, Guy Scarpetta defines cosmopolitanism in *Éloge du cosmopolitisme* as an attempt to occupy the ever unstable position where we arrive by "systematically" stepping across boundaries, by assuming an "essential exile" (exil essentiel) and "eternal diaspora, motility, and detachment from all that forces us to strike root and holds us back," (une diaspora sans fin reconduite, . . . une mouvance, . . . un arrachement à tout ce qui enracine, qui fixe et qui fige) by realizing, finally, that "no value is wholly tied down to a

place and no language is whole" (aucune valeur n'est localisable et
. . . aucune langue n'est toute) (1981, 25). Salman Rushdie is right
to call this "essential" exile part of our "common humanity."[34]
True, New York is the new "imperial center," and English "the Espe-
ranto of the modern world" (Hoffman 1990, 251). But "centrality
of control" has never been more "presumptuous," hence more in-
dicative of modern era's globalizing twilight, as Martin Albrow suggests (1997, 192): globalization need not mean—and ought not to
be—economic and cultural homogenization exclusively, the putatively neoliberal triumph that so many decry. There exists, in other
words, no center, but centers, competing nuclei; no language but
languages in the global Babel, so many dialects of the "globalbab-
ble." Analogously—and it is the awareness of this analogy that
"heals"—there is no single language in which the psyche can
"truly" represent itself and by which it can be claimed exclusively,
but a plurality of tongues and idioms. "Entered" by many voices,
Eva makes them "hers"—and *her*—and she is "being remade, fragment by fragment, like a patchwork quilt" (Hoffman 1990, 220), a
"script," "written in a variety of languages" (275). These languages
interpellate, inflect, and articulate each other. Together, they cir-
cumvent, mark out not an original core but a kind of Lacanian absence, a "loss which is the model of all loss" (274) and, as such,
provides the negative, "non-transcendent" (274) matrix of every
subjectivity, all the more so under globalization. Again, this recognition gives comfort, "is large enough to *cradle* a tenderness for everything that is always to be lost—a tenderness for each of our
moments, for others and for the world" (274). I must call attention
to Hoffman's memorious-intertextual trope of the "patchwork
quilt," but I would also stress that "loss" or "lack," the constitutive
if fantasmatic nucleus of being, plays here a major epistemological
role. "The gap," she says, "has also become a chink, a window
through which I can observe the diversity of the world" (274), a
unique angle and "Archimedean leverage" from which a "multiva-
lent consciousness" can make out and embrace an equally multiva-
lent world, the very "chinks between cultures and subcultures"
(275). For

> [m]ultivalence is no more than the condition of a contemporary aware-
> ness, and no more than the contemporary world demands. The weight
> of the world used to be vertical: it used to come from the past, or from
> the hierarchy of heaven and earth and hell; now it's horizontal, made
> up of endless multiplicity of events going on at once and pressing at each
> moment on our minds and our living rooms. Dislocation is the norm

rather than the aberration in our time, but even in the unlikely event
that we spend an entire lifetime in one place, the fabulous diverseness
with which we live reminds us constantly that we are no longer the norm
and the center, that there is no one geographic center pulling the world
together and glowing with the allure of the real thing; there are, instead,
scattered nodules competing for our attention. New York, Warsaw, Tehran, Tokyo, Kabul—they all make claims on our imagination, all remind
us that in a decentered world we are always simultaneously in the center
and on the periphery, that every competing center makes us marginal.
(274–75)

Eva is uniquely positioned to grasp this heavily mediatized Babel
because she is writing from a non-position of sorts, from the "white
blank center, the level ground that was there before Babel was built,
that is always there before the Babel of our multiple selves is constructed" (275). This is "ground zero" (276), what in *Memorious Discourse* I often identify as "groundless ground" (*Grund*) in which the
Barthesian zero degree of autobiographical writing grounds itself—
and fails. Yet this failure is redeemed by its own narration, through
which it acquires a voice. Notably, the voice comes into being memoriously, in conversation with other voices and their stories as *this*
story chugs on and in the process sprouts an identity, Eva's. As I
point out in the epilogue, Lee Siegel's also memoriously Nabokovian novel *Love in a Dead Language* associates the worldwide interlock-
ing of stories—the narrative integration of the global world—and
translation. Hoffman does the same when she reaches the "point"
to and into which she has tried to translate herself, to "triangulate"
all along (1990, 276), a "point of calibration" where she finds her
intertextual and supralinguistic voice above, under, or, more befittingly still, in all natural languages, past voices, and stories. None of
these can monopolize the representation of the self in the new
Babel. None can "translate," "assimilate" (276)—à la Mary Antin—
and speak, textualize, "construct" us completely in the postmodern
epoch, and it is in this sense that Eva claims that "we exist not only
within culture but also outside it" (276). Like in Siegel, translation
does not erase the differences among idioms, voices, and stories. It
does not yield absolute equivalents or renditions. It just suggests a
cultural and textual modus vivendi, a way in which texts and cultures
can coexist while overlapping, intersecting, interacting, and cross-
fertilizing each other, thus giving rise to new narrative forms and
subject "formations," to selves and identities.

Postmoderns like Siegel, Hoffman, Acker, or Charles Johnson
show that singularity, the idiomatic, and the idiom of the self overlap

with the transidiomatic and the transcultural, open onto the global and its swarming, Bakhtinian heteroglossia. Indeed, Eva defines her "voice" as "mastery" of her time's "voices" (1990, 276), incorporation of, and ability to play, this time's games of multiplicity, to let her "voices" talk to each other. There was another time, when she thought that her self's halves had to be glued back together linguistically. She learns now that, reinforced by the disjunctive logic of modernity, the "halves" in fact were, and are, more than two within a broader and shifty mosaic. Nor must the fragments and their voices be "welded" or the boundaries policed, and in this regard no "reconstruction" of the former paradise takes place here, as some have claimed (Friedrich 1999, 161). It would be futile, anachronistic, and a major inconvenience to the welfare of the self. Above, I called *Lost in Translation* a "transitional" text. We can see now, this text is "in transit," too. It grows, evolves in memorious collision with other texts, and ends up giving rise to a postmodern model of becoming attuned to a global problematic and awareness.

The Theater of Genre: Narrativity and Selfhood in David Antin

> *narrative lies at the core of my ideas about the structure of the self*
> —David Antin, *what it means to be avant-garde*

> the self itself is emergent in discourse
> —David Antin, *talking at the boundaries*

> [Prose is] "a cultural and ideological notion"
> —David Antin, "Thinking about Novels"

Like Hoffman, David Antin tells selfhood's postmodern saga, complete with its re-presentational double bind: to present itself, to "originate" textually, the self must take the memorious high road of otherness. In Nabokov and Hoffman, this "deviation," as I call it apropos of *Speak, Memory*, means essentially re-presenting others and their stories. In David Antin, this happens, too. But we shall see below that there are also moments when the narrating self views itself as (an)other, so much so that what this self revisits is its own past and the stories documenting it as if they were somebody else's. Thus, David Antin suggests that true selfhood obtains like a quantum leap of sorts as older moments, episodes, and stories are revealed and relived. Stemming from this is a unique type of "narrativity," which he sets up against conventional understanding of genre.

If a genre is "a theater of expectations," David Antin argues in a commentary on Toby Olson's novels, then that genre marks off "a site of possible operations within which these expectations can be satisfied, deferred, deflected, frustrated or transferred." This theater itself, he goes on, "can be regarded as a concrete structure satisfying a particular building code, or merely the promise of a place" occupied by "unexpected objects" or "unimaginable happenings" (1991, 210). Further, in "the structuralist," a poem from *what it means to be avant-garde*, the author puts his theatrical-performative concept of genre in historical perspective. "A genre," he offers, "is a theater defined by a history of the performances you remember taking place within it and any work seeking to play that theater will be judged in relation to the history of performance youve constructed for it" (1993b, 159).

In this chapter's final part I cast light on a certain dimension of David Antin's genre poetics—or, "counter-poetics," to use the term employed by Henry M. Sayre apropos of David Antin's talk-poems (1982, 432). In my own terms now, what interest me here are David Antin's memorious view and practice of narrativity, along the lines the author himself draws above and elsewhere in his work. That is, I will be pursuing narrative representation not as a traditional "building code" that keeps, for instance, metaphoric inflections of discourse at bay, but as a multigenre strategy of summoning, recollecting intertextually, the unexpected and the unimaginable, the unpredictable and the uncanny—ultimately, as a modality of tracing the dynamic, culturally controlled production or "origination" of the self. Significantly, David Antin has both worked out and reflected on this modality in his poems. As Hank Lazer has observed, "[a]n investigation of narrative lies at the heart of Antin's considerations of what it means to be a poet" (1995, 124). Following critics such as Lazer, Marjorie Perloff, and David Antin himself, I take a closer look at the practical results of this "investigation"—at the "theoretical" inquiry into narrative representation as well as at several texts growing out of this inquiry—and see how they bear upon David Antin's postmodern genealogy of selfhood, his invariable project. To reconstruct David Antin's representation model, I focus primarily on texts from *talking at the boundaries* (1976) and, to a lesser extent, *what it means to be avant-garde* (1991).

The writer evolves this model, I submit, across and against the classical tripartition of genres. More to the point, he effects a performative (onstage) conjuring up of life's strangeness and multifariousness, which are evoked essentially by narrative means as David Antin's memorious performances reel out sumptuous, long-winded narrative flashbacks.[35] It is equally worth observing, though, that these prose-based protocols of discourse also function like metaphoric structures as defined by most theories of metaphor. Namely, in spite of their prosaic and realistic appearances, they overflow preset categories of objects to shed light on the unknown, on the terra incognita of the self's unique experiences. As Paul Ricoeur insists in the preface to the first volume in his series *Time and Narrative*, such "illumination" may occur both through metaphoric language and plot. "The productive imagination at work in the metaphorical process," Ricoeur maintains, "is thus our competence for producing new logical species by predicative assimilation. It 'grasps together' and integrates into one whole and complete story multiple and scattered events, thereby schematizing the intelligible signification attached to the narrative taken as a whole" (1984, x). Moreover, the French philosopher notes, since metaphor is a staple of poetic discourse and plot an utmost feature of narrative, the two genres appear "closely bound up with each other" within "one vast poetic sphere that includes metaphorical utterance and narrative discourse" (xi).

David Antin's post-Aristotelian view and enactment of memorious narrativity are not incompatible with Ricoeur's phenomenology of genre and other, postmodern attempts in criticism, literature, or the arts to break away from the tripartite scheme classical poetics has handed down to us.[36] But the American poet takes a step further. He declines to rehearse the distinctions between "fact" and "fiction," and "poets" and "thinkers," respectively, as we learn in an interview with Larry McCaffery (David Antin 1996, 41–42). Nor does he differentiate between prose and its storytelling repertoire, on the one hand, and poetry and its tropological arsenal, on the other.[37] In effect, he proposes in the same interview that "[n]arrative action may be similar to the way metaphor functions in some kinds of poetry— the difference being that storytelling is grounded in an event more widespread, common social practice" (41). Furthermore, he mentions the development of Wittgenstein's style and thought—the enduring influence of which David Antin has often acknowledged[38]—to point out that the very language of *Notebooks, Zettel,* and *Philosophical Investigations,* whose texture itself constitutes a metalinguistic meditation, becomes "enchanted with the subversive tendencies of language and its multiple discourses." Notably, this enchantment obtains through narrative and metaphors that increasingly come to shape Wittgenstein's later work (50–51).

But, cutting as he does across established genre boundaries to do away with arbitrary and, as theorists like Gérard Genette have argued in a broader context, apocryphal classifications (1979, 65), David Antin introduces a new one. There is no clear-cut term to describe it since his syncretic "performances"[39] straddle the traditional divisions between genres, representation modes (fiction versus nonfiction),[40] discourse types (literature versus criticism; psychology and philosophy versus aesthetics and, again, literature), expression forms (writing/textuality versus speech/orality/"improvisation"),[41] and adjacent vocabularies. For lack of a better word, I will call this distinction phenomenological. This "classification principle" is most clearly brought to the fore, simultaneously described and applied, as Lazer has observed (1995, 124), in "the price," a piece performed in San Francisco in 1986 (David Antin 1993b, 92–119). "Poem-rap" (Alpert 1995, 188) and critical essay at the same time, the text expounds David Antin's notion of intertextual selfhood, in a discourse lodged at the crossroads of all the domains, forms, and paradigms listed above. It starts off, in point of fact, with a typically phenomenological move, with that sort of self-reflective opening protocol that speaks eloquently to the phenomenological legacy of poststructuralism and even of certain forms of cultural analysis such as identity studies (i.e., Foucauldian and cultural-materialist critiques of "disembodied subjectivity"). Thus, David Antin publicly owns that the self, the actual object of his performative "thinking" out loud or "questioning," and the very notion of question(ing) are intimately tied together. This realization alone would give the lie to the critics contending, as the author ironically paraphrases them before long, that he "had not enjoyed the benefit of french deconstruction which should have disabused [him] of [the] illusion of . . . the unitary self" (1993b, 93). Quite to the contrary, he tells us. "[I] have always thought," he explains,

> the idea of the self was surrounded by questions   and
> in fact what i was interested in were precisely those
> questions   which were questions i spent a lot of time
> asking   because i didnt know the answers   for if i
> knew the answers i wouldnt have any reason to ask the
> questions   and one of the questions im interested in
> asking is   what is the locus of the source or ground of
> the self   so when i thought of the title for this talk
> as "where are you?"   what i had in mind was to look for
> the place where the self   or what i take to be the self
> has   its ground. (93)

What the writer envisions here is something far less nebulous than the ontological concept of *Grund*, which Heidegger and others after him have employed to probe the "essence of poetry" and its illumination of the foundations of being. In the poem under scrutiny, the "ground" designates the place from which the self emerges, comes or is brought to the fore, into the open, or discourse. To Heideggerians, this constitutes an utmost feature of poetry as a particular language form. Yet David Antin prefers to call this process *narrative*. It integrates the self as structured identity and the self as becoming or "identity in-the-works," so to speak, trading upon—while declining to "solve"—the Parmenides-Heraclitus dilemma of classical metaphysics. Thus, on the one hand, the unrelenting disclosure of the self warrants a sense of identity or "coherence-granting" continuity within the same individual entity that we refer to by calling him or her by the same name throughout his or her life. On the other, we see this identity undergo experiences so different—so "differentiating"—that they threaten to unravel the fabric of the entity they are meant to weave (1993b, 94). Consequently, it might be more appropriate to talk—again in a fairly Wittgensteinian tone[42]—about one's "selves" rather than one's self as much as there are so many ways of talking about the same self or "I" (162–63).

To put the matter otherwise—or get closer to the memorious core of the matter, rather: for David Antin, identity and the self are two different things. The latter is the broader category, springing, as he specifies, out of a "collision of the sense of identity with the issues of narrative" (95). It is at this juncture that, the obvious "overlap" notwithstanding (Lazer 1995, 126), the poet puts forth the demarcation I was referring to above, one which sets off *narrative* from *story*. "i would like to distinguish," David Antin continues,

> between two   things one i would call narrative and the
> other story   and as i see it theyre related   but not
> the same   story is a configuration of events or parts
> of events that shape some transformation   but narrative
> or so it seems to me   is a sort of psychic function
> part of the human psychic economy and probably a human
> universal   at least we identify it with being human
> and it involves a particular paradoxical confrontation
>
>   consider the possibility of being confronted by a
> potential transformation   think of some thinking mind
> some subject   some experiencing human being   even a
> very elementary one

        at some point this being encounters the
    possibility the likelihood of transformation . . .
        now my sense is that the center of narrative is the
    confrontation of experience   an experiencing subject
    with the possibility of transformation   the threat of transformation or
    the promise of transformation. (1993b, 95)

This is not the sole place, in "the price" or elsewhere, where David
Antin originally parts company with critics and thinkers on aesthetic
and philosophical issues. It is, though, one of the most consequen-
tial because it theorizes, against structuralism and rather along
poststructuralist and postmodern lines, memorious narrativity as understood and practiced by the author. According to this understanding and practice, narrative is the subject's internalization of his or
her potential change, human mind's confrontation with the alienat-
ing-annihilating possibility of the Rimbaldian "*JE est un autre.*" In
discourse, and in memorious discourse in particular, such a possibility translates into a phenomenology of continuous development,
flux, growth, crisis, and change, in short, transformation. While
story suggests completed cycle, closure, *structure,* narrative stands
for—and brings about—*structuration,* repeated reconstruction
("grounding") of selfhood on the heels of decisive critical moments
and in socioculturally determinate, transformative contexts. As the
writer specifies,

    what narrative at its core celebrates or ritually
    reenacts is this grounding of self   over the threat
    of its annihilation   and here is where my distinction
    between narrative and story comes in
        because i would hold that a story is merely
    the configuration of events or parts of events that
    shape a possible transformation   a temporal
    configuration of events that mark the passage of one
    articulated state of affairs into a significantly
    different one   which when it engages the desires and
    fears of an experiencing subject represents the external
    shell of surface manifestation of a possible narrative
    but it is the engagement with the possibility of change
    that is the fundamental issue
                        because any event that is of
    any significance at all must change you. (98–99)

In view of this forthright statement, David Antin's whole work
strikes me as an ongoing narrative meditation on the self, a ceaseless
interrogation of the metamorphosis and heterogenous "becoming-

Other" grasped as the inner logic and inescapable drama of being. Of course, "the price" itself is paying the price for this vision, along with numerous other poems by David Antin—as many splendid illustrations and celebrations of change. For, to be sure, change—and being, selfhood therewith, ultimately—"comes at a price" (99). And so does the poem, the "price" for which is David Antin's postmodern "balancing act" or relentless negotiation of structure and structuration, story and narrative, identity and self, homogeneity and heterogeneity, text and intertextuality. Notably, various personas of his narratives run the risk of disintegration as they evolve: "[t]he degree to which [a significant event] changes you is the degree to which it is a threat to your existence" (99), the author himself acknowledges. But, if this prospect is real, can then the text itself, no matter what we choose to call it—poem, narrative, performance, "talk poetry" (Altieri 1986, 13), and so forth—head off the same mortal danger, in other words, dissolution, amorphousness? Traditional poetics would probably give us a skeptic answer here. But David Antin's performative, antiprescriptive, and memoriously "transgressive" discourse hints at something else. A category different from story and other literary forms, narrative operates as an integrative, coherence-building principle of his performances/texts rather than as a centrifugal force. Paradoxically as it may seem, narrative—vehicle and symptom of existential change, difference, and cultural hybridity—works to provide David Antin's own narratives with continuity and "flow." In this sense, "the price" itself is again an example.

I use the word example advisedly. The writer develops his "theory" of narrative by narrative means, through concrete examples— what he calls "thinking by way of example" (1993b, 111), and a very explicit thinking to that.[43] He thinks narrative through, represents (theorizes) it memoriously or "exemplarily," by renarrating previous stories ("examples"). In doing so, he acts out the venerable truth that oral cultures have for long been living by: knowledge is as manageable in narrative, in particular examples, as in abstract categories (Ong 1982, 140).[44] Thus, in David Antin, the theoretical text—in principle, a model that formalizes, conceptualizes knowledge—is shaped *as* narrative intertext. Accordingly, to instantiate his model of the self as cultural intertextuality or "social construct" (1993b, 98) growing out of the "series of accommodations"— adaptations and (per)mutations—the self has to undergo, the author reprises the story of a "famous russian journalist" (99) who went through momentous "accommodations," personal as well as collective. David Antin's character "came to terms" with himself and more or less the entire twentieth century of Russia and its successor, the defunct Soviet Union: the Bolshevik revolution, various leaders and dictators "from kerensky to brezhnev," and the collective nightmare they have been responsible for. Only "coming to terms," survival as moral and political compromise, costs quite a bit. And both the self of this writer—and spokesperson for the former Soviet Union to boot—and this self's narrative chronicle bear out such a transaction. Realistic, pragmatic, or just "cynical," this antiheroic self is endowed with a "shiftiness," a malleable texture that enables it to "fold itself around whatever comes without tearing   the mensheviks the bolsheviks the   constitutionalists the bolsheviks again the leninists   and in the end the stalinist imperium" (101).

No doubt, there is a *story* here. Yet it does not quite honor the self. This is a dismaying account of successively aborted narratives, of "narrative crises" and "situations" (102) that the self's survival instinct warded off, denied, or "forgot," and in so doing failed the test of responsibility, as the character's writings testify. In "what i am doing here," the opening piece from *talking at the boundaries*, David Antin is very adamant about this relation between self-perception— one's sense of one's own "personality"—and ethical, "self-interrogating" memory, which staves off the temptation of "selective" recollection. "[T]he only way   that i can conceive of myself   as a personality," he states in an important confession, is "by an act   of memory   by an act of interrogation of my memory   which is also talking   the self itself   is emergent in discourse   in some kind of discourse   it is probably available   but it comes up under dialogue   and the dialogue   is   conducted with it   and then the self emerges even though the self   may not have been there until you called upon it." (1976, 10)[45]

To go back to "the price," a similar albeit less self(-)incriminating case than the Russian writer's provides the author's father-in-law. As a young boy, he witnessed the execution of a soldier whom Trotsky sent to death for having "commandeered" a herring. "Whenever he [the poet's father-in-law] tells that story," David Antin writes in another definition/enactment of narrative,

> he comes to the edge of a narrative in which he stands
> at the brink of a terrible transformation   which if he
> chooses to experience could prove horrifying   and which
> he characteristically deflects with a laugh   but by
> repeatedly approaching and resisting the transformation
> that entering this narrative would force on him   what
> he approaches in this story   at least in its repeated

tellings   is very much like narrative as i have defined
it   but it is a narrative of the narrative situation
of the threat and terror of a narrative which could if
experienced transform my father-in-law's self beyond his
own recognition

   and yet at the same time if i am right   his
continued resistance to this threat is a fundamental
self constituting act. (105)

Revealingly, the father-in-law's story is interwoven with its telling.
They cannot—and should not, David Antin insists—be kept apart.
The delivery does not "distort" the tale.[46] In fact, it makes the delivered episode be what it is, mean what it does, for the teller, the characters, as well as the audience. In and through the very act of
storytelling, the storyteller takes up not only a narrative position but
also an ethical stance. Unlike the Russian writer, who in his stories
chose to ignore crisis and thereby the narrative "constitution" of his
self as culturally and politically inflected by certain critical moments
in his life, the father-in-law confronts such moments in his story.
And again, the story bears out this personal engagement, through a
unique dynamic of "discourse" and "story," as the structuralists
would say.
   One should keep in mind, though, that David Antin takes aim
precisely at this terminology and the arguably formalist mind-set
couched in it. Here is his critique, which merits extensive quotation:

   now this act of confrontation is almost entirely
absent   from the accounts of narrative given by the
structuralist thinkers like propp or bremond or lévi-
strauss or todorov or roland barthes   because they are
fundamentally externalists concerned with the
articulation of story as a kind of abstract and
generalized social production   and while they sometimes
illuminate elegant symmetries in the shapes of plots i
dont think they are really relevant to a study of
narrative at all   mainly because they begin from texts instead of tellings
and even if they come out of
tellings they come out of more or less ritualized
occasions that tend to obliterate the narrative centers that
arise from human experience but stories that
arise from ordinary social occasions are always
narrative   because they arise out of a circumstance in
which you are talking and trying and failing to make
some kind of sense

> and the stories that they have collected are
> usually nobody's telling and often a kind of synthesis
> of several people's tellings   or else they treat them
> as nobody's telling   where nobody is trying to make any
> particular sense. (110–11)

David Antin rebuts above an entire tradition of "folklorism" (111), formalist ("morphological") poetics (V. I. Propp), and its heir, French structuralism. He calls this "objectivist" or "neopositivist" line of thought "externalist." Opposed to it is his "internalism," which interlocks the tale, the telling and its cultural-historical context, and the teller in a single discursive apparatus.

This apparatus is intriguingly memorious, both a subject *in* David Antin's "text"—as inscribed in the book I am quoting from—and its shape. For the text is, after all, the "(tran)script"—"notations" or "scores"[47]—of an oral performance through which David Antin delivered ("told") it, even though, it goes without saying, "whatever winds up on paper is never exactly like whats in the air" ("the price," from *what it means to be avant-garde* [1993b, 124]). Theme and form are, here as elsewhere in his oeuvre, the two faces of his Janus-like talk-poem. Accordingly, change, which narrative represents, fashions not only the selfhood of his characters, whose metamorphoses ("change stories") he feeds into his work, but also this work itself. The latter opens a window into an autobiographical space where the reader witnesses how the author's own life has been in its turn more or less molded by these metamorphoses/texts. Doubtlessly, David Antin's talk poems commemorate—in both senses—transformation. They orchestrate a phenomenology of inner becoming, of self-acknowledged crisis, change, and growth, unfolding as they do a poetic panorama the main instruments of which are, oddly enough, narrative as well as dramatic: narrative in that the "poems" basically consist of/re-present stories told mostly in denotative language, and dramatic because the author delivers his "stories" by performative means, *coram populo*.

"[t]he river," which follows "the price," is in point of fact change itself, a Heraclitean, "ongoing enterprise" (123) as much as a poem *about* change. Its inevitable flip side, stability—identity features that remain unaltered while the self evolves—is also present throughout the poem but chiefly in its latter half, which tells another story of the poet's father-in-law. "[T]he river" raises the "question of beginning" (126) and answers it by meandering through a few narratives exemplifying—in all senses—the leitmotif of beginning, which the author reiterates verbatim at strategic moments. Actually, he uses the plural "beginnings" instead of the singular, and the distinction is noteworthy. The poem recounts, among other things, a series of "starts" in the author's and his father-in-law's life as so many occasions for the people involved to experience narrative at critical turns in their lives: the speaker's decision to move to California and teach in San Diego or the father-in-law's decision to emigrate to the U.S. following traumatizing experiences in Hungary. In part, the poem derives its consistency from the organizing presence of the symmetrically deployed theme (126, 134, 142, 153), the latter being part of the explicit commentary on the narrative episodes in the poem.

More remarkably still, the piece is held together by the aforementioned undergirding narrative phenomenology. The text shows how people face out dramatic transformation and thereby deal with who they are or are about to turn into. Change—or the prospect thereof, at least—may be brought about by experiences such as voluntary relocation, hasty self-exile, the learning of a new language and its use in one's writing, a new career, one's discovery of a new artistic talent, and so forth. These may be solemn exploits or anecdotal moments, such as the comic encounter between one of the poet's co-workers and her tattooed date in "what am i doing here" (1976, 8). In hindsight, however, they all turn out to be *meaningful.* That is, not only are such episodes memorable; they also carry memorious potential. They constitute postmodern memory cases where the personal and interpersonal (intertextual) aspire to equivalency, hence dispute the same discursive space. This is why they are worth "remembering recording representing," to quote the title of another poem from *talking at the boundaries.* Prone to re-presentation in David Antin's text, these prior representations of life prompt narrative "self-representation" and hermeneutic revelations à la Nabokov, recollection as self-understanding, in brief, a fundamental sense of identity. Again, David Antin's postmodern stories do not reflect this identity mimetically. They do not build it from scratch but scratch it together, not unlike Nabokov, Hoffman, and other memorialists of postmodernism. They "compile" identity out of a rich repertoire of extant stories and their cultural intertexts. The next chapter carries on the chronicle of this identity construction by focusing on postmodernism's onomastic discourse.

2

Naming, Representing:
Postmodern Onomastics

[L]et us activate the differences and save the honor of the name.
—Jean-François Lyotard, *The Postmodern Condition*

[N]o word exists alone, and the reason for choosing each word
had to be explained with a story about why it must be said this
certain way. That was the responsibility that went with being
human. . . .
—Leslie Marmon Silko, *Ceremony*

AT THE CROSSROADS OF LINGUISTICS AND ANTHROPOLOGY, ETHNOGRA-
phy and folklore, history and geography, onomastics has traditionally raised complex issues regarding the origins and meanings of
names. In the wake of structuralism and its poststructuralist fine-
tuning, Continental thought and criticism have further compounded
this interdisciplinarity by putting a cultural, ethical, and political
spin on onomastic analysis. First, this chapter reviews some of these
developments. Then, drawing loosely from them, it goes on to examine the memorious use of names by postmodern writers of back-
grounds as diverse as Auster's, DeLillo's, Acker's, and Morrison's.

The reader of the postmodern memory chapter might wonder,
What does "memorious" mean here? It means that the postmoderns are drawn to the literary and cultural intertextuality of names,
that they treat names as intertexts, onomastic re-presentations. In
postmodernism, I submit, names, too, re-present. They say other
names while saying themselves, and by the same token flaunt their
own "positionality," their place in a culture's or literary tradition's
nomenclature. All poems are positional, we have learned from
Nabokov. And so are names. Underlining the "poetic" value of
names, Kenneth Burke notes in *The Philosophy of Literary Form* that
this value or function operates alongside names' descriptive role
(1967, 147–48) to suggest an "interpretation": a certain "attitude"

(149) toward the thing named, a "command" (294) or "recipe for wise living" (295). Where philosophical or philological onomastics dwells typically upon the formal relationship between the name and the named, Burke deems naming a social "strategy" (300), contending that the semantic analysis of the onomastic sign's two units does not tell the whole story. We begin to tell this story once we look into the poetic employment of the name, which accounts for the latter's social impact. That is to say, semantics alone is powerless, hence it must be accompanied by a pragmatics capable to gauge the public effectiveness of an onomastic "style" or "poetic" twist.

Is postmodernism one of pragmatism's avatars? *Memorious Discourse* does not purport to answer this question, although it does not dodge it either, in this chapter and elsewhere. Not unlike Burke and other pragmatists, I believe in the social resonance of speech acts, signs, words, and names. A naming act is, indeed, an *act*, an "action" form. But what I mean to emphasize on a more Bakhtinian tone throughout this chapter is that this action's form shapes the social signification, the politics of action itself, because this form is rather a memorious *formation*: as a name is created and used—always *relationally*—other names are reprised and, with them, a whole spectrum of texts, discourses, and representations.

To tell a name's story, then, as Leslie Marmon Silko observes in the epigraph above, is to tell other names' stories. Consequently, to understand a name is to understand its interonomastic "origin," the intertextual stuff it is made of, in short, the name's memorious nature. Names do represent certain identities. But, as I maintain, a name's articulations with other names and the narratives underpinning them, then with the histories, cultural sediments, and politics embedded in those narratives, are also "packaged" with that representation. To be sure, names are like "label[s] of the mental file[s]" we keep on people (Margolin 2002, 109). Or, as one of DeLillo's characters puts it, names—proper names, to be more precise—are our "badges," and we will come back to DeLillo's insight. But all these labels and badges, all these names and chunks of text are linked to other labels, badges, texts, and the chunks of life they organize into otherwise ever-intertwined nomenclatures. We will be better prepared to come to grips with this distinctive onomastic "mess" in DeLillo and other postmoderns after a detour through Derrida and Lévinas for, long-winded as their answers may be, these thinkers have asked questions not unlike those posed by DeLillo himself, as well as Auster, Acker, Morrison, Updike, Roth, Pynchon, Silko, Louise Erdrich, and other contemporary writers.

"WE EMBRACED EACH OTHER BY OUR NAMES": THE NAME, THE OTHER, AND THE POLITICS OF ONOMASTIC INTERTEXTUALITY

When you name yourself, you always name another.
—Bertolt Brecht, *Mann ist Mann*

More pointedly than other kinds of discourse, postmodernism shows that names are like texts, that many names, including literary names, *are* texts; that naming a character involves a fictional and ideological decision leading to a "fable of identity," which tags as much as enmeshes the name-bearer in history—in the history of a community, of a place, of an obsession—or, intertextually, in literary history. In other words, our names are memorious because they carry the comforting or painful memory of others and their names, real or imaginary, other "badges," barely visible or conspicuously incised, palimpsestlike, underneath our own. Names are hardly surface, "free-floating signifiers." Nor do they betoken the alleged superficiality of the postmodern subject. Postmodern onomastics illuminates this subject's cultural "thickness" and historical moorings. In a sense, postmodern names do represent our being's outer layers or garments, our linguistic in-vestment. Yet in another, this investment runs deep culturally and politically, for our names weave us into other layers of social life and history, into otherness, ultimately, and our responsibility toward it.

Etymology and its sister, onomastics, lie at the core of Derrida's deconstruction. The latter may not be a method, as he often insists. But onomastic dissection is certainly a favorite technique *of* deconstruction. In this view, the French philosopher has always been an onomastician of sorts. With *On the Name* (1995), though, names no longer are solely, or primarily, a method of inquiry. They become subject matter. Interestingly enough, *On the Name* is *de facto* an American book because it gathers English translations of three short texts independently elaborated and originally published in French in 1993: "Passions," "Sauf le nom," and "Khora." They make up, their author tells us, "a sort of *Essay on the Name*—in three chapters or three steps" (1995, xiv).

To take the first step, Derrida concedes that something or someone bears our name, and we may in fact nourish the illusion that, as he says (12), "all that returns to X," to that named something or someone, naturally returns to, bears upon, and in some way honors us. Yet we, the named, are not, nor do we become, our names, possibly except, as DeLillo warns us, when culture's fame ("renown") apparatus manages to "reduce" the "being" (*être*) of some among us, what they actually are, to their "re-noun" (*renommée*), to the "Name" (*le Nom*)—a "renamed" name, it usually turns out, irrelevant to the named (2003b, 81). Either way, the name does quite well in our absence, in the absence of an organic tie to the named, to "the place toward which something could return" (Derrida 1995, 12)—without in fact ever completing the return and thus reaching its putative origin.

Or, to the contrary, the named itself may simply break free from the name we gave him/her/it. The latter can therefore "disappear *in [our] name*" (13), in which case the relation between the name-giver and the named corroborates the poststructuralist dynamic of originless trace: the subject is hardly the ultimate "source" our name or the names we give the world can refer to or fall back on safely. The name's destiny appears, in this light, "destinerrant" (30), to use another Derridean coinage. The name "errs" on its way back to the elusive source, a source which in his/her/its turn is not coextensive with the name he/she/it bears. The secret of our being, of a subject or object (a text, for example), can be, and usually is, successfully *spoken in other names, cross-onomastically or memoriously, by way of onomastic intertextuality*. Being is indeed "irreducible to the very name which makes it secret" (26). All we can do, I would suggest following out Derrida's thought, is paraphrase being, go around it in onomastic circles that cross other beings and their circles. Around being, and in order to name it, we draw the circles of otherness; around our being, and in order to talk about it, we speak through other(s') names, in (their) tongues. Great responsibility comes with this memorious realization.

On the heels of this understanding, step two becomes possible, if "obliquely," as Derrida lays down an ethics of reading that constructs the reader as "friend." We will see momentarily how the philosopher conceptualizes the dynamic of friendship and naming. For now, let me just say that, according to Derrida, Augustine's *Confessions* or Silesius's religious poems issue a remarkable invitation or prescription. "The friend," the French philosopher specifies, "is asked, recommended, enjoined, *prescribed* to render himself, by reading, beyond reading: beyond at least the legibility of what is currently readable, beyond the final signature—and for that reason to write" (1995, 41). Analyzing one of Silesius's addresses to his audience, Derrida shows how the reader is entreated to reach, through the reading of the poem, beyond the poem and to become writing himself, indeed, that essence (*Wesen*) the "writ" embodies. Importantly, this essence does not predate reading, and here we witness,

again, the postmodern/poststructuralist resistance to any suggestion
of source, origin, or founding authority/anteriority. The essence is
that which the "friend-reader" instantiates, bodies forth during
reading; it is, as Derrida argues, "born from nothing and tends
toward nothing" (42), pure "becoming" (*Werden*) and "becoming-
self" that allows for an "engendering *of* the other" (43).

Khora marks the third step toward *On the Name*'s poststructuralist
philosophy of naming. Derrida stresses here that the complex Platonic notion of the *khora* reaches us basically as a mass of sounds, as
a name. But, he goes on, "when a name comes, it immediately says
more than the name: the other of the name and quite simply the
other, whose irruption the name announces," an "imminence" of
a continuously postponed presence. The term's name, let alone its
translation, lays bare an ambivalent, rather paradoxically fruitful "incapacity for naming" (89). That is, it names without naming because
it breaks the noncontradiction rule enforced by traditional logic.
Further, it is both sensible and intelligible—or rather neither—a
"genre beyond genre" yet a site or "receptacle" for oppositions and
distinctions, thus a space giving (lending) itself to naming, a place
where naming can take place. It does not remain beyond naming,
much though we shall never be able to come up with the right name
for it, with *le mot juste* (93). "Not having an essence," Derrida asks,
"how could the *khora* be . . . beyond its name?" (94). At this juncture,
he distinguishes between common and proper names to argue that,
if the notion cannot be named (renamed, translated) by a common
name, by an all too specific, category- or genre-bound denomination,
the proper name might be the solution. As Derrida proposes, *khora*
should be understood as *the khora*, a unique entity without a referent
that one might locate in a *class* of objects.

This impossibility of identification and localization of that which
allows other things to take or have a place renders reading possible
(98), and the next chapters will ponder this paradox more extensively. Here, it is the *khora* and the scholarly body accumulated
around it that problematize the very process of reading, of reading
as a perpetually recommenced act of naming and renaming, entail-
ing endless "permutations, substitutions, displacements" (111). As
a matter of fact, this might very well be one of *On the Name*'s main
lessons: naming is just another . . . name for reading, for comprehension in general. People and texts are not very different in this
respect. The name is a dynamic reality. Its body launches invisible
tentacles to other onomastic bodies. Its history and makeup call for
careful perusal because the name always says more (names) than itself and that which it points to, labels, or identifies.

On the Name gives it to us straight: onomastic issues are "urgent" (16). *Politics of Friendship*, a translation of the 1994 French original, *Politiques de l'amitié*, reaffirms this urgency as it draws from the most traumatic collective experiences of the twentieth century, the Holocaust and communism, to foster a new "onomastic politics" where, simply put, naming no longer provides a bureaucratic tool of controlling the other, but a way to "embrace" him or her, an occasion for friendship. The suggestion of this alternative—onomastic, ethical, political—gets somewhat "lost in translation." Importantly, Derrida is talking about *politiques* of friendship, and the plural makes a whole lot of difference. Specifically, he is contrasting two kinds of politics: a unifying, authoritarian, enslaving one and another where friendship as a response to the call of the other works through names, involves them deeply. The clearest, albeit extreme illustration of the former sort, which has recourse to names to discipline the named and hence the identity of the other, is twentieth-century totalitarianism from Hitler's national-socialism to Milosevic's socialist-nationalism. The alternative, Derrida's, is memorious twice: first, due to the argument itself Derrida is making, and second, because he is building it through a Lévinasian reprise.

This is not the first time he looks to Lévinas's thought, as *On the Name*'s summoning of otherness has shown. In fact, Derrida's entire philosophy, particularly its spectacular, renewed emphasis on ethical matters, could be seized as an unremittingly memorious dialogue with Lévinas, with his Husserlian and Heidegerrian interpretations, to be more precise. This exchange commences with the frequently quoted essay "Violence and Metaphysics" from *Writing and Difference.* There, Derrida dwells at length upon how Lévinas takes up Heidegger to sketch out a philosophy—especially an ethics—of being more effectively revolving around the presence of the other and the responsibility we bear for this presence (1979, 134). No doubt, Lévinas's thought is an important source for him—and ambiguously so. It is, as a matter of fact, both a target and a guide for what will come to be known as deconstruction, the critique of the binaries or conceptual dualisms shaping, according to Derrida, the whole history of Western metaphysics and culture from Plato to Descartes to Husserl (Lévinas's major inspiration), to Lévi-Strauss's structuralist anthropology.

I am rehearsing this textbook definition deliberately, for the distinction or hierarchical opposition between the self and the other is among the dichotomies Derrida renders unstable—with Lévinas's help. In *Totality and Infinity* (published in 1961) and elsewhere, Lévinas explains how and on what level—the level of "sensibility" as opposed to "totalizing" reason—we are likely to meet the other,

whence act "responsibly"/"altruistically" in a world we must share
with other selves. If it is to occur, this meeting has to take place outside the stereotypes and categories of traditional metaphysics. Simply put, Derrida sets out to dismantle these rubrics of thought by
showing how that which they claim to isolate (de-fine) is already "in-
fected" by the elements they purport to keep out: their conceptual
other. The self is already on the way to the other as his/her *alter ego*,
according to Derrida's reading of Lévinas (1979, 187). We will see,
this situation bears upon who we are and upon how our names bear
out, in their turn, our identity.

While less explicitly conjured in *Politics of Friendship*, Lévinas's
figure looms high in the memorious backdrop of Derrida's thoughts
on names, naming, the interpersonal, and history. It is worth recalling that Lévinas's *Proper Names*, a translation of *Noms propres* (1975)
and *Sur Maurice Blanchot* (1976), which comprises essays the French
philosopher published between the late fifties and the midseventies,
was released by Stanford in 1996, just a few months prior to *Politics
of Friendship*. Furthermore, Lévinas's book appeared in the same series in which Derrida's *On the Name* had come out the year before.
Thus, all these titles make up a fairly coherent discourse on onomastics, philosophy, and culture. In this discourse, Lévinas's approach
to otherness and history, on the one hand, and Derrida's analysis of
naming as a political act, on the other, play a major role and call for
a discussion that must not lose sight of their mutual implications.
They do provide illuminating, unavoidable contexts for each other.
Hence, a quick look at Lévinas's book is in order before delving into
the memorious onomastic intricacies of *Politics of Friendship*.

Proper Names celebrates the "great names" that have placed themselves on the line of European intellectual history from Kierkegaard,
Proust, Martin Buber (the other great modern philosopher of otherness), Edmond Jabès to—no surprise here—Derrida himself (Lévinas 1996, 55–62). In this view, the book is a commemoration. For
so are proper names, after all: we resort to them to remember and
commemorate, to recall those no longer with us but still close to us
in ways that more often than not defy immediate comprehension—
and, we will observe, Derrida picks up, through Michel de Montaigne, on this fundamental function of names. For now, let me note
that Lévinas seems to be distinguishing between linguistic signs in
general and names while addressing the crisis of language and representation in our time. "Signifiers" and "signifieds," he contends like
so many other theorists and critics after structuralism, play a "sign
game" that has "neither sense nor stakes" anymore (4)—"Hence
the wearing away of the signified, releasing a system of signs, of signi-

fiers without signifieds, of a language that no full meaning guides,"
as he concludes in his own essay on Derrida from *Proper Names* (58).
In effect, the celebrated names enumerated above have earned their
names for having admirably accounted for our "general alienation
from the meaning" and the corresponding "painful break with discourse" as reflected in the modern obsession with "the inexpress-
ible, the ineffable, the unsaid" (4). Still, there is hope. Perhaps "the
names of persons whose *saying* signifies a face—proper names, in the
middle of these common names and commonplaces—can resist the
dissolution of meaning and help us to speak." Thus, proper names
"will enable us to divine, behind the downfall of discourse, the end
of a certain *intelligibility* but the dawning of a new one" (4). "What
is coming to a close," Lévinas ventures, could be a "rationality tied
exclusively to the being that is sustained by words, the *Said* of the Saying, the Said conveying fields of knowledge and truths in the form
of unchanging identities, merging with the self-sufficient Identity or
a being or system—complete, perfect, denying or absorbing the differences that appear to bear or limit it" (4–5).

The end of this Hegelian type of identity wherein the identical
and the nonidentical are made to coincide has been ceaselessly announced, however, by countless names worth recalling, from Ga-
briel Marcel to Buber, Bakhtin, Derrida, and Lévinas himself.
"Being," they tell us, is "relation to the other than self, and awakening" (Lévinas 1996, 5). If we *are*, we are born into an interpersonal
ontology and fundamental accountability for and to the other. And,
as a whole series of twentieth-century critics and writers have insisted, literary language, in its profound intertextuality, is the medium per se in—and through—which this ontological, relatedness-
derived responsibility redeems its implied, generous promise.[1]

Lévinas's reflection on the bonds between the self and the other furnishes the ethical template for Derrida's *alternate* ("other") politics
of friendship where the Greek love (*philia*) and friendship as commemoration and remembrance through names open up unforeseen
possibilities. One "answers for self"—for what we are, do, say—
Derrida writes. But this basic statement holds true, he reminds us in
Politics of Friendship, "beyond the simple present" (1997a, 250) because the "'self' supposes unity" defined as "memory that answers." My name, my proper name, plays a major role in endowing
this unity with ethical consciousness. I may be, empirically speaking,
a compound personality (Dostoevski), a "multiplicity" (Nietzsche),
or a "split" subject (Lacan). But my proper name formally assigns a
unique "source" to all my deeds, becoming as it does "the agency

to which the recognition of this identity is confided." "'I' am assumed," Derrida specifies, "to be responsible for 'myself'—that is, for every thing imputable to that which bears my name" (250). This liability, he continues,

> presupposes freedom, to be sure—a non-present freedom; but also that which bears my name remains the "same," not only from one moment to the next, from one state of that which bears my name to another, but even beyond life or presence in general—for example, beyond the self-presence of what bears that name. The agency called "the proper name" cannot necessarily be reduced to the registered name, patronymic or social reference, although these phenomena are most often its determining manifestation. (251)

The last specification would have remained obscure had the philosopher not cleared it up by another memorious move—a return to Montaigne. For the author of the *Essays* explains in the famous section "On Friendship" how proper names "sponsor" the encounters among the named, between me and you, the self and the other. Names unfold a "friendly" world where the named are already inscribed in an emotional partnership before they actually get to meet and formally "make friends" by introducing themselves to one another. "I met [La Boétie]," Montaigne writes, "and first made me acquainted with his name, thus preparing for that loving friendship. . . . We were seeking each other before we set eyes on each other—both because of the reports we each had heard, which made a more violent assault on our emotions than was reasonable from what they had said, and I believe, because of some decree of Heaven: we embraced each other by our names" (qtd. in Derrida 1997a, 251).

What we are facing here is the imperative of (re)thinking names in general and proper names in particular as inseparable from friendship. Linguistics, semiotics, onomastics, ethics, politics: they all merge into a seamless continuum of thought. It is inherently onomastic, one could argue, to respond to the call of the other and thus prove our responsibility toward others through friendship. Proper names both precede and foster friendship, care, and commitment. Through them, we "register" socially at the same time that they lay down a model of social behavior, of how we should treat others and of how, in being what we are, we relate to other human beings. This relation is, I would point out, synchronic, linking us up to our contemporaries, as well as diachronic, connecting us "intertextually" to those before us, to history and culture in general. *Onomata* designate both those we know, the "known," as well as those we do not or did not know. The name as an exemplary case of *noun* goes down in history and reaches up to us from it. As such, yielded up by a historical process rather than "radically made over" by celebrity hysteria, the name becomes a sign of effective *renommée* and thereby an instrument of public memory—one more time, an essential way of reconstructing a tradition, of representing, organizing, and preserving (archiving) a culture. For the "vertical" ethic of remembrance reconstitutes the "horizontal" ethic of social intercourse as the dead prove our friends as much as the living.

Friendship toward the former is as crucial to the survival of a culture as friendship toward the latter. Drawing from Aristotle and Cicero, Derrida observes that since we cannot have an infinite number of friends, it is those whose names we remember that count as friends. They may be people whom we have known personally or who have gained a name for themselves. These are intertextual (yet no less "real") beings of sorts, "those whose legendary friendship tradition cites and emulates, the name and the renown, the name according to the renown" (3). The renowned (*renommé*) whom I may not have met and properly "made friends with" is the friend that offers his or her friendship—a book, a style, a thought, or an image—even after he or she has passed away. This is how the renowned, having re-named themselves through their achievements (texts), become heritage, tradition, culture, subject of posthumous re-presentation, of reading, writing, and rewriting.

Thus, it seems to me that, much like living *in* a society, inheriting one and its culture is inheriting, and responding to, a roster of proper texts/names. Culture implies the survival of long gone—if never met—friends, their "testamental *revenance*" (3). It is through their names that they come back to guide and nurture us, their "legatees" (291). Derrida uses the last word advisedly. Playing on its Latin etymology, he wants to underscore not only the cultural legacy bequeathed to us, or the obligation that comes with this inheritance, the ethical compact or law (*lex*) *binding* us. He also means to highlight the very bind itself (*ligatura*), not least the fact that this is a memorious com-pact, involving as it does a textual rapport, a pact of reading (*lectura*), of reading the absent friend, of what, under his or her name, has been handed down (*traditus*) to us. Indeed, etymology helps us understand why the legatee (*legatus*) must be a reader (*lector*) of *traditio.* A recollection form, commemoration is not just idle remembrance but also reading (*lectio*), vigorous engagement with the names of tradition—with past texts. As I stress repeatedly, names are more than "indexes," means of pointing to or at people, of sorting them out, and so on. I also reiterate throughout this chapter, our names, our texts—and the names they "make" for us, their authors—place us alongside others, living or dead. Names weave us into the names and the texts of the present and other presences as much as into the texts of the past because names also "presentify" the past, re-present it to us, present us with the gift of its presence.

We shall see, to give itself successfully, this gift and the gift of naming generally must overcome the predicament of postmodern onomastic representation and postmodern representation *tout court*: they must cope with that which in a name resists naming, and must equally fight off the lure of "transcendental" reference and its *mis*-naming consequences. In fact, the postmodern writers I discuss below show that, paradoxical as it may seem, this resistance, the specter of the unnameable looming high behind names, of the failure to identify, to pinpoint the named through a name, sets up in a fashion similar to Derrida's "supplemental" lack the very premise of excessive, intertextual (over)naming. This is conspicuously a memorious or "circuitous" premise as postmodern names name through other names, and we cannot but follow them about while avoiding the trap of the referential yet fallacious shortcut. Further, these writers insist in the same Lévinasian-Derridean vein that the "chain of names" argument does not raise a "merely" linguistic, onomastic or textual, point. A whole ethics and politics are in play here, a way of understanding identity, the self, and its relation to others.

"Nom de Nom": The Unnameable and the Unspeakable

> My name is Paul Auster. This is not my real name.
> —Paul Auster, *City of Glass*

> I have appropriated for myself the nom de nom Elux Troxl. This is not my nom. This is merely the sound-identity I have assigned to my nom.
> —Don DeLillo, *Ratner's Star*

> There may be no gods, but there is a pattern: names by themselves may have no magic, but the *act* of naming, the physical utterance, obeys the pattern.
> —Thomas Pynchon, *Gravity's Rainbow*

Names, Justin Kaplan and Anne Bernays write, "are what anthropologists call cultural universals." "Apparently," the critics go on, "there has never been a society able to get along without them" (1997, 16). The "cultural universals" notion presupposes a descriptive value of names, which in turn rests upon a reliable logic of representation and coherent model of identity. People can "get along," function socially, because society has worked out ways of *identifying* its members, in a twofold sense. First, we are assigned names through which we are recognized, told apart, categorized, and even controlled, for naming and linguistic representation, the "wording" of the world and the resulting linguistic mapping, the "columbarium of the concepts" in general are political if inherently misleading and arbitrary operations, according to Nietzsche (1989, 245–56). "To impose names," Toril Moi comments,[2] "is, then, not only an act of power, an enactment of Nietzsche's 'will-to-knowledge'; it also reveals a desire to regulate and control reality according to well-defined categories" (2001, 160). Second, this onomastic operation assumes that the object identified through the name— somebody's identity—is largely stable, noncontradictory, unified, a *je unaire*—and again, Nietzsche and his postmodern heirs greet this assumption with skepticism.

Along these lines, a contemporary writer like Auster urges us in his *New York Trilogy* (which includes *City of Glass*, *Ghosts*, and *The Locked Room*) and virtually throughout his work to ask ourselves, What happens to the "cultural universals," to all the existential and social assumptions behind names and naming, when more and more people seek *a-nonymity* as a critical reaction to our celebrity culture and its obsession with popularity and the limelight? Whether real human beings or fictitious characters, they give up their sometimes well-known—and well-publicized—names and, by the same token, lifestyles, careers, public personas, even their homes and families. A growing number of cultural theorists, philosophers, artists, and writers are raising this question. Here, I am posing it, too, in relation to the emerging culture of anonymity in narratives by recent American writers. Pynchon, Roth, Acker, Kingston, Leyner, Powers, Marilynne Robinson, Auster, and DeLillo immediately come to mind, with the last two as possibly the more striking cases and therefore worth some closer examination below. To anticipate my argument a little, the relation of Auster's onomastic fictions to Thoreau's politics of social "withdrawal" and especially to Beckett's "unnamable" might suggest a possible answer. But, before teasing out the bearings of these intertextual ties upon Auster's and DeLillo's postmodern discourse of names and naming,[3] let me provide some aesthetic and ideological context by making two points.

The first concerns celebrity, high visibility, and "name recognition." In the wake of the social cooptation of the historical avant-garde, artists and writers, including the most famous, have become increasingly aware that our stardom culture has turned, through its apparatus of mediatic production and reproduction, into an ominously ambiguous notoriety machine. This machine makes and undoes success—financial and otherwise—reputations (*renoms*), names, public images, "bodies of work," to quote a title by Acker, and even, symbolically, bodies of authors, to recall a scene from DeLillo's early novel *Great Jones Street*. In that book and practically everywhere in his fiction, DeLillo shows how this culture and the market logic underlying it construct the writer as much as they "deconstruct," tear him or her apart. In DeLillo, artists, no matter how "experimental" and "cutting-edge," are ultimately turned into fetishes, popular icons of mechanical reproduction and consumption. A previous paradigm of interpretation, reader-response criticism à la Wolfgang Iser, Stanley Fish, and Norman Holland hinged on the public's involvement, through reading, listening, viewing, and so on, as necessary "completion" or "rounding off" of the artist's "project." Yet to DeLillo and Pynchon, two of the most characteristic—and famous—writers of our time, this model no longer appeals.

Their reaction strikes me as a telling cultural symptom. The authors themselves have spent very little time in the spotlight. As is well known, Pynchon has practically vanished, which has quite naturally enhanced the mystery aura surrounding him, and his appearance of sorts on a January 25, 2004, *Simpsons* episode has done no damage to this aura—quite the contrary. DeLillo, another recluse, has actually turned an illustrious writer's "disappearing act," the avoidance of publicity, of readership and its consumptive reflexes, into the very plot of his 1991 novel, *Mao II*, as we will see later on in chapter 5. Some have suggested that his protagonist, Bill Gray, the celebrated writer who changes his name and goes underground, hints at Rushdie's living in hiding after Khomeini's *fatwa*—and I should observe in passing that in *Fury* (2001), his first "American novel," Rushdie seems to respond to *Mao II*'s authorial self-erasure theme.[4] But Joseph Tabbi has persuasively argued that "Bill's *self-chosen* isolation is reminiscent" chiefly "of J. D. Salinger or Thomas Pynchon, whose long-awaited fourth novel, *Vineland*, also appeared within a year of *Mao II*' (Tabbi 1995, 194). Salinger, we will recall, has not published anything since 1965. I might add that some have gone so far as to see in "Pynchon" Salinger's nom de plume and that, in a brief note, Pynchon declined to dismiss this hypothesis.

At any rate, Pynchon's 1963 novel, *The Crying of Lot 49*, revolves around the "calculated withdrawal, from the life of the Republic, from its machinery" (101) of a whole subculture and system of power and cultural production, of a whole America. This "with-

drawal" and the "namelessness" or the real or putative anonymity
that it fosters are fundamental themes in his and other postmoderns' works. As we will notice in Auster, this self-removal is oppositional because it rejects a certain routine, social status quo, not least
individual identity status. This rejection entails a specific handling
of names and onomastic elements in general. Names, pseudonyms,
Kabbalah-like treatment of personal and place names, brand names
colonizing our collective unconscious and wiping out the individual
marks of the psyche, noted or notorious, cartoonish or nonsensical
names—all bear out, in DeLillo, Pynchon, Auster, Leyner, Acker,
and others the drama of an identity threatened by mass culture, advertising, publicity, crowds, fame, PR manipulation, and "spin."
People make a name for themselves and wear their selves out in the
process.

And here is my second point. With it, we go back to Lévinas and
Derrida at the same time that we move on to Auster's work, and to
his social philosophy first. In *The Art of Hunger* he insists, in the spirit
of Paul Celan and Lévinas (1993, 43–44), that the poem must be a
"going-toward, a moving toward the Other" (22). But so is his own
work: a genuine "moving toward the Other" and forms of otherness
shunned or eclipsed by our mythology of success, that is, as he specifies in *Hand to Mouth,* toward "the downtrodden, the dispossessed,
the underdogs of the social order" (1997, 13). He undermines this
mythology in *The New York Trilogy* (1985–86), *In the Country of Last
Things* (1987), *Moon Palace* (1989), *The Music of Chance* (1990), *Mr.
Vertigo* (1994), *Timbuktu* (1999), and, most recently, *The Book of Illusions* (2002) and *Oracle Night* (2003).[5] Throughout his work, in novels, autobiographies, movie scripts, poems, Auster "sanctif[ies]
failure," to quote from *Hand to Mouth* again (1997, 38). "Challeng
[ing] the American way," as Marco Stanley Fogg, the drifting protagonist of *Moon Palace,* says (1989, 60), Auster targets the dominant
narrative of social Darwinism. Repeatedly, he tells a story that carries
his characters toward the other and thereby a "higher stage of consciousness" (61), which also is a higher stage of onomastic intertextuality—let me note that the character's name is truly remarkable:
Marco, from Marco Polo, Stanley, from explorer Henry Morton
Stanley, David Livingstone's partner, and Fogg, from Phileas Fogg,
Jules Verne's protagonist in *Around the World in Eighty Days*—a bunch
of "vagabonds" without exception.

If some of us, Auster thinks, are "born into a state of *otherness*"
(1993, 42), others must go through a "spiritual initiation" and take
up, accordingly, egregious ways of living: "dangerously" and on the
run, on the outside and outside institutions, families, careers, and

publicity. They become, *Moon Palace*'s main hero ascertains, "an instrument of sabotage, a loose part in the national machine, a misfit whose job was to gum up the works." "No one," he tells us, "could look at me without feeling shame or anger or pity. I was living proof that the system had failed, that the smug, overfed land of plenty was finally cracking apart" (1989, 61). Jamming the "national machine," people like Fogg thwart the social narrative woven by it. But how does this happen? More to the point, what role do Auster's names play in the construction of this "antinarrative"?

To answer the question—and thus see how Auster's critical onomastics honors, with remarkable social insight, Derrida's and Lévinas's other and its names—let us go back to *The New York Trilogy*, more specifically, to *City of Glass*. There, Auster's hero Peter Stillman assumes the name of one of his own "figments," a character in a book Stillman wrote before vanishing: Henry Dark. The other major character of the book is one Daniel Quinn, author of mystery novels and Auster's omnipresent "intrafictional" alias. Quinn publishes his work under the telltale pseudonym William Wilson, but, oddly enough, gets a call from somebody that mistakes him for one . . . Paul Auster.[6] Asked about his name, Stillman tells Quinn, who manages eventually to track Stillman down, that it refers to Humpty Dumpty, not to Henry David (Thoreau)—the master of "disobedient" withdrawal, as Quinn presumes. Yet I would not dismiss the latter's guess completely either. Auster informs us that Stillman, a former Columbia professor, had published a book, *The Garden and the Tower: Early Visions of the New World*, which focuses on utopian thought, in particular on one Henry Dark, a late seventeenth-century Bostonian Milton scholar. Stillman himself suggests that Dark and his "prelapsarian" nostalgia foreshadow Thoreau's individualist utopia. Moreover, Fanshawe, another famous name and recluse in Auster's *The Locked Room*, lives in Boston under the assumed name of *H*enry *D*ark. The novel becomes heavily intertextual as it rewrites Hawthorne's own *Fanshawe*—Hawthorne, the reader will remember, is another master of "disappearance" for Auster, who repeatedly plays upon the plot of "Wakefield" in the *New York Trilogy*, *The Book of Illusions*, *Oracle Night*, and elsewhere. And finally, let me note that one Denis Walden is among the narrator's and Fanshawe's former friends.

What does all this mean? What are we to make of the frequent references to the darkness surrounding Auster's heroes in their half-enlightening, half-exasperating solitude? I submit that Stillman, Fanshawe, Quinn, Marco Stanley Fogg, Dark, and all who dramatize Thoreau's postures from *Walden*'s "Solitude" embody Thoreau's "dark side," so to speak. Auster does not fall back idealistically on transcendentalism and the romantic mythology of untainted nature. His Thoreau is an odd one because Auster re-presents his transcendentalist "model" through modern writers and philosophers of solitude and anxiety: Kierkegaard, Norwegian novelist Knut Hamsun, Kafka, and Beckett. Auster's narratives of fasting and abstinence, for example, with their emphasis on indigence and hunger as sources of revelation and forms of resistance to the "feasting" society, tap Hamsun's 1890 novel *Hunger*, which features a starving young writer, and Kafka's famous short story, "The Hunger Artist." In effect, the essays in *The Art of Hunger* specifically expound the outcast's refusal to consume and thus participate in society's symbolic production-reproduction cycle. "To eat," Auster writes, "is a compromise, since it sustains him within the context of an already discredited and unacceptable world" (1993, 33). Fasting designates, as the author contends apropos of Hamsun's hero, a breach of the social contract, a political statement. Rejecting the routine of consumption as self-preservation and preservation of certain values and ideologies, the "art of hunger" is, Auster tells us, an "existential art." As such, it brings forth an entire phenomenology of "need" at the end of which, like in Kafka, we may or may not find ourselves.[7]

It seems to me, though, that Beckett's discourse of negativity, his characters' loneliness and ceaseless crawl "on [their] face" in the "existential" "mud" of the "dark," to recall Beckett's *How It Is*, not least the illogisms and paralogisms plaguing his dramatis personas' language, have left a more enduring trace in Auster. As I suggest elsewhere, Auster "beckettianizes" Thoreau. Take, for example, *City of Glass*, which is, in a way, Auster's response to Beckett's 1956 novel, *Malone Dies*. Like Beckett's narrating hero, Peter Stillman, son of Peter Stillman, sits "alone in the dark." His compulsory references to darkness and solitude during his meeting with Quinn—"Dark. Very dark. As dark as very dark. . . . An entire childhood spent in darkness" (Auster 1990, 19, 31)—rehash Beckett's themes, language, and the split identities of his characters. Stillman, Jr. makes and immediately retracts his statements, names and unnames himself: "I am Peter Stillman. This is not my real name" (21). On a deeper level, this is true: the son's name is and is not his because it names, points to the father. But through the father—and in his name—P(eter) S(tillman) becomes Auster's post-scriptum to Peter Stillman as Henry Dark as H. D. (Thoreau)'s precursor. For we discover that the father had run, à la Henry Dark, a most bizarre experiment on his son, keeping him "alone in the dark" in hopes to make him speak the pre-Babel, perfect language. Yet the son did not grow up in the Thoreauvian, revitalizing solitude, but in its opposite, symbolic, Beckettian darkness, and the son now speaks the language of Beckett's heroes. So Auster's memorious writing itself, while drawing from Thoreau, speaks in tongues, and one of this is Beckett's. Writing in his "red notebook," private-eye Quinn uncovers the Beckettian authorial identity through which, intertextually "naming" Thoreau's, Auster builds his own: "All I can say is this: listen to me. My name is Paul Auster. This is not my name" (49). Yes, let us listen to Auster's other (Auster): this is not his name but somebody else's: Thoreau's, Beckett's, and others'. Yet through others' name(s), and in the name of the lesson of dissent they teach us, Auster tells a story that moves while "moving toward the Other," representing it, acknowledging its presence and our responsibility toward it.

I return now to DeLillo's vision of names as personal badges to better understand what it reveals about postmodern identity. Critics of psychoanalytic persuasion like Luce Irigaray maintain that "a proper name, even a forename, is slipped on the body like a coating—an extra-corporeal identity card" (2000, 418) we are issued right after the umbilical cord has been cut. Hence, it is naming itself that in a certain sense cuts the cord, so the name "replaces the most irreducible mark of birth, the *navel*" (418), quintessence of our birth-as-incorporation, of our body.

But does the name remain wholly separate from the body if the navel, the symbolically central body part supposedly displaced by the name, is still there, witness to what went on? In the 1976 novel *Ratner's Star*, DeLillo declines to sever the umbilical cord between body and name: "[N]ames," a character offers, "are the animal badges we wear, given not only for practical necessity but to serve as a subscript to the inner person, a primitive index of the soul" (1980, 396). Further, to quote from *Ratner's Star* again, there are certain "names that go back to the very dawn," names that "*tell stories.*" They "have greater *storied content* than modern names, most of which are merely convenient denotations packed with noise value" (155; emphasis added). In an article, later on incorporated into a book,[8] Paul Maltby addresses the "metaphysics" of this "noise value" in—where else?—*White Noise* (Maltby 1996). Below, I cast light on the memorious relation between onomastic representation and identity in *Ratner's Star*, possibly DeLillo's least discussed work if we leave aside the 1980 novel *Amazons*. Since DeLillo's entire work—novels, plays, the 2001 novella *The Body Artist*—betrays a steady fascination with names, naming, and language in general, and since this work has been viewed as a paragon of the postmodern discourse on subjectivity, I will also refer to other texts such as the 1982 novel *The Names*, another title, another name—and indisputably DeLillo's major name book—that says it all. I am basically interested in how DeLillo portrays posthumanist subjectivity, a postmodern issue the next chapter will take up more closely. To draw this picture, the author makes massive and inventive use of fictional onomastics. Importantly, he turns to names in an age that has lost faith in what *Ratner's Star* refers to as "the principles of scientific humanism"—and this is, I argue, a memorious turn.

To clarify this point, I would underscore that like other postmoderns, DeLillo sees names as repositories of stories. Names are fictions, fables, texts encoding—textualizing—the subject's identity and yoking it to other identities past and present. Likewise, according to another character of the novel, names—and numbers—constitute "the secret source of entire cultures" and thereby "give us power over the world." Still, neither "numerology" nor onomastics enables the scientists in *Ratner's Star* to reach the "thing beyond naming," that is, to get in touch with their selves. There are always names beneath names and numbers beyond numbers. Names are memorious badges: "circumlocutions," paraphrases, Kabbalistic permutations intertextually deferring that which names name. According to Irigaray, the name is always "late" with respect to identity (2000, 418). While DeLillo and the French critic agree on this account, the American writer does not consider onomastic "belatedness" a deterrent but a narrative stimulus rather, a memorious incentive, as it were.

The Names, Ratner's Star, White Noise, Underworld, and other texts in the DeLillo "onomastic canon" put representation on trial, representation as expected effect of the classical (transcendental) understanding and practice of language. This is not without radical consequences, but let us see first how this radicalism has come about. For a long time, language was seized as a "see-through" kind of garment of things, a docile medium where a sign was thought to lead straight to its object. In fact, this was, and is, not just a matter of language. It is also an anthropological and humanistic issue. It has everything to do with "scientific humanism" as a discourse that turns up representations of the world and, as an effect of this discourse, with how the human sees, represents itself in this world. In *The Order of Things*, Foucault traces the logic behind this linguistic-anthropological dynamic back to the "original form" in which, according to Judeo-Christian tradition, language "was given to men by God himself" (1994, 36). In this form, words were "transparent signs for things" (36) because the former resembled the latter in a very intimate, material way. "The names of things," Foucault says, "were lodged in the things they designated, just as strength is written in the body of the lion, regality in the eye of the eagle, just as the influence of the planets is marked upon the brows of men: by form of similitude" (36). In the Babel episode, a vengeful God rescinds the semiotic transparency of representation by severing the ontological cord uniting representation and the represented, name and named. Consequently, the object is not "present" in its name anymore. Vice versa, the name is no longer materially, physically rooted in, and thereby "motivated" by, what it designates. The resemblance law is abolished. As a result, the initial, resemblance-based sign-object relation, the only one legitimate and imaginable because sanctioned by God, gives way to a multitude of relations, and language is replaced by languages, although, as Kabbalistic tradition has it, Hebrew still contains examples of the "original name-giving" system (36). So, when we attempt to name something or somebody, we, moderns, no longer identify, pin down the "essence" of the thing or person named.

In the prologue, I touched on Foucault's analysis of origin, and I must get back to his conclusions because they fully apply here: through naming, no origin or referent is reached directly, but through other names and onomastic compounds, through other names and words surrounding and intersecting them *in praesentia*, not least through those connecting up with them *in absentia*, whole paradigms of notions, texts, discourses, and ideologies. This is how bare referentiality, grounded in the sign-object "transcendental" nexus, is deposed memoriously, by intertextuality, that is, by the chain of onomastic signs. And this is the resulting world, in Italo Calvino's description from his short story, "A Sign in Space": "In the universe now there was no longer a container and a thing contained, but only a general thickness of signs superimposed and coagulated, occupying the whole volume of space; it was constantly being dotted, minutely, a network of lines and scratches and reliefs and engravings; the universe was scrawled over all sides, along all its dimensions. There was no longer any way to establish a point of reference" (1968, 39).

Further, when reference, depth, direction, stable center ("point of reference") go, the former anthropological centrality of the human goes with them: we become unable to *identify* the world with the same old unerring confidence because no name takes us to the *identity* of the named anymore. The human "drifts" from name to name, sign to sign—signifier to signifier, as we say after Saussure—

from text to text, or, even more accurately, "glides" on them, *horizontally*, having lost the aptitude for a *vertical* plunge, for breaking through the word into what the word names. We are de-centered drifters whenever we try to comprehend, grasp, represent. In our humanistic endeavors, we keep slipping off our former center. Therefore, it is these endeavors themselves that "aggravate" our posthuman condition, keep displacing us from the mythical seat of one and truthful language at the very moment of our discourse—the intertextual, erratic post-Babel babble and stutter that David Malouf has captured so vividly in *Remembering Babylon*.[9] This discourse, the names we assigns objects, can no longer identify objects and their "truths." Deposed masters of transparent names and discourse, we find it difficult to identify ourselves.

This is as much as saying that we do not name the world but ever its badges, others and their names. Lévinas and Derrida explain why this *should happen*; DeLillo and other postmoderns retort: this *cannot but happen*. Nor, they also claim, do our names "identify" us, or help us represent, "understand" ourselves as they did in classical times—or in realistic fiction, for that matter. Balzac's and Dickens's character names purport to tell us who and what kind of people their heroes and heroines are. Balzac's "Vautrin," to take an example, portrays the bearer of this name morally and otherwise (cf. Fr. *se vautrer*, "wallow"), and this speaks to the onomastic philosophy underpinning *Père Goriot* and the entire *Comédie humaine* for that matter. Even later authors like Joyce and Proust (Moraru 1995, 121) imply that names are forthright expressions of identity. Moreover, for Faulkner and his *Light in August* hero Byron, "a man name, which is supposed to be just the sound for who he is, can be somehow an augur of what he will do, if other men can only read the meaning in time" (33). So realists and moderns alike assume by and large a substantial, mimetic ("Cratylian") link between the name to the named.

In *Mimologiques. Voyage en Cratylie*, Genette calls this assumption "semantic fallacy" (1976, 328), a modernist staple that, I would stress, postmodernism targets. The fallacy implies a subject's preexistent, coherent, already-structured identity, which the name reflects, echoes somehow. But in his preface to Žižek's *Sublime Object of Ideology* Ernesto Laclau turns this argument on its head by emphasizing "*the retroactive effect of naming itself.*" "[I]t is the name itself, the signifier, which supports the identity of the object," he insists (1989, xiii). Furthermore, "if the unity of the object is the retroactive effect of naming itself, then naming is not just the nominalistic game of attributing an empty name to a preconstituted subject. It is the discursive construction of the object itself" (xiv). The rejection of the descriptivist-indexical onomastic model is not without political consequences, as Laclau and other recent theorists contend. "If the descriptive approach were correct," Laclau suggests,

> then the meaning of the name and the descriptive features of the object would be given beforehand, thus discounting the possibility of any discursive hegemonic variation that could open the space for a political construction of social identities. But if the process of naming of objects amounts to the very act of their constitution, then their descriptive features will be fundamentally unstable and open to all kinds of hegemonic rearticulations. The essentially performative character of naming is the precondition for all hegemony and politics. (xiv)

In postmoderns like DeLillo, onomastic meanings and the meanings of our identities are not "given beforehand." Names do not simply reproduce identities and their worlds. DeLillo's identity "badges" are not transparent ID's, "descriptive" mimesis of our identities, social status, character type, or "inner self." They are complex texts, social and cultural intertexts, and starting from their end and with their reading, we may begin—quite "antihegemonically"—to "construct" (fathom) and even reconstruct the named.

Rendered possible by memorious naming, onomastic reconstruction—renaming—is a daunting task, though. As a *Ratner's Star*'s character declares, our names are *pseudo*nyms, names of names, or, "nom[s] de nom," to recall DeLillo's ironic phrase, tropes of a Beckettian "unnamable" name. There will always be "levels of unspeakability," the same hero says, that we must peel away to get to the "true name," to our(-)selves. When we finally think that we have ferreted out, retrieved the self, all we grasp is another name, another signifier. But this is not necessarily a dead end or disempowering because in the process, from the way we and our culture deal with names, we learn valuable lessons about ourselves, our world, and how our selves fit in it, about how they link (us) up to other selves. Reassuringly, older names made sense, or seemed to; they designated "us," pointed to "us" without delay or detour through other words, worlds, and cultural spaces. Postmodern names call for some sustained sense-making, instead, and often they may make no sense at all. The *meaningful* onomastic badges we used to identify with have yielded to commercial onomastics that our children, like Steffie in *White Noise*, mumble while asleep: "Toyota Corolla, Toyota Celica, Toyota Cressida." An absurd music of the deep while there is no "deep" anymore? The "I like Ike" ("ecstatic chant") of our consumerist unconscious? A "visionary moment," perhaps, for Gladney, Steffie's father, suddenly overwhelmed by names' "formidable power" (Matlby 1996, 261)? In any event, *White Noise* revealingly shifts the emphasis away from personal names to brand names, from differentiated subjects to serialized objects or consumer products. With this shift, the individual gradually ebbs and threatens to wear off, "immunized against the language of the self," as DeLillo writes in *Mao II* (1991, 8). It takes up a statistic identity and eventually gets sucked up into the body common of the crowds: the shopping masses roaming the discount nirvana of U.S. outlet malls, the millions of angry demonstrators in Tehran, the thousands of couples getting "mass-married" in ballparks as they "chant for one language, one word, for the time when names are lost" (16). Onomastic dramas are dramas of identity, speak critically to a loss that is more general, existential.

At first glance, it might surprise us that *Ratner's Star* does not actually deal with crowds but with individuals, moreover, with exceptional individuals: scholars, top researchers, even geniuses like math whiz Billy Twillig. Billy is fourteen years old and, according to the narrator, winner of the first Nobel Prize ever awarded in mathematics and thus already a legend in his own time. The novel opens with his flying out to a supposedly secret research center, where a group of physicians, astronomers, mathematicians, computer scientists, and other scientists expect him to lend a hand with the deciphering of what looks like a radio message from outer space. Billy's new home, "Field Experiment Number One," is a strange place. Its structure uses highly sophisticated, artificial materials yet suggests medieval, even ancient styles.

This is the fundamental paradox novels like *Americana, Ratner's Star, The Names,* and *Cosmopolis* rest upon: the interplay of late twentieth-century abstract science, on the one hand, and early, archaic, or prehistorical epistemologies, modes and ways of knowledge, on the other. The former has gone to great lengths to rid itself of emotional involvement and the reality of the body—of corpo-reality altogether. Largely marginalized if not completely displaced, at least in the West, by modernity's sober, antiseptic, Cartesian rationality, the latter carries us in the opposite direction by stressing—and pointedly overstressing—the ignored role of the nonrational, the magic, the body, the visceral, the animal, materiality generally in the post-Enlightenment pursuit of knowledge. As one of DeLillo's scientists argues, this epistemological displacement is largely a result of "scientific humanism." While expanding rational knowledge and methods of inquiry, scientific humanism has managed to discount or even do away, we understand, with the human itself, with its concrete presence as blood, flesh, sex, dream, and desire. Admittedly, mathematics, modal logic, nuclear physics, chemistry have dug the discursive grave of the human, of the body-mind unit. Likewise, lab research, the development of scientific models, and technological advance overall have also posited the irrelevance of the cultural environment, of the political affiliation of the researcher, and so forth. But this is precisely what DeLillo's scientists dispute by obsessively setting off the context and the subtext of the scientific text, the biological, political, and economic "construction" of "innocent," in-vitro discovery.

Needless to say, we do not have to buy indiscriminately into this gloomy critique of modern science despite the latter's dehumanizing record. What really intrigues me here is, simply put, DeLillo's onomastic imaginary and the fictional possibilities his postmodern epistemological critique opens up. Also remarkable is that these two aspects are interwoven. For it is the name, our "animal badge," that allows DeLillo to highlight the nonrationalist, corporeal, and political bearings of what otherwise passes as "pure" discourse. The name is an anthropological caveat. It tells stories. It tells, that is, of the "impure" circumstances, assumptions, procedures, and ends of astrophysics and anorganic chemistry. It is of course noteworthy that DeLillo's mathematicians and computing specialists are fascinated by objects, materials, and facts reminiscent of a world symbolically opposite to the nature of their business. Hence DeLillo's odd, playful oxymorons: abstraction and abjection; calculus and steamy sex; absolute research rigor and utter sloppiness of researchers, who walk around badly dressed, dirty, ungroomed; the lofty sphere of scientific exploits and the humble abode of Endor, the scientist who resides in a muddy hole and subsists on a diet of worms; "the archreality of pure mathematics" and the typically DeLillean obsession with waste, trash, junk, feces, and the "guano market." The writer deconstructs modern scientific enterprise by laying bare the crude materiality of abstract work, the repressed and impure underbelly of "unsullied" thought. In *Ratner's Star,* the triviality of the body, the biological in general come back with a vengeance to debunk logicians' denial of "the evidence of our senses." Outrageous as the political and physiological undergirdings of logic and algebra may seem, they draw our attention to the divorce of reason and matter, mind and body, spirit and senses that underlies the humanist project.

This is where names and, with them, numbers come into play. They are the shifting ground where the utopia of modern rationality and order, objectivist and abstract mode of inquiry, and related humanist linchpins come loose and turn topsy-turvy only to let us glimpse their non-Cartesian, blood-smelling flip side. DeLillo plays off the intrinsic ambiguity of letters, numbers, and their combinations. He shows how they fuel both the triumph of reason and its failure, both algebraic acrimony celebrating the autonomy of human inquisitiveness *and* pseudo-Kabbalistic euphorias bespeaking submission to a cruel and elusive divinity. Like Andrei Codrescu's 1999 "antiapocalyptic" novel *Messiah,* where some believe that the wheel of fortune from the popular TV show can be employed as a sort of high-tech, Kabbalah-inspired tool to uncover God's secret name, *Ratner's Star* catches the scientific community at the peak of this dilemma. In effect, most of Billy's colleagues have already "recanted." Responding to the alienating upshots of research, to humanism's often dehumanizing consequences, they hark back to alternative forms and sites of knowledge. They know letters can shape into both rational structures such as computer language *and* into "the secret power of the alphabet, the unnameable name, the literal contradiction of the superdivinity, fear of sperm demons" (DeLillo 1980, 215). And now they choose the latter, that is, the quasi-Talmudic worshipping of names and numbers over modern mathematics; ritualic onomastic lists over equations; the magical power of these "elemental lists" over "provable" facts; the ancient, the savage, and "what he accomplished in his instinct for pure space and the mathematics of motion" over modern methodologies and their high-tech gadgets.

Furthermore, the development of mathematics, or philology for that matter, can be construed to reflect the continuous yet unrevealed presence of a premodern, magical mentality. As Endor claims, "the whole history of mathematics is subterranean, taking place beneath history itself, misunderstood, ignored, ridiculed, unread, a shadow-world scarcely perceived even by the learned." Therefore, *Ratner's Star*'s scholars now "muse on latent history." As we learn, "latent in any period's estimation of itself as an age of reason is the specific history of the insane" (387) and, I should add, of the silenced, ignored, uncommon, bizarre, marginal, alien, "uncivilized," in- or less-than-human, de-humanized bodies. Numbers and names are living testimonies of this unacknowledged knowledge. Modern mathematics and linguistics approach them in largely descriptivist terms, assume, that is, their transitivity and instrumentality, and study them as means to grasp and control the reality they "express." On the contrary, DeLillo's scholars take names as realities in and of themselves, unlimited to the mimetic function. As Billy reflects,

> among the things beyond expression in various cultures have been the names of deities, infernal beings, totemic animal and plants; the names of an individual's blood relatives of the opposite sex (a ban related to incest restrictions); the new name given a boy at his initiation; the names of certain organs of the body; the names of the recently dead; the names of sacred objects, profane acts, leaders of cults, the cults themselves. *Double substitutes* must be used. Carefully devised code words. Taboo variants. Oaths are dully taken. An entire bureaucracy of curse, scourge and punishment is set up to discourage utterance of the unspeakable. (38)

The history of modern science can be rewritten, DeLillo implies, as the chronicle of our failure to speak the unspeakable, to read (through) the name. Theory manipulates names, kicks them around, and squeezes them into smart formulas, but the named retains its a-nonymity. We crack the signifier open, yet the signified reveals itself as another linguistic shell. Names have lost their exchange value, as Baudrillard would say. They no longer *exchange* for meaning but mean (name) other names instead. So they ceaselessly put off their meaning by putting forward strange names that invite further perusal and connections, and launch us into the unspeakable and the unknown, into the terra incognita of our being where the unnameable does allow, odd as it may seem, for naming and representation—of us and the world, anew. Like Umberto Eco's infinite semiosis, postmodern onomastics is infinite onomastics. As somebody in the novel says, "to bear a name is both terrible and necessary. The child, emerging from the space-filling chaos of names, comes eventually to see that an escape from verbal designation is never complete, never more than a delay in meeting one's substitute, that alphabetic shadow abstracted from its physical source" (DeLillo 1980, 19). We come again to understand why DeLillo's characters are almost morbidly attracted to the physical, the body, and its most impure forms. They sense the failure of reason's attempts to "abstract" the name from the named, so they try by bodily means, by their own material lifestyles, to bring physicality back into the epistemological picture. In doing this, they also set forth the homology of the studied and the student, object and subject. Not only have we lost access to the named. We have also lost access to ourselves—our selves—so we do not know what our names name. That is to say, we do not know who and what we are anymore.

On the other hand, modern onomastics has forfeited its anthropological meaningfulness. True, DeLillo does his best to think up unique, sometimes weird-sounding names for his scientists: Eberhard Fearing; Barnaby Laporte; Ottum; Hof; Byron Dyne; Endor; Shlomo Glottle; Cyril Kyriakos; Una Braun; Mimsy Mope Grimmer; J. Graham Hummer, "widely known as the instigator of the MIT language riots" and also a member of "Cyril's subcommittee on phrasing"; Howie Weeden; Beveridge Kettle; Simeon Goldfloss; Robert Hopper Softly; U.F.O. Schwartz. Thus, *Ratner's Star* achieves an onomastic tour de force well served by irony, cultural allusions, various etymological plays, and daring alliterations, bringing out somewhat the individuality of the named. But, for the most part, this uniqueness remains irretrievable. Aware of this loss, some characters change their names or rather give up names entirely. Gerald Pence, for example, becomes Mutuka. A former futurologist, previously sold on the notion that historical developments can be anticipated (named) through abstract thought, he lives with nomadic tribes in the outback. His new people do not use names but circumlocutions (intertexts), a name-free language in form of "pure narrative" (106). Another character, Siba Isten-Esru, admits that "I like literally to segment a name until nothing remains." Onomastic anatomy ultimately leads us, she believes, to "blank space and silence," not to an immediate increase in self-knowledge. As noted earlier, names take us to other names so that the "true name," Ratner himself ventures, is always an illusion prompting further "substitution, abbreviation, blank spaces, utter silence" (221). We speak the name, and as we do so, we go through infinite layers of "unspeakability" (221), a DeLillean concept to which we will return in chapter 5. We wallow in the "unnameable" (215) that occasions and inspires naming. To Ratner's mind, the "thing beyond naming" is not a thing actually, the named, but a "state." We read names and we "fall" into that state.

DeLillo's characters employ numbers and names while operating computers to decode a supposedly extraterrestrial message. But all they unearth is just another swamp of numbers and names: the uncountable and unaccountable, the Kabbalistic unspeakable and the Beckettian unnameable both in one. They look ahead into the future yet are beset by the remote past, by Egyptian, Mesopotamian, and ancient Chinese cultures and their names, their onomastic cultures. They start out with sophisticated software yet wind up handling stone tools in the bush. And, to complete the circular irony of the novel, Ratner's star proves to be Earth, as Billy discovers. It turns out, in an "untold past" a group of humans had sent a message in outer space, and the message has now circled back to its source, with cosmic and semiotic irony. Billy cracks the message code not through superior mathematics but through "junk mail." So, the solution to the conundrum of communication, signs, names, and their meanings is contingent, of the *hic et nunc* kind, impure, historical. To understand the name, we need to "historicize" it. We must look for the context or ensemble in which the particular name is a part, a moment in a sequence, naming other names as it names itself, telling other stories as it tells its own—that is, ours. If DeLillo's names name anything at all, they name—tell the story—of this memorious realization.

WOMEN'S NAMES: ACKER, MORRISON

> [A] name doesn't tell you what something is so much as it connects the phenomenon/idea to something else. Certainly to culture.
> —Kathy Acker, *Bodies of Work*

> Names both identify and constitute identity.
> Molly Hite, *The Other Side of the Story*

Postmodern women writers reinforce this onomastic contingency by underscoring the multiple engendering of names. Both a private and a public, collective operation, the production of names and their meanings is in their works intertwined with individual and social production and re-production. Accordingly, naming here encroaches upon, and is in turn inflected by, the hotly disputed and diversely enacted categories of gender, sexuality, and body, as well as community, race, class, ethnicity. This discourse typically recapitulates the biography of these "formations," and so a whole web of histories actually comes to the fore enmeshed with narratives of names and naming. These are histories of female dispossession and pain, defeat and triumph, no less than histories of collective, racial, and ethnic struggles. Across this spectrum, reality and fiction intersect, dovetail, fuse, and swap their own names, much to our confusion.

This confusion has deep-running existential and epistemological ramifications, as we will see in chapters 4 and 5. For now, I will call attention only to the ontological scandal that breaks out as female writers' onomastic discourse tears down the wall convention erects between reality and fiction, "raw facts" and their imaginary "double." If the imagination "repeats," somehow "refers" back to a preexistent ontological datum—if the imagination is memorious, as I maintain—that does not necessarily mean that it rehashes some pre-cultural, pre-textual reality. The "imagination feeds on [the] previous imagination" instead, as Robert Scholes assures us (1979, 214), and, I argue, it is postmodernism that has privileged this modus operandi, has constituted itself around this "parasitic aesthetics"— around the aesthetics of new, paradoxical type of originality. Let us forget, then, about Harold Bloom's anxiety of influence, Scholes also urges. Let us, writers and readers alike, "enjoy," à la Žižek, postmodernism's prime symptom and celebrate the literary imagination's memorious feast on the archive of the past. After all, this is what countless contemporary artists and writers encourage us to do, with the proviso that not only does their imagination borrow, steal, and otherwise draw from previous imaginary worlds, but it also shows off, quite purposefully, this intertextual appropriation. To be sure, purpose—goal, sense, direction, "agenda"—must be underscored here to set this type of postmodern intertextuality apart from the freewheeling, debonair, intertextual-for-intertextuality's-sake acrobatics that prevail on the more jocular side of postmodernism.

This purpose becomes evident in one of the most intriguing arenas of postmodern plagiarism and pastiche: contemporary writers' use of names of characters from former works. This intertextual onomastics has been among memorious discourse's most popular ploys. Postmoderns like Pynchon, Auster, Heller, Doctorow, Coover, Leyner, Charles Johnson, John Irving, Samuel R. Delany, Gibson, Sterling, Siegel, Rushdie, Coetzee, as well as Cynthia Ozick, Angela Carter, Maryse Condé, Bharati Mukherjee, Rebecca Goldstein, Karen Tei Yamashita, to list just a few, borrow and variously manipulate proper names from Dickens, George Eliot, Disraeli, Defoe, Poe, Hawthorne, Melville, Ellison, Heinrich von Kleist, Kafka, Nabokov, Jean-Jacques Rousseau, or Proust. Still, this recycling of literary history's "cognominal archive" has been largely ignored in scholarship on contemporary fiction, postmodernism, cultural representation, and in "theory" generally.

Acker's reception is a case in point. While dwelling at length upon her rewriting of others' texts and styles, critics have shown little interest in her valiant appropriation of literary names. I find this surprising. Acker's character names such as *Great Expectations'* M. de Clèves and the Duc de Nemours (1989, 78) should be the first to raise the red flags of postmodern bricolage and, more broadly, of memorious discourse. We do come across such names in her fictions, but they are hardly fictional; the author did not quite dream them up. To baptize her dramatis personae, Acker "steals" from Cervantes, Sade, Mary Shelley, Dickens, Hawthorne, Melville, Rimbaud, Lampedusa, Colette, Genet, and others. She does it systematically, as part of a larger program, which I find worth examining more closely. I propose, therefore, that we turn to Acker's work now—primarily her essays and, secondarily, her fiction—to cast some light on its onomastic feature and see why it operates "quotationally," rehearsing a well-known literary nomenclature and thus rendering her creations *re*creations.

Acker develops a full-blown onomastic theory in two essays from her anthology *Bodies of Work*, "Seeing Gender," first published in 1995, and "On Delany the Magician," 1996. Like the latter, initially a preface to Delany's science-fiction book *Trouble on Triton*, the former builds its argument (twice) obliquely, as a commentary on Judith Butler's own commentary ("Bodies That Matter") on Irigaray's essay-manifesto *Ce sexe qui n'en est pas un*. Here, Acker identifies "naming" and "renaming" as fundamental strategies of cultural appropriation and determining features of her identity politics. Theory and criticism are very personal acts everywhere in Acker, so it comes as no surprise that in this piece, too, the author talks about her life. Her childhood, we find out, gave her early on a sense of exclusion, of being shut out, barred from expression and self-expression, language use, and naming ultimately. Acker seizes patriarchy as gender-based asymmetry of onomastic discourse, that is, as linguistic environment where woman may be object of naming yet never naming subject. Others can name, talk about, and represent her while the right to language and representation, including self-representation, is being denied to her.

For Acker, the *Timaeus* is one of the earliest texts formulating the metaphysics of this denial. Plato's dialogue, she maintains, teaches us that women lack "essence" and "form." Therefore, women cannot reproduce or "repeat" themselves (Acker 1997, 166). Thus, they possess no independent "capability of mimesis," so they "can neither be named nor discussed" (160). Yet others (men) do name them while self-naming, language, hence the whole world remain outside women's reach. "I knew this," Acker confesses,

as a child, before I had ever read Plato, Irigaray, Butler. That, as a girl, I was outside the world. I wasn't. I had no name. For me, language was being. There was no entry for me into language. As a receptacle, as a womb, as Butler argues, I could be entered, but I could not enter, and so I could neither have nor make meaning in the world.

I was unspeakable, so I ran into the language of others.

In this essay, as yet, I am only repeating those languages.

Though I couldn't be named, everyone was naming me: "This naming of what cannot be named is itself a penetration into this receptacle that is at once a violent erasure, one that establishes it as an impossible yet necessary site for all further inscriptions" [Butler, "Bodies That Matter"]. That is, the name *female* acts to erase the presence of women.

When I was a girl, I wanted to do anything but be a girl, for both *girl* and *woman* were the names of nothing.

Now that I am no longer nothing, now that I have run away and so thrown off the names *girl* and *woman*, I am left not even with that. Not even with nothing. With a name such as *pirate* which seems solely metaphorical. I want to *see* my body. (161–62)

To recapitulate: as a woman, Acker cannot name herself and the world, and her very name names just this inability. Yet others can name her, *mis*name and practically "erase" her, deny her language and her humanity in the process. There is injustice here, resulting in the Beckettian unspeakable and unnameable, but also as in Auster, a predicament that she is turning to her advantage, odd as it may sound. For onomastic oppression drives her to piracy, to stealing others' languages and names, to intertextual onomastics as a form of memorious discourse. But these languages leave her "unspoken," shaped as they are by patriarchy. The one language disputing the latter, its underlying hierarchies and binaries such as male-female, good-evil, rational-irrational, subject-object, and their mimetic logic is, Acker contends, the language of the body, of her body, her flesh, blood, sexuality, and desire. Consequently, what Acker actually sets out to do is use *this* kind of expressive medium to appropriate, inflect, rework, de-code, and re-encode "other" languages and, along with them, their whole set of values, hierarchies, power structures, and beliefs by sexualizing them, suffusing them with female corporeality—the hitherto excluded, silenced, or unnamed—by running them, not unlike DeLillo, through the "impure" filter of desire, obsession, and calculated, if shocking, obscenity.

"Seeing Gender" takes to task traditional metaphysics of gender by pinpointing the historical resilience of its mortal foe, a linguistic ontology that reinscribes language into woman's world—"for me, language was being," says Acker—at the same time that it uncovers women's semiotic and ontological exclusion ("as a girl, I was outside the world. . . . I could neither have nor make meaning in the world"). The 1996 essay belabors the ontological argument with additional stress on the social inscription of names. "Naming is always a metonymic process," Delany has stated. In her comment, from which I have excerpted the first epigraph to this section, Acker points out that "a name doesn't tell you what something is so much as it connects the phenomenon/idea to something else. Certainly to culture. In this sense, language is the accumulation of connections where there were no such connections. And so, to Delany, names such as 'science-fiction' form a web" (1997, 61–62). "Web" is Delany's own word, along with "weave," "net," "matrix," and other members of the *textus* family (62). They all pinpoint etymologically the "textile" makeup of society, the materiality of its texture. To no negligible degree, this materiality is of onomastic nature. As we have learned throughout this chapter, names are "woven" into the social fabric. They make up for privileged linguistic units where language and, by the same token, culture appear as what they fundamentally have always been, "accumulation of connections" between me and you, self and other, à la Lévinas and Derrida. Thus, names also reinforce, in Delany's and Acker's onomastic poetics and politics, the postmodern certainty that culture is a web of relations, an inter-text, and, more notably still, that by reweaving a "matrix" text, one may intervene in structures of aesthetic, social, and political nature.

To sum up, names unearth a paradox in society and Acker's own writing: on the one hand, there are "unnamed" and thereby outcast individuals; on the other hand, these individuals, Acker herself as a writer, for example, can take up others' languages, texts, and names and impact the larger assemblages ("textures") these are part of. Using others' words or names in textual or oral form takes Acker into the very heart of the social, into its living textuality and concurrently into the vivacious sociality of texts. Her characters' names are cognominal texts laid into the fabric—the larger "textum"—of society. Since "the world is word" (62), this world—which, notably, is the "world of men" (68)—can be changed through rewording, renaming, and re-signifying. A semiotic overhaul of society and its engendered hierarchies seems within the writer's reach because, as "discourse," language use enables meaning making, not just meaning reproduction (4). "Political, economic and moral forces," Acker contends,

> are major determiners of meanings and values in a society. Thus, when I use words, any words, I am always taking part in the constructing of the political, economic, and moral community in which my discourse is taking place. All aspects of language—denotation, sound, style, syntax, grammar, etc.—are politically, economically, and morally coded. . . . Whenever I engage in discourse, I am using given meanings and values, changing them and giving them back. A community, a society is always being constructed in discourse if and when discourse—including art—is allowed. (4)

Raiding the "cognominal archive," Acker casts light on an essential dimension of identity in our time: its cultural-historical mediation, its dependence on—or "construction" by—the already said, written, expressed, by the already named. The name is just another argument for the memorious condition of the self in postmodernism. That is, the name shows that this self is fundamentally relational, intertextual, further, that there is historical and social depth to it. Onomastic representations link up with other onomastic representations as much as they do with people, objects, and facts. Thus conceived, onomastic intertextuality is the sociocultural flip side of intertextual onomastics understood as a linguistic and literary "web" made up of names, signifiers, words. As such, the manipulation of names is a particular case of rewriting, which, as I have shown elsewhere, implies rewriting of textual materials as well as rewriting of the social texture.

Acker's fiction teems with examples of intertextual onomastics, which her books usually flaunt in their very titles—in their names: *Great Expectations, Empire of the Senseless* (which plays upon Nagisa Oshima's movie *In the Realm of the Senses*), *My Death My Life by Pier Paolo Pasolini,* and *Don Quixote, Which Was a Dream. Don Quixote*'s protagonist, for instance, is Cervantes's hero, who becomes, ambiguously enough, a hero-heroine in Acker and therefore can have an abortion. Having thus "achieved knighthood," s/he sets out to "save the world" (10). This is undoubtedly ironic given the chivalric institution's aggressively masculinist history. But Acker's pseudo-Quixote deploys a kind of frame narrative—*anti*narrative, to be more precise—within which the writer retrieves many other fictional characters and their names from Lampedusa, Wedekind, Emily Brontë, and others, in a mix of literal reproductions and pastiches. These intertextual appropriations, transformations, and displacements aim at "infecting" the ideologies of gender and power that the onomastic intertexts epitomize and in which they are embedded. Punning on her own name in the very opening of the "novel," the author renames herself, and identifies herself, as (*h*)*Acker,* a writer who steals from others and their onomastic treasure chests. At the same time, others are stealing (life) from her by means of a catheter (*Kath*)eter, as the abortion is being performed on "Kathy' "'s body. Yet Acker turns this violent scenario upside down: the abortion, assumed violence to the female body, gives Kathy a new body. As a result, and with a wink at Charlotte Lennox's 1752 book, *The Female Quixote, or, The Adventures of Arabella,* she becomes a "female-male of a night-knight . . . no longer anonymous [as] she receives a name," and so "she's able to have adventures and save the world" (10–11).

Playful as this intertextual onomastics may be, it nevertheless drives home Acker's serious "purpose," her unambiguous politics of naming, and politics in general, which begins, and is carried through, as a memorious story of stories and their names.

According to Cynthia Davis,[10] in Morrison "power is largely the power to name." This self-acknowledged[11] onomastic politics is steeped into the African American "ritual" of naming (Fabre 1988, 108). Black names play a vitally memorious role throughout Morrison's work, particularly in her 1977 novel *Song of Solomon*, my focus here. As in Acker, names tell stories, with other stories inside them, which collectively bear witness to a history of naming—history of language—as part and parcel of African American history. As Lucinda H. Mackethan observes, the novel "emphasizes names and naming in ways that place the novel squarely within Black American literature's dominant tradition." The critic goes on to explain, "Works in this tradition enact quest for identity within a culture which systematically denies the black person's right to both name and identity as a means of denying his or her humanity" (1986–1987, 200).[12]

Commentators have not been insensitive to *Song of Solomon*'s intertextual onomastics, pointing out that the novel's names encapsulate "legacies" to be "traced" (Fabre 1988, 109). Pursuing this suggestion from the vantage point of my book's argument, below I will be "look[ing] at names as signs registering something more important underneath" (Carmean 1993, 47). Undoubtedly, this is a daunting task since, the same critic warns, "for African-Americans, the issue of names/identity/heritage may be infinitely complicated by the loss of an original family name" (47). Indeed, in antebellum America black proper names were a cruelly ironic sign of onomastic "impropriety": the name bearer was first un-named, stripped of his or her original African name, then assigned a new name (renamed) by the "proprietor" (the slaveholder) in utter disregard for the "property'"s identity. Moreover, the new name usually included, if not simply was, the slave owner's. Thus, the slave's name automatically defined (named) the slave's status, classified him or her as a slave. In *Beloved*, another major onomastic narrative, Morrison is surely right to remind us that "definitions belong to the definers—not the defined" (190), which contention corroborates in African American context Nietzsche's insight into the politics of naming: "Die Mächtigen sind es, welche die Namen geben" (It is the powerful people who name) (1978, 88).

It would be only fair to say that most African American names initially signified the oppressive other, erasing the self and its name.

With the abolition of slavery, a whole semiotic overhaul of the name becomes possible, and along with it a personal remaking, socially and politically speaking, of the name bearer. African Americans re-appropriate—redefine and adapt—the proper names once imposed on them, "correcting" them yet usually without abandoning them. Abusive naming ignores the named person's right to express, by name, him- or herself, to name his or her unique essence, *ousia*, in the ancient Greeks' ontological terminology. A name is "unsuit-able" or "incorrect" when it does not reflect a voluntary, conscien-tious option, also when it arbitrarily denies/ignores the named the right to have his or her individuality inscribed in the name. On the contrary, "a name is correct," Michael D. Palmer writes in his com-mentary on the *Ur-text* of Western onomastics, Plato's *Cratylus*,

> not only if it successfully (and directly) refers to a real unit or kind of object, but if it also discloses the *ousia* of the thing, or correctly describes it. A name is correct, as Socrates says, if "the *ousia* of the thing named remains in force and is made plain in the name." . . . Since *ousiai*, and not the namemaker's preconceptions about reality, provide the only basis for any distinctions that can be called natural, and since names are given for the purpose of discriminating among things on the basis of these distinctions, Plato's view of the correctness of names may properly be called a "nature" theory. Names are correct if and only if they are given in accordance with nature and adequately describe what they name. (1989, 127)

Thus, on the one hand, slave names were "natural," or "motivated" ("Cratylian") in that they did designate slave status. On the other hand, they were unnatural, and arbitrary ("Hermogenic"), because they overlooked the identity (essence, *ousia*) of the named while be-traying slavery's unnatural nature instead.

The black community in Morrison's Mercy, a town on the border of Lake Superior, has developed a sophisticated onomastic culture pivoting on memorious names. As Guitar, one of Morrison's main heroes, says, African Americans got and may still be "getting their names the way they get everything else—the best way they can" (1978, 88). Nevertheless, he urges his friend Milkman, *Song of Solo-mon*'s protagonist, "You should hang on [to your name], for unless it is noted down and remembered, it will die when you do" (333). Naming could have been an accident, or even an incident, and a violent one at that. Names could have been won or could have been imposed in battle, actual or symbolic, to recall Derrida's "Battles of Proper Names" chapter from *Of Grammatology*. Stemming from the mapping of a geography and its citizenry, proper and place names simultaneously bespeak and act out a politics, a power configuration embedded in a cognominal signifier of lineage, kinship, belonging, ownership, and so on. No doubt, toponymic and patronymic discourse is hardly innocent, much less so when race plays into it, and Morrison's characters know this full well. All the same, fundamentally memorious, postmodern onomastic representation is re-presence, to rehearse Said. Names present us with mementos where onomastic reference references texts, stories. They honor by their very connection to the named the latter's inscription into the past and the present, into an ancestry and a place. Therefore—and here Derrida comes to mind again—names must in turn be honored and commemorated, regardless of what they initially stood for and how people ended up bearing them. Double signifiers of historical injustice *and* pride, names may seem absurd or ludicrous, but there are no meaningless names ultimately because people can give them *new* meanings, can legitimate them. Morrison's characters understand that, while they may not be necessarily responsible *for* their names, they are still responsible *to* them, and all they do in life is done, as Derrida writes in *Otobiographies,* "in the name of the name . . . , put [ting] one's name on the line (with everything a name involves)" (1985, 10, 7).

Consider, for instance, the long list of proper names the narrator provides toward the end of the novel:

> [Milkman] closed his eyes and thought of the black men in Shalimar, Roanoke, Petersburg, Newport News, Danville, in the Blood Bank, on Darling Street, in the pool halls, the barbershops. Their names. Names they got from yearnings, gestures, flaws, events, mistakes, weaknesses. Names that bore witness. Macon Dead, Sing Byrd, Crowell Byrd, Pilate, Reba, Hagar, Magdalene, First Corinthians, Milkman, Guitar, Railroad Tommy, Hospital Tommy, Empire State (he just stood around and swayed), Small Boy, Sweet, Circe, Moon, Nero, Humpty-Dumpty, Blue Boy, Scandinavia, Quack-Quack, Jericho, Spoonbread, Ice Man, Dough Belly, Rocky River, Gray Eye, Cock-a-Doodle-Doo, Cool Breeze, Muddy Waters, Pinetop, Jelly Roll, Fats, Lead-belly, Bo Diddley, Cat-Iron, Peg-Leg, Son, Shortstuff, Smoky Babe, Funny Papa, Bukka, Pink, Bull Moose, B.B., T-Bone, Black Ace, Lemon, Washboard, Gatemouth, Cleanhead, Tampa Red, Juke Boy, Shine, Staggerlee, Jim the Devil, Fuck-up, and *Dat* Nigger. (Morrison 1978, 333–34)

"Angling out from these thoughts of names was one more," the narrator goes on, Guitar's own name. When Milkman brings it up, Guitar refers him to the name's story: "I do accept it. It's part of who I am. Guitar is *my* name. Bains is the slave master's name. And I'm all of that. Slave names don't bother me; but slave status does" (161). There would be no point in calling himself "X," like that famous "red-headed Negro" (161). He does not disown the name in whose name his ancestors were enslaved and oppressed. Even in this name's name he can make a name for himself.

Nor does he repudiate his nickname, with roots in a childhood episode—another name story—"down home in Florida" (45). In fact, most of the proper names above are memoriously derived, nicknames, stories in a(n) (onomastic) nutshell. These *cognomina* were also received, conferred by others, usually for reasons unfathomable to outsiders. Results of "blind" (71) or "foolish misnaming" (18), some of the nicknames were plucked by relatives, masters, or authorities from lists and texts that bore no specific relevance to the named, or were only a "joke," a "disguise," a "brand name" (17). Macon Dead, for example, is a "name scrawled in perfect thoughtlessness by a drunken Yankee in the Union Army" (18), who mixed up the person's place of birth and status of parents (they were "dead"). The name was recorded as such in the register of the Freedmen's Bureau, meant to include, ironically enough, the freed slave and thus *mark* his liberation. In a way, this irony is canceled out by another, which suggests that, in the named, only the former slave has died while the human being lives on.

The Bible is another repertoire of odd names. As Ruth Rosenberg tells us, "it was the custom for the father," in the house of Morrison's grandparents, "to open the scriptures at random and allow his finger to travel the page so exposed. Whatever configuration of letters it stopped on, regardless of their meaning, was conferred upon the newborn child" (n.d., 196). In the novel, parents make "blind selection of names" (Morrison 1978, 18) for their sons and daughters by choosing clusters "of letters that seemed" to them "strong and handsome": Magdalene, whom everybody call Lena, Hagar, and even First Corinthians. Pilate's father "copied out of the Bible" (53) the only word he ever wrote, his daughter's name. This happens to be, of course, a man's name. Still, the proud, powerful, and mysterious Pilate treasures, literally "bears" her name, keeping it written on a paper scrap in a little box she wears like an earring (168). Continuing the family tradition, and redefining it as a tradition of strong women, she taps the same sacred nomenclature for a name for her own daughter, Rebecca, or, Reba (147–48).

Pilate, Reba, and others like them, both men and women, generally do not abandon but keep such names, trying to "dignify" them, to resignify their onomastic signifieds while rescuing the signifiers.

What they are after is, again, what Laclau identifies as the "retroactive effect of naming." You may already have a name, but it is your behavior that makes it mean one thing or another, and always after naming has occurred. Creating their own lives, Morrison's people recreate their names. Retroactively, these names reflect a "deep personal pride" (Morrison 1978, 38). Therefore, they are treated with "respect" and "awe" (19), *as if they had been a matter of free choice.* Or, as Lucinda H. Mackethan comments, from his relationships with black women Milkman comes away with the realization that the power to give a name is less important than the power to give the given name its meaning, which is "the power over life itself" (1986–1987, 206). This explains why the character becomes very "possessive about his name" (Morrison 1978, 38), which he hated at first (88) as much as he detested the nickname "he was never able to shake" (15).

His father, Macon Dead, also loathes his son's nickname, "which stuck in spite of his own refusal to use it or acknowledge it." In fact, "it was a matter that concerned him a good deal, for the giving of names," he thinks, "was always surrounded by what he believed to be monumental foolishness" (15). His son's nickname, for example, sounded suspicious, somehow "impure":

> Without knowing any of the details, however, he guessed, with the accuracy of a mind sharpened by hatred, that the name he heard schoolchildren call his son, the name he overheard the ragman use when he paid the boy three cents for a bundle of old clothes—he guessed that this name was not clean. Milkman. It certainly didn't sound like the honest job of a dairyman, or bring to his mind cold bright cans standing on the back porch, glittering like captains on guard. It sounded dirty, intimate, and hot. He knew that wherever the name came from, it had something to do with his wife and was, like the emotion he always felt when thinking of her, coated with disgust. (15)

Macon is not completely off the mark. There is a story behind his son's name. As a grown boy, Milkman was still nursed by Ruth, whose relationship with her father carries over into the oedipal scene involving her son. Proper names are no longer secret once they circulate, but they do shroud secrets, they name other names, the anecdotes and incidents to be shared only with those close to you. The same holds true for place names such as the name of the southern town where Guitar and Milkman wind up: "Everybody in this town, is named Solomon, [Guitar] thought wearily. Solomon's General Store, Luther Solomon (no relation), Solomon's Leap, and now the children were singing '*Solomon* don't leave me' instead of

'*Sugarman.*' Even the name of the town sounded like Solomon: Shalimar, which Mr. Solomon and everybody else pronounced *Shalleemone*" (305). Traveling to the South, the two friends embark on a journey in space as well as time, in a mythical time that preserves the precious memory of names. Down South, where "collective memories [are] kept alive through names" (Fabre 1988, 113), names and the stories of naming—names' past, their "genealogy" or memorious, if invisible, body—live on side by side. Unlike the North, where the main characters of *Song of Solomon* had migrated, the rural South of their ancestors rests upon a memorious ontology, upon the co-presence of reality and myth and uses the latter to ceaselessly rework and rename the former and its names. No wonder Milkman is at a loss. All he can do is surmise, conjecture, venture a guess. Where a Southerner like Calvin seems able to orient himself in the surrounding world "as a blind man caresses a page of Braille, pulling meaning through his fingers" (Morrison 1978, 282), Milkman feels shut off from things and their names. Starting off as a search for Pilate's "gold," Milkman's quest for the past, for his own past and the stories behind his family's names, turns into an initiation to a language "before language, . . . before things were written down" (281). This "original" idiom, in which there was no gap between the name and the named, survives and becomes audible in certain African American names provided that we hear them right—provided that we understand the stories they whisper. Closest to this "natural"—yet how culturally sophisticated, how intertextual—form of communication, children's songs usher Milkman into a wholly new universe:

> He almost shouted when he heard "Heddy took him to a red man's house." Heddy was Susan Byrd's grandmother on her father's side, and therefore Sing's mother too. And "red man's house" must be a reference to the Byrds and Indians. Of course! Sing was an Indian or part Indian and her name was Sing Byrd or, more likely, Sing Bird. No— Singing Bird! That must have been her name originally—Singing Bird. And her brother, Crowell Byrd, was probably Crow Bird, or just Bird. They had mixed their Indian names with American-sounding names. Milkman had four people now that he could recognize in the song: Solomon, Jake, Ryna and Heddy, and a veiled reference to Heddy's Indianness. All of which seemed to put Jake and Sing together in Shalimar, just as Circe had said they were. He couldn't be mistaken. These children were singing a story about his own people! He hummed and chuckled as he did his best to put it all together. (307)

This is the ultimate challenge: retrieving the name's memorious body, putting together names' "unbelievable but entirely possible"

(35) stories by finding these narratives' "many missing pieces" (308). Milkman becomes suddenly attuned to a whole onomastic world, to names of people, places, and roads, "wondering what lay beneath the names, how many dead lives and fading memories were buried in and beneath the names or the places in this country. . . . the other names . . . [u]nder the recorded names" (333). This wonder outlives the tragic ending of the novel and much like Milkman's final jump, signifies a leap into consciousness, indeed, an invaluable, memorious recognition.

3

Remembering the Posthuman:
Intimations of Heterogeneity

As we have seen, the crisis of onomastic reference betokens the crisis of the human. No longer *identifying*, the name calls into question *identity* itself. To "find" the latter—to name it—we straggle, wandering from name to name and self to self. But, I have also submitted, it is the initial failure of naming, of "finding ourselves," that carries us toward others. This is how the memorious name uncovers our inescapable ties to them no less than the otherness woven into our selves, assuring us that, written by our names and the stories behind them into the social narrative, we are intertextual, *hence* social beings.

This postmodern—"post-original"—realization empowers us. But it comes *after the human*, at the very least after its crisis has broken out and has been acknowledged, thought through. Taking stock of this plight, postmodernism's onomastic theory and fiction fuel the expanding discourse of posthumanism. In Derrida, DeLillo, and other postmoderns naming and knowing are synonymous; if the noun does not dole out, lay hold of the known, if it does not identify as it used to or we imagined it did, then human identity, the human itself traditionally conceived are in trouble. And so are the humanities because they do not put out reliable knowledge anymore, do not manage to pin down, name the world but other names, and the names those are made of, in a process that hardly recovers a "truth," "origin," or "presence." According to Derrida, the very "name of the human" (*l'homme*)—the human's representations, worldviews (Weltanschauungen), the human sciences altogether—is the "name of that being which . . . has nursed the illusion of full presence, of a reassuring foundation, origin, and finite play" (le nom de cet être qui . . . a rêvé la présence pleine, le fondament rassurant, l'origine et la fin du jeu) (1979, 427). Tirelessly puncturing this "onto-theological" pipedream throughout his career, Derrida has been struggling to figure out how we might move beyond the human; indeed,

125

how to account for a move that, as I insist below, has already taken place; how to conceptualize the posthuman, in other words—truly in *other* words, that is, in new terms, which might help us deal with, if not swerve around, older conceptual traps.

More intently than the previous chapter, this segment of the book joins in the effort to come to grips with the posthuman, an increasingly defining concern not just for Derrida. In fields as diverse as philosophy, political science, theology, information technology, robotics, medicine, critical theory, aesthetics, and literary studies, this endeavor has involved rethinking the human and humanity, and by the same token modernity's—and modernism's—legacy, broadly speaking. Core categories of the "universalist" narrative of the Enlightenment and therefore, as Donna Haraway points out in her "Manifesto for Cyborgs," prime "modernist figures" (1990, 86), the human, humanism, humanity, and the humanities[1] are now undergoing deep-reaching reassessments and displacements. Unavoidable as they may be, such changes need to be tackled critically, for posthuman physicality, sexuality, and sociality, their politics, genealogies, historical formations, and present reformations are anything but predictable.

Revolving around various *posts*, contemporary theory has sought, too, to understand the posthuman before its advent proper. The Saussurean view of language as speaking through us, its presumed masters, a view essentially shared by Heidegger (1975, 197); also in Heidegger, the famous "Letter on Humanism" and, more recently, Peter Sloterdijk's reply, which "sketches a brief history of humanitas as literacy network" (Apter 2001a, 78); the critique of the author as "origin," "presence," "center," or language "owner," argument put forth by Barthes, Derrida, Kristeva, Jean Ricardou, Marcelin Pleynet, Sollers, and other *Tel Quel* group members, and traceable to Saussure and Bakhtin; Deleuze and Guattari's disassembly of "desiring-machines" in *Anti-Oedipus*'s momentous unseating of the Freudian paradigm; Lacanian psychoanalysis, in particular the roles it assigns to lack and absence in the overall architecture of identity, and to language in the mapping of the unconscious and in the "positing" of the subject (2000, 80); Lyotard's take on humanism in *The Inhuman*, but also, if less directly, his definition of discourse in *Just Gaming*; Foucault's pronouncement on "man" as a "recent invention, a figure not yet two centuries old, a wrinkle in our field of knowledge, [which] will disappear again as soon as that knowledge has discovered a new form" (1994, 23); the hyperreality epidemics in Baudrillard; Derrida's deconstruction, which ultimately targets the human and its time-honored, "logocentric" self-representation also known as humanism; late feminist, gay, lesbian, ethnicity- and race-based critiques of traditionally white, male, masculinist, and heterosexist notions of identity, with Butler, Sedgwick, Fuss, Hayles, Bordo, Delany, hooks, and Haraway as first names that come to mind: they all have attempted a full-fledged, posthumanist critique of the Cartesian subject undergirding modern representations of humaneness in the West. Nonetheless, the discussion of textually and culturally specific displacements of the human and humanist discourse is just getting in high gear. In this view, it is important to stress, as Halberstam and Livingston have in their anthology *Posthuman Bodies*, that the posthuman does not complete teleologically the "human story," does not simply finish up—nor does it finish off, break out of—modernity's number one grand narrative. It would make more sense, the critics add à la Lyotard, to revisit the human and its history as the posthuman "in the works," and, in so doing, to concede that the *post* in the *post*human both resists and triggers the complex implications of the *inter, infra, sub, trans, pre,* and *anti.*[2]

It comes as no surprise that the newly emerged posthuman symptomatology has surfaced predominantly in cybernetics (Wolfe 1995), cyberculture (Gray 2001, Haraway 1990), cyberpunk (Bukatman 1993), cyberfantasies of fetishism (Fernbach 2002), monstrosity, and aliens (Graham 2002), as well as in related areas of postmodern literature, science fiction, popular culture, the "avant-pop," and film.[3] It is in these territories of the contemporary imaginary that the most shockingly posthuman possibilities have been tried out through various challenges to inherited representations of the self, principally of the human body and its multiple, culturally-historically set boundaries. The body unfolds a site where the human as a whole and part of a greater whole becomes something else, undergoes significant transformations, or, as noted above, reveals that such mutations have been under way for quite some time now. Accordingly, the human body, a major focus of posthuman representations, cannot but renegotiate the interplay and hierarchies of reason and flesh, "spirit" and materiality, "naturalness"—the reason-governed body as given, made once for ever and going through "organic" growth— and "constructedness"—the body as material object shaped by competing discursive forces, the body as subjectivity, the human as *subject.*

For the sake of terminological clarity, I offer at this point a distinction between "posthuman" and "posthuman*ist.*" Where physical metamorphoses and generally speaking physicality are at issue; where these changes affect primarily, if not exclusively, the human body, deforming it, de-humanizing and stripping it of the expected human features, rendering it monstrous or inhuman, excessively organic (biological) or insufficiently, partly so (cyborg-like), I propose that we witness a *posthuman* becoming. But where critics try to come to terms with this process by theorizing posthuman developments and debating their implications *in* and *for* the human sciences; where, relatedly, they run up against the limits of classical humanism in defining the human and its posthuman mutations, and in response critique the cultural-philosophical, "humanist" roles the human has played as a rational entity in the West;[4] where, last, this critique lays bare the unexamined, universalist albeit Eurocentric and masculinist assumptions underpinning the human subject, I deem *posthumanist* a better choice. Further, the posthuman is depicted chiefly in the arts, supplies raw material to fictional discourse; the posthumanist is a matter of metadiscourse instead, a topic chiefly for critics, philosophers, and scientists working toward a revisionist rethinking of the human outside the humanist box. Otherwise, the dichotomy is fairly undependable. Bodily changes bear upon the mind, too, upon the rational subject capable of "reflection." Nor does thought—the thought of the posthuman included—occur solely in scientific or philosophical-speculative form. After all, postmodernism merges language and metalanguage, reflection and self-reflection.

One more time, the aforementioned posthuman shifts and renegotiations belong to a process already in place. Yet the process has accelerated of late, has become impossible to ignore. Arguably, the postmodern is the metadiscourse where this posthumanist reflection or realization obtains, as well as that which, within the contemporary, provides the instruments—tropes, themes, vocabularies—for the discursive production, for a picture of the posthuman, so much so that for some critics the *post* in postmodernism and posthumanism is the same.

I submit, this picture is memorious. That is to say, posthuman representation underscores the cultural and material-technological intertextuality of the human, its infiltration by, inscription into, and continuous "referencing" of, larger representations, texts, networks, assemblages. Additionally, this representation comes about while it re-presents previous characters, foregrounding literary intertextuality as the human's "origin," which is precisely what we will learn from Roth, McElroy, and Leyner in this chapter's second section.

To illuminate the memorious condition of posthumanity in postmodernism, I turn to Derrida again. His analysis of the subject and its ethics will help us get a handle especially on the Pynchonian post-human, which I examine first. More broadly, a Derridean, intertex-tual-cultural notion of subjectivity orients the whole chapter, including the final considerations on postmodern ontology in De-Lillo and Gibson.

In his interview with Jean-Luc Nancy, " 'Eating Well,' or the Calcula-tion of the Subject," Derrida underscores the uneasy relationship of ethics and the deconstructive idea of subjectivity.[5] He is wrestling here with a larger and hotly debated problem: the contested ethical dimension of poststructuralism and postmodernism. As is well known, the Nietzschean genealogy of moral values and Heidegger-ian ethical "supplementarity" guide his "deconstructive approach to the logocentric structure of moral dualism" (Kearney 1993, 32). We are often reminded, too, both Nietzsche and Heidegger ques-tion the possibility of "actual" ethics.[6] Therefore, this "dimension" has struck some as hypothetical at best. Nor am I unaware myself of poststructuralism's and postmodernism's controversial ethical ma-neuvers.[7]

I would argue, though, that Derrida's philosophy of subjectivity does not rule out a certain ethics, further, that his "apocalyptic" dis-course is a place where this ethics arises in response to the subject's memorious makeup as evinced in its technological making, un-making, and remaking. For, far from ascertaining the " 'demise of the ethical' " in a " 'post-deontic' epoch" (Bauman 1993, 2) irrevo-cably marred by the "technological di[sa]ssembly of the moral self," the subject's tribulations help us think about a new, "postmodern ethics" (195). As explicated in Derrida and allegorized in Pynchon, this "di[sa]ssembly" holds reconstructive potential and so is worth some closer scrutiny. I seize it in *Gravity's Rainbow* as both *"discursive" representation and "metadiscursive" critique of the human at a turning point in its history*, as a step in the ongoing posthuman reinvention of the subject. Pynchon enters a major chapter in the narrative of posthuman becoming undergirding postmodernity, a story that McElroy, Leyner, and Gibson carry on and retell. As they do so, they enact the ambivalent logic at work in authors like Pynchon and De-Lillo, the double gesture of postmodern representation that both sets the stage for, and puts forth critical responses to, the subject's ethical trials.

THE SUBJECT IN THE ZONE

Gnostics who have been taken in a rush of wind and fire to cham-bers of the Rocket-throne . . . Kabbalists who study the Rocket as

Torah, letter by letter—rivets, burner cup and brass rose, its text
is theirs to permute and combine into new revelations, always unfolding . . . Manichaeans who see two Rockets, good and evil . . . a
good Rocket to take us to the stars, an evil Rocket for the World's
suicide, the two perpetually in struggle.
                                —Thomas Pynchon, *Gravity's Rainbow*

[T]he frontier is more undecidable than ever, as it is between
the good and evil of all nuclear technology.
            —Jacques Derrida, "No Apocalypse, Not Now (Full Speed Ahead,
                                      Seven Missiles, Seven Missives)"

[A]t present the exploitation of a man for the purpose of science
is accepted everywhere without the slightest scruple. Who still
ventures to ask, What may be the value of a science which consumes its minions in this vampire fashion?
            —Friedrich Nietzsche, *The Future of Our Educational Institutions*

"Bookmatching" *The Crying of Lot 49* and *The Post Card*, and *Gravity's Rainbow* and *Les Fins de l'homme: à partir du travail de Jacques Derrida*, respectively, Alec McHoul and David Wills (1990) have brought into view some of the benefits of reading Pynchon "with" Derrida. The American writer, we are told, is "deconstructive" in that he breaks down binaries such as cause/effect, stimulus/response, real/fictive, immanent/transcendent, and textual/contextual. In principle, this could "amoun[t] to annulling the ethical qualification and to think-ing of writing beyond good and evil," as Derrida warns in *Of Grammatology* (1976, 314). Yet, interestingly enough, this does not happen; there is, to recall de Man, an "ethical tonality" to the inter-play of the subject and technology in *Gravity's Rainbow*. Derrida's in-terview "'Eating Well'" and his lecture "No Apocalypse, Not Now (Full Speed Ahead, Seven Missiles, Seven Missives)" urge us to tune in to this tonality, and in so doing furnish a revealing theoretical framework for the following discussion of Pynchon's novel. I rein-force this framework with Heidegger's "Question Concerning Tech-nology" since the technological impacts, quite visibly in Pynchon, agency and accountability. More generally, as Lisa D. Campolo maintains, "both the relation between Derrida and Heidegger and their questioning of the system of humanistic ethics can be effec-tively explored by considering their respective critiques of technol-ogy" (1985, 435). I bring these critiques to bear upon *Gravity's Rainbow* so as to sketch out the novel's own ethics, which inheres, it seems to me, in showing how human agency collapses as "modern humans [become] technological objects" (Bauman 1993, 195), how technology's "destination" (193) sends the subject off on an "er-

rant" destiny, but also how embedded in this situation is the prospect of a posthuman subject and its ethics.

In *V*, *The Crying of Lot 49*, *Vineland*, *Mason & Dixon*, and, we are
about to see in detail, *Gravity's Rainbow*, technological proliferation
affects the subject and agency through particular figurations of the
body. Much like the dislocation Derrida's deconstruction performs,[8]
Pynchon's work acts out posthuman and posthumanist displacements of the traditional subject. Yet, one more time, this does not
lead to a definitive "repressi[on]" of the ethical, as some commentators would have us believe. Pynchon's memorious imagination
foregrounds the cultural fabric of the subject, uncovers the "unnatural" morphology of what philosophers from Aristotle to Heidegger
and Derrida designate as *hypokeimenon*, a certain structure of "sub-
jection." It is the tragic-comic "dehiscence" of the subject (Derrida
1992, 103), its "dissipation" as former *substratum* that Derrida conceptualizes and Pynchon narrates through the symbolic assault of
technology. In light of the Derridean notion of a subject *deprived* of
substratum, the main questions I wish to ask à propos of *Gravity's
Rainbow* are, What kind of moral agency may the characters still
claim as their own once their bodies and minds have become sites
of technological mapping? What is the ethical stance of a literary
text that divulges this mapping, this cultural-technological "infec-
tion" of the human, now prone to reification and dehumanization?
What type of "ethical choice" (Booth 1988, 8) does the novel make
by playing up the workings of "vampiric" *techne*? And last, What is
the ethics of a reading that focuses on Pynchon's technology theme
and its memorious bearings?

The "interfac[e] between bodies and technologies" (Hayles
1993b, 165) is the novel's ethical linchpin. Specifically, the technological ties into the ethical through the former's symbolically re-
working the human in its various, eccentric embodiments, which
ends in a whole phenomenology of corporeal disruption and manipulative reincorporation. It is much more than one's individual body
that various machines disassembly and reassembly in Pynchon. It is
the body's metaphysical, epistemological, and ethical horizon, the
realm of the "spirit" (*Geist*), that technology collapses, setting in
motion both posthuman and posthumanist displacements. Inspiring
"elaborate terror," technology takes up demonic forms in *Gravity's
Rainbow* (1973, 230). It threatens the organization of the human
and humanist subject by hatching a corporate plot to "dismantle"
"Man" (712), and, I might add, the masculine marker notwithstanding, the threat concerns all humanity. In the "Zone," the region of
northern Germany where Nazi scientists have produced the famous

V-2 rocket, American soldiers sing bacchic "Rocket Limericks" (305) that picture the relations of humans and technical devices as sexual encounters resulting in castration, alteration, maiming, violence done to the body: "There was a young fellow named Hector, / Who was fond of a launcher-erector. / But the squishes and pops / Of acute pressure drops / Wrecked Hector's hydraulic connector" (306); "There once was a fellow named Ritter, / Who slept with a guidance transmitter. / It shriveled his cock, / Which fell off in his sock, / And made him exceedingly bitter" (334); "There was a young man from Decatur, / Who slept with a LOX generator. / His balls and his prick / Froze solid real quick, / And his asshole a little bit later" (335). People and machines, tools and weapons—mainly missiles and missile parts—make up strange conglomerates. Humans turn into "Raketenmensch[en]," Rocketmen (366). They worship the mystic bomb, "becom[e] one" with it (403), "both aggressor and victim, rocket and parabolic path," "extension of the Rocket" (402), squeezed up in the missile's fuselage, symbolically swallowed up whole by the new Leviathan.

Technology, especially belligerent technology, weaponry, is glaringly masculinized and sexualized. Aggressive, therefore "male" and overly sexual, it turns on, subdues, and finally supplants human sexuality, men's and women's alike. Potence that renders humans "impotent" and desireless, *techne* makes itself into their sole object of desire while making them want to be possessed by it. It cancels out their prowess, carries out unspeakable acts on women while enfeebling "maleness," "disarm[ing]," "de-penis[ing]" it, and "dismantl[ing]" the human (712) more broadly. The phallic Rocket is the ultimate "erection." Enzian, a member of the African Schwarzkommando,[9] suspects that

> love, among these men [doing scientific research], once past the simple feel and orgasming of it, had to do with masculine technologies, with contracts, with winning and losing. Demanded, in his own case, that he enter the service of the Rocket. . . . Beyond simple steel erection, the Rocket was an entire system *won*, away from the feminine darkness, held against the entropies of lovable but scatterbrained Mother Nature. . . . He was led to believe that by understanding the Rocket, he would come to understand truly his manhood. (324)[10]

Pynchon figures the subject as a cultural space eroding the binaries of inert and alive, static and mobile, material and intellectual, physical and nonphysical, natural and artificial, biological and anorganic.[11] The novel displays staggering combinatory capability, foregrounding what Donna Haraway has identified as "leaky distinctions." While the modern age was obsessed with the "specter of the ghost in the machine," in postmodern culture, Haraway maintains, machines encroach upon the realm of the "spirit" (1990, 193) only to render the latter a mechanism, scheme, artifact, material construction with a cultural history—a memorious past—behind it. Even though Pynchon's characters are not cyborgs like Philip K. Dick's or Gibson's, they feature a similar structure. Mechanical parts and instruments are built into people's brains, undermining the site of the "spiritual" and along with it the notions of reason, mind, individual autonomy, and agency: "Inside their brains they shared an old, old electro-decor—variable capacitors of glass, kerosene for a dielectric, brass plates and ebonite covers, Zeiss galvanometers with thousands of fine-threaded adjusting screws, Siemens milliammeters set on slate surfaces, terminals designated by Roman numerals, Standard Ohms of magnese wire in oil, the old Gülcher Thermosäule that operated on heating gas, put out 4 volts, nickel and antimony, asbestos funnels on top, mica tubing" (Pynchon 1973, 518). Thus, the novel unearths a frail, heterogeneous structure of the subject, of a fragmented subject colonized and practically displaced by technology, by the fruits of its own "runaway" rationality, as Anthony Giddens would say. While the human body is relegated to the status of "hardware,"[12] *techne*, in the modern, "perverted" sense Heidegger takes aim at, stands for the actual subject, enjoys a "vitality" of its own (Pynchon 1973, 401) unnoticed by the managers and plutocrats who still nourish the illusion of controlling "[le] *technologique*" (401). Ironically, it is an inanimate object like "Byron the bulb"[13] that boasts of having a "soul," and Pynchon plays here upon the complex meaning of the German *Seele*, the Hegelian counterpart of *Geist*. Likewise, manipulating cultural references and blurring the boundaries between human and nonhuman, Pynchon fancies a Proustian

> metal-ebonite-and-plastic young Marcel . . . , a mechanical chess-player dating back to the Second Empire, actually built a century ago for the great conjuror Robert-Houdin, very serious-looking French refugee kid, funny haircut with the ears perfectly outlined in hair that starts abruptly a quarter-inch strip of bare plastic skin away, black patent-shiny hair, hornrim glasses, a rather remote manner, unfortunately much too literal with humans . . . , no fakery inside to give him any touch of humanity at all. (675)

As this Proustian reprise shows, humans are in *Gravity's Rainbow* fraught with non-humanness. At the same time, devices, appliances,

and parts vaunt a compensatory identity of sorts. Realm of omnipo-
tent technology, the Pynchonian Zone operates a symptomatic
transfer of subjectivity, structure, autonomy, and coherence from
"real" subjects to mechanisms—to the Great Mechanism gearing everything to its purposes. Literally and metaphorically, people are
"transmitters," components of a larger, all-comprehensive network
or apparatus. Pynchon's text simply turns the modern view of technology as "extension of the human body" upside down: it is humankind that now functions as a "prosthetic device."[14] To recall one of
Walden's social comments, "men have become the tools of their
tools" (Thoreau 1992, 29)—or, as Henry Adams, one of Pynchon's
masters, says, it is "motors" that "drive the men. . . . The New American [i]s the servant of the power-house" (1999, 352, 388). Fragments of a system the proportions of which they hardly fathom, the
humans are now entangled in *techne*'s gigantic web. No longer self-
determining, self-representing, and *stand-alone* entities, the human
signifiers stand for, signify something else always outside themselves.
They serve as links, "transmitters," or, with a term often used in
chapter 5, relays in a chain or memorious carousel of re-presentations whose meaning lies beyond the human unit. People supply the
pieces of the big technological puzzle, cast contours on a map impossible to comprehend—grasp in its entirety and read—and are
concurrently crossed, decentered as subjects, by this inhuman chart
of materiality, hardware, and energies. Subjects to a superior authority, they have lost their subject status, hence no longer count as
moral agents.

   Drifting along radio waves, sliding up and down the network's
power paths, indeed, witness—and victim—of the "nascent network
society" (Shaviro 2003, 148), the self, or the ego, as Pynchon says, is
part of a "grid," of a memoriously relational world, and eventually
becomes a grid itself, "flows" following the rules of modern religion, electricity.[15] Tellingly, a character "thought of himself . . . as a
radio transmitter of some kind, and believed that whatever he was
broadcasting at the time was at least no threat to them. In his elec-
tro-mysticism, the triode was as basic as the cross in Christianity."
"Think of the ego, the self that suffers a personal history bound to
time," Pynchon's hero tells himself, "as the grid. The deeper and
true self is the flow between cathode and plate. The constant, pure
flow. Signals—sense-data, feelings, memories relocating—are put
onto the grid, and modulate the flow" (1973, 404). The subject as
grid and flow between electric poles, technologically deterritorial-
ized through war, colonization, deportation, and violence, is more
than a poststructuralist insight. It thematizes, to quote Giddens

again, the "consequences of modernity," its effects on a subject structure otherwise presumed to be anchored in reason, hence consistent, coherent, autonomous, in control. Repeatedly, Pynchon plays up the tropes of a disrupted and erratic subject, a groundless (Grund-less) and heterogenous subject ever differing from itself, unable to regain its former strength and exercise ethical agency. He dramatizes an agonal ego that technology parasitizes and consumes while eating into its metaphysical and moral foundations. As a result, and much as in Derrida, in Pynchon formerly "certain predicates" of subjectivity are now "deconstructed"; among these, "the sub-jective structure as the being-thrown—or underlying—of the substance or of the substratum, of the hypokeimenon, with its qualities of stance or stability, of permanent presence, of sustained relation to self, everything that links the 'subject' to conscience, to humanity, to history . . . and above all the law, as subject subjected to the law, subject to the law in its very autonomy, to ethical or juridical law, to political law or power, to order (symbolic or not)" (Derrida 1992, 99). Subjected to devouring, objectifying technology, the subject loses in Gravity's Rainbow its traditional, humanist ethical identity. It finds itself stripped of ontological substratum and, by the same token, of the moral, "sub-jective" infrastructure that brings subjectivity "before the law," of the Heideggerian Geworfenheit (from the German werfen, "to throw") that "casts" the subject into the realm of responsibility.

"Re-found[ing] a discourse on the 'subject,' on that which will hold the place (or replace the place) of the subject (of law, of morality, of politics)" (Derrida 1992, 107), the "experience of deconstruction" makes possible a nontranscendent, "nonsubjectile" reinvention of the subject's ethical structure. This reinvention lays down a specific "duty" of deconstruction (108) and, pace Paul Smith (1988, 55), an affirmation, a necessary validation of responsibility since "there is no responsibility, no ethical-political decision, that must not pass through the proofs of the incalculable or the undecidable" (Derrida 1992, 108). In which case, one could say, the subject's definition as "affirmation without closure, trace, différance from self" paves the way to a new, "post-metaphysical" ethics, one which "would not be predeconstructive" (103), that is, premised on the metaphysical transcendence and coherence of the subject.

Pynchon's text allegorizes—and hyperbolizes—at length this inner displacement and the ensuing ethical "repealing" of the subject. I find it significant, in this regard, that the self appears in the novel as a mere "electric" phenomenon. This mode of appearance is the ultimate, if metaphorical, outcome of *différance* as alterity pervading and fragmenting the subject's place, injecting the human with artificiality and heterogeneity, substituting machine components for organs, turning the self into a grid, and plugging it into a larger, transsubjectively memorious network. Thus, this "différential" maneuvering troubles the binaries that have informed the human subject and guaranteed its cohesion and moral agent status. Pynchon repeatedly exposes the unethical penchant of technology, highlighting the "instrumentalization" of this subject, the annihilation of its agency and responsibility. His text teems with images of a humanity (geopolitics, economic infrastructures, etc.) woven into a global plot meant to ensure technology's supremacy. Pynchon deliberately reverses—"deconstructs"—the relation between ends and means, showing how history is "staged" for technological purposes:

> It means this War [World War II] was never political at all, the politics was all theatre, all just to keep the people distracted . . . secretly, it was being dictated instead by the needs of technology . . . by a conspiracy between human beings and techniques, by something that needed the energy-burst of war, crying, "Money be damned, the very life of [insert name of Nation] is at stake," but meaning, most likely, *dawn is nearly here, I need my night's blood, my funding, funding, ahh more, more.* . . . The real crises were crises of allocation and priority, not among firms—it was only staged to look that way—but among the different Technologies, Plastics, Electronics, Aircraft, and their needs which are understood only by the ruling elite. (1973, 521)

As late as Sartre, humanism insisted that humankind is what it makes of itself. It turns out, the human is in Pynchon quite literally made, produced, as it is *un*made by technology. To further, reproduce itself, *techne* produces and reproduces the human by usurping its former "making" position, and this applies to the "elites," too. True, as certain members of the "Schwarzkommando" put it, "Technology [is made to] respon[d]," and it is people who are held responsible for its progress and upshots, especially those involving warfare. "Go ahead," Pynchon has personified Technology reply, "capitalize the T on Technology, deify it if it'll make you feel less *responsible*— but it puts you in with the neutered, brother, in with the eunuchs keeping the harem of our stolen Earth for the numb and joyless hardons of human sultans, human elite with no right at all to be where they are" (521). However, the self-absolving argument is too abstract, too general-anthropocentric and "residually humanistic" (Tabbi 2002, xvi, 48) to boot. After all, it is isolated amid *Gravity's Rainbow*'s so many scenes and metaphors hinting at technological developments above human design. Further, Gabriele Schwab has shown that the "impact of technology on the formation of the egos, the bodies, and the unconscious of historical subjects" (1994, 178) bears especially upon "peripheral" selves in *Gravity's Rainbow*. The Hereros belong to these marginal and repressed groups, which also include, Schwab says, the woman, the primitive, the Jew, the revolutionary. Notably enough, they are the first technology attacks, vampirizes, tries to co-opt. Their drama speaks to the twilight of the humanist subject, to its entering a post-Enlightenment age where the rational notion of responsibility no longer holds sway. So the search of "younger Schwarzkommando" for some sort of human responsibility behind the spectacle of technology is bound to remain purely theoretical. Like other labyrinthine texts by Pynchon such as *V* or *The Crying of Lot 49*, *Gravity's Rainbow* features a utopian quest. The Hereros fall short of their goal because there is no ultimate ethical center, instance, or source to be exposed and held accountable. On the contrary, the search decenters the seeker. If Pynchon does adopt a moral stance in this respect, this aligns here with the ethics of Derrida, de Man (1979, 188–220), J. Hillis Miller (1987, 41–60), and poststructuralism in general. For he seems to suggest that any ethical "referentialization" that would strive to "reinvent" the traditional, "pre-deconstructive" subject as a source of responsibility is self-defeating.

To de Man and Hillis Miller, this temptation—no less than its necessary failure—marks a defining ritual of reading. *Gravity's Rainbow* takes up this ritual by fancying the technology of the "Zone"[16] as a text plotting its own encoding, inviting interpretation at the same time that it foils it. Spreading out like a gigantic text, technology writes itself across ethical subjects, "cutting across every agency human and paper that ever touched it" (566). Consequently, the meaning of the resulting "structure" (566) "lie[s] in a conspiracy beyond human agency," as Joseph Tabbi observes in *Cognitive Fictions* (2002, 43). Corporations from two continents and seemingly opposed military alliances, public and secret organizations, governments, ethnic and racial groups take part in the writing of this "Zonal" Kabbalah of technology, which certain characters haplessly strive to decipher. They suspect, for instance, that the ruins of "Jamf Ölfabriken Werke AG" make up a secret—and sacred—technological discourse. Through his "English interlocks," Director Krupp employs the "8th AF bombers" as "special tools" of reading and writing. "Bombing," we learn, is "the exact industrial process of conversion, each release of energy placed exactly in space and time, each shockwave plotted in advance to bring *precisely tonight's wreck* into being thus decoding the Text, thus coding, recoding, redecoding the holy Text" (Pynchon 1973, 520–21). Writing, reading, rewriting, and rereading trace the endless life cycle of a technology intent upon preserving its all-inclusive textuality at all costs. As for the humans in the Zone, they "are supposed to be the Kabbalists out here, say that's our real Destiny, to be the scholars-magicians of the Zone, with somewhere in it a Text, to be picked to pieces, annotated, explicated . . . this holy text had to be the Rocket, . . . our Torah. What else? Its symmetries, its latencies, the *cuteness* of it enchanted and seduced us while the real Text persisted, somewhere else, in its darkness, our darkness" (520). As Joseph Tabbi points out elsewhere, "the rocket, worshipped by many characters in *Gravity's Rainbow* as 'Holy Text,' provides a sublime uplift *as* text, a disembodied web of information that floats above nature's gravity and belies its potential for causing real, material destruction" (1995, 75).

Transnational corporations, technocratic groups pushing "National Socialist chemistry" (Pynchon 1973, 578)—plastic is "fascist"[17]—freemasons and latter-day alchemists, Harvard eggheads, Argentine anarchists, and Russian intelligence officers are involved in the production of an absolute form(ula): the Zone's megatext, the new Kabbalist synthesis (590). The Germans and the Allies unknowingly work together, beneath the "superficial," obvious—and hence "misleading"—text of history, in the hatching of the technological plot, the "real" yet elusive text that employs its more visible strata as pre-texts, camouflage or "decoy" writing. The Zone unfolds as a textual, or, better still, intertextual cobweb of plots (603), geographic writing of delusive "paraphrases" (625), perpetually modified, rewritten, "edited" by "Them" (694), the invisible "writers."[18] Most remarkably, "They" engineer or "write" a geopolitics (727) at the expense of the people, now textual units or agents through which writing takes place. In this world and as a result of this writing, the ethical option is placed under erasure, unwritten. Although the Rocket seems to stand as a morally ambiguous sign, beyond good and evil and so unreadable as *either* good *or* evil, the novel shows—and this is one of its ethical moves—that the unethical *technologique* has the upper hand. Definitely, the Rocket does not "take us to the stars." One cannot regain access to transcendence, to the Kantian "starry sky"—the correlative of the "moral law." In actuality, the V-2, the central "paragraph" of the Zonal discourse, pre*scribes* the "World's suicide" (727). Technology plots war as a means to revise, edit, and so perpetuate its own text.

A technological paragon of the novel, the missile claims the place of the Enlightenment subject, occupies the topology of selfhood in its most private manifestations. Symbolically, the map tacked to the wall of Slothrop's office in London pinpoints both his love affairs and the spots hit by V-2 missiles. The Rocket thus gradually becomes central to a strange technomythology. The soldiers and technicians working on, or firing, it are the new "gnostics."[19] Their bodies are literally and metaphorically "enclosed" by the Rocket's fuselage. There is, in *Gravity's Rainbow*, a violent transfer of subjectivity from humans to the mystic missile. The latter mimics transcendent subjectivity by hurling actual subjects "beyond themselves," by turning them into fuel and instruments. The Rocket is Pynchon's "fallen angel," evil *messenger* of an absent "above" ("the medium is the message"). It quotes, and mocks, Rilke's angels as symbols of a supernatural world that provides mortals with the Kantian "ontotheological" justification of the law.[20] The "pro-jectile" reveals itself as a sort of fraudulent, *absolute* sub-ject besieged, Derrida says, by "the problematic of the *je* [*c*] *t* (above all subject, object, project)" (1992, 100).

Autotelic, following a circular trajectory, the Rocket has no other target (finality, transcendence) than itself, much like the technology it epitomizes. It is, it seems to me, a caricature of the former, rational subject. The missile is self-sub-*missive*, as Derrida would put it, a self-reflexive text referring to itself and textualizing/fictionalizing the human in this process. It gives the human, Pynchon suggests, the appearance of being what the humanist subject has never been *other than theoretically*, in its humanist representations (*humaniora*): a "grand narrative"—"the subject is a fable," Derrida reminds us (1992, 102)—a story or fiction whose coherence obtains at the expense of the "real" subjects' being remade into "surface effects," "fallout" (103). No wonder Pynchon's people roam the Zone, condemned to relay status, to picaresque "destinerrance," (sub-)missives without destination and destiny, or whose destiny is to eternally rewrite ("maintain") the Zonal technotext. Unlike them, the Great Missile is self-centered, a self-addressed "missive" throwing itself toward itself. It mimics the Heideggerian "*Geworfenheit* (thrownness) of *Dasein*" (110), parodies the ethical-metaphysical re-centering of the "responsible" subject as an *erected* missile, a "phallogocentric" symbol *par excellence*. In actuality, the missile has displaced, sub-mitted the human sub-je[c]t by "throwing [it] beneath." Technology has replaced—as Textology—the topology of *Dasein*, the map of existence: Being has been "(en)framed" and has become "Zone."

Derrida's lecture "No Apocalypse, Not Now" brings into play the couple missile-missive and by implication the technological "liquidation" (1992, 96) of this subject. Here, the philosopher dwells

upon apocalyptic (nuclear) technology, and this can help deepen
our understanding of Pynchon's novel. In brief, he puts forth the
curious hypothesis that atomic weaponry[21] is "*fabulously textual
through and through*" (1984, 23).[22] It exerts, he goes on, a rhetorical,
persuasive function, the famous "deterrence" ("diplomatic power"),
which, notably, "would not exist without the structure of a text"
(26). The missiles are both reality and figment, fable, discourse, "to
the extent that, for the moment, a nuclear war has not taken place:
one can only talk and write about it" (23). Much like the Zonal air
strikes in Pynchon, the technological text washes away the previous
textuality of the world in order to write itself. The nuclear attack
brings about a "remainderless [*sans reste*] destruction of the archive" (27), of extant referentiality. Therefore, apocalyptic[23] technology appears[24] as the "only possible referent of any discourse and
experience that would share their condition with that of literature"
(28). Both real and textual, the A-bomb renders itself its own "absolute" referent, the only thing one can talk about, or, as Derrida sees
it in *Psyché, la seule trace ineffaçable*, the trace that cannot be erased
(379). Where humans do not represent themselves anymore, the
missile stands for the sole, self-representing missive/message
(*envoi*).[25] It wages a war "in the name of [*au nom de*]" what is "worth
more than life," the . . . "name itself" since one cannot name the
"apocalyptic" referent of the name—as we saw in chapter 2, the unnameable and the unrepresentable are synonymous in Derrida.
Again as in Pynchon, the self-referentiality of lethal technology affects, in fact suspends the relations among *socii* (Derrida 1984, 23),
among subjects making up a society, a *socius* or *ethical body* (people
bound by certain values). Self-referential, "self-addressed" technology breaks up this body and the bodies constituting it, turns once
"whole onto themselves" human subjects and nature into relays,
tools, objects, *parts.*

It is this process of object- and relation-becoming, this instrumentalization that Heidegger takes issue with in his critique of *Ge-stell,*
or, technological "enframing." As David Farrell Krell remarks in his
introduction to Heidegger's "Question Concerning Technology,"
the "supreme danger" of *die Technik* stems from "enclosing all
beings in a particular claim—utter availability and sheer
manipulability . . . , reduc[ing] man and beings to a sort of 'standing
reserve' or stockpile in service to, and on call for, technological purposes" (Heidegger 1977, 285). The German philosopher argues, basically, that both the "instrumental" and "anthropological"
determinations of technology are incomplete. Technology is neither
solely "a means to an end" nor just "human activity" (288). "Cor-

rect" as they may be, these definitions are not necessarily "true" (289), especially if one takes into account modern *techne*'s tendency to evade human control (289). Similar to Pynchon, Heidegger underlines the seemingly paradoxical "monstrousness" (297) of modern *techne* (and modernity in general), its unethical character.

It bears noting, along these lines, that Heidegger links up responsibility and instrumentality. In humanist tradition, the former characterizes the subject while the latter is an attribute of technology. However, modern technology, as opposed to its pre-modern forms, mounts a deadly "challenging setting-upon" (das herausfordernde Stellen) (Heidegger 1962, 16), by which "what we call real is revealed as standing-reserve" (Heidegger 1977, 299). As "no mere human doing" (300), technology instrumentalizes people and "cancels" them as responsible subjects although its initial mission was the exact opposite, that is, to empower them. In its newly acquired sense that has supplanted the original meanings of *poiesis*, *techne* sets up the subject as *Bestand* (298), "standing-reserve" (308). Nature, history, humanity have become, *Gravity's Rainbow* shows, technology's warehouse, instrumental reserve "ordered" by *techne* (Heidegger 1977, 299). The prevalent logic of our time is techno-logical. This may as well be the supreme "danger" (309) humans have to face, no easy challenge, for we have been deeply involved in "driving technology forward" (300). We have brought this threat upon ourselves; it is "human doing" (300) and therefore "perverse," "unethical." While in Heidegger technology as such is not necessarily "demonic" (309), it nevertheless presents a real threat insofar as it "has already afflicted man in his essence" (309).

Our "radical responsibility" (Campolo 1985, 433) in light of Heidegger's analysis is a revaluation of *techne* as *poiesis*.[26] Heading off the "(en)framing" technology holds in store for us, *poiesis* may redeem, Heidegger hopes, our destiny through art. On the latter's terrain, one can confront technology and unearth its essence—an essence that, importantly enough, is *not* of technological nature (Heidegger 1977, 317). It is through art that we can pursue this essence, bring it into the open and thus engage head-on with the alienating "objectification" (Mark 1987, 161) technology threatens to bring upon us. This is why art bears a great responsibility.

Gravity's Rainbow does not ignore this responsibility. Dramatizing the collapse of the humanist, ethical subject in the deadly clasp of "vampiric technology," Pynchon joins in the contemporary effort to rethink the subject, its new structure and site—the displaced place of its responsibility. To be sure, Pynchon does not pine for a prelapsarian metaphysical coherence of the subject. The "ethical model"

Pynchon seems to drive at entails coming to terms with the posthuman condition embedded in the memorious relatedness underpinning the textual-technological network in which his characters find themselves enmeshed. This condition and the ethical problems it raises, he suggests, must be acknowledged, first. Then, they must be thought through from a new, post-transcendental position founded—"re-founded," in Derrida—on "difference and not identity" (Siebers 1988, 97), or, in Pynchonian terms, on the realization of the cultural-technological constructedness and relationality sanctioning the subject and life generally under postmodernity. As Christopher Norris comments on Deleuze's reading of *Kant's Critical Philosophy*, this conjunctural and decentered subjectivity breaks with the traditional constitution of the moral subject (1986, 14). Pointedly, Pynchon calls our attention to the "vampiric" character of the new, sham transcendence, of the "subjectile" subjectivity that turns humankind into an *available* object and assigns perpetual "dehiscence," "destinerrance," and lack of destiny as its "mission."[27]

It would be all too simplistic either to merely celebrate Pynchon's "attack" on technology or, conversely, to dismiss his work as another example of the "disempowering habit of demonizing technology as a satanic mill of domination" (Penley and Ross 1991, xii). I do find the novel's representation—and critique—of the unethical, hegemonic technological particularly appealing. But *Gravity's Rainbow* lays down an ethics by focusing on infernal technology at the same time that it declines to fall back on a putatively pre-technological paradise of untainted, pure subjectivity. Technology "posthumanizes" the human, uncovers its cultural-memorious makeup, but it has been doing it since day one. Technology has always been embedded in the structure of the self, inlaid and reproduced in the structure of our bodies. As objects of technology,[28] we take it in, so to speak, we become—already are—it. "We have never been modern," Bruno Latour proclaims in the title of one his books. To paraphrase him, one could say, "We have never been human"—and Slavoj Žižek has said it in *On Belief*, where he urges us that "One should claim that 'humanity' as such ALWAYS-ALREADY WAS 'posthuman'" (44). It appears that we have always been "impure," material, "constructed." On the other hand, the advent of the posthuman does not "eradicate" the subject. Nor is the latter "killed off" by the poststructuralist logic warranting this advent: the *human* subject (and the subject of *humanism*) is instead de-centered, and its formerly "unexamined agency" is "questioned" (Spivak 1999, 323), as I have done here by looking at the role technology plays in the "de-centering" process.

Transformed by this process, Pynchon's characters may seem "unnatural," and the situations they are caught in have struck readers as offbeat, eccentric, even destructive. Yet we need to remember that these situations are the bitter fruit of "scientific progress." Ironically, this progress has not resulted in the humanization of technology, but in the technological posthumanization of the human, which has somehow "naturalized" technology, turning it into a bodily drama. The distinction between human bodies and body parts no longer operates once the mechanical, the artificial, and the discursive have been embodied—corpo*realized*—and work as such. They have decentered the self, and this postmodern/posthuman decentering leads to an ethical crisis. As Zygmunt Bauman explains in *Postmodern Ethics*, the technological erosion of the "moral self" (1993, 195) defines the age of "pervasive technology," *our* age.[29] Positing us and the world as "environment" (186)—as "storehouse," Heidegger wrote—technology heralds the "sovereignty of means over ends" (Bauman 1993, 188), of tools over the subjects supposed to operate them. Whether the planet as a whole or the "human self" as an entity (195), former "totalities" break apart because the only totality technology

> systematically constructs, reproduces and renders invulnerable is the totality of technology itself—technology as a *closed system*, which tolerates no alien bodies inside and zealously devours and assimilates everything that comes within its grazing ground. Technology is the sole genuine individual. Its sovereignty can be only indivisible and exceptionless. Humans, most certainly, are not excepted.
>
> Like anything else, modern humans are technological objects. Like anything else, they have been analysed (split into fragments) and then synthesized in novel ways (as arrangements, or just collections, of fragments). (195)

Unable to cope with fragmentation, the moral subject of humanism is "the most evident and the most prominent among technology's victims" (198). It is this victimization that Pynchon's text depicts while suggesting that the time has come to think about another ethics reflecting the new age—posthuman—of the subject, of the subject as flow and heterogeneous materiality.

But how does Pynchon's own discourse respond to the discursive invasion of the human body, to the unethical suspension of the subject? What does the novel as narrative, as "form," do in reaction to what it tells of, possibly against what technology does to humans? In short: what kind of textual ethics obtains in Pynchon? I would argue that as a text, *Gravity's Rainbow* does not replicate the text of technology, and this is the Heideggerian, *poietic*—"artistic"—thrust of Pynchonian representation. A foremost example of postmodern *poiesis*, the novel fosters an ethics of its own, which can be best grasped in textual terms, as an ethics of writing and reading. So the questions *Gravity's Rainbow* raises are not only, How does Pynchon's writing represent, how does it react to the technological dystopia it describes?, but also, How do we react, as readers, to this reaction? In what sense is our reading, our dealing with Pynchon's writing, different from what Pynchon's Kabbalists accomplish as "writers" and "readers" in the Zone?

For one thing, *Gravity's Rainbow* is not, its intimidating bulk notwithstanding, the voracious totality, the hegemonic and all-embracing textual sprawl technology purports to turn into in the book. For another, our reading of Pynchon's Kabbalistic text further chips away at this totality, decenters and multiplies it: there is a war *in* the novel, and then there is the postmodern "war on totality" (Lyotard 1993, 16) waged *by* the novel itself. Joseph Tabbi has asked, and rightly so, how effective this antitotalist resistance is (1995, 76–77). Arguably, the novel's multiple centers and the overall "indeterminacy" stemming from its shuttling back and forth between paranoid totalities and ironic-relativist debunking thereof (77) ultimately undercut the authoritarian all-inclusiveness of technology. There is considerable evidence in favor of the argument that Pynchon's narrative declines to be the "metanarrative" totalistic and totalitarian *techne* aspires to become. What we are dealing with is rather an unstable, protean, unyielding—many would say, unreadable—text, *a text that insists on remaining open* à la Eco's *opera aperta*. This openness goes against the closure totalist-totalitarian technology struggles to bring upon Pynchon's world, as much as it proves incompatible with a former totality, humanistic, rational, subjective and subjectively coherent, reassuringly grounded in transcendent values. To put it otherwise, there are disjunctions between what the novel represents, how this is represented, and how we ourselves may represent—read—Pynchonian representation. It is in these gaps, differences, and asymmetries that *Gravity's Rainbow*'s morality thrives.

ENGENDERING GAMES: THREE STEPS
ON THE LADDER OF POSTHUMANITY

Following the discussion of the posthuman and its ethical ramifications in *Gravity's Rainbow,* I want to shift gears a bit and focus on three literary models of posthuman becoming—three models of memorious transgression or metamorphosis of the human through what I would call engendering games. I use the term metamorphosis advisedly for my first example, Roth's 1972 novella, *The Breast*, undertakes a daring rewriting—a textual metamorphosis—of Kafka's own "Metamorphosis."[30] The second will be McElroy's novel, *Plus* (1977), a text closer to the cultural form most posthuman interrogations tend to privilege: science fiction, whether in literature, theory, or film—where *Blade Runner* and the *Star Trek*, *RoboCop*, *Alien*, and *Terminator* series remain the classical illustrations. Finally, I turn to Leyner's more recent refiguration of the male body as posthuman corporeality. I propose that these are three "posthuman fables" that reprise and revise previous fables and discourses of the body, gender, and humanity—as many symbolic steps on the ladder of posthumanity. The modus operandi of all three is, programmatically and conspicuously, *intertextual.* Here posthumanity "originates"— quotation marks are required here, too—in these writers' responses to previous works, artifacts, and cultural discourse: Kafka, Beckett, and pop culture, to name just a few.

The textual strategies, the intertexts these strategies are brought to bear upon, and, lastly, the obtaining posthuman projections all vary. But, I will show, such differences can be so organized as to trace a certain development or "radicalizing" of posthuman discourse and its expanding critique of the human and humanism over the past three decades. To anticipate a bit, Roth's and McElroy's posthuman visions still tolerate the notion—either comic or tragic—of human(ist) restitution. In their posthuman stories, the human is still the broader, accommodating narrative or paradigm, if not the ideal. Already embarked upon posthuman metamorphoses, their characters strive to regain a lost humanity. Thus, in a sense, both writers allow for a "rehumanizing" of the *Kreatur* formerly known as Gregor Samsa, and Imp Plus, respectively, whereas Leyner's avant-pop, technology-driven fantasies of "hypermale" identity seem to resist more emphatically human and humanist nostalgias.

In Roth and McElroy, the relation between rationality and physicality—a dialectic tension marking our inherited notion of the human—is basically reinvented. The two authors shed light on the very construction and historicity of "humanity" at the same time that they set about painting subjectivity with a different, posthuman brush. Their protagonists query their own humanness, see the extraordinary, multiply traumatic transformation affecting them as an occasion to reflect (especially in Roth) on the unavoidable and inseparable themes of humanity and modernity, of humanity and the humanities, as noted above. Significantly, Roth's hero looks back on modern literary and cultural history, on the "great Western authors" he has taught and who, he suggests, have made him into what they fancy. A literature instructor, Roth's character David Alan Kepesh ironically instantiates ("turns" into) that which modernity abhors, rejects, ignores, or has not managed to come to terms with, that is, Kafka's nightmarish view of the subject. According to Roth's rewriting of the Kafkaesque metamorphosis, one cannot rule out the possibility that some day we might transform into what we teach. To paraphrase an old saying: tell me what you lecture on and I will tell you what you may become—or something of that kind. Unlikely as it may sound, it might be the humanities we fell for a long time ago that are leading us unaware down the transgressive path of posthumanity. In McElroy, on the other hand, a different if acknowledged intertext—Beckett, this time—brings to the fore, through the "cellular" body, a similar possibility of "reinventing the subject." If Roth lays bare an excess of organicity—the subject appears as a huge body organ—McElroy stresses the loss of corporeal substance, a dramatic decrease in the traditional materiality of the subject deemed, also traditionally, as "embodied reason." His hero comes to embody—we shall see, the inverted commas are not out of place here, either—Deleuze and Guattari's "body without organs." Very much like in Roth though, we witness the same startling "growth into humanness" (Porush 1985, 181), while Imp Plus refuses to be a mere "terminal identity," to quote Scott Bukatman's title (1993). And it is this refusal, this spectacular reassertion of identity, that entails a radical questioning of humanist assumptions.

But who is Imp Plus? Or, to rephrase the question à la Lyotard: "Can thought go on without a body"? That is—also Lyotard: "[H]ow [can one] make thought without a body possible . . . thought that continues to exist after the death of the human body?" (1991, 13–14). McElroy's novel tries to answer such posthuman questions by telling the story of an engineer who is dying of exposure to radiation. His human body becomes irretrievable, a "total loss," but his brain keeps working while displaced onto a new, "post-organic" or "postbiological" environment. That is, he agrees to have the brain removed and serve as the intelligent center coordinating a space lab whose mission would be too dangerous for people. Placed in a glucose pool, hooked up to computers, measuring devices, communication systems, and other instruments, the engineer's brain is meant to function as a sort of "ghost in the machine": human software controlling nonhuman hardware, its whole environment, gauges, biological supply sources, and propelling mechanisms. This ensemble is "perhaps the most complete embodiment in American literature of Donna Haraway's cyborg" (Tabbi 1995, 154). And it works, but only for a short time. The success of the experiment hinges on Imp Plus's becoming a Pynchonian communication device himself, a transitive object no longer subject(ive). Imp Plus would forfeit the perception of the self as *his* self; his "mission" depends on how effectively corporeal loss—his disembodiment—would cancel out his sense of identity.

A self-acknowledged fan and critic of Beckett, McElroy works the portrayal of impaired, defaulting, and receding physicality from *Molloy, Malone Dies,* and *The Unnamable* into his two-story story, if I may say so. A first narrative level consists of several flashbacks. Here, we learn how the engineer has lost his humanity by "shedding" his body. Interwoven with this epic layer is a second one, which unreels Imp Plus's posthuman evolution. Beckett's protagonists somehow relinquish their bodies, "go liquid" in *Malone Dies* (1965, 225), turn into "vegetables" in *The Unnamable* (329), find their "substantiality" a mere hypothesis, and appear largely cut off from their surroundings. Imp Plus, though, moves in a different direction. He grows a new, bizarre corporeality by simply *willing* it. His newly, *self-engendered* body is an act of will, a psychological, not a biological outcome of physical, genetic developments. After all, "he [is growing] a body from a mind, reversing the normal route of evolutionary phylogeny and foetal ontogeny" (Porush 1985, 174). Shockingly enough, Imp Plus creates himself by multiplying his brain cells, pulling stalks as his new, weird limbs. And his bodily self-generation parallels the rise of a novel, critical self-awareness on the ruins of his former submissiveness as an instrument inside the software-hardware unit. So, he achieves—intertextually and tragically—what Beckett's hero can only dream of in *The Unnamable*: "to become human" (1965, 315). Indeed, the process is tragic as Imp Plus's "becoming" or, even better, "rebecoming-human" amounts to suicide: he refuses to comply with the orders received from the earth-based experimenters and finally burns his ship up by allowing it to reenter the terrestrial atmosphere at deadly velocity. He grows into a new humanity, into *post*humanity actually, along the lines of an ambiguously "progressive" narrative, to recall N. Katherine Hayles's observations on the posthuman in "The Life Cycle of Cyborgs" (1993a, 153–54). This narrative assembles a new type of subjectivity by offsetting the initial "remission" of the body, of the embodied subject, his freedom, autonomy, and other humanist elements. This memorious narrative re-presents Beckett's dehumanization and alienation story, integrates it into a broader text where the unprecedented posthuman interface of body and machine does preserve empowering possibilities.

Unlike McElroy's, Roth's rewriting of the human is more conspicuously postulated on a regressive model. *The Breast*'s protagonist, professor of Comparative Literature at Stony Brook, changes, as the title foretells, into a breast. Doctors describe the amazing metamorphosis to the hero "'as a massive hormonal influx,' 'an endocrinopathic catastrophe,' and/or 'a hermaphroditic explosion of chromosomes' tak[ing] place within my body between midnight and four A.M. on February 18, 1971, and convert[ing] me into a mammary gland disconnected from any human form, a mammary gland such as could only appear, one would have thought, in a dream or a Dali painting" (1972, 5). "They tell me," Professor Kepesh carries on, "that I am now an organism with the general shape of a football, or a dirigible; I am said to be a spongy consistency, weighing in at one hundred and fifty-five pounds (formerly I was one hundred and sixty-two), and measuring, still, six feet in length." The detailed description of his shape and features is important, too:

> Though I continue to retain, in damaged and "irregular" form, much of the cardiovascular and central nervous system, and excretory system described as "reduced and primitive"—tubes now help me to void—and a respiratory system that terminates just above my midsection in something resembling a navel with a flap, the basic architecture in which these *human characteristics* are disarranged and buried is that of the breast of the mammalian female. (13–14; emphasis added)

"Human I insist I am, but not that human," he owns (21), or, as he puts it later on, "I am only human" (72). His affliction is a "symptom" of humanity. That is, he implies, "normal" humans must be *more than (just) human* to cope with their traumatic condition, maintain their human appearance, identities, and places in their culture. In sum, the human is the posthuman-to-be. *Post*human longings make us what we are while telling us that what we happen to be at a certain point is never enough, hardly the "end," or, à la Derrida, (at) our destination. We are, rather, perpetually on the way there, struggling to out-human the human, much like Professor Kepesh has "out-Kafkaed Kafka," as he recognizes, and has therefore changed into the topic of his well-attended lectures. His own metamorphosis, he also acknowledges, might be his own way of *being* Kafka, or Musil, or Swift, or Gogol ("The Nose"), or any other canonical object (text) the teaching subject has come to identify with—in all senses. He has simply become the "marvelous transformations" (Roth 1972, 72) fancied by these authors. Giving the lie to Harold Bloom's "anxiety of influence," Kepesh has followed them faithfully if a bit too far. His "posthumanization" bodies forth physically a crisis that besets, according to many "culture wars" combatants, the *humanities.* Kafka's "Metamorphosis" is "directly descended from classical traditions" (Clarke 1995, x), both Western—running from ancient "metamorphic allegories" (Plato, Ovid, Apuleius) through postmodern "re-engenderings" à la Calvino and García Márquez[31]—and Jewish, or Hassidic to be more precise (Bruce 1996, 107).

The upshots of this odd intertextual metamorphosis are notably different from what happens in McElroy. First off, if Imp Plus becomes pure intelligence before getting himself a new, posthuman body, Kepesh turns into the absolute body, as it were. In effect, he loses but a few pounds and his height remains unchanged. To McElroy's "body without organs" able to "will" itself a disseminated, rhizomic corpo-reality, Roth's hero responds by "hyperorganicity." The latter presupposes hypersensitivity in general and a comically portrayed hypersexuality in particular. It is true, he has trouble seeing, smelling, "experiencing [him]self as speaking to others" (Roth 1972, 52), "buried" as he stands in the huge lump of flesh. On the other hand, he is as aware as Imp Plus of being watched and means to resist the "experiment" he is subjected to.

Second, I have referred to Imp Plus as "it"—formerly a "he"—and to Kepesh as "he" consistently because there are important gender distinctions to be made here. Admittedly, these distinctions are somewhat hard to draw. McElroy's engineer is deprived of his maleness while losing his body and/or humanity. To him, brain excision is basically castration, all the more so that he painfully recalls a remarkably erotic "pre-posthuman" past. Imp Plus does grow a body, but this process unfolds along nonsexual, posthumanly self-engendering lines: he (or it, rather) engenders itself at the same time that it de-genders *him*-self.

Roth's character is less ambiguously positioned. Granted, his posthumanity does not lend itself to definition in terms of gender easily. After all, he is a breast. This indicates that his posthuman reembodiment has followed a feminine model, possibly as a result of his equivocal infatuation with his girlfriend's breast, which one could analyze—and psychoanalyze—at great length. All the same, his feverish sexuality manifests itself, for all his feminine shape, as masculine: Kepesh attempts to employ his female body, a nurturing and nourishing symbol originally, as a male organ. And finally, the narrative style is radically different in the two works. McElroy's memorably reflects the plight of his hero through narration, while Roth's story flows without hurdles, originated in a first person who has not lost any of the cultural, logical, and psychological features that render storytelling possible. Reprising Beckett's, Imp Plus's story is told from the odd perspective of a narrative instance that has trouble perceiving and naming objects, not least representing itself and identifying itself as narrative subject, distinguishing between subject and object, and so on. These are additional signs, semiotic "ailments" that overall tag McElroy's (post)discourse as posthuman.

If earlier authors such as Roth and McElroy anticipate a host of posthuman and posthumanist issues, recently risen to fame avant-pop writers like Leyner take us a step further. It seems to me, his fictional project dovetails with current arguments around information, materiality, and cultural embodiment. As Mary Ann Doane points out, "the concept of the 'body' has traditionally denoted the finite, a material limit that is absolute" (1990, 163). The body is presumably born, "produced" once for ever. Any intervention in its structure seems "unnatural" since bodies supposedly grow according to an organic, intrinsic algorithm of psychosomatic development. In fact, their growth cannot overrun the "finite limitations" (163) laid down genetically. Commenting on this model of corporeality, N. Katherine Hayles reiterates the postmodern belief that "the body is primarily, if not entirely, a linguistic and discursive construction" (1993b, 147). Indeed, in postmodern culture and theory the body no longer stands as a paragon of the "finite." One does not stop producing, building, and building it up long after it has already been produced, so to speak. Further, once the corporeal has become a process, bodily limits keep shifting, are steadily redrawn as a result of what Hayles calls "inscribing and incorporating practices."[32] The examples she adduces to illustrate inscribing practices, "Boys don't walk like that" and "Girls don't sit with their legs open," show how "culture produces the body" at the same that the body generates culture. Moreover, they shed light on the gendered embodiment inscribing practices effect while tracing the body's social boundaries. It is exactly this mutual articulation of the cultural and corporeal in terms of gendered, or, shall I say, hypergendered modification that I am here interested in. Focusing on Leyner's 1992 book *Et Tu, Babe*, I examine the mock-science fictional techniques the author employs to carry out such a modification and, most importantly, to determine—and critique—it as human, indeed, humanist *commodification*.

Leyner has published five books of jazzy, experimental, and highly provocative fiction. Their titles are fairly relevant to their style: *I Smell Esther Williams and Other Stories* (1983), *My Cousin, My Gastroenterologist* (1990), *Et Tu, Babe* (1992), *Tooth Imprints on a Corn Dog* (1995), and *The Tetherballs of Bougainville* (1997). Finding traditional narrative "too prolix and discursive," Leyner aims at writing "a kind of fiction that the reader can't skip, because it's so dense with pleasure, so unrelentingly enjoyable, so packed with event" (Grimes 1992, 64). Ostensibly, Leyner's interest in his readership is crucial to his writing. As William Grimes also observes, "Leyner takes the idea of an audience seriously" (64). Unlike the "defiantly noncommercial" Fiction Collective, Leyner finds the "commerce rather exhilarating" (64). Yet he is not just another avant-garde renegade domesticated by the "market" and conveniently turned into a "sellout" (64). His work has always been fascinated with the ideas of publicity and the public arena in which authors make their "appearance." What is at stake here, though, seems to go beyond authors' narcissistic obsession with their social image, and the reactions to their books. In *Et Tu, Babe*, Leyner enacts the notion of authorship to carry out a postmodern/avant-pop critique of the human and humanism under consumerism. To do this, he dramatizes the interaction of the writer and the market, the utmost tropes of the private and public spheres. This dramatization should be taken in a performative sense, for *Et Tu, Babe performs* the author's public persona: Leyner's protagonist is a writer named Mark Leyner, anxious to *produce* himself and so "overcome" his humanity.

This production means, again, first and foremost, performance. Leyner-the-character, the target of the irony of Leyner-the-author, acts on the social stage, turning himself into the ultimate commodity people crave. The modification of the body in *Et Tu, Babe* is an odd prerequisite for such a commodification. The author-in-the-novel produces his body, "metamorphoses" it to better fit the pattern of marketable icons stardom culture routinely promotes and feeds on. In this view, Leyner's immensely playful and satiric take on the "marketability" of the writer may very well be as effective as any serious cultural analysis. Coming from the market's margin, as avant-garde writers usually do, Leyner the-author-*of*-the-novel lays the terms for a mordant anatomy of the market's both captivating and repellent center. Intensely allusive and ironically bookish, his text provides unique, if hilarious, insights into the contemporary mechanisms of publicity, success, and star system.[33] Unlike certain mainstream writers drawing upon the sociocultural apparatus of commodification, Leyner bases his critique on the author myth.

DeLillo's *Ratner's Star* and *Mao II* also play out the recluse author's "iconology," as we shall see in chapter 5. Yet DeLillo's author loathes his commercial image. He toils to protect his privacy, his identity ultimately, by refusing to "be understood" (1980, 411), to publish, even to write, to *produce*. On the contrary, everything Leyner's author does is geared toward cultivating and re-producing his public figure. In point of fact, his books as such are less important, which explains why we do not learn much about their content. But there is a perplexing relation between the writer's texts and body, a curious exchange of materiality between textual reality and corporeality: the less material the character's works, the more physical and real the corporeal (the corpo-*real*).[34] The author-protagonist literally embodies the classical ambiguity of the *corpus*. He is obsessed with his body (see Lat. *corpus*) as his actual work, writes and rewrites it. Roth and McElroy show how their heroes' bodies are affected by "negative" metamorphoses they hardly welcome or control, whereas Leyner willingly "edits" his body as a science fiction text and advertises it as such. He strives to render his magnificent bulk his true masterpiece, a famed *corpus*—a "body of writings." Thus, as in *My Cousin, My Gastroenterologist*, "identity merges with typography" (Hayles 1999, 45), denaturalizing human corporeality.

In this light, Leyner's vision of texts' paradoxical devaluation under the pressure of the market and publicity may be another symptom of "fast capitalism."[35] One can argue, actually, that Leyner uses his posthuman caricature of identity and authorship to expose artistic commodification by turning the market logic on its head: it is not the author—the rational-humanist, "creative subject"—who puts forth, promotes his work; it is this work, promoted in turn by the media, PR staff, and other market forces, that "hawks" its author. In a textually oversaturated world, books' significance as aesthetic and textual objects diminishes. Poems and novels are not ends but means to upgrade the author's "marketability." Then, the writer has to live up to his social double, the famed author. A suitable image helps him close the gap, so he builds his body, re-producing it at the gym for further public (iconic) reproduction. Ironically again, textual production is a warm-up for the production of the author's body and, by implication, for a mock-Nietzschean "overcoming" of his humanity.

To suggest this bizarre and ultimately posthuman processing of the body, and to critique commodification in a world that claims to make good on its "humanist" promises, Leyner humorously, and memoriously, taps the myth of the super-(hu)man: Superman himself as a superhero but chiefly as a supermale.[36] Here, *Et Tu, Babe* sets in train a twofold, spectacular displacement. On the one hand, it intervenes in the culture of hypermasculinity, of hyperbolic male-ness associated with the Superman/Rambo stereotype. On the other, it undermines the institutionalization of the public person, satirizing celebrity culture's commodification machine. Essentially, this is how, drawing from pop culture, Leyner manipulates the post-human imagery of the body for critical purposes. Leyner, the-author-as-character, modifies his body to adapt it to the media's imaginal code and peddle his icon with a higher profit. McElroy turns to sci-ence fiction to limn Imp Plus's corporeal "regeneration"; Leyner "feigns" the genre, rather, employs it as a pop form allowing him to incorporate clichés, motifs, and procedures from popular culture itself.[37] He operates in the interstices of genres and cultural strata, targets the artificial seclusion and hyperrefinement of "elite" cul-ture at the same time that he parodies, pastiches, mimics, or ventril-oquizes multiple areas and languages of popular artifacts, consumerism, and mediatic "hypervisibility."

I cannot help repeating the prefix "hyper," and for good reason, for it epitomizes *Et Tu, Babe*'s high-speed, overinflated style, its poet-ics at large and especially the poetics of the male body, its hyper- and super-masculinity. The fast-forward mode of social life and the magnified body go hand in hand in Ben Agger's "fast capitalism," suggesting a total overlap of the private and the public, of biography and bibliography. Leyner's body is not endowed with common sensi-tivity but with "hypersensitivity." "My whole life," the protagonist of *Et Tu, Babe* discloses, "has been one long ultraviolent hyperkinetic nightmare" (1992, 4). Hysterical pace is typical of the "career code" "timing" the construction of posthuman hypermasculinity in *Et Tu, Babe*.[38] "Do I always conduct my business with this kind of nonstop indefatigable intensity and zeal?" he asks. "You bet I do. Do I make any distinction whatsoever between my personal life and my career? No, sir, I do not. I work and play at one speed: hyperdrive—Mach 9, adrenaline OD, total warp. It's the only way I know how to live" (77).

Like movie stars, our writer gets fan letters. "[Y]ou'd be sur-prised," he reveals, "at how many young people write in with the same basic question: 'How do I know if I'm great or if I'm the victim of megalomaniacal delusions?' My standard reply is: 'Sorry, kid, you're probably the victim of megalomaniacal delusions because only an infinitesimal percentage of the species is truly destined for greatness'" (77). This passage strikes an ironic and even a self-ironic note if we take into account the confession Leyner makes right after it: "Since I was a small child, I've had that feeling that simply by clenching my jaw and visualizing an explosion, I could blow up plan-ets or stars in galaxies thousands of light-years from earth" (77).

"Megalomaniacal delusion or fact?" he asks again. The answer deserves to be reproduced entirely because it highlights Leyner's capability of parasitizing popular culture genres, stereotypes, and techniques. "I've been lucky enough over the past few years," he says, "to have developed a very close friendship with the acclaimed theoretical physicist Stephen Hawking. I first became acquainted with Stephen when his secretary wrote a letter to my editor at Harmony Books, to say that Hawking didn't feel completely comfortable publishing *A Brief History of Time* until I'd reviewed the book's fundamental theorem and given my critical imprimatur." We further learn that "Leyner" "was seated ringside next to Stephen at the Evander Holyfield/George Foreman bout in Atlantic City, and I mentioned my suspicion that I had the ability to destroy celestial bodies simply by willing it, and not only did Stephen find this plausible in the abstract, but actually correlated it with several heretofore unexplained supernovae" (78). Fairly different from Roth's and McElroy's literary reprises, Super(hu)man and, more broadly, popular culture intertextuality do not stop here, though. The author throws in autobiographical details to ironically amplify and model the success of avant-garde writers on stardom stories. Otherwise, it is quite unlikely that Leyner's style—experimental fiction at large—will ever enjoy the popularity of a movie, his rising cult figure status on some campuses notwithstanding.

The author's existence is hyperintense, dominated by the science fictional, immensely aggrandized public image of the author. More than a mere case study in megalomania, *Et Tu, Babe*'s posthumanity casts light on celebrity culture's mediatization of authorship. Students of postmodernism may find somehow intriguing, though, Leyner's projection of the posthuman subject through a hyperbole of the body, more precisely, of the male body. Whereas philosophers and critics have pointed to "transparency" (Baudrillard 1987b, 33) and "disappearance" (Kroker and Kroker 1987, 20) as "rituals" laying down the body's postmodern condition, Leyner seems to hint at a more complex process. He does dislodge inherited corporeal structures but just to paranoically upgrade the body's visibility and corresponding semiotic capability. Leyner-the-character literally forces his body to signify through "manipulative biology" (Helen N. Parker 1984, 49–60) and other similar practices. For instance, he undertakes "self-surgery" to get a more profitable, "temporary new Look," although his "dimpled, clean-shaven face framed by blond-flecked chestnut tresses combed back into an undulating pompadour had become an instant icon to millions of fans" (1992, 25). But Leyner ("Leyner") does not "rewrite" only his face at "The

Hyatt Self-Surgery Clinic." He also rewrites his organs through "visceral tattoo[ing]."[39] Screening his X-rays, "female medical technicians and nurses . . . go nuts" over the sexy tattoos engraved on his heart. Moreover, he rewrites, "interpolates" his body by grafting artificial muscles onto it. Writing and working out, text building and body building, geniality and genitality: it is always physicality and sexuality that take precedence. The market is fully sexual, the author ascertains (6). It is sad, he also maintains, that folks like Melville, Flaubert, or Conrad did not write to "enhance their fuckability." "My books and my body," he declares, "—my status as a reckless writer and a gorgeous male—are my iridescent plumage; they're the equivalent of the male. . . . My books and my body: my not-so-subliminal advertisement to women that I will make a primo contribution to the genetic makeup and survivability of their children" (127). As a hypermale and superhero, the author is an ubiquitous symbol of sexual prowess: only special spermicides can overpower his spermatozoids.

Leyner's private life is a hot subject on talk shows. He employs a PR "Team Leyner" at "Team Leyner Headquarters" and is protected by a "phalanx" of aging female bodyguards.[40] His wife, Arleen, and Leyner, we find out, "took them in, treated them as members of our own family, administered large dose of synthetic human growth hormone and testosterone to each woman, and replaced her atrophied musculature with powerful artificial muscles made out of polymer gels that contract when electricity is applied and expand when the current is turned off" (16). As one of the staffers briefs Leyner, Pepsi is ready to "remunerate Team Leyner with $750,000 in cash, plus $250,000 in stock" (78) should the writer mention Diet Pepsi in his new book. He is not only a topic of "oral history" (151), a favorite subject for Connie Chung, Carl Sagan, or Christian Barnard. His body is an urban landmark. There is a "huge neon Team Leyner sign at 2 Times Square . . . simulating positron emission tomography images of Leyner's brain function as he writes, laid over a magnetic resonance image of his brain anatomy—so pedestrians below can actually observe glucose metabolism at various sites within Leyner's cerebral cortex as he's producing one of his critically acclaimed best-sellers" (164). Nor does D.C.'s skyline fare better, for it is redesigned to simulate "building blocks toppled in a toddler's tantrum" while "looming over the city, dramatically illuminated by floodlights, was a huge 1,000-foot white marble baby in diapers, arms akimbo, smugly admiring his own vandalism" (75).[41] The "Überkind" is Leyner himself advertising Diet Cola and perhaps more than that: a new age of high marketability where ultrafetishis-

tic hypermasculinity supplies a blueprint for posthuman corporeality.

Where Roth and McElroy set out to reinvent the human memoriously by re-collecting modernist texts by Kafka and Beckett that for-
mulate the human and its modern crises, Leyner's avant-pop
recycling of contemporary culture reprojects the human along the
crisscrossing lines of consumption and gender. Roth and McElroy
do not rule out the possibility of regaining lost humanity either, no
matter how serious their heroes' troubles. This is how the two writers
react to posthuman transformations and anxieties under way for
quite a while. Leyner's hypermale, superhuman antics intimate instead that such changes run deeper than we may think. He acknowledges them overtly and urges us, in postmodern fashion, neither to
disregard nor to welcome them uncritically.

HOLOGRAMMATOLOGY: POSTHUMANITY AND POSTMODERN ONTOLOGY

"The sky above the port was the color of television, tuned to a
dead channel." And: "Another postmodern sunset, rich in romantic
imagery. . . . We stood there watching a surge of florid light, like a
heart pumping in a documentary on color TV." What postmodern
fiction fan would fail to recognize the passages? The first opens William Gibson's *Neuromancer* (1984, 3). The second is from the third
section of DeLillo's *White Noise*, "Dylarama" (1986, 227). Strange as
it may sound, the section's title makes sense if one recalls "Waves
and Radiation" and "The Airborne Toxic Event," as DeLillo entitles
the previous parts. "Dylarama" combines "Dylar" and *horama*.
"Dylar" is a medication supposed to alleviate the fear of death, a pill
developed with help from volunteers like Babette, protagonist Jack
Gladney's wife. *Horama* means "sight" in Greek. Further, one can
take "Dylarama" to parallel "panorama," "a complete view of an
area in every direction," as *Webster's* defines it. "Dylarama" would
designate then a panorama of death, a totalizing "view" shaped by
the viewer's thanatic fears.

Yet hardly anybody dies in *White Noise*, and even Gladney botches
comically his attempt to kill Gray. Death does not survene as we may
expect, although everybody seems obsessed with it, and there is
never a shortage of volunteers for exorcising simulations of disasters. Death is nonetheless omnipresent as an ongoing, stealthy process. This omnipresence impacts postmodern ontology, DeLillo's
fictional world in particular. What *White Noise* uncovers, and memo-

rably—as well as memoriously—critiques, is a different kind of death, namely, the accelerating erosion of inherited reality. Subjectivity and its formerly "natural" environment are the categories most decisively refashioned by such an ontological displacement. To be sure, the rhetoric of death, decay, and dissolution has changed, no longer deploying the tropes of its traditional visibility. Death still entails a "terminal" scenario, but in a sense that sets DeLillo's dark imagination, cyberpunk, and, as we saw earlier, Pynchonian depiction of subjectivity in an interesting dialogue: *White Noise*'s subjects and objects have been made into "terminal identities." People's lives do not "terminate" due to "fatal" accidents or diseases. Instead, death is in-scribed, literally *written* into the very structure of subjects once the "system" (the market, technology, the government, etc.) has turned them into "terminals" of various networks, as Baudrillard insists in "The Ecstasy of Communication." Humans and their milieu have lost the ontological foundations, and beliefs therein, that had so far underwritten their sense of reality and autonomy. They are not self-sufficient, rationally "originating" entities anymore but effects and even side effects, *fallout* in a technology-saturated environment. This is the point both Pynchon and DeLillo make, and they make it through astonishing hyperboles, ironies, and caricature, through an "extreme" style that speaks to a fact of postmodern life: we are less and less what we think we are; we are "constructed," and posthumanly so. Nor have we ever been otherwise. But we have never been so thoroughly under the sway of a world that we had set out to build as a token of our supremacy. Nature—human nature included—has become artificial performance and is now being staged as a play, a mediatic make-believe. The anthropological notion of subjectivity no longer holds water, as we noticed apropos of *Gravity's Rainbow.* Also like in Pynchon, the subject has changed into "a bunch of electronic dots," as DeLillo puts it in his 1978 novel *Running Dog* (31).

At the end of this chapter, I want to look closer at the representation of reality, of people and objects in *White Noise,* and eventually locate the point where postmodern and cyberpunk modes of representation intersect. Also, I address the relation between "mainstream" fiction and genres like cyberpunk, which is still peripheral in postmodernism at large. As Brian McHale suggests in *Constructing Postmodernism,* these two may share more than we assume. Cyberpunk works like *Neuromancer* and others by Gibson, Bruce Sterling, Pat Cadigan, Neal Stephenson, Walter Mosley, on the one hand, and texts by Pynchon (*Gravity's Rainbow, Vineland*), DeLillo (*Ratner's Star, White Noise, Mao II*), or Powers (*Plowing the Dark*), on the other, all

bring forth the transformation real people and environments undergo under the pressure of technology in contemporary society.
Needless to say, there are important differences between DeLillo's
and Gibson's views of this process. But, again, what I am primarily
interested in is the area in which mainstream and not-so-mainstream
postmodern representations of reality and subjectivity overlap and
talk to each other.

The ontological premises belying these representations demarcate
such a zone quite visibly. Alongside Pynchon, McElroy, Auster,
Coover, Barth, Federman, Clarence Major, and Ishmael Reed, or
younger, avant-pop postmoderns like David Foster Wallace, Leyner
and Curtis White, both DeLillo and Gibson address chiefly ontological issues. In doing so, they raise epistemological questions to a
lesser extent, and, we shall see in the next chapter, critics have seized
ontological concerns as postmodern hallmarks. Further, the treatment of reality in *White Noise* and *Neuromancer* goes to show that the
two writers' specific takes on these problems are compatible, although they are not identic either, as I will demonstrate below. In
both texts, natural reality gets dislodged, "deconstructed" as reality
because it is produced, written—which threatens to wipe out the distinction between the natural and the artificial. Likewise, the human
subject appears in DeLillo, to recall the poststructuralist terminology applied to *Gravity's Rainbow*, as a "fable" (Derrida 1992, 102),
"a surface effect, a fallout" (103). It is the result of a "plot" that
"writes together," mixes up heterogeneous data or "pocket litter,"
to quote a famous phrase of *Libra*. "You are the sum total of your
data" (141), *White Noise*'s Gladney learns during a "simulated evacu-
ation."
    This type of subject lies at the core of DeLillo's intriguing *oeuvre*.
In *White Noise* it is less the CIA "plotters" and "writers" who concoct
the story of the subject, of the subject *as* object and hence instrument. DeLillo tells us how subjectivity and its agency get processed,
"written" by other, less visible "agencies" and "agents," which sets
off another aspect of DeLillo's cultural critique, more broadly postmodern discourse's unique ability to take on the postmodern world.
"Dehiscence," "intrinsic dislocation," "*différance*," "destinerrance"
mark the subject in Derrida (1992, 103), in Pynchon, not least in
DeLillo, despite the more realistic, everyday-life type of fictional setting. Arguably, Pynchon's Zone and DeLillo's suburbia do not differ
radically. In both, the poststructuralist dissection of the human subject and its worldview helps us come to terms with an inherent process of posthuman becoming: *différance*, inner dislocation, and

multiplicity have always been human attributes, and it is time now, in the postmodern age where such features are more conspicuous than ever before, to reinvent ourselves—our selves, capacities, and values—starting from these features, "re-membering" them, taking them into account. As one can see, drawing upon postmodern fiction's memorious discourse, I am entering an equally memorious plea on behalf of a certain kind of criticism. For this type of analysis may help us pinpoint and perhaps resist the rise of new, all-embracing totalities on the ruins of the human subject and its humanist myths of progress, control, and instrumentalized, if "natural," nature.

To come back to the section titles now, it is noteworthy that the human and its "natural" surroundings have been transformed into "unnatural" objects, upshots and spin-offs of various technologies. Once affected by "waves and radiation," "airborne toxic events," and the like, people and nature have gotten "dehumanized," to use a more traditional word. The subject is nothing more than an ersatz, an afterglow. And so are its environs. The characters suspect, natural phenomena are "by-products"; chemistry has taken over. In response, the formerly "genuine" perception of nature yields to a hermeneutics of suspicion that routinely reads the natural as technological setup. Heinrich, Gladney's son, surmises that what we assume to be rain may be "sulfuric acid from factories across the river" or "fallout from a war in China" (DeLillo 1986, 24). The unexamined belief, the "false consciousness" or delusion of "nature-as-natural," he argues, provides a sort of unacknowledged compact holding together social life, or the illusion thereof. In other words, we are simply expected to take the visible's natural origin for granted. But besides and underneath "spills, fallouts, leakages" (175) lie less conspicuous yet more ominous phenomena. "The real issue," Heinrich says, "is the kind of radiation that surrounds us every day. Your radio, your TV, your microwave oven, your power lines just outside the door, your radar speed-trap on the highway" (174).

There are at least two important implications here, physical (or physiological) and intellectual (or ideological). First, humans are literally impacted by exposure to "constant rays" (175), are radiated, and changed, à la Pynchon, into "fields" themselves, dissolved as bodies and self-sufficient, Cartesian entities once they have been brought under the sway of external sources of energy. At a less symbolic level, this can result in "nerve disorders, strange and violent behavior in the home," "deformed babies" (175), and the like. Second, an analogous deformation may affect people's minds, turning them into "Tubeheads," as Pynchon says in *Vineland.* TV-watching is, in fact, the utmost ritual of Gladney's household. Hypnotically gazing at catastrophic reports amid no less catastrophic developments worsens the subject's plight, makes it dependent on what above I call newly emerged totalities, in that while the subject is no longer one, "whole," the media induce a dependence on other grand totalities, stories, and mythologies. Intellectual radiation—intellectual eradication—matches physical radiation, whether by design or accident, nuclear or otherwise. Exposure to TV rays or TV information, to X-rays or atomic radiation, to the media or "toxic events" has basically the same outcomes. Therefore, physiology functions in *White Noise* and elsewhere in DeLillo as an intellectual allegory. Our thinking is—or can become—the sum total of the information the TV screen "radiates" as much as our identity is, Gladney realizes, a computer file, a chemical formula perpetually "rewritten" by technology, or a "contract," a "capitalist transaction" (194). So DeLillo's book stages the drama of a "digital subject" held captive and refashioned in a "digital world" (Ruthrof 1990, 196). The subject and its surroundings obtain, to use Gladney's own term, as "texture," writing effects, whether we are talking about humans or their "natural" and "commercial" landscape (the omnipresent supermarket). To reproduce Derrida's observations from "No Apocalypse, Not Now," reality is "fabulously textual," "constructed by the fable" (1984, 23). Both Derrida's nuclear criticism and DeLillo's catastrophic imagery uncover a reality deprived of original substance, a reality as aftermath and effect—writing effect, to be more specific. Subjects and objects are transformed into holograms through radiation, radio waves, toxic and TV emissions—amusingly enough, *émission* is French for TV "show" or "program."

Not only does DeLillo's narrative render the body—the nature's body included—a technological performance, simulation, specter, chemical sunset, a picture "developed" technologically. *White Noise* is more than such a simulating writing that defines reality, according to Jonathan Culler's analysis of Derrida's grammatology, as "already written," produced as *text* (1979, 75). Like other books by DeLillo, this novel foregrounds the ontological displacement such a writing brings about. Its hologramlike narrative, its "hologrammatology," pinpoints the lack of "substratum," of "Aristotelian substratum," as DeLillo says half seriously, half ironically elsewhere. Such lack characterizes his people and places. Not only are these images, computer simulations, or "toxic events" *holograms*; they are also generated through a "referentless" writing of sorts, to recall Gregory Ulmer's *Applied Grammatology* (1985, 7). This deliberate "writing of emptiness" gives birth to "empty" (*hollow*) subjects, sites, déjà-vu situations, staged disasters, and, conversely, disastrous events that look like perfect simulations.

Cyberpunk hologrammatology plays up this engineered demise of the real, takes it to a higher level. *Neuromancer* performs, as Veronica Hollinger points out, a radical "cybernetic deconstruction" (1990, 29). To a larger extent than *White Noise*, it blurs the boundaries between the real and the simulated (the fictive), the "natural" and the "written." DeLillo's world still carries the painful memories of a natural world. It remembers, "quotes," as it were—if not relies on—the humanist notion of a subjectivity once thought to be more than just a "field" and "contract." It shows off twilights that did *not* look like fallout. Disenchanted, "constructed," postmodern as it may be, this universe is not simply accepted. The characters argue over its architecture and meaning, a sign that resistance and dissent are not a moot point.

Unlike DeLillo's, Gibson's writing of the fallout calls this possibility into question. For one thing, *Neuromancer* does not challenge the ontological texture of cyberspace. The latter has become, famously, "a consensual hallucination experienced daily by billions of legitimate operators, in every nation, by children being taught mathematical concepts. . . . A graphic representation of data abstracted from the banks of every computer in the human system" (51). "Criminal ecology" is hardly an exception, caused as it is by "leakages" and other accidents: it represents "naturalized" negativity, the "normal" state of things in the wake of the ecological disaster. If DeLillo narrates catastrophes—real or simulated—in-process, as well the process of their writing/reading, Gibson spins out a postcatastrophic world where one can hardly fancy further deteriorations. A crucial paradigm shift has taken place: Gibson's "matrix"— omnipresent and all-comprehensive writing—has replaced the fallout as "accidental" writing. "Dylarama," a basically individual, idiosyncratic hallucination bordering on the paranoid, has become consensual. The sky does not look *like* a hologram—it *is* a hologram and nothing else, above Night City, the Sprawl, everywhere.

But, of course, subjectivity is the landscape undergoing the most spectacular transformations. Subjects have turned into holograms themselves, pseudopresences, pictures. More radically than in De-Lillo, they are "discursive constructions," to recall N. Katherine Hayles (1993b, 147). They embody both technological and cultural texts, even though Gibson's *Neuromancer* underscores the obsolescence of "the written word" (88). The body is an intersection of grafted muscles, artificial organs, implants and "holographic memory" (170), which a character compares to an "ancient television . . . , a vacuum tube," but also to his own DNA (171). Subjectivity and its environment seem to spring from such a core vacuum and substratum without substance, from an "original," "founding" emptiness. Countering some of mainstream postmodernism's realistic relapses, literalizing certain of its most daring yet somewhat still anthropological allegories, narrativizing various poststructuralist concepts, Gibson sets the stage for a posthuman rearticulation of reality where humans and nature no longer are what they used to be and where no humanist nostalgias or ethical judgements are meaningful anymore.

On a deeper level, though, Gibson's and DeLillo's fictions meet, on a ground Pynchon, McElroy, Roth, Leyner, and others have also staked out in their posthuman stories. These authors' insights into the makeup of reality, of the self, the body, the natural may well vary. But the memorious emphasis they all place on the heterogeneous materiality, intertextuality, and overall discursiveness laid into the architecture of "natural" bodies, on technological and cultural formations as practices that "inscribe" and "incorporate" (Hayles 1993b, 156) both nature and the human, brings these authors under the authority of the same posthuman logic and fuels the same postmodern critique. In the next chapter, I propose that we look more closely at postmodern, fictional, and theoretical models of reality, and discuss in more specific terms how this critique stems from, or at the very least is implied in, the ontology underlying these models.

4

"The Collapse of Distance": Ontological Frameworks and Enframing Games for a Disenchanted World

MODES OF BEING, MODES OF DOING: "HIGH THEORY" AND THE POLITICS OF REPRESENTATION

[T]ruth demands that we bestir ourselves.
—Jacques Lacan, "The insistence of the letter in the unconscious"

Reality is not what is "given" to this or that "subject"; it is a state of the referent (that about which one speaks) which results from the effectuation of establishment procedures defined by a unanimously agreed-upon protocol, and from the possibility offered to anyone to recommence this effectuation as often as he or she wants.
—Jean-François Lyotard, *The Differend*

[L']*écriture est la continuation de la politique par d'autre moyens* [Through writing, political struggle goes on].
—Philippe Sollers, "Écriture et révolution"

BUT HOW DO ONTOLOGY, CRITIQUE, AND REPRESENTATION INTERRELATE? After all, tradition teaches us that they speak to distinct domains of life and are by the same token couched in discrete discourses: existence, or, the things that "are" (*ta onta* in Greek metaphysics), and the philosophy thereof, respectively; social space and the engagement with the ideologies vying to adjudicate it; and textuality-at-large, poems, stories, movies, any representation and its aesthetics, hermeneutics, stylistics, semiotics, psychoanalysis, and so forth. In this book, I take aim at this compartmentalized view of culture and discourse. As I insist throughout, postmodernism's memorious dis-

163

course broadly and postmodern criticism in particular pivot on relationality, are inherently cross-disciplinary.

Following in the footsteps of Borges's hero much like the postmodern writer, the postmodern critic makes out connections among
things, texts, and fields. Under postmodern scrutiny, a world asunder, arguably a modernist legacy, becomes a cluster-world. Nor is
this world a *transgressive* totality, which reading might cross over into
the misty beyond of "origins," but, as I stress ever so often, a *digres-
sive* world of linkages, ramifications, and reverberations across subjects, paradigms, and inquiries. For it is not the "vertical" myth of
the *root* that guides me as, *en postmoderne*, I seize upon representation
as re-presentation, but the "horizontally" sprawling *rhizome* (Apter
2001a, 71); not the "archeology" of the signified but the Lacanian
chain of signifiers. Indeed, it is not the discourse's fabled underside,
the mythic trans- and non-discursive that lure the postmodern critic
of postmodern discourse but quite the opposite: it is this discourse's
imbrications and implications, the other texts, representations, and
discourses with which a particular novel links that, like Funes, I "remember"—spot, descry, further represent to me and others—as I
read Pynchon and DeLillo, Guy Davenport and Morrison, Octavia
Butler and Michael Cunningham.

The matter at hand is not "only" literary, nor "only" literarily intertextual. Attuned to the wider memorious logic of postmodernism, postmodern reading splices up not "just" texts, but also
contexts. In the name of an enlarged, cultural intertextuality, postmodern criticism propounds that a text—and a postmodern text
more systematically than others—assimilates, re-presents a context
because textual representations come about in collision with fictions, constructs, and representations of a more general kind, with
the "texts" of race, gender, sex, ethnicity, with the whole panoply of
textuality writing our identities into a culture. But this also means
that the context is always-already textualized, comes somehow pre-
represented, deployed unstably on both sides of the fictional-real divide, charted as a textual domain and by texts, packed in various
representations and formulas. These could be of the "general" discursive type or of a more narrowly textual sort such as previous novels, poems, and other forms of literary and artistic representation.
Either way, postmodernism takes in and on a context through critical references to other texts that have already textualized, addressed
this context, "hard fact," or "slice of life." This is the fruitful paradox of postmodern representation into which we run ever so often:
the memorious constitution of the world, the world's intertextual
"packaging" and seemingly *distancing*, interposing textual and fic-

tional garments actually deliver the world's living body to us, bring it intimately *closer*, provide for its representability in texts by giving these texts something to latch onto, namely, a textually mapped, hence *compatible*, analogically constructed con-text to which they can "relate" and speak.

Consequently, a whole lot hinges on representation so understood; representation is an issue as sociocultural and political as ontological and aesthetic. A certain ontology, a certain grasp of the dynamic of representation and the represented, fictional and real, does presuppose a politics.

This correlation remains an apple of discord among students of postmodernism to date although as early as in the mideighties critics like Brian McHale opened the door to a less insular—postformalist—approach to this issue by emphasizing the postmodern ontological turn and its consequences beyond the usual concerns of ontology. McHale claims that postmodernism marks "a change from an epistemological dominant to an ontological one" (1987, 10). In contrast to modernism, postmodernism shifts its focus away from "problems of *knowing*" to "problems of *modes of being*" (10), asking, "What is a world?; What kinds of world are there, how are they constituted, and how do they differ?; What happens when different kinds of world are placed in confrontation or when boundaries between worlds are violated?; What is the mode of existence of a text, and what is the mode of existence of the world (or worlds) it projects?" (10). Although any ontological interrogation, when "pushed . . . far enough . . . , tip[s] over into an epistemological" one (and vice versa) (11), the "dominant" postmodern thrust is ontological.[1] Postmodernism still bares a certain logic of reality, putting forward as it does "explanations" and "interpretations"—admittedly, modernist "residues." However, in response to the conflicting, often deceiving answers modernist aesthetics has given to knowledge-related questions, postmodernism tackles primarily ontological issues. Unfolding as it may within the same postromantic culture of the idiosyncratic, the obscure, and the elusive, it nevertheless pays attention chiefly to problems such as worldly framework, limit, and the erosion of the boundaries between distinct worlds or reality regimes. Postmodernism characteristically ruminates the troublesome multitude of these worlds, the ontological scandal of their simultaneous existence. In sum, it thematizes the ontological status of the represented world(s), forefronting the interplay of different and frequently divergent "rules of reality," dramatizing the tension between, and the intertwining of, fiction and reality.

The shift McHale locates in fiction also occurs in "high theory," which has systematically mulled over "postmodern reality," namely, over the very fabric of our world. This chapter examines, first, Lyotard's and Baudrillard's pictures of this "reality," weighing their answers to a question that I deem unavoidable, if not necessarily ontological. As I remind the reader in the prologue, McHale himself contends that the foremost postmodern questions are, "Which world is this?" and, most significantly, "What is to be done in it?" Now, it seems to me that the latter takes us in a pragmatic-political direction since a certain ontology presupposes if not calls openly for a certain behavior, for specific acts. I might point out, too, the ambiguity of the second question, which plays upon both what we *can* do at present and what we *need* to do so as to have a say in how things will be, in what the world will be like. Hence a third question: "Can we change this world?" And a fourth, perhaps: "If so, how?" Granted, the scope of *Postmodernist Fiction* and, to a lesser degree, *Constructing Postmodernism,* McHale's second book on the topic (1992), is rather different. I think, though, that a postmodern answer to the ontological question "How is this world possible?" implies, if not spells out, a model of political action. As an intertextual dynamic of text and context, as memorious discourse, postmodern representation supplies a cultural arena where this model is both brought into relief and acted on; "high theory" provides another site for the same purpose. Analogously, not only is postmodern representation thought out, "theorized" here. Not only do Lyotard and Baudrillard lay down an ontology. Theirs are *critical* ontologies for their thoughts on "postmodern reality" open up unforeseen, social and political possibilities. To tease out these possibilities, I revisit some of their earlier, classical texts.

Before I get started, let me clarify that "postmodern reality" designates, first, the sociocultural environment typical of our (postmodern) time, and this is apparent especially in Baudrillard, although he has refrained from calling postmodernism by its name.[2] In this sense, and for the sake of argument, the stress is on "reality," on the "world," in other words, on the "content," or, as Lyotard says below, "referent" of representation. In a second sense, *postmodern* reality emphasizes that this world is somehow produced, imagined, fictionalized, treated, narrated, and otherwise con-textualized in a specific, postmodern fashion. Representation—postmodern representation—is here the privileged element. In both cases, with respect to representation no less than to what it represents, the two philosophers distinguish an individualizing "condition," an ontology. My point is that a particular sociopolitical critique is embedded in this condition or can be inferred from it. I ascertain this model in Lyotard's and Baudrillard's *critical worldviews*, but also, albeit perhaps somewhat unexpectedly, in a writer like Nabokov later in this chapter.

Lyotard's trailblazing "Answer to the Question, What Is the Postmodern" (1984, 71–82; 1993, 1–16) is as good a place to start as any. The essay yokes together the postmodern and the sublime with help from Kant's *Critique of Judgement*. And since the notion of *presentation* is key to his move, Lyotard also addresses the "presented," the object of artistic presentation, or, "reality," and the kindred concept of realism. Thus, his theory of postmodern representation becomes a theory of reality in, and for, the postmodern age, the sketch of an ontology that both partakes of, and parts with, modern (modernist) representation of the world.

I want to propose, and thus anticipate a later contention, that this conceptualization of postmodern reality implies a theory of social action or "events" (Lyotard 1993, 15). The theory cannot be dismissed offhand as "young conservatism" and simply charged with promoting "political indifference" (Benhabib 1984, 123). In effect, Lyotard's essay replies to "Professor Habermas" and others who have "urged us," sometimes in defense of modernity's "unfinished project,"[3] "to give up experimentation, in the arts and elsewhere" (Lyotard 1993, 1). These injunctions may sound alike, but they make different claims. "It is not necessarily the same thing," Lyotard cautions us,

> to demand the provision of a referent (and objective *reality* [italics mine]), or a meaning (and credible transcendence), or an addressee (and a public), or an addressor (and expressive subjectivity), or a communicative consensus (and a general code of exchange, the genre of historical discourse, for example). But in these various invitations to suspend artistic experimentation, there is the same call to order, a desire for unity, identity, security, and popularity. (4)

Declining the peremptory invitations to "liquidat[e] ·the legacy of the avant-gardes" (4), Lyotard makes two points. First, these requests assume the (pre)existence of an objective, non-imagined, a-textual, "original" reality whose presumably transparent meaning can be, and should be, handed out or conveyed to the audience "as is," mimetically, without substantial change. Therefore—and this is his second point—artistic treatment of this reality premises an ontological or referential status quo. In Lyotard's view, "recognizable meaning" (5) contained in nonexperimental discourses "stabiliz[es] the referent." In the typical line of French avant-garde thought, Lyotard ranks formal practices politically. Thus, he would certainly agree with Deleuze and Guattari, who in *A Thousand Plateaus* see "no difference between what a book talks about and how it is made" (4). Yet, Deleuze and Guattari also conclude, "Therefore a book also has no object" (1994, 4). On this account, and precisely because the philosophers make no distinction between its politics and its style, I would submit here—and Lyotard would probably agree—that a book does have an object yet not in the traditional-mimetic sense. The book constitutes necessarily an action, *a verbal action with the "world" as a direct, albeit obliquely impacted, object.* Any style entails a politics as much as, Sartre lets us know, there is a metaphysics to any form. Accordingly, de-stabilizing the referent through aesthetic discourse *is* politics, political action. Reacting to Terry Eagleton's and Peter Dews's critiques of Lyotard, Richard Beardsworth disputes—effectively, to my mind—the contention that "the 'postmodernist' and 'post-structuralist' fascination with art and literature as metaphor and substitute for, or supplement to, politics points to its utter lack of credentials in the political domain, if not to its latent fascistic 'aestheticisation of politics'" (1992, 45).[4] Art, art that Lyotard values, operates politically in that it performs a transformation of reality, provides us with the symbolic rules of the latter's "rewriting," which in turn challenges a specific time and space *in their essence,* in their ontological makeup. Fictional worlds theorists like Doležel tell us that literary texts "are ensembles of non-actualized possible states of affairs" (1998, 16). As the critic exemplifies, Hamlet is not a person from the "actual world," but *Hamlet,* a fictional world, makes him possible in ours. Hamlet is a "transworld identity" (17) whose textual possibility sets forth a prospect for the full, politically transformative reimagining—re-originating—of the "original" world.

Memorious discourse in particular constitutes a *radical* form of politics because it takes the undermining logic of the avant-garde and tones it up further. Postmodernism does not simply overhaul reality. It also exposes reality's "imposture," as it were, the "unreal"—intertextual, constructed, ideological, sometimes "policed"—state of things, which state reflects the system's functioning. Capitalism, Lyotard remarks, "has such a capacity to *derealize* familiar objects, social roles, and institutions that so-called *realist representations* can no longer evoke *reality* except through nostalgia or derision—as an occasion for suffering rather than satisfaction." To be sure, "Classicism seems out of the question in a world where *reality is so destabilized* that it has no material to offer to experience, but only to analysis and experimentation" (1993, 5; emphasis added). In a postclassical environment, postmodernism's "antirealistic" poetics challenges reality politically. For realism can be "defined only by its intention of avoiding the question of reality implied in the question of art" (7).[5] I would pinpoint here the obvious: Lyotard, a leading postmodern advocate and poststructuralist philosopher, accuses realism itself of dodging the reality question and its related referent issue, a charge that positivist realists and their recently self-appointed executors, the "postpositivist realists," have been known for leveling against postmodernism and poststructuralism.[6]

Of course, according to Lyotard, modernity is already postmodern—and conversely, a future anterior logic inserts postmodernism into modern discourse. Modern science, economy, and philosophy spoke to a fundamental "discovery of the *lack of reality* in reality," a discovery otherwise inseparable from the compensatory invention of "other realities" (9). Modernity inaugurated an "era of suspicion," to quote Nathalie Sarraute, or, as Lyotard maintains, "whenever [modernity] appears, [it] does not occur without a shattering of belief" in "reality" (1993, 9). No doubt, modernity gave up its mimetic ambitions, the age-old fable of realistic representation. That is, modern art did not just cease to *present* reality, but, under the pressure of new artistic practices, reality itself underwent an evolution, became unpresentable through former discourses. "I shall call modern," Lyotard announces, "the art that devotes its 'trivial technique,' as Diderot called it, to presenting something that is unpresentable" (11). With modernism, that which had initially been supposed to be an *ancilla realitatis* gained the upper hand. The copy refashioned the original, so to speak—and, we will see shortly, Baudrillard does speak so. Modern art forced the referent to adapt to, and "look like," the new artistic vision, to uncover the void at its core; the realistic surplus of reality was played out as lack of reality, modernity "unfold[ing]" as it did "in the retreat of the real" (13).

In this respect, postmodernism goes further, in a way "completing"—pace Habermas—the transformative, ontological and formal, project of modern representation. The postmodern builds on the modern, which tells us that they must be compatible in some regards. But this does not mean that we should not differentiate between them, and Lyotard does just this by stressing that postmodern discourse seeks to overcome the nostalgia for absent reality, for "presence" (13), that modern "derealization" (12) or "unpresentation" thereof somehow posits. Thus, Lyotard famously specifies, the postmodern would be that which in the modern invokes the unpresentable in presentation itself, that which refuses the consolation of correct forms, refuses the consensus of taste permitting a common experience of nostalgia for the impossible, and inquires into new presentations—not to take pleasure in them, but to better produce the feeling that there is something unpresentable. The postmodern artist or writer is in the position of a philosopher: the text he writes or the work he creates is not in principle governed by preestablished rules and cannot be judged according to a determinant judgement, by the application of given categories to this text or work. Such rules and categories are what the work or text is investigating. The artist and the writer therefore work without rules and in order to establish the rules for what *will have been made.* (15)

Critics have singled out this fragment for its aforementioned future anterior logic, for its *post modo.* Now, the theory of the unpresentable postmodern elaborated in this passage and throughout the second half of the essay could also be read politically, and I intend to work out this reading against some of the harsher political judgments passed on Lyotard's theory of postmodernism.

First, he tells us, postmodern representation, too, mirrors the "weak ontology" of our age, the "lack of reality of reality." But, second, the postmodern is more radical aesthetically and politically than the modern because it conveys this precariousness of reality through representation itself. As the opposition Proust versus Joyce suggests, unlike the modern, the postmodern brings forward its unrepresentable object in the structure of representation, or, "in the writing itself, in the signifier" (14), which is not without broader consequences. For, third and most important, postmodern representation contests and reworks, as Lyotard notes in several places in *The Postmodern Explained,* the rules of artistic production, reception, circulation, recognition, and canonization. So postmodern representation does not limit itself to redefining artistic principles and norms alone, to inventing new techniques and devices. These "rules" (15) are definitely transaesthetic. Vice versa, any attempt to "fulfill the phantasm of taking possession of reality" (16) without discursive mediation ought to be suspected of a totalitarian agenda. "It should be made clear," in fact, "that it is not up to us to *provide reality,* but to invent allusions to what is conceivable but not presentable" (15).

What are these allusions? They are memorious re-presentations. That is, they constitute, as I put it above, "oblique," intermediary, "secondhand" if often first-rate references, cultural constructions, intertexts, or, Lyotard writes in *The Differend* à la Wittgenstein, reality as "protocol effect" (4), upshot—post factum, after the literary fact or "event," *post modo*, postmodern—of the rules identified above. This is postmodernism: memorious discourse that inheres in the future anterior effectiveness of a representation model, paradigm, or rule that turns retroactively the text into an "event." Let us reiterate Lyotard's statement: the postmodern author works with rules *that can be laid down only in hindsight*. Therefore, postmodern representation is *anything but mimetic (imitative)*. À la Heidegger, representation sets the represented up, "founds" it, but in a non-foundational fashion, allusively and intertextually, by the roundabout way of other representations. Thus, postmodern representation presents us— again paradoxically—with an unprecedented and formerly un-presented *world* while *re-presenting, working with, and re-working, prior wordings or representations of this world*. One more time, the postmodern text is an event, a re-presentational event—"the text can take on the properties of an event" (Lyotard 1993, 15)—not a reproduction of existing events and rules.

This *is* political. Representation—be it representation of the "unpresentable"—incriminates not only the formal stagnation, the complacency of "correct," "canonical," "mainstream" discourse, tastes, and promotion tactics. Postmodern poetics is also a politics, caught as it stands in a web of imbrications and implications that integrate text and context, representation and the represented, representation and foregoing representations. The apparently odd logic of the future anterior at play in "the rules for what *will have been made*" acts out the political, transforming thrust of the artistic event with respect to its presumed referent. It bears repeating: the text does not illustrate the principles, customs, values or the world already in place. By and large—and here Lyotard's argument sounds very *Tel Quel*—it comes up with discursive norms of its own, in and by the very "event" of its own deploying. The text ratifies, abides by the law of its production only retroactively and by taking itself as the sole criterion, legislating body. It follows that no extrinsic authority can control postmodern representation. But this does not imply that the text "happens" in a vacuum, randomly, and I must underscore this proviso more emphatically than Lyotard. The text's own generative axioms, on the one hand, and sociocultural norms, on the other, intertwine, are spliced together, both being adopted "after the fact"—after the discourse. Indeed, no mimetic (realistic) code could a priori channel postmodern discourse since the latter announces its codifying system while pro*nouncing* itself, *naming* itself and the world at the same time. There is no "nude," "given" "reality" to be mirrored mechanically by postmodern representation, but always a reality to be instituted, invented, set in motion, and disputed by it, characteristically in memorious dialogue with similar pronouncements.[7]

On this account, it is probably the place to highlight the double bind of invention—of *postmodern* invention. For, on the one hand, invention, which is usually thought of as bringing out something new, does alter the *preexistent* real and in so doing speaks to a politics that is anything but "neoconservative," "reactionary." On the other hand, invention acts out a circumlocutory logic, the logic of representation as reprise, which defines the "new" as aftereffect of an intertextual engagement with the already-said and already-written, with literary and cultural memory—with the history of representation.

Despite, or, *due* to this memorious engagement, rather, many postmodern painters, novelists, and critics decline to be "apologists for what exists" (Lyotard 1993, 6). Then, not only do they need to question the "rules" of discourse. It would also help if they grasped the greater assumptions behind these rules, in which case they would "soon find that such rules are so many methods of deception, *seduction*, and reassurance that prevent them from being 'truthful'" (qui leur interdisent d'être "vrai") (6; cf. Lyotard 1986, 20). Lyotard's approach to the concept of reality in postmodernism intersects here, if indirectly, Baudrillard's, especially the Baudrillardian theory of seduction. This theory, I argue, is both descriptive and, although less manifestly, critical. It takes apart postmodern reality to foster an awareness thereof, an ontological understanding that might afford a critical approach to this reality. To tease out this possibility, a quick outline followed by a critique of Baudrillard's reality model is on order.

To begin with, *De la séduction* judges seduction diametrically opposed to production (1988, 56), the latter's project being to "set everything up in clear view, whether it be an object, a number, or a concept" (érige[r] tout en evidence, que ce soit celle d'un objet, d'un chiffre ou d'un concept). "Let everything be produced, be read, become real, visible"—any productive gesture seems to urge us (Baudrillard 1987a, 21). Seduction "withdraws," instead, something from the "visible order," de-realizes the world by proclaiming the irrelevance of all distinctions and oppositions (Baudrillard 1988, 143), including the contrast between true and untrue, real and unreal. This particular distinction disintegrates once artists knock up against the impossibility to achieve "true" representations, to be "truthful." When this happens, we are left with *peu de réalité*, "little reality." The collapse of the same "binary scheme" and, in particular, the thwarting of the "contradictory process of true and false, of real and the imaginary" lead to Baudrillardian *hyperreality* (1983a, 122). The spreading practice of simulation heralds, according to the French thinker, the end of polarities (1988, 144), and with it, the crisis of the map, of the repertoire, of the register. As a result, we return to the in-distinctness prior to the birth of the paradigm, prior to metaphysics, hence "No more mirror of being and appearances, of the real and its concept. No more imaginary coextensivity. . . . The real . . ., since it is no longer enveloped by an imaginary, it is no longer real at all. It is hyperreal," *Simulations* teaches us (1983b, 2–3).

Lyotard's "shortage of reality"—reproduced and thereby "aggravated" by the English translation as "lack of reality"—is only apparently the flip side of Baudrillard's hyperreal. His ontological deficit, as it were, actually matches Baudrillard's ontological inflation. On closer inspection, the latter is a metaphor of the former, reframing the Lyotardian "void" as "surplus." Besides, both draw, and acknowledgedly so, from Nietzsche. Still, Baudrillard's simulation strikes me as more radical than the dialectic of sublime presentation. "The Hyperrealism of Simulation" (1983b, 138) chronicles a more advanced, "terminal" phase in reality's "illness," incriminates more directly the tactics meant to cover up this ontopathological state. There is, for sure, in Lyotard's description of reality no residual nostalgia for truth, no metaphysical yearning for a reality ("presence") lost in a disenchanted, cartoonish world. As we have noted and will see in the last chapter again, according to the logic of the unpresentable sublime reality cannot be coveyed, "reproduced." It can still be conceived, imagined, however.

Baudrillard rules this alternative out, for simulation "threatens more directly the difference . . . between 'real,' and 'imaginary'" (1983b, 5, 142). True, Baudrillard integrates Lyotard's contribution to an issue of *L'Art vivant* on hyperrealism into his own argument (1983b, 47). Moreover, the two critics share common sources—I have mentioned Nietzsche, and I could add theories and practices of the avant-garde, or Walter Benjamin's classical essay "The Work of Art in the Age of Mechanical Reproduction," among other references. But the two philosophers operate on somewhat different levels, which marks the "politics" of their worldviews. We have just noticed, while resisting realistic presentation, that which is unpresentable remains in Lyotard nonetheless "conceivable." Reality is still *darstellbar*, no matter how sublime Kantian *Darstellbarkeit* (representability) might be. In Baudrillard, on the other hand, simulation gnaws at the representational root of conceivability and "referentiality," rendering images simulacra, pseudoimages that stage an empty resemblance—the semblance of resemblance—the eerie likeness of the real and its absent body. So any attempt to represent sets in train a "ritual of extermination" that secretes hyperreality while canceling out the "object of representation" (1983b, 142). In this respect, the contrast between Lyotard and Baudrillard replicates that between surrealism, or, the historical avant-garde, and postmodernism. This distinction informs Baudrillard's account of simulation. "Realism," he maintains in *Simulations*, had

> already begun this tendency [of becoming the "allegory of death," of self-denegation]. The rhetoric of the real already meant that the status of the latter had been gravely menaced (the golden age is that of language's innocence, where it doesn't have to add an "effect of reality" to what is said). Surrealism is still solidary with the realism it contests, but augments its intensity by setting it off against the imaginary. The hyperreal represents a much more advanced phase, in the sense that even this contradiction between the real and the imaginary is effaced. The unreal is no longer that of dream and of fantasy, of a beyond or a within, is that of a hallucinatory resemblance of the real with itself. (142)

In Baudrillard's opinion, surrealism—Lyotard's avant-garde—has not gone all the way. It gestures, if reluctantly, toward an utopia of what earlier I called the discourse's "beyond." Surrealist representation, modernist representation at large—cubist, futurist, constructivist, minimalist, and so on—have not gone the limit, have not carried through the demolition of reality with all that it implies culture- and politicswise. It is simulacral representation, or, resemblance that debunks the very notion of resemblance and thus triggers off the self-mirroring of the nonexistent, indeed, manages to threaten, ontologically and politically, the very existence of things that are (supposed to be) (*ta onta*) "as they are" and hardly otherwise.

Therefore, simulation can be put to some positive work. Its theoretical virulence, its unforgiving, seemingly despondent antirepresentational radicalism can be retooled as a critically useful concept once we become aware of its deconstructive modus operandi. Simulation can be "turned around" and adopted as a critical strategy for its sobering, "disenchanting" effects. "More disenchantment is still needed," claims one of Baudrillard's interviewers (Baudrillard 1993, 149), and I agree. We are living in a disenchanted, post-Weberian world, but this is not a dead end; postmodern representation is not a "decadent" symptom. We need more of that which is "putting an end" to traditional representation, to the way things have been represented, and *have been*, plain and simple. This would be a way to revoke, and rewrite, the solidarity (complicity?) compact between us, as imaging and imaginative beings, capable of representing our world, and the world itself.

An important line is crossed here—as in Lyotard, as we have seen—but what allows us to take a more decisive step is Baudrillard's blurring the divide between the real and the unreal. Baudrillard's philosophy addresses head-on the collapse of this distance, of the chasms that historically have kept apart ideas, discourses, paradigms, and ideologies. This ontological implosion, it has been contended, has "catastrophic" effects on any representation and utopia—and what is utopia if not an apogee of representation, a supreme *Darstellung*? But inherent in postmodern ontology is another paradox, a particular limit notion—a shifty, problematic, "unpoliceable" border that exposes any self-sufficient, firmly marked-off entity as a myth or, even better, a cover-up of sorts designed to conceal connection, overlap, and intertextuality, that is, cultural and historical construction as reality's mode of being in the postmodern "clusterworld." Spreading on both sides of, and thereby deconstructing, the real/unreal rift, hyperreality becomes not u-topian, but rather a-topian. It gets, that is, impossible to demarcate, locate, and stabilize in a de-limited topos, inside (or outside) a certain ontological framework. It has usurped the site of Pascal's God: its center is everywhere; its circumference (and also reference, "referent," à la Lyotard), nowhere (Baudrillard 1983b, 11).

As Roger Luckhurst observes, "the announcement of the effacement of the boundary is a consistent element of definitional postmodernism" (1991, 359) from Leslie Fiedler to Ihab Hassan and Fredric Jameson. In this view, Baudrillard's simulation trades upon the same postmodern logic, straddling as it does the ontological hiatus between reality and its image by foregrounding the hyperreal world and its intentionally deceiving forms: "the deconstruction of the real into details," "endless reflection," "properly serial form (Andy Warhol)," "reduplication," "reproduction," "digitality," and so forth. All these conspire to make us believe that there *is* something of the "order of the real," of an ontological—social, cultural—establishment. But what if the latter is, like the "real" Los Angeles, one of Baudrillard's favorite examples, a fiction, a motion picture, a huge script, a script (and a crypt), that is, of reality (and its absent corpse)?

A caveat: this does not mean that Los Angeles does not exist, that its place is an illusion and its people delusional. It means, from a critical standpoint not alien to Baudrillard's postmodernism, that L.A. is hardly what a dominant representation—artistic as well as political—would have us think that the "true" L.A. is or should be. It means that L.A.'s urban and sociocultural "truth," being, or structure is not "natural" and "given," untainted by discourse, projections, and fictions, unmapped textually, culturally and ideologically. Therefore, as an already textualized space open to all sorts of structurations throughout its history, as a memorious structure, L.A. cannot be beyond re-structuring, beyond change. Above, Baudrillard points out the obsolescence of the map, of the repertoire, the paradigm, and other textual formations. What I would emphasize in my turn is that they become inoperable, irrelevant only if we place them, and the work they do, exclusively this side of the represented/representation divide, if we seize them as tools to map, organize, shape, express, and otherwise represent a textually untouched, unmapped, unrepresented reality. The philosopher offers that these tools' accelerating use hides the fact they have since long fallen in disuse because they have nothing to be used on anymore. Organized around pointless representation practices, culture thus comes off, ontologically and aesthetically, as a major cover-up operation one more time, admittedly not much of a "vision" to go on.

But fictionalizing and textualizing instruments are not immaterial, outworn, beside the point if we look for their workings where traditional ontology and aesthetics would not, and Baudrillard's own mention of *language as reality effect* (1983b, 142; italics mine) does recommend that we step beyond classical ontology and aesthetics. What Baudrillard ultimately designates in that formula is rather the opposite: *reality as language effect,* with language a catchall term for the complexly discursive forces that have already impacted and processed reality, have given it a configuration that actually ensures—no matter how strange this may sound—reality's presence, sets up an ontology discursively, writes the world into being. In sum, Baudrillard's outrageous contention that "reality" and its "expression" are superannuated holds water only within the transcendental framework of mimesis-as-imitation, which deems the objects of representation textual-cultural tabula rasa. However, in the memorious context of what earlier I called "postmodern reality," reality no less than our transforming participation in it might, quite the contrary, just get another chance.

We can now circle back to my starting point and put McHale's question, "What is to be done in this [postmodern] world?," in more pragmatic terms. What is, I would ask à la William James, the "cash-value" of these extreme and, some say, self-defeating visions of postmodern reality? (1978, 32). Which are their "practical consequences" (28) and the other "vital satisfactions" "the possession of truth" (98)—the "truth" about L.A., for instance—would likely bring us?

"Truth" is key here. I think William James's pragmatic view of truth, on the one side, and Lyotard's and Baudrillard's approaches to the same, on the other, are not incompatible. A host of postmodern and poststructuralist truth notions in thinkers from Foucault (1984, 51–75) to Derrida (1972, 275–324) and Derrideans like Philippe Lacoue-Labarthe (1971) to de Man (1979, 79–230) turn on the same Nietzschean model,[8] which, notably enough, overlaps with William James's. The pragmatic philosopher, too, defines truth "genetically"—if not "genealogically"—as having grown "petrified by antiquity" (1978, 37). Implied here is the sociocultural formation and discursive "formatting," the historicity of truth at play in Nietzsche and his followers, including Lyotard and Baudrillard. Both seize truth, what reality is and means, as an "effect" of linguistic-discursive protocols. To go back to the conspiratorial metaphor of culture as "cover-up" operation, one could also, and quite sensibly, argue that the truth culture masks has to do with the truth's own "true" nature, is the truth about truth. Underpinned by mimetic representation's hallowed doctrine, Western culture has been denying constantly its own involvement in the making of a category that it goes out of its way, instead, to advertise as "pure," "original," "natural," uncorrupted by time, allegiances, ideologies, representations, texts—by culture itself. Western culture strives, largely speaking, to represent itself as set apart—ontologically—from that which it has represented, "originated" all along. Culture, we are told, may evolve, is subject to time, to history and its "constructing" effect, whereas truth, the truth of what representation represents, remains immune to the representational and fictionalizing textual-discursive arrangements, somehow lies outside them. This is what makes it identifiable as truth. And this is the reassuring bedrock, the assumption on which classical representation, writing, and reading have been operating.

Nietzsche and post-Nietzschean thinkers retort that this theory is treading on thin ice. Once we admit that truth has a memory, a cultural biography of becoming and adjustment within textual-material circumstances, we can no longer defend the hypothesis of monolithic and stable truth, of truth as a datum, meaning handed down to us as if authorized by an authority above history, an authority who tautologically refers to itself, asserts itself in the very process of authorizing the notion of transcendental referentiality of discourse. Thus, modern, "disenchanted" culture is marked, for Baudrillard, by the Nietzschean "death of the divine referential" (Baudrillard 1983b, 9). This bears upon Lyotard's ontology, upon the substance of the surrounding world, its truth, and how we represent it. In this view, Western culture can also be defined as a systematic, if unconscious, struggle to exorcise (Baudrillard 1983b, 9) and dissimulate this death and all the deaths, disappearances, and reality crises derived from it. As a result, representation in the inherited sense is a pointless, because objectless, if not fraudulent epiphany, and this situation can be geared toward a "spectacular manipulation of consciences" (10), toward a "*culture* of the spectacle" with a very political agenda.

But seduction and simulation do not serve this agenda because they demolish, as noted earlier, the binary system underwriting it. One more time, at the system's core there lie the semiotic, ontological, as well as political distinction between sign, or, representation and its presumed truth or content, and related to this distinction, the "wager of representation" (10), namely, the belief "that a sign could refer to the depth of a meaning, that a sign could *exchange* for meaning and that something could guarantee this exchange—God, of course" (10). But since in the modern world, this guarantee has lost its former "cash-value," simulation of presence, including God's presence, lords it over by default. And if God himself becomes a simulation effect, then the whole mimesis-as-imitation-based traditional system is rendered "weightless," a "gigantic simulacrum" where no representation (sign) is ever again exchangeable for its reality (referent) or meaning (signified), but only for itself (11), hypersemiotically. Classical representation postulates the difference, and thereby the possibility of exchange between the sign and what the sign stands for. Simulation, on the other hand, rejects this principle, negates "*the sign as value*" (11), and so blocks the semiotic exchange insofar as a sign, a representation, is traded for some truth or meaning in the sense discredited after Nietzsche. Simulacra forswear this sort of metaphysical bartering by collapsing the epistemological and ontological distance between representation and represented, symbol and symbolized. Against Western culture's cover-up pressure, the members of these pairs are revealed as homological, structurally alike, equally coming on the heels of a long history of fictionalization, symbolization, and textualization. I submit that this memorious move clears the road for critique.

In "Baudrillard and the Politics of Postmodernism" chapter from *What's Wrong with Postmodernism* (1990, 164–91), Christopher Norris alleges that Baudrillard propounds

(1) that theory is a discredited enterprise, since "truth" has turned out to be a fictive, rhetorical or imaginary construct; (2) that this prevents (or ought to prevent) our engaging in activities of "rational" argument or *Ideologiekritik*; and (3) that we must henceforth drop all talk of the "real" as opposed to its mystified, distorted or "ideological" representation, since such talk continues to trade on old assumptions that no longer possess any force or credibility. (171)

Norris agrees with the first axiom but rejects the rest, concluding that what we ultimately learn from Baudrillard is "that any politics which goes along with the current postmodern drift will end up by effectively endorsing and promoting the work of ideological mystification" (191).

There is more to Baudrillard's politics, I would answer. "Baudrillard's Bad Attitude," to quote Andrew Ross's essay title, is more complex than it seems; I find it, as a matter of fact, ultimately encouraging. Interestingly enough, Norris, too, praises Baudrillard for being "much nearer the mark in his characterisation of present-day society" (1990, 180) than "neopragmatists like Richard Rorty and Stanley Fish" (178), even though, incidentally, in an interview with Sylvère Lotringer Baudrillard states that pragmatism is "the same as simulation pushed to the limit" (1993, 105). At any rate, Baudrillard's truth "diagnosis," we gather from Norris's commentary, is, for one thing, correct. But the political passivity Norris distinguishes in this verdict—what Jameson takes to task as the "depoliticizing theory of postmodernism" (1984, 65)—is a different story. On the face of it, Norris makes sense. No doubt, Baudrillard does not call openly for an intervention in reality since he sets out, in the first place, to "dismantle the reality principle" (1993, 123), to leak out its "secret"—"truth does not exist" (124). Norris's rationalism balks at this hypothesis.

What is at issue here, though, is the extent to which this rationalism itself and *Ideologiekritik* as its militant twin risk replicating the fictions they struggle to unsettle, if they ignore the "artifice" at "the very heart of reality" repeatedly pointed out by critics like Baudrillard (1983b, 151). Turning the tables on Norris, one could say that Baudrillard's theory in a sense carries through, while retooling radically, an older "false consciousness" analysis. His hyperreality critique is a *Kritik* of sorts, updated for the postmodern age. First, this critique establishes the fictionality, "constructedness," and intertextual nature of inherited truths; second—and this is a fairly pragmatic gesture—it conjectures that truth does not "exist" at all if its existence is transcendentally postulated on an external reality or presence ("referent") prior to representation, "construction," or "expression"; if the antecedence of the pristine pre-textual goes, then the represented and representation (construction, staging, expression, etc.) do indeed become one. And third, as in Lyotard, representation puts forth the represented, brings something new into the world, more broadly represents the world into being, hence it can be seized politically, as an instrument of change precisely because it tends, in our postmodern times, to take precedence over the represented quite literally as the represented comes already textually and culturally processed, re-presented.

Indeed, "it's the tail wagging the dog" (M. W. Smith 2001, 2), but in a good way. Rex Butler writes that Baudrillard's "essential argument" is that "the world conforms," indirectly expressing an "intention" hidden behind the world's "seeming appearance" (1999, 137). But is Baudrillard's reading of this "conformity" conformist itself, politically acquiescent? Not at all. Representation is re-presentation, memorious, as I have been defining it consistently, but not in the sense that it repeats, re-states, shores up the established "state of affairs," and so does the bidding of that whose picture it paints, of that which thus lies safely outside, prior to, and unaffected by a poem or video. Hard as it may be to wrap our minds around this notion, re-presentation institutes and makes the "real" what it is and means to us. Enabled by the re-presentation model of discourse, representation critique is *Ideologiekritik*.

"Plagiarized by Life": Nabokov's Pendulum

" 'The Assistant Producer' is based on actual facts. As to the rest, I am no more guilty of imitating 'real life' than 'real life' is responsible for plagiarizing me."
            —Vladimir Nabokov, Appendix to *The Stories of Vladimir Nabakov*

[L]ife had been real before, life will be real from now on, I hope.
            —Vladimir Nabokov, " 'That in Aleppo Once . . .' "

I'd like the boundary between fact and fiction to be as unstable in my work as it is in my experience. Yet at the same time I have a strong desire to get at something I would call reality, however indeterminate that may be.
            —David Antin, 1996 interview

Nabokov marks a turning point in the modern history of fictional representation, as I suggested in the opening chapter. There, I discussed this turn by focusing on the intertextual dynamic of fiction and autobiography, which results, we noticed, in a specific configuration of memorious discourse. Back to Nabokov, I propose that we resume the discussion with an eye to the "obliteration of the boundary between fiction and reality" (Grabes 1985, 269) occurring in his short stories and impacting, I contend, not only his ontology, but his historical and cultural outlook more broadly.

If the typically "modernist," "subjective determination of reality" (268) still draws a "shadow-line between fiction and reality" (268), postmodernism steps across this border. As a consequence, fictional discourse is "no longer a representation of discrete versions of a given reality, but merely a range of synthetic constructs which may, at certain points or in certain habitual guises, touch on and even evoke what we conventionally take to be 'real,' but which can with equal justification be termed 'fantastic' (or 'fictive') *or* 'realistic'" (269). Grabes's conclusion squares with McHale's. Drawing upon a similar "boundary-violation" in contemporary narrative, McHale places "the crossover from modernist to postmodernist writing" in the "middle years of Vladimir Nabokov's American career" (1987, 17, 18). We have noted, this crossover involves an ontological turn and raises, accordingly, a host of issues on the "real" and the "fictional," "origin" and "copy," their interplay and boundaries. I want to propose here that, whether entirely postmodern or not, this move could be traced back to texts older than *Lolita* (1955) and *Pale Fire* (1962). More remarkably perhaps, it is in the short story rather than in the novel that it happens, although *The Real Life of Sebastian Knight* (1941), according to Grabes (1985, 270–71), or even *Laughter in the Dark* (*Kamera obskura*) (1932) already attempted to break down the barriers between the real and its image. Using Erving Goffman's "frame analysis" as well as theories of fictionality and possible worlds (Thomas Pavel, Lubomir Doležel), make-believe (Kendall Walton), and "storyworlds" (David Herman), I will show that Nabokov's first short story in English, "The Assistant Producer" (1943), playfully enacts this breakdown. The text brings to the fore a whole narrative strategy of reality-fictionalizing—or reality-textualizing, as I say apropos of Lyotard and Baudrillard—at the same time that it sets out to ironically "naturalize" the fictitious. A true watershed in Nabokov's career, this story offers a fictional site for various, biographical and autobiographical, linguistic, cultural, aesthetic, and political transactions. The real (the [auto]biographical, the historical) and the fictional, the past and the present both of the writer and his work are rendered, also with a term used in the previous section, homological, equally textual in their build. Thus, they can be, and are, spliced together. As such, they engender in "The Assis-

tant Producer" a vision and narrative practice that lay the groundwork for later, more innovative ontological undertakings such as the
novels *Pale Fire* (1962) and *Ada* (1969).

Now, in view of my argument, the first epigraph above could mis-
lead us if taken at face value. As Gennady Barabtarlo comments, the
"true events" the story is based on, "slightly adjusted for better
focus and concatenation, are wrapped in the arrantly fictitious tin-
sel-foil of a Hollywood production, employing available sundry Russian émigrés as supers and consultants" (qtd. in Alexandrov 1995,
105). Stemming as it may from "actual facts," this text is a memorious tour de force, for not only does Nabokov show how reality "originates" in fiction, becomes fictional, staged as it is by textual devices
and genres, in brief, by discourse. In turn and, as we shall see below,
not unlike some of Borges's stories, Nabokov's represents "real" life
as "plagiarizing" fiction and ultimately the literary text itself. As we
shall discover, this representation reaches beyond mere mimesis—
or, "imitation," to quote Nabokov's more limitative term. "The Assistant Producer" does chronicle a "true" episode from the life of
Russian singer Plevitskaya, as Roy Johnson tells us.[9] However, the
story resists this representation-as-imitation by enacting life as memorious "discourse formation," more precisely, as a reflex of performative (dramatic, cinematic) discourse. If life spins off literature
as its "impersonation," this is possible, as we observed above, only
because the former has already taken on a textual-performative
structure able to generate the latter. Life produces fiction as an "assistant producer" produces—etymologically, "brings forward"—a
movie, as any fictional mechanisms give rise to fiction. Thus, Nabokov tears down the wall between life and its double; his gesture is
both the theme *and* the outcome of the performative act, of the text
titled "The Assistant Producer."

I find it noteworthy that Nabokov employs the very tropes and
representational modes of performance to thematize, and bridge
concretely, through writing—the writing of *this* story—the ontological cleft between facts and images of facts. One could safely call this
a *mise en abyme* in Lucien Dällenbach's sense. The story abounds with
"homologies" ("resemblances," "coincidences," "relations") between a component or aspect of the narrative (episode, character,
motif, utterance) and the narrative in its entirety (Dällenbach 1977,
46). So, the part acquires a "metatextual" significance (98–101) as
it foreshadows, duplicates, and otherwise reflects—and reflects on—
the whole it belongs to. The author sets forth this significance from
the outset, in the title itself. The latter starts the story out dialogi-
cally, a sign that the dialogue the narrator carries with the reader or

the "narratee" is going to play an essential role in "The Assistant Producer." The opening paragraph, in fact, seems to begin with the narrator's answer to a potential query about the title, a question the story's readers may raise, as the narrator implies. The response rhetorically rephrases the question before giving a clue for the text's interpretation: "Meaning? Well, because sometimes life is merely that—an Assistant Producer. Tonight we shall go to the movies. Back to the thirties, and down the twenties, and round the corner to the old Europe Picture Palace" (Nabokov 1995, 542).

This passage sheds light on the whole story and is illuminated by it in exchange, so both the quotation and its larger context call for some rereading in view of this mutual decoding.[10] The fragment's opening word responds to the title, "reads" it and the piece it names: the capitalized Assistant Producer is simply life. Accordingly, narrating a life episode resembles movie-watching ("Tonight we shall go to the movies"). In spite of the "Bibliographical Note," the writer already defines the "real" as "production" and the story's narrative apparatus in cinematic terms. Not unlike *Speak, Memory*, where the magic lantern motif plays, as we saw in chapter 1, a central role, "The Assistant Producer" turns to the silver screen world. Specifically, the text provides us with an essential reading tool, pointing to the performative analogon of narrative discourse: film as a "master trope" in the story.[11] Ostensibly, "Nabokov never lets his reader forget that he is the conjuror, the illusionist, the stage-manager, to whom his characters owe their existence" (Merivale 1967, 209). In our story, though, he promotes life itself to stage manager and from offstage comments on the "production" as if his own job were to simply summarize and explain the "show" for us.

The fragment also points to the multiple, temporal and cinematic layers of the text, once again recommending a way of "unreeling" the narrative web. The intertwining of these strata muddles a great deal the actual plot in the first two sections of the story. In its third part, though, we come to realize that "The Assistant Producer" reconstitutes the mysterious disappearance of a White Army leader in Paris, by ironically modeling the mystery of the whole affair on a movie script. What might have become a detective or spy narrative is being reencoded—and analyzed—as motion picture, to wit, as a series of movies or movie styles. The main characters, "la Slavska" and Golubkov, are both actors and agents (plotters of General Fedchenko's kidnapping) in more than one film, and, we shall notice, both in the show and in reality. Most intriguingly, as the spy narrative gets under way and generates less suspense, cinematic discourse takes over, becoming more intricate and disorienting. Thus, we travel back to the 1930s, that is, to a Hollywood production on la Slavska's really dramatic career, then farther still, on to the events of the 1920s, which the American movie features prominently. At last, we wind up in the symbolically named movie theater and, "after the show is over" (Nabokov 1995, 555), out into the "solid world" of Paris, a "reality" (555) wherein a character of the performance that has just ended (Golubkov) apparently lights up a cigarette. Starting off with reading guidelines that call our attention to the cinematic fictionalizing of life, the narrative loop ends with a complementary "naturalization" of the fictional: Golubkov's "Lookee," fictional object in the movie-in-the-text, is as "tangible" as the cigarette the narrator gets ready to enjoy "after all that trashy excitement" (555). The general himself becomes a sort of "metaphoric traveler" (Pavel 1986, 85), a "fictional hero" "visit[ing]" our "real" shores (85) and thereby encouraging us to reconsider both *his* fictionality and *our* actuality.

This is how reality and the imaginary frame each other successively, make the reader respond to them as to their ontologically "absolute" other, that is, force us to treat the real as fictitious and vice versa. Thus the text veers from a whole "schizophrenic" (Walton 1993, 191) line of Western thought, which tells us that "fictional worlds and their contents [are] insulated or isolated in some peculiar way from the real world, separated from it by a logical or metaphysical barrier" (191). Breaking through this barrier, Nabokov sets off ontological traffickings, allows, that is, his characters to leap across the "barrier between [the] worlds" (192) usually separated by the fiction/history divide. Following Nabokov, postmoderns like Leyner, Woody Allen, and Jasper Fforde further "soften," as Fforde writes in his *Eyre Affair*, "the barrier between reality and fiction" (2003, 206) so that Victorian heroines roam the "real" world and, conversely, crossing the "fictional" landscapes of *Jane Eyre* and *Martin Chuzzlewit*, "real" people threaten to "alter" (157) the books' plots and even the original manuscripts themselves.

Reading "The Assistant Producer" requires placing the story's textual units within various "frameworks or schemata of interpretation" (Goffman 1986, 21), and we must face a serious challenge as the text keeps playing with these frameworks, switching them repeatedly and without warning. Nabokov's narrative pendulum swings back and forth across the fictional/real ontological watershed, suddenly divulging to the reader the presence of discourse, the motion picture set in the background of a "historical" scene, or, vice versa, the historical surroundings of an event presented as invented, "purely" discourse. The "theatrical frame" of the story's performative universe (theater, opera, film, etc.) encompasses and denaturalizes "reality," places it within quotation marks, as it were. Simultaneously, fictional elements naturally "fit" into the environment of "life-as-life." In this view, it hardly surprises us that the "theatrical frame"—the sociocultural convention transforming "an individual into a stage performer" (Goffman 1986, 124)—no longer demarcates the fictional territory and, as a result, may not get an adequate response form the reader. The performer nonchalantly crosses over into the narrator's "tangible" domain. In doing so, he or she ignores the "spatial boundaries" (139) meant to "cut off the depicted world from what lies beyond the stage [or the screen] line" (139), to police the frontiers of the "storyworld" as "projected environment" (Herman 2002, 17). The fictional and the nonfictional now overlap, mingle, mirror each other. Thus, in la Slavka's performing "style" and, as a matter of fact, in the character as a whole the two realms symbolically intersect:

> She was a celebrated singer. Not opera, not even *Cavalleria Rusticana*, not anything like that. "La Slavska"—that is what the French called her. Style: one-tenth *tzigane*, one-seventh Russian peasant girl (she had been that herself originally), and five-ninth popular—and by popular I mean a hodgepodge of artificial folklore, military melodrama, and official patriotism. The fraction left unfilled seems sufficient to represent the physical splendor of her prodigious voice. (Nabokov 1995, 542)

In acting out her socially and culturally assorted identity, the great singer displays a "corporeal style" (Judith Butler 1990, 139) that, as an involuntary parody, recovers no "original" identity, mocking, in fact, the very notion of "original."[12] La Slavska might once have been a peasant girl, closer, that is, to what she tries to copy. The "overstyling" of popular songs and performance, on the one hand, the influence of other "styles," and her aristocratic pose and aspirations, on the other, taunt rather than retrieve that remote source. The character is nothing more than a performing "agent," an embodied voice without origin and originality whether on stage or in "real life." A persona par excellence, she gradually becomes a textual index of sorts, so much so that the reader comes to associate her presence with counterfeited emotions, fabulation, melodramatic make-believe. The photograph in Chaliapin's dressing room conveys precisely this sense of artificiality and unreality (542), of fictitiousness creeping upon the "actual" world. Significantly, it is the vanishing of her "true personality" in the motley of kitschy modes

of impersonation that secures her a leading role in the plot cooked
up by her husband, General Golubkov. Apparently, la Slavska is destined to be a "spy," that is, to carry out her impersonations in the
"real world." Moreover, her disarmingly eclectic, fake style translates into multiple political allegiances following her husband's
"fluctuations of double-crossing" (546).

"Double-crossing" is a governing figure in "The Assistant Producer," a text that hops with aplomb across stylistic, political, and
ontological borders. I have remarked that Nabokov takes up cinematic motifs and devices to suggest that these borders are as porous
as they appear to be pervasive. As a result, the story reads like a narrativization of several film episodes preceded by a "historical" introduction, episodes deployed throughout the text and separated by
the narrator's commentary. Intriguingly, the commentary takes us
beyond the "movie" into the "real world," or, in the narrator's own
words, into "that vile script . . . enacted in reality" (543), yet only to
bring us back to the "spectacle." As critics have noticed, Nabokov
already masters "the sort of narrative mode of rapidly switching
forms of address and points of view" that later novels will refine.[13]
However, despite swift narrative pace and perspective shifts, the alert
reader discovers that the "Assistant Producer" produces, so to
speak, different motion pictures, which vie for setting up the story's
main narrative frame. The narrator describes the most obvious in
explicitly cinematic terms. Here is its first, abruptly introduced episode:

> Ghostly multitude of ghostly Cossacks on ghost-horseback are seen
> charging through the fading name of the assistant producer. Then dap-
> per General Golubkov is disclosed idly scanning the battlefield through
> a pair of opera glasses. When movies and we were young, we used to be
> shown what the sights divulged neatly framed in two connected circles.
> Not now. What we do see next is General Golubkov, all indolence sud-
> denly gone, leaping into the saddle, looming sky-high for an instant on
> his rearing steed, and then rocketing into a crazy attack. (543)

The passage epitomizes Nabokov's "enframing game" with the
reader, a game usually giving rise, according to Goffman, to an "ambiguity of the frame" (1986, 303). Unless it is cleared up through
textual clues, this "vagueness" or "uncertainty" may yield "mis-
frames," that is, "beliefs, uninduced and erroneous, as to how
events at hand are to be framed" (303). Here, though, these enframing misjudgments are deliberately and playfully induced. The narrator plays tricks on us, recommending a mode of framing—of

reading—that proves a *mis*framing. Consequently, objects and events waver between two ontological territories, oscillate between the realms of "life" and representation (film) depending on the framework—"real" ("historical") or "fictional" (cinematic)—within which we place the whole scene. The quotation marks I have just used flag, however, the double, postmodern articulation or "fictionalization" of the two ontological domains: the "real" and the "fictional" are *already* memorious, fictionally pre-fabricated, which, needless to say, makes the reader's job even more difficult. Ostensibly, as we read, we move from represented life to a represented representation of life, or, an *ekphrasis*, in classical rhetoric a description of an art object within an artistic discourse of a different kind.

Suspecting a setup, the reader automatically goes back to check the first reading—that is, the framework he or she has employed first time around—through a second or even third perusal that will basically be on the lookout for any rupture or switch in the framework applied initially. In this light, it bears pointing out that the fragment I am discussing commences by unseating the interpretive frame one has most probably used to read the previous passage, which contains the narrator's comments on la Slavska's life after the Bolshevik Revolution and the war between "the Reds and the Whites." The *unreal*, spectral ("ghostly," the narrator says) mass of no less immaterial Cossacks on equally "ghost-horseback" opens out *ex abrupto* onto a totally different world: the world of fiction-as-fiction, of cinematically ordered biography (la Slavska's "destiny") or history (Russia's "destiny"). The ekphrastic passage exposes the wooden nickle, the artifice in the film shot "somewhere in Ventura County" (Nabokov 1995, 543) as the movie episode is interlarded with ironic stabs at genre clichés, at the movie itself ultimately. These metatextual intrusions seem to suggest that the fictional warriors literally dislocate "reality," which fades away as they are "charging through the fading name of the assistant producer" (we recall that the "assistant producer" had been identified as life itself in the story's first line).

Nonetheless, Nabokov takes here on another boundary or framing problem by explicitly focusing on the interface of the fictional and the real. The Cossacks—the shapes on the screen—may literally swarm through the actual name of the assistant producer as the film credits roll. Consequently, the movie's first scene (which "denounces" the artifact *as* artifact and therefore requires a fictional framing by the audience),[14] and the introductory presentation of the movie (the title, the cast, the director's and the producers' names, etc.), which entails a totally different response, overlap.

What is more, the narrator-commentator draws our attention to the film's heavily conventional apparatus of "production," to the memorious *scripting of reality*. The cinematic "gaze," its "prismatic" treatment of "seen" (filmed) objects and the ways these objects look and are viewed by the audience cannot be separated. This connection is all the more obvious as we go "back to the thirties, and down the twenties," that is, to the origins of the motion picture, an art whose development has been influenced by the progress of the "technology" of seeing and recording/framing the seen. General Golubkov, for instance, "is disclosed"—as the Cossacks "are seen"— "scanning" the battleground through a pair of "opera glasses." No doubt, "what we see" while watching a movie is no longer "neatly *framed*" (italics mine) by the two "connected circles." As the narrator says, the old enframing was replaced by a more "discreet" one, likely to enhance the cinematic make-believe.

In fact, the verisimilitude effect has depended in motion pictures and literature alike on artists' ability to camouflage the devices—the discourse—employed to *produce* such an effect. Effacing the "form," hiding or, as above, "covering up" the rules and conventions shaping the "content," has been seen, at least in works resting upon mimetic-realistic assumptions and scopes, as a way of upgrading, and vouching for, "content" and its "truth." In this regard, by focusing on the mutual framing of the "real" and the "fictional," on the frail boundaries between the two, and on the representational conventions constructing the represented, "The Assistant Producer" mounts a critique of realism, to wit, a critique of sentimental-heroic-exotic discourse laying mimetic-realistic claims. The movie is from the outset framed as movie, as artifact; one easily makes out the calculated disruption of the "viewed" by the technology of viewing, by movie-making. The clumsy presence of the medium and its optical machinery in the film gives the lie to the film's narrowly mimetic pretenses. The characters and situations are blatantly conventional, shadows of reality ("ghosts"), which the director summoned from his unreliable "files" (543), from cinematic discourse's memorious stockpile. Teeming with kitschy stereotypes, the sequence is predictable for the discriminating moviegoer (or story reader), ruling out the "unexpected" in the confrontation between the "Reds" and the "Whites." Along these lines, the paragraph following the longer passage on the "spectral" Cossacks tops any of Nabokov's previous ironies:

> But the unexpected is the infra-red in the *spectrum* [italics mine] of Art: instead of the conditional *ra-ta-ta* reflex of machine gunnery, a woman's

voice is heard singing afar. Nearer, still nearer, and finally all-pervading. A gorgeous contralto voice expanding into whatever the musical director found in his files in the way of Russian lilt. Who is leading the infra-Reds? A woman. The singing spirit of that particular, especially well-trained battalion. Marching in front, trampling the alfalfa, and pouring out her Volga-Volga song. Dapper and daring *djighit* Golubkov (now we know what he had descried), although wounded in several spots, manages to snatch her up on the gallop, and, lusciously struggling, she is borne away. (543)

The "impromptu" appearance of la Slavska (Masha, as Golubkov calls her) confirms the melodramatic pattern of the genre, carries over details from previous paragraphs, and foreshadows later developments. The "extreme," least inspired artistic solution, which chooses the "gorgeous contralto voice" over the more reasonable "*ra-ta-ta*," belongs, we learn, to an "infra-Red." Nabokov thus ironically makes the *extremes* of the aesthetic and political spectrum meet and convey the same inconsistence ("spectrality") and contrivance. At the same time, the *fictitious* passage alludes to la Slavska's *real* political allegiances—the "more practical party . . . her wily peasant soul chose" (543)—allegiances that the story will corroborate before long.

The movie we are "watching" in the fragments so far discussed furnishes just one cinematic layer of the story. To our confusion, the narrator pinpoints the fictitiousness of all layers in the same ostentatious manner. He emphasizes the mediation of the information we are being given and invites us to partake in his memorious discoveries or predictions: "we get a gloomy glimpse . . ." (543); "we are now going to witness" (545); "you will see her next" (549); "we get a few last glimpses" (554), and so forth. Nor will the reader fail to notice that identic ceremonious formulas, exposing the movie *as* movie, actually introduce *different* movies or at least different cinematic styles. A first one, insistently described as conventional, "unrealistic," features Russian battle scenes, stock sets displaying "the self-conscious samovar reflecting distorted faces" (544), and Golubkov's presenting his officers his war capture, the former "infra-Red" leader, as his "bride" (544). Toward the end of the first section, a new kind of movielike treatment of narrative information takes over, so different that one might suspect that another movie is being shown at that point. Clearly, the storyteller's comments turn the Ventura County-shot motion picture into a performance where the gap between fiction and reality (history) is closing fast. The text chooses the same cinematic trope to account for the narrative selection of facts (discourse or "subject," in the terminology of narrative poetics): as we are told, "indeterminism is banned from the studio" (544), which means essentially that the "Paris movie" carries on the plot of the "Revolution show." For Masha's capture was not quite haphazard; as the narrator reveals, "when the great exodus began, . . . the General and his wife already formed one team, one song, one cipher" (544).

The "team" stars from now on in a less picturesque and romantic film. The Russian steppe makes room for the urban set of Paris, and the heavy-handed, civil-war intrigue is replaced by a truer scheme, Golubkov and his wife's plot to kidnap the president-to-be of the White Warriors Union. The heroic-folkloric clichés live on solely in la Slavska's performances, which are themselves being incorporated into the larger show of "effacement" (547) and impersonation she and her husband put on as triple agents. Otherwise, the movie borrows the patterns and techniques of a new genre, the detective or secret agent narrative. This time around, it is the narrator who controls narrative speed—"my reel is going too fast" (545), he warns us. If he previously distanced himself from the Hollywood melodramatic production—the cinematic fashion in which he chose to present Golubkov's and la Slavska's encounter—now this critical distance is shorter. The "Paris episode" lends itself to a more realistic and economical presentation as well as faster narrative pace. It dredges up more reliable "facts"—a "most weirdly monotonous series of events" (545)—and correspondingly fends off any romantic digressions, superfluous ornaments or "dreams" that "may well strike the film pruners as an excrescence upon the main theme" (546). More importantly still, the narrator is now also a witness, a character in the movie whose plot he is outlining, as we find out in the opening of the third section:

German film companies, which kept sprouting like poisonous mushrooms in those days (just before the child of light learned to talk), found cheap labor in hiring those among the Russian émigrés whose only hope and profession was their past—that is, a set of totally unreal people—to represent "real" audiences in pictures. The dovetailing of one phantasm into another produced upon a sensitive person the impression of living in a Hall of Mirrors, or rather a prison of mirrors, and not even knowing which was the glass and which was yourself.

Indeed, when I recall the halls where the Slavska sang, both in Berlin and in Paris, and the type of people one saw there, I feel as if I were Technicoloring and sonorizing some very ancient motion picture where life had been a gray vibration and funerals a scamper, and where only the sea had been tinted (a sickly blue), while some hand machine imitated offstage the hiss of the asynchronous surf. . . . A venerable but worldly priest, with his cross gently heaving on his ample chest, sits in the front row and looks straight ahead. (547–48)

Foregrounding the story's aesthetic themes and mechanisms at the plot level, the passage supplies another ideal example of *mise en abyme*. First, it once again blurs the demarcation between reality and fiction: seeking realistic effects, movie companies employ "real" people, yet the "figurants" turn out eerily "unreal," stuck as they find themselves in their spellbinding past. In other words, "reality" unfolds itself memoriously, as "consensual representation" (Couturier 1993, 370) and "prismatic glamour" (Nabokov, qtd. in Jan Stephen Parker 1991, 68). It is "always refracted,"[15] mediated, and constructed, a discourse ("vile script") or performance (film) structured by fictionalizing techniques processing "*un*real" raw materials yet pursuing, and achieving, uncannily make-believe effects.[16] As the narrator concludes, one finds oneself unable to tell the represented from his or her deceiving representation since the represented already leads a fictitious life, and in this respect Nabokov's ontology squares with Baudrillard's and Lyotard's. Second, despite the autobiographical aspect of narration at this juncture, the narrated movie is not—not simply—realistic recollection but remake and intertextuality, a projection of an older movie, which automatically reworks ("modernizes") a "very ancient," silent, black-and-white motion picture. As *Speak, Memory* also helped us realize, there is no ultimate life truth our memory retrieves, but another movie, production, trope, cultural and intertextual fashioning and refashioning of things past, which remembrance recalls and redoes, if not invent, simultaneously. And third, the reader may come to witness the erosion of another distinction between reality and fiction as he or she may spot, among the "right-wing festival"'s attendees, the narrator himself in the "venerable but worldly priest" who "used to hear Golubkov's confessions" (Barabtarlo in Alexandrov 1995, 106, pointing to a passage in Nabokov 1995, 551).

As we saw earlier, a performative event in itself, the festival featuring la Slavska's "tremendous sonorities" (548) attracts a "cinematic" ("unreal") audience. Conversely, the tape the narrator's memory plays for us revolves around a host of dramatic scenes. In fact, the central couple of the story is continuously performing. Masha sings while her husband acts "artistically," in the same "overstressed" (547) manner, the part of the "hired lackey" (547). Most notably, artistic performance goes hand in hand with "political

performance" as Masha and Golubkov mastermind General Fedchenko's kidnapping. But if Golubkov allows himself just one "dramatic treat" (549) during the whole operation, his wife is immersed
in various "passable imitation[s]" (550) even after the conspiracy
has been uncovered. When charged by the police, Golubkov even
complains that "somebody has been impersonating" him (553),
while la Slavska puts on a great show of "grief-stricken innocence"
(553).

   Finally, after "we get a few last glimpses of the Slavska in prison"
(554), the storyteller brings us back to the largest narrative frame of
his story, which does not insist on separating fiction (motion picture) from reality (history) either. This third frame or ontological
confine is as provisional as the previous ones. Contrary to the narrator's delusive observation, the show is not over. The encouraging ex-
clamation, "Welcome reality!" (555), is certainly just another
enframing trap. The movie goes on, invades celebrated reality as life
and its cinematic duplicate are undergirded and constructed by
the same ambiguous, fictional mechanisms. The "mirrors of possibility" (555) spin out both imaginary representations and "real"
events. On his way to an appointment on rue Descartes (!), General
Fedchenko vanishes in the fictional abyss of rue Pierre *Labime* (italics
mine), the name of which, it goes without saying, one cannot find
in any Paris street guide. Crucial information we have been fed in
the story turns out an "optical trick" (551) in hindsight. But if the
"assistant producer" can manipulate facts at will, if "Dr. Puppen-
meister" can play with Golubkov's life and with the "actual" movie's
five endings as he pleases, so can the inventive narrator. In the story's last lines, he actually lets on that the movie's protagonist (Golubkov) and the "dapper" man walking down the Parisian street may
be the same person.[17] It is the unpredictable logic of the "Puppen-
meister" that lies behind the "actual" world and "maintains" its realistic makeup. In other words, by welcoming reality the narrator
welcomes us to a new film, perhaps more lifelike but essentially
based on the same cinematic principles.

Concurrently, if independently, Nabokov and Borges turn over a
new leaf in the history of modernist representation. A whole "memorious revolution" breaks out in their works, a sea change that, as
noted previously, writers like Barth, Pynchon, Coover, Reed, Perec,
Peter Carey, and Danilo Kiš will bring to postmodern fruition. In all
likelihood, Nabokov's story and Borges's "Funes" (dating back to
circa 1942 and published in volume in 1944) were written around
the same time. Also, the famous "Tlön, Uqbar, Urbis Tertius" came

out in 1940, was reissued in *Ficciones* (1944), and was appended a "Postscript" in 1947. Likewise, "The Theme of the Traitor and the Hero," a narrative "artifice" (Borges's term) of the "Funes" type, is flanked in the same 1944 collection by two texts dated 1942, one of which is the better-known "Death and the Compass."

As readers of these early Borgesian gems, we must play the same ontological games as in Nabokov. We must learn, that is, to avoid enframing traps. And we do so, no question about it, the hard way as we mistake "reality" for its "fictional" double, and vice versa. In Nabokov and Borges, writing, writing-as-game-playing, constitutes fundamentally a readerly setup. This setup is memorious on two accounts.

First, it implies relationality where traditional ontology and its aesthetics posit rupture, discontinuity *across ontological realms* that classical metaphysics keeps distinct. Memorious writing launches connections, ties, overlaps, effects place-swaps, conversions, mutual mirrorings, and otherwise collapses the distance between the represented ("life") and representation, its "double." As we have remarked, the represented is already represented, a representation, a discursive construct, hence already its own double. Therefore, I insist in this chapter and throughout the book, representation is memorious, re-presentation. It may "reflect" the world, but this is itself a world of reflections, texts, and stories. So, representation, and postmodern representation more emphatically and self-consciously than other representations, captures the *déjà*-written and represented, limns *a world pregnant with fiction.* "Tlön," "Death and the Compass," "The Theme of the Traitor," and other Borgesian texts play precisely upon the ontological impasse stemming from the postmodern fictionalizing of this world. They take us repeatedly into the same Cartesian cul-de-sac, into the same rational and representational abyss—the deceptive rue Labime—where we have a hard time sorting out the copy and the original, the double and the doubled. In "Tlön," an acknowledgedly fictional world represented in an equally imaginary text "intru[des] . . . into the real world" (Borges 1998, 80). As in Nabokov, we find ourselves at a loss to determine what is real and what is made up, which copies what. We look for a "distance" and the usual ways of measuring it, for the expected, reassuring "signposts" and "milestones," and we find none. Nor does "The Theme of the Traitor" help much. Is literature truly "copying" (Borges 1998, 144) history? Or is it the other way around, as the assassination of Fergus Kilpatrick—which "plagiarizes" (145) *Macbeth* and *Julius Caesar*—seems to imply? As in Nabokov, life plagiarizes texts. Reality comes into being by imitating fiction, repre-

senting that which is supposed to be less "real," derivative ontologically speaking.

Second, yet related to this fictionalizing of reality, to the unmask-
ing of its discursive makeup, Nabokov, Borges, after them Pynchon,
DeLillo, Acker, Leyner, and a number of postmodern critics and theorists more methodically graph—write, chart—an ever-outspreading
textuality. If life and text are ontologically homologous architec-
tures, of the same order, as Nabokov and Borges contend, then life
and text interface, dovetail, are "plugged" into each other. They are
not separated "vertically," into different strata or degrees of existence. Nor are they, as a result, cut off from each other "horizontally," on the social level and *in* the field of social action. This is
another way of saying what this chapter's first half in particular and
Memorious Discourse in general have been saying over and over again:
as memorious enterprise, re-presentation, or textual maneuvering,
the postmodern text works over not only other texts but also social
life itself. The last chapter argues that this remains a way of reading
postmodernism even when at issue is the postmoderns' wrestling
with the "unreadable" itself.

5

Representation, Unreadability, Intertextuality: Reading the Postmodern Sublime

THE UNPRESENTABLE AND THE UNREADABLE

THE PREMISE OF POSTMODERNISM'S REPRESENTATIONAL POLITICS LIES buried in the earlier fictional ontologies of authors like Nabokov and Borges. It is their postmodern heirs who think it through and spell it out, but, as they do so, they must reckon with the adverse pull of modernist tradition in fiction writing, representation more broadly, and criticism. Indeed, Joseph Tabbi observes in *Postmodern Sublime*, "the literary criticism of the past few decades, at least in the United States, has inclined toward partial and minimalist forms; it has afforded little room for the un-ironic, expansive gestures that are traditionally associated with the sublime. Equating master narratives, and total conceptual systems of any kind, with political totalitarianism, literary theorists have never been comfortable with writers who speak directly to power" (1995, ix). Now, the postmodern no longer sees irony and the sublime as mutually exclusive. To paraphrase a French symbolist, postmodernism does not wring irony's neck. In fact, one would be hard put to find an anti-ironic fine print in the new lease on life the category of the sublime gets from postmodernism. If anything, the postmoderns upgrade irony, so much so that when they re-present, à la Funes—when they evoke the other representations intertextually tied into whatever they may invoke—they often do it with an ironic twist.

But irony in postmodernism designates more than the classical figure listed in rhetoric handbooks. It does pertain to language, but—*hence*, the postmoderns would say—it is also a form of cultural critique; pastiche, which Jameson deems *the* postmodern hallmark, is another. Together, they stamp memorious style in literature, advertising, film, or fashion, as well as in the critical conversation around this style inasmuch as this debate does not dwell just upon the stylistics of representation as re-presentation but also upon its politics. Thus, irony and other amphibological, antitotalist "gestures" do not die out in the wake of the sublime's revival in postmodern culture and theory. This happens not simply because postmodernism is an accommodating paradigm—and it is—but because the postmodern retools the sublime, rendering it compatible with the ironic from the standpoint of a certain philosophy of representation. According to this philosophy, the difference between irony as a way of making representation slippery, difficult to pin down, to *read,* and the sublime as a form of bringing forth the unrepresentable and the ungraspable of representation is of degree, not of essence. One witnesses within the postmodern a continuity, or, negative progression, as it were, from the ambiguity and multiple readings of the ironic to the sublime's unrepresentable-unreadable domain. As I have submitted previously and I am reiterating in this chapter, this space allows for open-endedness, multiplicity, heterogeneity, literary and cultural intertextuality, and by the same token for the very condition of representability and readability.

This may also explain why Jameson (*Postmodernism*), Lyotard (*The Postmodern Condition*), and other American and Continental, particularly postmodern and poststructuralist critics interested in issues of representation and reading have turned repeatedly to the sublime.[1] Listening to them, one does get the feeling that the concept is "à la mode" (Nancy 1992, 37), an intellectual symptom of our postmodern age, true imprint of our cultural "now" (*modo*)—although this present is able to paradoxically determine itself as *post*-modern, as "coming after," in the aftermath of its own mode, *mode* (Fr.), and epoch. Otherwise, the fashion of the sublime may speak, indeed, to the "retro" drive of the postmodern, to our recycling urges. This *mode* is venerable, but of late it appears to have become more than a theoretical fad. After Kant, and especially with Kant's late twentieth-century commentators, the sublime has taken on new meanings and prerogatives. Like irony, it constitutes a larger, discursive, philosophical, and cultural problem and, as such, has left its mark on aesthetics, literary theory, and art criticism.[2]

Irrespective of discipline or focus, ongoing disputes over the sublime end up reexamining representability and related topics: presentation and representation, the presentable and the representable, and so forth. I would go even further and offer that issues such as the nature and limits of representation, then, bordering on these limits, the unrepresentable itself are inseparable in postmodernism from perception and comprehension, more specifically, from reading, readability, the readable, and its opposite, the unreadable. We shall see, the unreadable and the "unpresentable" sublime as grasped by contemporary thinkers make up a particular kind of memorious dynamic, which I tackle below by focusing on works by Lacoue-Labarthe, Nancy, de Man, and, again, Lyotard. Last, I go back to DeLillo's fiction and its persevering forays into a similarly sublime, if differently approached, problematic: reading, readability, and the sublimely unreadable cultural text of postmodernity; responding to this expanding textuality, rising "postmodern literacy"; and, attuned to the latter, the evolving structure of the subject, a cardinal concern in *Memorious Discourse.*

Revisiting Kant's *Critique of Judgement,* Lacoue-Labarthe's "Sublime Truth" deconstructs Kantian language with help from Derrida's "white mythology" (Derrida 1972, 72–128). Lacoue-Labarthe focuses primarily upon the figures of Moses and Isis in Kant, where they are charged with conveying the divine word to humankind. Yet all they communicate is God's "unpresentability." For God, Lacoue-Labarthe glosses, does not speak in his own voice. He does not speak at all, actually. His word is passed on indirectly by the inscription (the figures) upon the temple. This is God's "utterance," which also utters God's "nonrepresentation." Thus, either through a prohibition against representation (Do not represent me!) or through a more general "opinion" on the "impossibility" of representation overall (I cannot be represented), God calls himself "unpresentable." What we have here is the canonical definition of the sublime, the sublime as the presentation of the unpresentable, or, à la Lyotard, the sublime as the "presentation" of the fact that there is "something unpresentable." Lacoue-Labarthe's reference to Lyotard's unpresentable goes hand in hand with the whole argument advanced in "Sublime Truth" even though the main references are Heidegger and Heideggerian readings of Hegel and Nietzsche.

The status and limits of presentation are at stake throughout. So Lacoue-Labarthe distinguishes the "presentational" significance of the figure ("graven image") in the biblical context invoked by Kant from the determinant role unveiling plays, through presentation, in the engraving upon the Temple of Isis. He takes his point of departure from Heidegger's reconstruction of the phenomenology of the aesthetic on a nonrepresentational basis in late works such as "The Origin of the Work of Art" and *Nietzsche.* According to the French philosopher, Kant's examination of the beautiful and the sublime is still unable to shake off the vocabulary of "eidetic presentation" or the "imagination," which presumably captures the Idea, being's "eidetic truth." But on a deeper level, Lacoue-Labarthe asserts, Kant anticipates ways of breaking out of the Hegelian "closure of aesthet-

ics." Analyzed by Heidegger himself and traced by some back to
Hegel's "end of art," this closure rests upon a mimetic-representa-
tional understanding of art. As *Memorious Discourse* often reminds
the reader, art's "truth," or, "message" has long been regarded as
adequacy (*homoiosis*) to an external, preexistent, discursively transcendent object, model, or origin. Heidegger parts company with
this tradition by arguing instead that art puts forth a different kind
of truth: "unconcealedness" displaying itself by means of beauty—
phainesthai. As most historians of aesthetics ascertain, with Hegel a
new notion comes to the fore: art's incapacity to represent. But,
again, Lacoue-Labarthe contends that Kant's sublime already breaks
new ground in this direction ("Sublime Truth [Part I]" 1991, 20).
Viewed by Hegel as an accord between form and content, the beautiful "completes" the sublime ("Sublime Truth [Part I]" 1991, 23)
since the latter presupposes an incongruity between form and content, a "nonrepresentation" that precedes yet warrants, we shall observe, the representation performed by the beautiful. The figure of
Michelangelo's Moses, famously interpreted by Freud, epitomizes
the paradoxical status of the sublime, "representative" as it is of the
taboo against representation, or, of the "possibility or impossibility
of art" (Lacoue-Labarthe 1991, 25). As a *figure*, Moses embodies the
aporia underlying the traditional conception of the sublime: the
sublime's "negative presentation" amounts to "the negation of presentation" (26).

Terminologywise, contemporary theory seldom sets presentation
apart from representation, and, as the previous chapter suggests,
they can be used interchangeably. Kant and his recent critics do distinguish presentation from representation, though. Unlike classical
representation, Lacoue-Labarthe's, Nancy's, Derrida's, and other
postmoderns' and poststructuralists' presentation notion has no
mimetic (imitative) relevance, no weight as picture (copy) of a particular material object or metaphysical idea. Conventionally, to represent is to copy, imitate, replicate an existent presence (thing or
fact), and both presentation and representation can copy, imitate,
and reduplicate. Sublime discourse in Lacoue-Labarthe and others
troubles this equivalence to the point that the quasi synonyms become antonyms. We can still call a sublime painting or poem a representation, a sublime representation. But, we are told, we need to
bear in mind that that painting or poem no longer represents or
repeats a prior presence in a common sense. It provides, rather, the
place or opportunity for an "absolute" presentation, like a sentence
in which a transitive verb is used "absolutely," with no direct object
or complement. This is, too, a presentation without object and

whose objective is not to render present, to "presence" something antecedent or external to itself. As Nancy specifies apropos of Hegel, presentation, sublime presentation, to be more precise, is "pure," "nonrepresentational presentation" (1992, 41). With a sublime painting or poem, there occurs a presentation that just presents itself, no referential strings attached.

In Lacoue-Labarthe's deconstructive reading, the Kantian sublime drives a major blow to the doctrine of imitation. But this is hardly the issue. Nor is imitation's demise at the hands of post-Kantian, postromantic modernity. My question here as elsewhere in this book is, rather, Can we still salvage reference from the wreckage of mimesis-as-imitation, of representation narrowly represented? On the face of it, sublime presentation leaves no hope for a positive answer since the aforementioned referential strings have been severed. Yet, as I have been maintaining, this negative response and more generally the negativity of the unpresentable ultimately play a quasi-foundational role, founding, or clearing the way for, representation, providing for the very possibility of referentiality, of a link to something to be represented.

But what kind of link are we talking about in the wake of the anti-imitative onslaught? Lacoue-Labarthe and other poststructuralists tend to seize the unpresentable sublime as an *ad quem*, tell us how it ends (cuts) the referential links so that a meaning of a higher sort can obtain, along with a reading thereof. In writers like DeLillo, the unpresentable sublime is more like an *ab quo*, originless yet originating point sending forth connections of a particular, memorious type. The postmoderns' sublime is not a semiotic cul-de-sac but a stepping stone for re-presentation, a memorious window into further representations. In other words, while critics like Lacoue-Labarthe contend that the sublime "un-presents," that it presents us with the notion that there is, in this or that representation, something representation cannot capture, artists such as DeLillo hint that the buck does not stop with that which in representation informs us of the latter's impasse. In DeLillo and others like him, the postmodern sublime lays the groundwork for the aesthetics of re-presentation as I describe it in *Memorious Discourse*. For, as I maintain throughout the book and as the second half of the chapter will corroborate, representation's traditional, immediately referential or "transitive" moorings have been replaced by relations of a different type, by links to other representations, paintings, or poems, less acknowledged in, say, realism, yet increasingly forefronted in modernism and more programmatically so in postmodernism. Through these links, art relates *to* the world so that it *both relates and relays the world*, launching relations to it always-already of the intermediary order of a relay. It is this logic of relatedness, this paradoxical distance-that-delivers, this memorious distance to, or deferral of, the represented in representation that, as chapter 4 also stresses, brings the represented world closer and dis-closes it to us. A negation of the world and its meaning makes them possible *in effigy*, in and through their originating representation.

Kant does underscore this paradox. Zeroing in on the writing upon the Temple of Isis, Kant's sublime reading leaves behind classical mimesis, art as reflection of some truth; truth be told—by Kant—truth is unpresentable. Further, the unpresentable is unrevealable; and unveiling, representing, speaking (about) truth boil down to un-speaking, un-representing, concealing it. Attempting to unveil, or, decipher writing further veils, enciphers it. Reading the words upon the Temple is fundamentally—"necessarily," Harold Bloom would say, from a different vantage point (1975, 97)—misreading and un-reading, failing to read them. Reading means facing, and "escalating," the unreadable. Thus, I would posit that the reading of the sublime inscription appears as a sublime process itself. In other words, reading constitutes—is, rather, constituted by—its own confrontation with the unreadable. At this crucial point, mimesis turns into its opposite to become Heideggerian "presentification" of truth, no imitation (*Nachahmung*) but *Darstellung* in a non-imitative (non-representational) sense, truth's appearance, its coming into *Unverborgenheit* (unconcealedness). Mimesis now designates truth's self-presentation. Truth reveals itself as re-veiling, sheer play of presentation that institutes the un-veiling of its reference. The revealed secret, the secret of the sublime, is the triumph of presentation over mimetic representation. Presentation is active—it simply *is*—but not (as) an analogon; it "takes place," Nancy concedes in "L'Offrande sublime," yet "it does not *present* anything. Pure presentation, presentation of the presentation itself, or presentation of totality, does not present anything. One could say, of course, using a certain vocabulary, that it presents nothing or *the* [*sic*] nothingness. To use another vocabulary, one could say that it presents the unpresentable" (elle ne *présente* rien. La présentation pure, présentation de la présentation même, ou présentation de la totalité, ne présente rien. On pourra dire sans doute, dans un certain lexique, qu'elle présente rien ou *le* rien. Dans un autre lexique, qu'elle présente l'imprésentable) (1992, 67). The unpresentable is here the unexpected driving force of the sublime, the content of the "sublime offering."

Appearances notwithstanding, this offer is generous, with notable consequences in postmodern discourse. Seemingly, we are hardly offered anything at all, but we get a lot—we get *the whole*. The "offrande" offers and opens that whole up at the same time: "*le tout* est offert" and "ouvert" concurrently (72). This offer/opening up also offers/opens up Funesian cultural memory, the "total recall," memorious representation as re-presentation. Lacoue-Labarthe stresses that the sublime signs upon the wall do not stand for God directly but for God's representation or discourse (his voice), hence they constitute re-presentations, figures one must figure out first when seeking to represent God. Thus, the sublime offer is also a memorious offer. The unpresentable is not an aesthetic and discursive blind alley, but the paradoxical *Grund* and the unlikely prerequisite for the semiotic wealth, the literary-cultural webs and representation networks that this or that representation (text) is intertextually "plugged" into and, visibly or less so, part of. From a readerly viewpoint, this *presents* us with a wide range of possibilities. At odds with the "servitude of representation" that tends to place mimetic (imitative) constraints on discourse production, on the response thereto, and on the experiencing of art more generally, sublime presentation empowers and liberates reception by making it aware of the representational plurality from which individual representations spring and to which they link up. This freedom, the very possibility of reading ultimately, is the positive flip side of the *un*presentable and the *un*readable. Implicit in postmodern theory's "sublime turn" is a particular theory of reading.

This theory becomes explicit in de Man. In his "ethics of reading," discourse as representation and discourse as readable object are at issue, and inseparably so, for reading turns on my ability as a reader to represent to myself and others that which I believe the text represents. I must attempt this critical representation doomed to fail as I am, but this would be a sublime failure, a failure of reading and representation, a failure of reading *as* representation. Here, Lacoue-Labarthe, Nancy, and de Man overlap. In de Man's view, the sole thing reading is able to represent is its own presentation. This means that in failing to enunciate ethical judgements, to represent, to "make language referential" (Miller 1987, 51), reading cannot but "pronounce"—"offer" us—discourse's unreadability. Reading manifests itself as a pure process, solely presenting itself without any irrevocable representational, or, ethical consequence. It just *takes place*. The only staunch truth it is able to proclaim is its own occurrence. In doing so, it "acts out" the carvings upon the Temple of Isis.

Referring to textual truth and the reading supposed to unearth it, de Man quotes in his foreword to Carol Jacobs's *The Dissimulating Harmony* Hölderlin's words, "Es ereignet sich aber das Wahre," freely translated as "What is true is what is bound to take place" (qtd. in Miller 1987, 51). "In the case of the reading of a text," de Man goes on, "what takes place is a necessary understanding. What marks the truth of such an understanding is not some abstract universal but the fact that it has to occur regardless of other considerations" (51). Reading *presents itself*, reading's truth is *Ereignis*, the Heideggerian "event" through which Lacoue-Labarthe defines sublime presentation in the "Sublime Truth" essay's second part (1991–1992, 211–12). Reading is "bound to happen" *eventually*, is, indeed, an *event*, a word that preserves the Latin word for "come" or "arrive." It sur-*venes*. Its gift to us, what it presents us with, is itself. What it gives us is itself only and nothing else beyond, so all we get, in actuality, is its unreadability. We cannot represent the unpresentable. All we can do is witness its "advent," or, sublimity.

In "Phenomenality and Materiality in Kant," de Man addresses the sublime in terms of a phenomenology of reading. Focusing on "the antinomies at play in the mathematical sublime" (1984, 126), he emphasizes Kant's failure to "articulate the number with extension" (127). This unravels Kantian discourse, rendering it a dialectical mess in which the "interplay between apprehension and comprehension in the mathematical sublime" is undercut by a "dramatized scene" that sets up the faculties of reason and the imagination as "personified" and "anthropomorphized" concepts. Therefore, de Man contends, we are not dealing with categories but tropes; Kant's is an "allegorical" tale told under the guise of a "philosophical argument" and so "determined by linguistic structures that are not within the author's control." "Figural language" is the supreme law of philosophic discourse, according to de Man. Rodolphe Gasché has replied that such tropological "disruptions" do not threaten Kant's "philosophical mastering of intraphilosophical problems" (1990, 111). But can Kant, or anybody else for that matter, tackle these problems outside language and its cultural memory, outside the inherited vocabulary of philosophy, outside *any* vocabulary? Can we approach the same issues in Kant, and Kant generally— can we read him?—without recourse to his text and its language? De Man's answer is negative, warranted by the homology of the sublime and reading, of the "resistant" figurality of the sublime and the allegory of reading—the allegory of reading's "impossibility" (1979, 77).

The sublime, then, is the reading object par excellence, or, *metaob-*

ject. For, in reading the sublime we glimpse (read) the profound nature of reading itself. We come, in other words, up against that which ultimately cannot be read (represented) completely because it has not been completely (mimetically) represented in the first place, falling as it does under the jurisdiction of the *unpresentable.* One more time, "sublime reading" plays out, in a fruitful tautology, the reciprocal articulation of the unpresentable and the unreadable. That is, sublime reading as interpretation of texts *about* the sublime poses particular problems to readers. But more broadly, any reading, regardless of its focus, must respond to the challenge of what Hugh J. Silverman calls the "textual sublime," must engage with its object as "textually sublime" (1990, xv). The latter, the critic maintains, can be seen as "the text protecting itself from the actions and attempts at closing it off, clarifying its meanings, reifying its vitality. The textual sublime gives hope to literary criticism because it defies reduction" to "concepts, to ideas, to textual components." On the other hand, "The textual sublime gives purpose to philosophy, for without it philosophy itself would be of diminished interest; without it, philosophy would have only definite descriptions, concrete particulars, and determinate relations. Unlike the beautiful, the sublime is without boundaries" (xii). Grasped rhetorically, as Silverman recommends, the sublime is the prime focus of de Manian reading and of deconstruction generally. Conversely, underpinning the dialectic of *Auffassung* and *Zusammenfassung* in Kant's mathematical sublime is, according to de Man, a phenomenology of reading (1984, 129). The "economy of loss and gain" inherent in the sublime dialogue of the imagination and understanding is allegorized in the syntagmatic/paradigmatic maneuvers of reading, built into the "model of discourse as a tropological system" (130).

This model obtains in de Man's "Hegel on the Sublime" with the same consequences. What *das Erhabene* means, its semantics, is the result of "semic" differences whose "play" overflows the limits philosophical discourse sets to them. This play "deconstructs" from within discourse itself the narrative dialectic this discourse purports to institute (1987, 146). Language is the means by which and the medium or place where the sublime un-presents and un-reads itself, makes it hard for us to represent it. Accordingly, the sublime in Hegel—and largely against the grain of the Hegelian text—"reveals the inadequacy of the Longinian model of the sublime as representation" (148), revokes itself as it appears to evoke, present itself. The sublime is neither a symbol nor an index, and, de Man concludes, the Hegelian discourse aspiring to pin it down falls short because this discourse sets out to "identif[y] what cannot be identified" (1979, 11).

De Man's famous "resistance to theory" is ultimately a theory of unreadability (Rapaport 1990, 139), an account of literature's sublime resistance to "theoretical" closure, "readerly identification," "consistency-building," and so on. By precluding the "determination of meaning," deconstructive reading lays bare its own "excessive" nature, its phobia of limits, textual or ontological, and thereby its postmodern "condition"—its Lyotardian sublimity as discussed previously. De-termination means establishing a term, a terminus. It hedges meaning in, checks its semantic display (dis-play), which "terminates" de facto the process of interpretation no less than the life of literature and its associated institutions. On the contrary, de Man's reading asserts the un-determinative power of the sublime in texts and textual interpretation. His position is, again, not unlike Lyotard's. De Manian reading tells, too, an anti-grand narrative of sorts. For, in answering the question, What is postmodernism?, Lyotard establishes, in slightly different terms, the same correlation between the sublime and the legible as de Man.

Modernity, Lyotard maintains, "cannot exist without a shattering of belief and without discovery of the 'lack of reality' of reality, together with the invention of other realities" (1984, 77). We learned in chapter 4, he describes this lack by turning to Kant's sublime, which category involves a conflict between the subject's capability to "conceive" of something and the capability to "present" it. Further, the sublime takes place "when the imagination fails to present an object which might, if only in principle, come to match a concept" (78). This kind of object is "unpresentable." Modern art strives to "present the fact that the unpresentable exists . . . to make visible that there is something which can be conceived and which can neither be seen nor made visible" (78). Accordingly, modernism brings out the "unpresentable" as discourse's "missing content" while sugarcoating this realization formally. Yet this sublime aesthetic does not induce the true sublime feeling that blends reason and the imagination. It is the postmodern *in the modern* that accomplishes it by putting "forward the unpresentable in presentation itself" and denying "itself the solace of good forms, the consensus of a taste which would make it possible to share collectively the nostalgia for the unattainable" and the "communicable" (82). The postmodern enacts its sublimity through language, which presents itself, by virtue of its figurality, as a presentation of the unpresentable and consequently as a great reading challenge. One can say, therefore, that postmodernism communicates—carries without elucidating—the incommunicable, conveys a de Manian, unformulable ethics, a "moral" or message beyond reception or reading. No consensus of meanings, values, and "communicable" truths or references underwrites readability in de Man's sublime reading model, in Lyotard's postmodern sublime, or, as the remainder of this chapter proposes, in a fiction writer like DeLillo.

What DeLillo presents or communicates is indeed the barrage of the uncommunicable and the unreadable, the ordeal of interpretation and reading in a postmodern space that calls ceaselessly for sense making while confounding, derailing, and defeating it. He portrays everyday life as confrontation with thought-provoking yet overwhelmingly sublime, mind-boggling textuality, with texts, discourses, cultural languages, symbols, and representations that appear immediately available for consumption yet remain mysteriously elusive and unfathomable.. DeLillo shows that this textuality cannot be read, that is, cannot be transcended, assigned a meaning *beyond* it, further, that if we try to do so, we are bound to go wrong, misread, delude ourselves. As I insist in *Memorious Discourse* ever so often, if there is meaning here, it cannot be accessed "vertically" ("archeologically," or, "geologically," as Barthes would say) because we cannot "cut through," we cannot make the classical move of hermeneutics anymore. We cannot read this world's "depth," "semantically." All we can do is attempt it "horizontally," "syntactically," for in this world meaning is not a matter of textual transcendence but same-level relation. Here representations and their meanings are memoriously—inter-textually—tied into other representations and their meanings. Or, these representations and meanings "front" for other images and significations, amazingly diverse, both textual and nontextual yet relentlessly crying out to be perused by us, their readers. In turn, the readers themselves are "read," tested by novel readings. Presented with the sublime text of postmodernity, the consumer-reader must learn the new alphabet of consumer goods, work with the ever-shifting codes of the market, take in the apostate iconography of celebrity culture. Thus, DeLillo registers—critically yet not hopelessly—the birth of a new kind of reading, a new breed of readers, perhaps a new literacy altogether.

SYMBOLIC OVERLOAD: DELILLO, LETHAL READING, AND THE RISE OF POSTMODERN LITERACY

DeLillo lets significance emerge indirectly. The multiple parallels, symmetries, and recursive patterns in [*Mao II*] do not re-

place a disturbing reality with something else (a private
psychology, mythic cultural totality, or some other sublime
image of the writer's own mind and imagination). Rather, and I
think this is crucial to DeLillo's postmodern aesthetic, they enable the author to find the places where language converges with
the real, the *unpresentable*, everything that does not conform to
formal pattern and syntax. (italics mine)

—Joseph Tabbi, *Postmodern Sublime*

—Hypocrite lecteur,—mon semblable,—mon frère!
[Hypocrite reader,—fellowman—brother!]
—Charles Baudelaire, "Au lecteur"

He didn't really think he would have ended among the dead, injured or missing. He was already injured and missing. As for
death, he no longer thought he would see it come from the muzzle of a gun or any other instrument designed to be lethal. . . .
Shot by someone. Not a thief or deer hunter or highway sniper
but some dedicated reader.

—Don DeLillo, *Mao II*

With "older" postmoderns like DeLillo, Pynchon, Barth, Federman,
and Acker, then with the younger generation of Leyner and David
Foster Wallace, textuality, discourse, language, representation and
their networks become inescapably landscape, "natural" milieu and
"reference" for any new texts, stories, and representations. This is
how a particular type of realism emerges under postmodern aus-
pices. I would call this realism memorious, or, better still, sublimely
memorious. For the surrounding signs, images, and idioms stand for
more signs, images, and idioms rather than textually unmediated
"contents," in a world aswarm with forms yet "lacking" reality, as
Lyotard maintains above. The postmodern environment overflows,
according to DeLillo, with texts and signals, with a symbolic glut that
puts our reading skills to test. This is also the test of the postmodern
sublime precisely due to this deceptive overabundance of legibility,
of readable objects calling out to us, a befuddling surplus that turns
before you know it into its opposite, into the illegible, the impossi-
ble-to-read that presents itself while remaining unrepresentable.
Quite unrelentingly, DeLillo has probed this postmodern aporia of
reading, both reading's protocols and their failure. In fact, his fiction can be seized upon as an allegory of reading, a chronicle of our
struggle with postmodernism's sublime textuality.

So, I would ask, How does DeLillo read reading? How does he represent representation making? How does he envisage the private
and public arenas in which we all are readers and cannot but read
the text around us, try to represent it? How does he deal with con-

temporary readership and literacy, with that which our culture judges legible and worth reading? How does he come to grips with postmodernism's legibility, with how and what postmodernism means, with how we read it but also with what reading signifies in postmodernism? The discussion below imparts my suspicion that according to DeLillo, what and how we read in postmodern culture, the meaning of postmodern reading ultimately, bears upon how we read the postmodern itself, upon the very meaning of postmodernism. Meaning making *in* postmodernism, DeLillo intimates, makes the meaning *of* postmodernism, tells us "what to make" of it.

The *Mao II* excerpt sets forth in a nutshell a poignant critique of mass responses to narratives in an age that has integrated "aesthetic production . . . into commodity production" (Jameson 1991, 4). Alongside a host of contemporary writers from, say, Paul Auster to Jonathan Franzen, DeLillo trades upon the predicament of narrative representation, showing how cultural objects in general and stories in particular are in turn represented by the public. The "fate of narrative" in our time, DeLillo suggests, reflects the "clumsy transposition of art into the sphere of consumption" (Horkheimer and Adorno 1982, 135), a displacement that has given rise to a "system of non-culture" (128). However, it is not "high culture"'s "debasement" at the hands of the "culture industry" that he deplores. Culture as a whole, as a collective apparatus of narrative misreading is here taken to account. Yet, we shall see, this misreading is not absolute, a flop without bearings upon how we think of ourselves and our world.

Even though DeLillo's work does not necessarily advocate resistance to *popular* culture, it nonetheless unveils an uncanny resistance to *popularity*. He ranks fame among "mass delusion" phenomena, to recall Horkheimer and Adorno again. Insofar as it requires social performance, popularity is backfiring and treacherous, and creators had better ward it off. For not only has the role of Baudelaire's hypocrite reader grown of late. DeLillo suspects that the consumer of texts has become, strange as it may strike us, somewhat burdensome to authors, a threat. Reading is menacing, foreboding. As I observed earlier in this book, the reader is no longer the "co-author" *Rezeptionsästhetik* posited. The audience, the media, and the publishing houses now make up a whole machinery of voracious consumption, a demonology of domestication, control, and alienation. Ironically enough, striving to preclude this alienation, the author further alienates and isolates himself or herself. More ironically perhaps, this resistance to popularity, which DeLillo himself practiced for a while,[3] the refusal to give interviews, go on late shows, make speeches, and even publish magnifies the remunerative legend of the author, foregrounding the power of cultural systems to contain and exploit artistic dissent.

But DeLillo's consumption imaginary and the cultural critique built into it teach us an important lesson about the memorious production and treatment of the sublime text of postmodernism, of postmodern narrative representation in particular. A sublime formation, this representation is hard to represent, to read in the traditional, "referential" or transcendent sense. Therefore, it is susceptible to misrepresentation, to misreading, so DeLillo's readers fail to read the postmodern sublime interpolating their lives in so many forms. They fail because this text or representation no longer presents us with a content beyond itself, with, again, a transcendent meaning and raison d'être, but with *relations* to other texts and representations. So, oddly enough, where reading flounders it also finds its footing, discovers its stumbling block as part of something bigger, of a larger ensemble of textuality and meaning: this is how the stumbling block becomes, as I say above, a stepping stone, emulating the postmodern text's own re-presentational logic.

After a closer look at *Mao II*'s model of fending off co-optation, I focus on instances of readerly reactions that characteristically falter as they garble, misuse, and abuse stories. In doing so, these misreadings appear to mount a "lethal" menace to cultural texts and their authors alike, eroding our inherited notions of textuality and authorship. As we have learned, the failure of reading in de Man and other theorists of the postmodern sublime was an inevitable concept, almost a necessity. DeLillo is not far from a similar realization. Nor is reading or misreading exclusively textual or literary in his novels. Reading here covers an entire paradigm of cultural metabolism as nontextual narratives can be read, too. Whether as a metaphor of domination through "plotting" and "perusing" of private lives (*Libra, Running Dog*) or as an apparently counterintuitive symbol of opacity, reading is an omnipresent yet flexible master motif in DeLillo. Again, it is the "wrong," "distorting," even "malefic" reading that chiefly concerns him—and will concern us, too, in what follows.

The *Mao II* motto bestows a particular emphasis upon this sort of reading, with novelist Bill Gray's quandary a case in point. A main character in *Mao II*, he vanished from sight after putting out two acclaimed books, and I agree with Joseph Tabbi's suggestion that Gray "would prefer to channel his own life into a wholly textual reality, to disappear, like Pynchon, into his books" (1995, 197). New editions of these volumes, however, as well as his reclusiveness itself have meanwhile enlarged Gray's mythic aura. There have also been rumors about his third book, whose publication he postpones by endless "corrections," like the hero of Thomas Bernhard's 1975 novel, *Korrektur*. Make no mistake: for Gray revision is not a Flaubertian, ever-incomplete, perpetual tinkering with "style." Charlie, Gray's publisher, surmises—and he is right—that Gray keeps "revising" and "rewriting" to put off publication and by the same token the reading, circulation, and assimilation of his work, of himself ultimately. Odd audiences—he received a finger in the mail from a reader!—greedy presses, and prying media assail his privacy, conspiring to turn him into a marketable icon.[4] True, Gray managed to "contain" his most diehard reader's endeavors to bring him back into the open. He pulled, in fact, this reader, Scott, into the black whole of his Pynchonian, quasi-underground existence by making him his "assistant." But Gray cannot withstand Charlie's efforts to coax him into "reappearing."

Gray's "comeback" brings together key themes in DeLillo: the glamour of media iconography and the authorial "appearance" ("publication") its intensely traded images enforce; the public ritual of misreading, of "getting it wrong"; and terror and death, which tie into an intriguing but typical notion of plot. Charlie tries to "upgrade" the novelist's myth by convincing him to read on TV French poems by Jean-Claude, a Swiss writer held hostage by Beirut terrorists. Gray is actually supposed to take Jean-Claude's place eventually, which should whet the public appetite for Gray's forthcoming book. To secure his involvement in this scenario—and so, deliberately or not, entangle him in a story leading up to Gray's death—Charlie suggests that Brita, a famous photographer, take Gray's picture. At first, the writer resents the idea but eventually gives in

> not because he wanted to come out of hiding but because he wanted to hide more deeply, he wanted to revise the terms of his seclusion, he needed the crisis of exposure to give him a powerful reason to intensify his concealment. Years ago there were stories that Bill was dead, Bill was in Manitoba, Bill was living under another name, Bill would never write another word. These were the world's oldest stories and they were not about Bill so much as people's need to make mysteries and legends. Now Bill was devising his own cycle of death and resurgence. . . . Bill's picture was a death notice. His image hadn't become public yet and he was already gone. This was the crucial turn he needed in order to disappear completely. . . . The picture would be a means of transformation. It would show him how he looked to the world and give him a fixed point from which to depart. Pictures with our likeness make us choose. We travel into or away from our photographs. (1991, 140–41)

Gray means to evaporate in the unpresentable sublime of his deceptively representational image. He acquiesces to a mode of appearance or public presentation prone, he figures, to un-present him, to reintroduce him to the world *apparently* while *de facto* writing his obituary, a visual farewell note to the domain of the visible and its hungry gaze. Scott realizes that Gray employs the photographs "as a kind of simulated death" (140). "Mao," Scott reminds us, "used photographs to announce his return and demonstrate his vitality, to reinspire revolution" (141). Gray, as a "second Mao," resorts to the Chinese leader's ploy only to effect the contrary: a complete "self-erasure." If Gray's myth has been paradoxically reinforced by his photo's absence from newspapers and catalogues, the hundreds of photographs Brita shoots might "hide" him completely, mark his irreversible disappearance and thus finally protect him. Gray hopes that absolute exposure, the Lacanian-Baudrillardian paroxysm of visibility—the author's iconic, sublimely fallacious hyperpresence—might provide the perfect hideaway of un-presentation. A textual embodiment of Gray's innermost self, the still unpublished story is thus ideally camouflaged in its author's photographic disclosure. As Scott owns, "the book disappears into the image of the writer" (71), indefinitely putting off its reading, its—and its author's—death in alien hands. In his excellent book on DeLillo, David Cowart quotes from a letter DeLillo's most talented follower, Jonathan Franzen, received from the master and where DeLillo addresses specifically the connection between public textual consumption and the authorial identity ensconced in the consumed text. "If serious reading dwindles to near nothingness," DeLillo states in that letter, "it will probably mean that the thing we're talking about when we use the word 'identity' has reached an end" (qtd. in Cowart 2002, 126). In this sense, Tabbi (1995, 194–207) and Cowart (2002, 114–19) are right to devote whole chapters to the "death of the author" in *Mao II*.

The photographed crowds attest to the private subject's "swallowing" by his or her sublime picture. They set off the herd instinct-driven, mechanical "body common" (DeLillo 1991, 77) whose "millennial hysteria" heralds the twilight of the private ego, now "immunized against the language of the self" (8). The mass images featured in tabloids or on TV speak to a tragic immolation of the individual. From its dust jacket, which displays twenty-four "photo-paintings" of Andy Warhol's *Mao* series, to the large images of Chinese and Iranian crowds throughout the book, DeLillo's novel obsessively zeroes in on masses. Hecatombs of privacy, these cannot offer Gray a solution. Spellbound by official effigies of power such as Mao's portraits, hooked on images and indiscriminate consumption, crowds are what the writer flees. On the other hand, the attempted retreat through photographic self-giveaway into the safe heaven of un-presentation, of paradoxical invisibility, sets off memorious relatedness, plugs the writer back into the world, its stories, and images. "Nothing" escalates, "snowballs," and leads to more, then to surplus, to narrative and representational excess, at last, to too much, to the unbearable. Allowing his picture to be taken, Gray steps into the tragic universe of plot, precipitates the plotting of his own death. As Hemingway says in *Death in the Afternoon*, all stories, if followed far enough, end sadly. A self-declared Hemingway fan, De-Lillo carries this insight through. In the process, he outdoes his model, as in *White Noise*, *Libra*, and *The Names*, where the intertextual dialogue with Hemingway is even more conspicuous—incidentally, not only does *The Names* play out the death-bound plot motif, but it also "rewrites" *The Sun Also Rises*'s American expatriate story as transnational corporate narrative.

Struggling to avoid beheading on the scaffold of the "market," Gray, too, takes a fatal, downward—"deathward," as DeLillo writes in *Libra* (221, 363)—path, of which he is not unaware:

> Something about the occasion [Gray tells Brita] makes me think I'm at my own wake. Sitting for a picture is morbid business. A portrait doesn't begin to mean anything until the subject is dead. This is the whole point. . . . The deeper I pass into death, the more powerful my picture becomes. Isn't this why picture-taking is so ceremonial? It's like a wake. And I'm the actor made up for the laying-out. . . . It struck me just last night these pictures are the announcement of my dying. (DeLillo 1991, 42–43)

Gray's analysis of Brita's snapshots reaches even deeper. It points out the destructive meaning of "photographic execution," which critics like Barthes (1981, 6) and Susan Sontag (1990, 64) have discussed with particular acumen. "Everything around us," Gray contends, "tends to channel our lives toward some final reality in print or on film" (DeLillo 1991, 43). We count only as virtual narratives, as "materials" for stories—"I've become someone's material.[5] Yours, Brita," Gray avows. We are not subjects anymore, but "subject matter" awaiting its "heightened version": the cover story the crowds so eagerly devour. In DeLillo's Baudrillardian universe "nothing happens until it's consumed. . . . Nature has given way to aura. A man cuts himself shaving and someone is signed up to write the biography of the cut. All the material in every life is channeled into the glow" (44). The spectacular narrative "double" gains the upper hand over the "original" beings or facts because the original is already narrative, discursive. In consequence, and in striking accord with the self-referential logic of the media so cogently laid bare by critics from McLuhan to Baudrillard, there are no facts in this representational inferno, but merely *events*: narratable, newsworthy, "storybound" and hence readingbound occurrences. The Swiss hostage's release in Beirut is memoriously "tied to the public announcement of his freedom. You can't have the first without the second" (129). Vampirized and literally consumed by its mediatic double, life has been converted into, ingested, and abolished by "the consumer event" (43). The latter symbolically feeds on the flesh of its subject while apparently "promoting" it by concocting and spreading its "story."

Fictive or less so, stories are ominous for they expose their subject—in *Mao II*, the authorial self—to *consuming*, "viral" publicity. Failing to hide out in the negative of his portraits, Gray gets "developed," exposed, woven into a "plot." As it "develops" itself, this plot inches the writer closer to death, rehearsing the thanatic narratology upon which a book like *Libra* particularly dwells. Photographic and narrative exposure in the media brings about a lethal "unveiling" that reading will follow out and complete. DeLillo deals with this whole process in terms that recall Robert Escarpit's etymological speculations on the "act of publication" as "brutal exposure" and subsequent "willful violence" done to authors and their work (1971, 45–46). No wonder, a character in DeLillo's *Ratner's Star* says, "the friction of an audience . . . drives writers crazy" (1980, 411). Fearing the "violence of reading," Gray has joined that "class of writers who don't want their books be read," "express[ing]" in their works "the violence of [their] desire not to be read" (DeLillo 1980, 410). As Scott tells Brita, "for Bill, the only thing worse than writing is publishing. When the book comes out. When people buy it and read it. He feels totally and horribly exposed. They are taking the book home and turning pages. They are reading the actual words" (DeLillo 1991, 53). Like E. L. Doctorow's narrator in *The Book of Daniel*, Gray dreads "the monstrous reader who goes on from one word to the next" (Doctorow 1971, 246).

The tabloid pseudoexposé or the newsreels' "eventful story" is the genre that builds up the expectations of the "monstrous reader." Only very few writers can fight the "horizon of expectations" fostered by this sensationalist narrative. As George, another intermediary between Gray and the terrorists, claims, "Beckett is the last writer to shape the way we think and see. After him, the major work involves midair explosions and crumbled buildings. This is the new tragic narrative" (DeLillo 1991, 157). Beckett designates the creator opposing cultural co-optation. At the end of a reading De-Lillo gave on the Duke University campus in April 2002, I asked him about Beckett's role in *Mao II*, and he confirmed my suspicion. The Irish author was, DeLillo told us, among the last to have created a universe, "Beckett's world," in which Beckettian readers could be said to "live." *Mao II* suggests that in the post-Beckett era it is the other way around, rather. No matter how original and talented, writers are more or less pulled into the weblike world of their readers, have to live in the space containing, flattening out, and misreading theirs. Indeed, after Beckett, "the artist is absorbed, the madman in the street is absorbed and processed and incorporated" by the coins got in the street or by the TV commercial featuring him (157). Only the terrorist remains "outside," for "the culture hasn't figured out how to assimilate him." And, surprisingly or not, the novelist is the only one who sees that terrorism, the rhetoric of absolute "eventfulness," speaks "precisely the language of being noticed, the only language the West understands" (157). The "outside" may have "disappeared," as postmoderns from Pynchon to Andrei Codrescu (in his 1989 book *The Disappearance of the Outside*) to DeLillo himself contend. Still, DeLillo also implies, the writer, the novelist in particular, may be capable of "wielding," *inside* the postmodern Babel and against its often mind-numbing static, a "defamiliarizing," attention-grabbing, *critical* language that "commandeers" the surrounding idioms, speaks them only to expose their entrails, workings, interconnectedness, automatisms, and power over us. This is, I think, what DeLillo ultimately urges and tries to practice: postmodern—memorious—resistance against postmodernism itself, against a certain dark side of postmodern culture, to be more precise.

In various forms, the sociocultural incorporation theme lies at the core of DeLillo's prose, in earlier novels such as *Great Jones Street, End Zone, Running Dog,* and *Ratner's Star,* as well as in later, celebrated texts like *White Noise, Libra, Underworld,* and *Cosmopolis.* In *Great Jones Street,* for instance, the art market is the dominant focus. It literally haunts writers' imagination, casting a spell on their lives. In this respect, Fenig (see German *Pfennig*, "penny"), a "two-time Laszlo Piatakoff Murder Mystery Award nominee," is an emblematic character. Introducing himself to rock-star Bucky Wunderlick, he fancies a whole market mythology:

> I'm in my middle years but I'm going stronger than ever. I've been an-thologized in hard cover, paperback and goddamn vellum. I know the writer's market like few people know it. The market is a strange thing,

almost a living organism. It changes, it palpitates, it grows, it excretes, it
sucks things and then spews them up. It's a living wheel that turns and
crackles. The market accepts and rejects. It loves and kills. . . . The market's out there spinning like a big wheel, full of lights and colors and
aromas. It's not waiting for me. It doesn't care about me. It ingests
human arms and legs and it excretes vulture pus. (27)

Cultural consumption tropes such as the author's physical immolation and ingestion abound in DeLillo. Here, the corporeal metaphors of predation and digestion uncover the market's bestial body,
whose metabolism, as with *Underworld's* and *Ratner's Star's* waste, re-
fuse, and feces fixations, sets forth a strangely scatological economy
(324). Fenig suspects that he has lately ignored what Charlie calls in
Mao II the "launching power of our mass-market capabilities" (127).
In fact, Fenig sees himself a victim of the predatory "big wheel." Unable to sell his new "brand of porno kid fiction" despite its "Aristotelian substratum" and the "lowest instincts" the genre caters to
(DeLillo 1973, 49–50), he turns to "fantastic terminal fiction"
(222). Significantly, at this point he comes to fathom the importance of his "privacy" (222), realizes that he has been "used" by the
"market,"[6] dehumanized, and dragged toward "fascism." "I failed
at pornography," he explains, "because it put me in a position
where I the writer was being manipulated by what I wrote. This is
the essence of living in P[orn]-ville," he goes on, "[it] makes people
easy to manipulate. . . . I the writer was probably more aware of this
than whoever the potential reader might be because I could feel the
changes in me, the hardening of mechanisms, the subservience to
lust-making and lust-awakening. . . . Every pornographic work brings
us closer to fascism. It reduces the human element. It encourages
antlike response" (223–24).

Deficient listening, viewing, and reading torment DeLillo's writers
and artists. Wunderlick struggles to escape, in his own words, the
reaction of "the crowd's passion and wrath," the "immense . . . pressure of their response . . . blasting in with the force of a natural disaster" (14–15). Similarly to Gray, he no longer agrees to "sell," to
perform, record, give interviews, or make public appearances that
would end up bolstering his charisma. Remarkably enough, his manager does not ask him to play but solely "appear" (198), invariably
a symbolic ritual in DeLillo. Wunderlick's "silence strike" is another
form of artistic rebellion corporate giants such as Transparanoia or
Happy Valley Farm Commune seek to rein in. Like the publishing
house in *Mao II*, they want him just to be seen, show up, and thus
acknowledge—respond to, as much as perpetuate—the "need to be

illiterate in the land of the self-erasing word" (139). Yet, speaking the "self-erasing" language of postmodernity, speaking *to* this language, to the un-presentable sublime embedded in postmodernism's cultural discourse, this illiteracy is more complex a "response" than it may seem to Wunderlick. Besides, at the Duke reading DeLillo made it clear that his characters' beliefs do not necessarily reflect his own.

At first glance, this complexity, more exactly, the prospect of a new literacy, of worthwhile ways of handling the text of postmodernism, is hard to document. Bungled reading and reading of trite materials seem without hope. Unable to rise up to the challenge of that which may defy deeply seated routines, of that which may resist us and decline to present to us as a "meaningful" and recognizable object, the quagmire of literacy in hypermediatized, market-oriented systems haunts DeLillo and fuels his critique. A "digital" temple of contemporary society (Ruthrof 1990, 195–96; O'Donnell 1992, 181), the supermarket simultaneously spawns and bares in *White Noise* a new, "postcultural" *docta ignorantia.* Life in media-saturated "consumerized space(s)" (Elizabeth Wilson 1995, 146) encourages regression toward a new form of "brilliant" ignorance. "[T]here are full professors in this place who read nothing but cereal boxes," *White Noise*'s Murray Jay Siskind tells Gladney, chairman of the "Hitler studies" department at the midwestern College-on-the-Hill (1986, 10). To be sure, not all consumers ought to be devout readers. Nonetheless, *White Noise* insists precisely on reading as consumption, on readers increasingly "originated" by surrounding textuality and reacting *as* consumers, perusing more and more solely what they literally consume for survival or leisure. The sublimely "unspeakable" intertextual supermarket is both consumer goods emporium and library where shopping and reading overlap. It is, more to the point, the place where the former profoundly subsumes the latter. The memorious store marks out the *readable locus* of our time, the seemingly "easy-to-read" ("reader-friendly") "catalogue"-domain in which, perusing smartly packaged goods, customers/readers shop for elusive meanings. As Siskind observes, in the supermarket

everything is concealed in symbolism, hidden by veils of mystery and layers of cultural material. But it is psychic data, absolutely. . . . All the letters and numbers are here, all the colors of the spectrum, all the voices and sounds, all the code words and ceremonial phrases. It is just a question of deciphering, rearranging, peeling off the layers of unspeakability. Not that we want to, not that any useful purpose would be served. (37–38)

Much as it may try to speak the unspeakable, reading does not manage to call forth the meaning of this or that "text." The supermarket is not necessarily meaningless, but it does not "unveil" meaning. In fact, it blocks it out. The interpretation attempted here leaves us *this side* of understanding. The mystical, pseudo-Kabbalistic reading of sorts Siskind describes models "Eating and Drinking," the "Basic Parameters" (171). Knowledge, expertise, and literacy have lost their original, transcendent sense and object, and cannot but refocus on the superficial, or, we shall see, *sur*facial world of consumption. Genres, practices, and fields traditionally peripheral in the economy of scholarly discourse reach unprecedented curricular status. What is more, teaching in a media-shaped world has become teaching *of* the media. As in Pynchon, the means have swallowed up the ends and are now setting themselves up as their own *telos*, as thriving "coupon analysis" (DeLillo 1980, 344), "car crashing," "Elvis," and "Hitler studies" programs at the College-on-the-Hill prove. People peruse candy wraps and religiously watch food commercials between reports on natural disasters and massacres. A wholly new, and unholy, blatantly secular philology is growing from the study of "package narratives." *White Noise* is undeniably DeLillo's most critical account of literacy in a marketplace-dominated "postliterate" age (Jameson 1991, 17). As John Frow writes, "the supermarket is the privileged place for a phenomenology of surfaces" (1990, 427), which throws the consumers-readers in a glowing, alienating "labyrinth" (Pireddu 1992, 140). Here, they face their own consumption, a curious disappearance not beneath surfaces, for there is no beneath or beyond anymore, but *on* them, which makes the consumer and the consumed switch roles. The mall and the media are structurally alike. "Full of psychic data" (DeLillo 1986, 37), the former demarcates the locus of the ultimate "event": consumers' metamorphosis into mediatic objects, their insertion into the commercial narrative as self-aware "products," "exposed" and "featured" on the same glittering surfaces. "My family,"[7] Gladney notices while on a shopping spree, "gloried in the event. . . . I kept seeing myself unexpectedly in some reflecting surface. . . . Brightness settled around me. . . . Our images appeared on mirrored columns, in glassware and chrome, on TV monitors in security rooms" (84). Conversely, he registers the weird humanization of the goods for sale, which look "self-conscious," "carefully observed, like four-color fruit in a guide to photography" (170).

The image-becoming of the subject shapes the life of the academic exiles in *White Noise*'s college town Blacksmith. It "reveal[s] precisely the epistemological crisis that affects contemporary reality" (Pireddu 1992, 129) once the opposition between commodities and customers, media narratives and the readers thereof is suspended. And because these distinctions have been abolished, the crisis is not just epistemological, but also ontological, and perhaps primarily so. It is the copy that underwrites, while engendering, reality. À la Baudrillard, the duplicate predates—in all senses—its model, enjoys a socially higher significance. Babette, for instance, becomes suddenly interesting for her family when they see her on TV, her body turned into an image, "second-order information" (King 1991, 72). Unlike Gray in *Mao II*, Babette must make a "detour" through mediatic representation to become "visible," for her children and friends react to information "rather than to entities" (LeClair 1987, 209). As delusive as in *Mao II*, the rhetoric of appearance is spellbinding because people live in a culture of spectacular narratives. Gladney, for example, puts his dark glasses on "automatically" when entering the campus (DeLillo 1986, 211). Similarly to Siskind's Elvis cultural studies project, he treats Hitler like a star. Gladney's "postmodern attitude toward history as a kind of museum" or "supermarket of human possibilities, where people are free to shop for their values and identities" (Cantor 1991, 41) approaches Hitler as a paragon of *appearance*. In his courses, Gladney deals with the Führer as a celebrity (Conroy 1994, 107–8), drawing upon superficial, anecdotal details of his biography. Grounded in specific (mis)readings of people, events, and texts as they are, teaching and research represent another case of aborted cultural response. Intriguingly enough, Babette herself teaches modes of "appearing." Her odd course in "posture" covers a peculiar kind of "inscribing practice" (Hayles 1993b, 156). Unsurprisingly, it is the media that control this practice: people learn to "appear," to assume different postures, to take on various positions and, implicitly, sociocultural "positionalities" from TV, the archmodel of appearance. Their bodies are gravely affected by, if not turn into effects of, television.[8]

Teaching and learning, reading, watching, discussion, and other forms of knowledge acquisition and intellectual exchange take place—and go amiss—inside the circular universe of superficiality undergirded by the autotelic logic of media narratives. Babette ritually reads out pornographic literature to her husband—an echo of *Running Dog*—and tabloid stories to her evening class of blind people. According to Ben Agger, such a "passive" reading denotes the "degradation of signification" (1989, 6–8) in "fast capitalism," where "books become things provoking their thoughtless readings as things become books" (5). One witnesses here the all-pervasive "narrativization" of the world, which people treat as a legible story. They do not read literature, Agger argues, but "different things— television, popular magazines, money" (75–76). For sure, reading and its objects, the entire readability realm have changed. Postmodernism is straddling the textual/nontextual division, for better or worse. Babette cannot help but peruse "the wrong things" (76). Overall, she prefers to pore over advertisements for "diet sunglasses," cover stories strangely entitled "Life After Death Guaranteed with Bonus Coupons," or accounts of "country's leading psychics and their predictions for the coming year." These are the new heroic sagas insofar as they fit, for a fleeting moment, the pattern of the "eventful" story: UFOs invading Disney World, "dead living legend John Wayne . . . telepathically" helping President Reagan "frame U.S. foreign policy," and superkillers surrendering "on live TV" (DeLillo 1986, 146). These are stories run by the media, but also stories *on* the media and entertainment industry, and thereby part of the same self-referential tactic that turns communication instruments into information to be communicated. Furthermore, tabloid stories' omnipresence may indicate "the current fate of several traditional forms of cultural transmission" (Conroy 1994, 97). "Master narratives," whether "discursive" or "scriptive," no longer provide the only readings. The "iconographic" (107) usually accompanies narrative information, catches the reader's eye, more often than not replacing reading with a sort of "blind" gaze lingering on the skin of things, on shapes and colors.

For one thing, these readings tend to disregard customarily readable objects, turning to uncanonical, offbeat, or paltry stuff instead. For another, reading itself changes, becomes mere repetition, mechanical recital of texts. It does not involve actual comprehension anymore although understanding remains its aim. Moreover, it carries negative overtones, is looked upon with suspicion and used as a metaphor signifying manipulation, political control, and intrusion. It is noteworthy, in this view, that Gladney's "first and fourth" wife, while working "part-time as a spy," reviews "fiction for the CIA, mainly long serious novels with coded structures" (DeLillo 1986, 213). The "reading" she performs does not differ fundamentally from what Selvy, a secret agent in *Running Dog*, does. He is a "reader," too (DeLillo 1978, 54)—he "reads," that is, surveils Senator Percival (28); when Selvy gets a new, "temporary assignment," he also receives copious "reading matter" (156). CIA "readers" in

Running Dog and *Libra* can even use Kafkian-looking "reading machines," which scan people's most intimate stories, translate their private meanings into "readable" graphics.

The reading habits of DeLillo's characters ultimately point to a postmodern crisis of literacy.[9] But the author addresses this crisis by postmodern means, by typically postmodern languages, techniques, and themes. There is no nostalgia in his work for the romantic myth of authorship, nor for the more recent Beckettian model for that matter. Also, DeLillo scarcely laments the post–World War II vanishing of modernism's "Great Divide," which, according to critics like Andreas Huyssen, used to set apart high art and mass culture in modernism. In *White Noise, Mao II, Underworld, Cosmopolis,* and elsewhere, he rather targets an expanding consumption mode that loses sight of the differences among distinct, albeit interrelated, readable domains. His work carries out a critique of contemporary reading customs and literacy. This critique stresses the importance of differentiated, pertinent reading practices likely to acknowledge the defining features of various types of texts. In other words, DeLillo works out, from within postmodernism itself, a critical analysis of styles and scenarios of public absorption that threaten to cancel out postmodernism's emphasis on "local," fine-tuned responses and forms of representation, production, and reception. It is the social disregard for such a contextual, nuanced treatment of readable objects, to wit, the postmodern failure to foster reading modalities attuned to its own writing modes that has brought about this crisis. More significantly still, in view of the present discussion, DeLillo takes up a sublime position by pointing to the "transcendental fallacy" of any reading searching for meanings "beyond" the readable. Time and again, he hints that this sort of response to the text of postmodernity is bound to fail, to yield false results or "presentations." This text, he implies, must be grasped on its own terms, by taking into account its memorious structure, in which, as I have been arguing, concern with relations among signs, symbols, and representations replaces the classical age's metaphysical fascination with what might lie past or before them.

DeLillo also pinpoints the postmodern asymmetry and political "lag" between "resisting" cultural production and co-optating, "disciplined" and "disciplinating," "consumptive" reading. Postmodern writers are still awaiting for their postmodern readers—for postmodern culture at large—to catch up, one could say, but the situation may be more serious than we think. Most of DeLillo's fictional readers are "intelligent and literate" yet somewhat "deprived of the deeper codes and messages that mark [our] species as unique." Even if they "turn against the medium" (1986, 50) and reject the "mystical" experience of TV-watching, they cannot completely sidestep "lethal" exposure, the "contamination" of minds and bodies. There is hardly any difference, certain characters come to realize, between broadcast "events" and the "toxic airborne event," between news updates and Blacksmith's environmental catastrophe.

The whole apparatus of mechanical reading, of false appropriation of images, texts, and other legible objects is even more meticulously decomposed in *Libra*. While it is always highly relevant what and how DeLillo's people read, Lee H. Oswald's readings deserve particular scrutiny. They exemplify that type of misreading that highlights and worsens the character's fallacious perception and self-perception. One could argue that his readings bear the responsibility for his acts, that Oswald has *misread* himself into the "lone gunman" story. He has furnished the ideal materials for "his own fabrication in the name of a given desired effect" (Michael 1994, 151) envisaged by the real plotters. Win Everett actually "understands that there is no difference between the scripted Oswald and the 'real thing'" (Mott 1994, 139), or, in Frank Lentricchia's words, between the "assassin as writer" (1990, 447) and the assassin *written* by Everett. Everett "reads," and then takes advantage of, Oswald's misreadings, which prove self-misreadings since the texts Oswald has "perused" give him a false image of himself. "My boy Lee loves to read," Lee's mother says (DeLillo 1989, 107). "Reading Marx as a teenager," Lentricchia maintains, "altered [Oswald's] room, charged it with meaning, propelled him into a history shaped by imagination" (1990, 447). Marx and Engels, Trotsky, George Orwell's *1984*, H. G. Wells, and military manuals have profoundly self-alienating effects. It is not that he becomes a "victim" of "revolutionary," "anarchistic," or "utopian" literature. Whatever he reads, he reads "wrong," "following the text with his index finger, word by word by word" (DeLillo 1989, 49). He falls prey to "affective" or "factual" fallacies—varieties of the "transcendental" error mentioned above—while "struggling" to grasp difficult texts—and failing:

> The books were struggles. He had to fight to make some elementary sense of what he read. But the books had come out of struggle. They had been struggles to write, struggles to live. It seemed fitting to Lee that the texts were often masses of dense theory, unyielding. The tougher the books, the more firmly he fixed a distance between himself and others.

He found enough that he could understand. He could see the capital-
ists, he could see the masses. They were right here, all around him, every
day. (34–35)

"Forbidden," "hard to read" books bring out, erroneously, "the
drabness of [Oswald's] surroundings, his own shabby clothes were
explained and transformed by these books. He saw himself as part
of something vast and sweeping" (41), performing "night missions
that required intelligence and stealth" (37). This is another instance of misreading by which Oswald manufactures himself a heroic, fantasmatic identity. He gradually becomes his own narrative
project, "plots" himself, and therefore stages, as we may expect in
DeLillo, his own death. Like *Running Dog*'s "project" or *White Noise*'s
and *Mao II*'s obsession with "deathward" plots (1986, 26, 199; 1991,
200), Oswald's misreadings and overreadings lay the first stone for
the actual plotters' "extending the fiction into the world" (DeLillo
1989, 50). These readings supply Everett with essential narrative material, with the "pocket litter" (50) needed to put Oswald together
credibly as the lone gunman and thus cast him in a plausible "production" à la Nabokov's "Assistant Producer," in a "realistic-looking
thing" (DeLillo 1989, 119). *The Communist Manifesto* and similar
pieces get woven into the plotters' strategy of narrative "make-
believe," a term Everett actually uses. Oswald is simply another
"character in the plot" (DeLillo 1989, 78), the reader made, by his
own readings and his cunning "readers" alike, into a character of a
literally homicidal story. Oswald unknowingly helps his readers write
him, *script* and in-scribe him and his readings into a deadly text, a
textual *crypt*.

An intertextual creature, Oswald is equally *real*, however, and this
is one of DeLillo's main points. "Constructed" he may be, by others
and by himself, read, self-read ("self-taught"), and written into a
certain cultural and political position. But exactly due to this dynamic of fashioning and self-fashioning, Oswald is part of history, a
text in a textual series and chapter of a broader narrative the writing
or rewriting of which he makes possible. "Unoriginal" and originating in fiction, scripted by other readers and writers out of paper
scraps—another *être de papier*—he proves nevertheless real. On the
other hand, the simulated realism of writing-as-plotting forestalls
any real explanation, any accurate account ("reading") of what hap-
pened in Dallas on November 22, 1963. Nicholas Branch, "a retired
senior analyst of the Central Intelligence Agency, hired on contract
to write the secret history of the assassination of President Kennedy"
(15), must deal precisely with this sort of writing if he wants to compose the "real story."

Branch is another writer-in-the-text, a fictive narrator that duplicates *en abyme* the figure of the postmodern author. Presupposed by
the writing of his story, the understanding (reading) of the assassination takes an enormous amount of reading. Before narrating his
own version of the Dallas "event," Branch has to go through the
"historical record," to recall the "author's note" on *Libra*'s last
page. Branch is overwhelmed by information, both real and bogus,
provided by the Agency to help him put together a "history [that
maybe] no one will read" (60). This (hi)story, Branch thinks, "is the
megaton novel James Joyce would have written if he'd moved to
Iowa City and lived to be a hundred," the "Joycean Book of
America . . . , the novel in which nothing is left out" (181–82). The
memorious scope, the indefinite "branching off" of Branch's story,
its failure to "furnish factual answers" (see again the mentioned
"author's note") are inscribed in his readings for the latter supply
him with entropic information whose excess obliterates the real data
that may have yielded a coherent story or explanation. The abundance of narratives, records, reports, and testimonies memoriously
overlapping and dovetailing with each other blacken out the
"facts." Meaning becomes the victim of information. The signified
perishes, vanishes—"slides," Lacan would say—under the signifier.
Too many readings undermine reading, render texts illegible, turn
sense into nonsense. The "revelatory" story outgrows itself and gets
more and more complicated, winding up in the swamp of language
and textuality:

> Everything is here. Baptismal records, report cards, postcards, divorce
> petitions, canceled checks, daily timesheets, tax returns, property lists,
> postoperative x-rays, photos of knotted string, thousands of pages of tes-
> timony, of voices droning in hearing rooms in old courthouse buildings,
> an incredible haul of human utterance. It lies so flat on the page, hangs
> so still in the lazy air, lost to syntax and other arrangement, that it resem-
> bles a kind of mind-spatter, a poetry of lives muddied and dripping in
> language. (181)

Endless, sterile poring over unextinguished, "censored," or spuri-
ous materials speaks to the same "superficial" phenomenology at
play in *White Noise* and elsewhere in DeLillo. Despite or, better yet,
because of the amount of readings, Branch gets stuck on the surface
of things, a prisoner in the huge narrative storehouse. Significantly,
the novel does not present him in the act of story-writing or storytelling, but as a custodian of the textual archive, of available files, photographs, and books, a librarian lost in *Libra*'s Borgesian library. An

extreme case in DeLillo's inquiry into narrative consumption, Branch is another consumer of texts, an author unable to move beyond the "research" stage of his unreadable readings. The story he is assigned to write—ever incomplete, never revelatory—just adds another chapter to the "Dallas narrative," makes him an instrument of an expanding, fundamentally opaque text. We may expect Branch to "disappear" à la Gray, "digested" by his own project while trying to absorb all the stuff he is getting, in hopes that he will tell his own story, present his own findings someday. He stands no chance of becoming a true author, though, for he will not finish his readings. Dumbfounded by so much writing, so many reports, accounts, and presentations, he will never get to turn in his own presentation: what seems to be too present, or, omnipresent, is in this case just the unpresentable's flip side.

With Branch, DeLillo's drama of authorship and reception has come full circle. But we need to remember that DeLillo refuses to identify with his characters even when he makes them artists and writers. They are hardly the authorial mouthpieces one might expect. They help him, instead, drive home a point, raise an issue. In this case, Gray, Branch, and others like them are symptoms, and casualties, of a cultural shift. To be more precise, they illustrate the representational syndrome of postmodernism, the postmodern drama of meaning production (writing) and meaning making (reading), a "sublime" drama that, in keeping with its own innermost logic, postmodernism stages and critiques at the same time. Held captive in the sublimely "excessive" postmodern library, Branch will not stop reading, as I remark above. He will never get under control, in a stable representation, the symbolic overload he has been fed, because he is doing it all wrong. In this regard, he is not unlike Oswald. But DeLillo is, or becomes so, rather, through his memorious narrative. That is, *Libra* shows how meaning—the answer to the question, Who killed President Kennedy?—does not inhere in the reference of a certain "revelatory" note, report, photo, or phone conversation to a particular fact or person but in how a range of texts and their meanings interrelate, come together, conspire to make up a network of agendas, motives, and interests, and thus afford a memorious possibility of reading the "Dallas event": the possibility of conspiracy.

Epilogue: Authors in Debt: Credit Lines in the Global Economy of Representation

> En quoi l'autorité et la dette sont-elles inséparable? L'autorité
> ... signifie un crédit.
> [To what extent are authority and debt inseparable? Authority
> implies a credit.]
>
> —Jean-Michel Rabaté, *James Joyce*

STITCHING TIME AND SPACE TOGETHER

> Stories stitch time and space together and give them structure.
> —Lee Siegel, *City of Dreadful Night*

"Nabokov Son Files Suit To Block a Retold *Lolita*," reads an October 1998 *New York Times* headline. The newspaper apprises us of the controversy around the scheduled release of the English translation of Pia Pera's *Lo's Diary*. In 1995, when the Italian "original" came out, it immediately struck its readers as an overt reprise of *Lolita*. As the article's author observes, Pera follows in the footsteps of the age-old tradition of writing as appropriation of extant writings—the tradition of memorious writing: "[L]ong before Shakespeare, writers appropriated each other's historical themes, plots and characters, refashioning them into new works" (Blumenthal 1998a, 9). All the same, the anticipated publication of a retelling of Nabokov's famous 1955 novel "from the nymphet's point of view" (Blumenthal 1998b, 7) set off a "legal battle over copyright infringement and the limits of artistic borrowing" (Blumenthal 1998a, 9). Despite Pera's claim that hers was a "transformative" response to Nabokov's "challenge" rather than an act of "aesthetic and literary vampirism," as the Nabokov estate had contended (Blumenthal 1998b, 7), the *New York Times* reports in its November 7, 1998, issue that Farrar, Straus & Giroux has canceled the publication of *Lo's Diary*.[1] To be sure, the fact that *Lolita* itself "vampirizes" Edgar Allan Poe, or that Kurt Vonnegut (*Slapstick*), Sorrentino (*Mulligan Stew*), and Steven Millhauser (*Edwin Mullhouse: The Life and Death of an American Writer, 1943–*

224

1954) had already reprised Nabokov played no role in the decision. While mentioning certain "flagrant" cases of modern reprise from *West Side Story*—which "poaches" on *Romeo and Juliet*—to Philip Roth's *The Ghost Writer*—which (ab)uses Anne Frank—the article highlights chiefly the legalistic offshoots. In doing so, it overlooks the cultural and historical ramifications of narrative re-presentation. The *New York Times* contributor hardly wonders what renders memorious discourse possible if not inevitable these days and, reciprocally, how it might affect the world in which it occurs.

Two points bear making here. First, both the "prototype" and its transatlantic rejoinder instantiate the intertextuality typical of moderns like Joyce, late moderns like Nabokov himself, and even more so of postmoderns like Pera who have unabashedly stolen from Nabokov. Memorious discourse may have a long history behind it. But it is in postmodernism that it becomes a widely self-acknowledged and multiply revisionary practice—a literary and cultural "dominant." Elsewhere, I single out this reprise as a symptom of, and often discriminate retort to, an age of recycling and cloning. Here, I would stress that all the works listed above, whether "originals" or "copies," modern or postmodern, belong to the same albeit vast and diverse Western tradition of literary borrowings, within which the postmodern remake or rewrite stands out as a particular, more salient case of reprise.

The second point is that such exchanges have accelerated and spread lately to an unforeseen and unprecedented degree. They have been spurred by, and in their turn have furthered, the global circulation, bartering, and overall reprise of goods, values, discourses, texts, and representations across cultures. In other words, this cross-literary conversation has gotten increasingly cross-cultural, too, carrying on and amplifying dramatically an otherwise long-standing process. Hence, the "interpellation" and appropriation of representations by new representations no longer obtain "intraculturally," that is, predominantly within a national culture or cluster of related, usually neighboring cultures. Memorious representation is also "intercultural" in a notably transnational, indeed, intercontinental sense. The representational hybrids stemming from this commerce are taking postmodern memoriousness to another level, of more conspicuously and capaciously sociocultural and geopolitical significance, and into other spaces, dramatizing the new dynamic, velocity, and scope of global transactions. These cross-cultural narrative re-presentations bear witness to—and increase—the already growing mobility of texts, values, and symbols, the "interconnectedness" of the late twentieth-century "world system," as Immanuel Wallerstein would call it. This "system" is not only economic but also literary, intertextual, re-presentational, or, according to Arjun Appadurai, "imaginary."

Inside this system, the position occupied by *Lolita* is twice relevant. For one thing, the novel is a major text in the Western late modern canon. For another, the book and its memorious legacy cast light on a certain progression, on the global integration and expansion of the system. As I have suggested, if one steps back far enough, one could argue that Pera's "Italian Lolita," coming about as it does within the Euro-North American continuum, gives an intracultural reply to Nabokov. In what follows, I propose that we take a quick look, first, at a more markedly *inter*cultural Nabokovian reprise: Lee Siegel's novel *Love in a Dead Language*. Where Pera employs the technique of the diary to let "Lo"'s voice be heard, Siegel deploys the complex trope of narrative "travel" and translation to unfold an ampler, more ambitious, and inherently cosmopolitan panorama of stories, cultural and erotic affinities, compatibilities, conversions, and traffickings, a vision attuned to our time's global developments. In Hoffman and other postmoderns, we have uncovered a similar outlook, also aligned with geo-cultural processes. In the epilogue's second half, I will throw more light on this telling correspondence.

A writer and professor of Indian religions at University of Hawai'i, Siegel shows both in his scholarship and fiction how discourse works as a vigorous agent of cross-culturally memorious exchanges that sets up a dialogue between Western and Eastern traditions through literary flows and narrative "vagrancy." I focus here on his fiction rather than on his anthropological and religious research—which, incidentally, also mixes academic and more unorthodox, personal forms of presentation.[2] His two novels, *City of Dreadful Night* (1995) and *Love in a Dead Language* (1999), pursue the role narrative representation holds in the fostering of cultural languages that cut across local idioms, geographies, and political-economic systems. Not unlike Mircea Eliade, another historian of religions who turned to fiction to flesh out scenarios of intercultural encounters, Siegel suspects that "stories unify the world," as he puts it in *City of Dreadful Night*. "Real stories have no end," his character Brahm Kathuwala assures his audience. "None of the storyteller's stories," he goes on, has

> a beginning or an end—the story he has just told is but an interlude in a larger story. . . . Though the weaver of tales often stops with *but that's another story*, there are no other stories, no separate, discreet tales. There

are no borders. All of the stories are intertwined and overlapping: characters from this one inevitably walk through that one, change this one, which suddenly gives new significance to the events in some other one. A bird migrates through this one to roost in that one, its call echoing across the interludes; a tiger pouncing in [t]his one lands in that one, is killed in this one and is reborn as some man or woman, good or wicked, in that one; those men and women, transmigrating from story to story, connect all ages of the past, great ages of story, with the present. . . . All of the stories, each one having limited versions, each with infinite recensions, are interlocked and interlinked episodes of a greater, amorphous epic, and each contains the whole in a mysterious, unexplainable way. . . . Every story is embedded in the middle of this great, circular epic. There's no way out of it. (49–50)

In Siegel's world, stories, plots, motifs, characters, images travel—they travel a lot but not necessarily "well," as we say of certain wines, for they change, are refurbished as they are exported to, or traded in, unwonted locations, faster and more profoundly than ever before. *City of Dreadful Night* places Dracula in India and redoes Bram Stoker's work by detailing the "influence" of "Bra[h]m Stokerji" on Indian narratives of vampires, ghosts, ghouls, and ogres. *Love in a Dead Language* reprises *Lolita* but also elements of Philip Roth's *The Professor of Desire* and *Operation Shylock*, and, especially, the *Kamasutra*. In Siegel's transcultural imaginary, Western stories and their characters turn up in Eastern garments and vice versa. Lolita is renamed Lalita (Gupta); one Leopold Roth, a Sanskrit scholar, does the "Humbert Humbert in India"; and the *Kamasutra* provides the erotic ideal to which Nabokovian fantasies fail to measure up.

Otherwise, *Love in a Dead Language*'s plot is deceivingly simple because, to adapt the classical distinction between *inventio* and *dispositio*, Siegel does not quite "invent." He does not "originate" his story. In memoriously postmodern fashion, he deliberately and ironically puts together an allusive, recognizable, intertextual and transcultural plot. Here, I can only begin to scratch the surface of its fabulously rich fabric. The reader might distinguish in it a basic metafictional convention, namely, the text and its "double" or "metatext," in the form of a translation, commentary, or both. Significantly, Siegel weaves two different formal traditions into this structure, Western and South-East Asian, and in this regard, he reminds me of Salman Rushdie, Bharati Mukherjee, Arundhati Roy, Maxine Hong Kingston, Gish Jen, Condé, Édouard Glissant, Nicole Mones, or the Chinese-French novelist Dai Sijie. They are just a few among the recent international, multiethnic, and postcolonial writers who draw narrative analogies, and thus straddle the divides, be-

tween West and East or North and South while engaging—some of
them more pointedly and more extensively than Siegel—with migration, diasporas, acculturation and transculturation processes, plane-
tary, human, and economic flows, communication technologies, the
growth of institutional structures such as transnational corporations
(TNCs) and nongovernmental organizations (NGOs), and other
global phenomena.

But what exactly happens in the novel? *Love in a Dead Language* is,
as its full title says, "a romance by Lee Siegel being the *Kamasutra* of
Guru *Vatsyayana Mallanaga* as translated and interpreted by *Professor
Leopold Roth* with a foreword and annotation by *Anang Saighal* following the commentary of *Pandit Pralayananga Lilaraja*." The "romance" re-romances, so to speak, Nabokov's *Lolita*: "Lalita Gupta is
the reason for this text," Roth confesses in his journal (Siegel 1999,
5). But *Love in a Dead Language* imitates structurally both *Lolita*,
which is, we will remember, Humbert Humbert's memoir prefaced
and edited by one John Ray, Jr., Ph.D., and *Pale Fire*, which uses even
more substantially the Russian-doll-like ploy of text-cum-commen-
tary-cum-commentary-on-commentary and, in Siegel, shows up in a
telltale reference to "Zemblan" language.[3] Furthermore, *Love in a
Dead Language* draws upon the *Kamasutra* of Vatsyayana (approxima-
tively third century C.E.), a real if elusive text, and upon the more
mysterious translation into Persian of the original Sanskrit and commentary in verse by one Pralayananga Lilaraja, a seventeenth-
century scholar and poet in the court of Shah Jahan at Agra. In the
foreword, Saighal tells us that, as an editor of Roth's work, he is primarily interested in Pralayananga's gloss of the *Kamasutra*, while Roth
was attracted chiefly by Pralayananga's translation, which Roth had
translated in his dissertation (xv). I could not find Pralayananga's
text—*Love in a Dead Language* includes a bibliography, much of
which has clearly been made up, à la Borges—and the fact that the
names of the book's editor as well as Lalita/Lolita's are anagram-
matically inserted into Pralayananga's strikes me as a serious deterrent to further efforts in this direction.

Nonetheless, Siegel wants us to play the literary detective, and
some things do raise relevantly "bookish" flags. As indicated in the
title and then clarified in the "editor"'s foreword, the "romance"
is built around Professor Roth's translation. But this textual undertaking's underbelly is blatantly memorious because the translated
passages are followed by comments where Roth does not discuss
the Sanskrit original, or he does so superficially and only to the
extent that the philological and pseudophilological glosses—
representation of the original—offer the occasion to represent to us

his extramarital pursuit of Lalita Gupta. Leopold Roth is an anagram of Philip Roth, and I can think of a number of Roth's books
in which the erotical plot runs parallel or suggests parallels to what
happens in *Love in a Dead Language* (it is noteworthy that Roth's
short novel, *The Dying Animal*, resembles Siegel's the most, but, of
course, Roth's book came out after Siegel's).

Briefly, Leopold Roth's commentary chronicles, à la Nabokov, the
relationship between a teenage Lalita and a university professor, her
instructor of Indian civilization and culture, with the rather touristic
discovery of India in lieu of Nabokov's transamerican journey, and
ending with Roth's peculiarly memorious and mysterious demise—an unknown attacker apparently hit him over the head with
a large Sanskrit-English dictionary. Before this, though, the word
about the affair gets out and Roth faces public opprobrium, like so
many of Philip Roth's heroes. Finally, a third layer of self-referentiality, as metafictional as philological, presents Saighal's notes to
Roth's Lolita/Lalita narrative, which also rework, as I have pointed
out, Lilaraja's Persian comments, real or imagined. Roth's literary
"executor"—and this is interesting because Roth dies "by the
book" and by a book—casts light on, and often attempts to expli-
cate, Roth's translation as well as the Lalita scandal. All in all, this
is a memorious "apparatus" that lures the reader into a Borgesian-
Nabokovian maze of mutually mirroring narratives, allusions (to Nabokov and Philip Roth primarily), genuine or fake references, onomastic puns, double-entendre games, and various doubles such as:
Leopold Roth and Lee Siegel; Leopold Roth and Philip Roth and
Paul Rotherberg, and Lee Siegel himself—the ultimate diabolic
double, à la "William Wilson," for another character, named Leopold Siegel, will take Roth's place as husband and faculty member
at Western University in California; then, Saighal, who studied with
the fictional Siegel at University of Hawai'i; Roth's own daughter,
Leila, who dies at Lolita's age, and so forth. But what does this all
mean, and how much weight does it carry beyond the book's seemingly self-sufficient, formal acrobatics?

LOLITA OUTSOURCED: MEMORIOUS DISCOURSE
AND THE NETWORK SOCIETY

Despite, or, quite the contrary, precisely due to its quips, jokes,
hoaxes, and plays, literary and otherwise, *Love in a Dead Language*
must be taken seriously for what it accomplishes stylistically no less
than for what it tells us about the defining ways in which we repre-

sent ourselves and our world, about ourselves and our world ultimately. Alongside other memorious authors variously classified as
postmodern, postcolonial, diasporic, transnational, or multiethnic,
Siegel raises the question of what Emily Apter has identified as "an
emergent internationalized aesthetics" (2001b, 1). But what his
work reveals about us and our time reaches beyond the aesthetic,
the comic, or the "ludic." Funny, jocose, and intertextually so,
Siegel may remind the reader of another dexterous Nabokovian,
John Barth, who indulges his humorous metafictional experimental-
ism and tackles issues of gender and power by lifting forms, settings,
and characters from *The Arabian Nights* (see, for example, his novella
"Dunyazadiad"). While working with a similar blend, Siegel assembles, more markedly than Barth, a cosmopolitan discourse that foregrounds, both in form and substance, the turn-of-the-millennium's
global assemblages, exchanges, and mobility. Acting out postmodernism's quintessential relatedness, Siegel's manifest and sophisticated narrative reprise addresses and reflects—suggests, à la Varsava,
the "mimesis" of—the global age's cultural interconnectedness. It
allows, that is, an insight into the "isomorphism" between how his
narrative representations represent, what they represent, and
where—the world in which they do it. This is how we stand to learn
a broader, serious lesson from Siegel.

The Funesian metaphor and the critical approach derived from it
help us distinguish this lesson in *Love in a Dead Language*'s twin models of narrative and cultural interconnectedness. These models simultaneously shape the novel's fictional world and convey the shape
of the "real" world. One is primarily, if not purely, narrative. It has
to do with stories, what they are, and how they *travel*. The other lays
emphasis on what inescapably happens to stories as they go around,
on the translation *travail* brought to bear upon them when they
enter the world of the other: another space, language, culture, and
the whole *Weltanschauung* set into this otherness. As we can see, the
two models are virtually impossible to keep part; for practical purposes only, I will take them one by one.

First off, Siegel teaches us that stories cover the world in narrative
so thoroughly that "There's no way out of it" (1995, 50). In this
memoriously postmodern sense, there is, indeed, "no outside anymore," a position Derrida's "generalized writing" theory endorses.
On closer, deconstructive inspection, Derrida contends, "outside"
and "inside" (1976, 44–65), "here" and "there," text and whatever
we usually assume that lies outside it, its putatively nontextual context, upset the "exorbitant" (157), "supplemental" logic that has
traditionally sought to prevent them from swapping places. As a re-

sult of the swap, *il n'y a pas de hors-texte.* Frequent misreadings of the famous place in *Of Grammatology* notwithstanding, this means, as Michael Bérubé specifies, that "there is no outside-the-text" (1994, 104), no pristine, pre-textual limbo where people and things roam immune to textualization, cultural inscription, representation. And there is no *hors-représentation, hors-texte* or *hors-récit*—"outside-story"—anymore because, with another Derridean suggestion, "text" or story, the form and vehicle of representation in this case, is, and acts as, a "hinge" rather than separate unit (Mowitt 1992, 93), or as a unit that holds together insofar as it *joins* other units akin in terms of both constitution and role. All texts are sites on which other texts swing and fasten onto each other, as Siegel's story-telling alter ego says. This is *why* and *how* they spread globally so that no place on earth is "safe" from them, left unclaimed by texts and representations, narrative-free. And this is also why *globalization emerges as a domain of worldwide and mobile narrativity*: in the very narrative enveloping, organizing, and unifying of the world, the global reveals itself, plays its makeup out. This global outspreading and intermingling of narratives across time and space is, in a very metafictionally postmodern vein, possibly *the* topic of Siegel's texts as well as their structural principle. These texts speak to, arise in, and widen the global "storyscape," to venture a coinage analogical to Arjun Appadurai's "mediascape."

In relation to this model, Siegel works out, and acts on, a second one, which encapsulates a theory of cosmopolitan writing as twofold translation: commonly understood translation, from one idiom into another, but also cultural translation, translation as *trans-latio*, narrative travel and splicing up across all kinds of boundaries. The *Lolita*-as-the-new-*Kamasutra* plot enacts, and speaks to, a transidiomatic paradigm of "attraction," a global erotics of language and communication that seizes both eroticism and textuality as memorious, cosmopolitan aggregates—the term "cosmopolitan," I might add, pops up frequently in the Sanskrit original reproduced in the novel, and hence in Roth's translation. The cross-cultural language of desire and pleasure, on the one hand, and the equally cross-cultural texture of language and discourse, its essentially dialogic-memorious nature, on the other hand, are what Siegel brings to the fore and performs. Here, love, being-with-the-other, is translation and transubstantiation of desire into pleasure and self into/as other, and so are language, writing, text, representation. Text is texture, commentary—never "original"—by condition, ever re-presentation. Writing is not reflection of an origin *this side* of the cultural and subjective divide (me/you; we/they; over here/over there) but entails translat-

ing from another text, from the text of alterity. The self "originates," accordingly, in translation, in a translation of the other('s
stories) and in the underpinning rustle of tongues and voices. As
Hoffman teaches us, this self can be found and "founded" there.
Also as in Hoffman, in Siegel translation annotates, scrambles the
letters—while preserving the "spirit"—of what it translates. Siegel's
cross-cultural reprise of Nabokov and of the *Kamasutra* is an "ana-
grammatical" feat where all fictional initiative is seen as a "relet-
tering" operation across a multitude of gaps, borders, and divides.

In *Speak, Memory, Lost in Translation,* and *Reading Lolita in Tehran,*
reminiscence, biographical and autobiographical *regression,* becomes intertextual *digression,* journey in time, in personal memory,
as much as a detour through textual space, through others' memoirs. Not unlike Nabokov, Hoffman, Nafisi, Acker, Morrison, Auster,
DeLillo, Leyner, David Antin, and other postmoderns, Siegel intimates that the narrative archeology of identity, if rigorous, "radical"
enough, brings to light the "impurity" of our origins or roots (*radi-
ces*), shows that they are entwined with or already engrafted into
other roots. While calling itself forth from the past and "saying" itself in the present, the "I" also says the "Thou," à la Martin Buber,
Lévinas, and Derrida, takes upon itself to tell its stories; my name
names other names, spins the other('s) stories. Accordingly, the
other is my "invention," an invention as rethought by Greenblatt,
though, that is to say, a representation effect that depends on how
effectively I ferret out, adapt, and weld available representations together. In turn, the "Thou" narrates the story of the "I." In this
sense, my "true story" is always told by somebody else. I am a version
of his or her narrative, a version or "versant" of the other, and how
I come across greatly "hinges" on how con-versant the other is with
storytelling in general since it is in his or her stories that my being
"originates," is represented and presented to the world. I can be the
only one speaking about myself, but as I do so, I still speak in
tongues, à la Hoffman, I ventriloquize the other and its idioms because "my own" will never be able to shake off, "forget" the innumerable traces of language, history, culture, and emotion
bespeaking that other. In this light, I translate from a foreign language as I utter words in "my own"—that which I will never fully
own. The *other tongue,* the other ultimately, is what my representation stems from, what represents me. So the other is also my "representative"; vice versa, I am his or hers.

   A fundamental, mutual indebtedness marks, then, the relation between me and others as authors of stories, texts, representations gen-

erally. Postmodern discourse shows, more insistently, explicitly, and with unprecedented awareness compared to other discourses, that the structure of memoriousness is also a structure of responsibility, has a whole ethics to it. As I have stated on several occasions, *Memorious Discourse* refutes the blanket charges of ahistoricity, cultural superficiality, "irresponsibility," "gratuitousness," "amorality," and political "helplessness" repeatedly brought against postmodernism. The rebuttal would have fallen flat, though, had this book not have also taken aim at the largely modernist notion of a world in fragments—a world asunder, as I call it in chapter 4. Pynchon, DeLillo, Powers, Charles Johnson, and other postmodern writers, artists, critics, and philosophers make us the gift of another vision. Like Siegel's, theirs is a memorious outlook. They unfold the canvas of a world multiply integrated "vertically" in time, as "recent" narratives prove pregnant with narrative history, repositories of the cultural past, and "horizontally," as one story leads to another and to the domain of otherness. The prologue cautioned that this distinction was not as clear-cut as it looked, but by and large it has helped throughout the book and, here again, does help us understand Siegel's hero when he insists that stories stitch time and space together.

Among countless other postmodern stories, Siegel's set out to further sew the world together. That is to say, not only do they feature fictional situations showing what this sewing or stitching means. As stories, these texts themselves entwine, interlace, and otherwise seam our world with stories. So not only do they betoken the global Zeitgeist; not only do they impart a feeling of global interconnectedness. *City of Dreadful Night, Love in a Dead Language,* DeLillo's *White Noise, Underworld,* and *Cosmopolis,* Gibson's *Neuromancer,* Leyner's works, Updike's Bech series, and many others like them act as agents of globalization, of a certain noncorporate kind of globalization. Memorious discourse and Castells's "network society" are, I submit, structurally compatible. The former reflects the latter's architecture, and its worldwide proliferation is both symptom, tool, and part of this expanding network, contributing to the speeding up of our age's "time-space compression." David Harvey has identified this phenomenon as a "postmodern condition." I agree with the diagnosis, but what this verdict implies, I would add, is one more time the formal homology of the memorious postmodern and the global.

This homology is far from perfect. Nor should it be perfect. On the one side, one can certainly make a case for an alliance, for memorious discourse as an "accomplice" of that globalization which threatens us with what Updike calls in his novel *Bech at Bay* "deep-fried homogeneity" (1998, 239) of the world. On the other side, the one I tend to situate myself, there are asymmetries and disjunctures whose oppositional potential cannot be ignored. For it is the memorious approach that helps us acknowledge this potential by seizing upon the structure of memoriousness, upon representation as representation, as a structure of responsibility. This is responsibility toward the other, an accountability deeply seated in, and posited by, the structure of otherness ingrained in postmodern representation. As I write, compose, represent as a postmodern author, I re-collect traces and testimonies of otherness, of textual and cultural difference, and for this difference, for, and to, *that which makes my representation, my work, and myself possible*, I cannot but remain accountable. My work, if true to what it is and what I am—if "original"—will always and paradoxically bear the marks of the other, will contain his or her memory as other. In this regard, one could claim that postmodern representation goes, or can go, against the grain of "globalization-as-homogenization."

Postmodern authors and critics, some of them examined in this book, suspect that authorship and indebtedness are each other's flip side, that to be an author is to go in debt, become indebted to other authors and others generally, to the Derridean "friends" who have extended generous lines of credit to them. In a way, postmodern representation is ever "on loan" from other representations even when the fine print of lease or loan agreement is hardly legible or presentable, as we have noticed in chapter 5. The "lines of credit" can be read "between the lines" of the postmodern novel or short stories, in fact are more often than not flaunted, shown off, like the credits rolled in the movie from Nabokov's "Assistant Producer." The postmoderns do not shy away from crediting the memoriousness of their works, disclosing that these have grown, as I say in the prologue, "in the margins" of other works. Above, I evoked the delicate, ambiguous isomorphism of this memoriousness and globalization. I close here with another type of correspondence, also assumed, suggested in the prologue, and practiced by this writer across all chapters: the similar homology of what I have been talking about and how I have done it. The reader may have noticed, I have produced marginalia to marginalia, and extensively so. At times, I may have tested the reader's patience, but the critical isomorphism growing out of those close readings and elaborations "in the margins" of others and their texts seemed and seems to me a matter of course, an adequate response to the call of the other.

Notes

PROLOGUE

1. In his book on the *mise en abyme* device, Lucien Dällenbach defines the "specular" (*spéculaire*) in antimimetic (antireflective) terms. According to the French critic, there lies, nested inside "specular narrative," an "inner mirror" (Dällenbach 1977, 52), a textual segment—episode, symbol, character—that somehow clarifies, repeats, or otherwise "reflects" the whole. The French Nouveau (Nouveau) Roman in particular and postmodernism in general, from García Márquez to John Barth and Acker to Michel Houellebecq have been abundantly "specular." I have discussed the "narcissist poetics" of *le récit spéculaire* in *Poetica reflectarii* (1990, 7–45, 70–110).

2. Andrew Hurley, who has offered the most recent translation of "Funes el memorioso," renders Borges's title as "Funes, His Memory." He calls "Funes the Memorious" "vaguely Lewis-Carroll-esque" (Borges 1998, 535). Personally, I like both titles, but I prefer the Lewis Carroll undertone over the "nod to JLB's great admirer John Barth" (535), which Hurley's choice implies. His solution recalls the French version, "Funes ou La Mémoire."

3. See my book, *Rewriting* (2001, 149), for a brief overview of literary responses to *The Scarlet Letter*.

4. In *The Ghosts of Modernity*, Jean-Michel Rabaté makes the case for a "haunted" modernism (1984, xvi). Where self-acknowledged, deliberate, and ideologically driven intertextuality is a concern—and a "cultural dominant"—postmodernism strikes me as even a more qualified candidate for "spectrality."

5. Both in substance and form, my "postmemoir" resembles Marianne Hirsch's "postmemory." Commenting on Eva Hoffman's *Lost in Translation*, the critic uses the term to explain how Holocaust survivors' children relate to the traumatic experiences of their parents, experiences that children "recall" merely "as the stories and images with which they grew up, but that are so powerful, so monumental as to constitute memories in their own right" (1993, 7). The postmemoir—postmodern autobiography—has less to do with traumatic memories than with life writing that re-writes somebody else's memoir, or, texts generally, instead of just chronicling one's own life. I will come back to Hirsch's postmemory notion in chapter 1's "Postmemoir" section.

6. Caldwell outlines Marr's analysis and also quotes Patricia L. Tenpenny, et al.'s article, "In Search of Inadvertent Plagiarism," which defines "cryptomnesia" as a form—and source, I might add—of unwitting plagiarism. I agree with Caldwell's conclusion: the "coincidence of plot, narrative and name" is not as "'striking'" as Marr claims (Caldwell 2004, 11).

7. Marie-Laure Ryan's essay on postmodernism and fictionality, which quotes a 1989 article where Dorrit Cohn debates the fictional vs. historical binary, purports to "salvage the distinction" (Ryan 1997, 179) yet, also like Cohn, provides little in

the way of analysis of postmodern texts. "Creat[ing their] own world," Ryan argues, "fictional texts do not share their reference world with other texts," nor can they "directly attack, disprove or supplant another text, be it fiction or nonfiction" (167). In a note, the critic adduces as an example Jean Rhys's *Wide Sargasso Sea*, which rewrites *Jane Eyre*. Many critics, myself included, have shown, though, that Rhys's text must draw from Charlotte Brontë's to "create its own world," "referring" deliberately, abundantly, and critically—"extensively" and "intensively," as I put it (2001, 23–37)—to *Jane Eyre*. In this and other postmodern cases, intertextuality displaces and supplants classical referentiality while predicating the "reality effect" of Rhys's novel upon a transparent, systematically pursued textual reference. This is how postmodernism gives distinction reinforcers a hard time: not by suspending fiction's "truth"—I am afraid *Gravity's Rainbow* does not "say 'I am not true'" (Ryan 1997, 181)—but by revealing this truth's cultural-material, fictional, and intertextual makeup and thus blurring the traditional dividing line between fiction (fictional texts) and history (historical truth, either personal or collective). *Speak, Memory* is among the first texts to thumb its nose at the distinction.

8. "In its encyclopedic scope," Molly Hite writes, *Gravity's Rainbow* "appears dedicated to the proposition that *everything is connected*: there are insinuated links between synthetic polymerization and the evolution of the earth; between astrophysics and psychic phenomena; between African dialects and Rilkean poetics; between international cartels and Freemasonry; between comic books and covenant theology" (1983, 95). At the same time, the critic adds, the novel refuses to accept the "totalizing tendency of the thematic connections" (96) launched in space and time, declines to endorse it or believe in it. Pynchon's work "dictates the terms on which totalization should be possible, even as it resists totalization" (97). It suggests a paranoid vision at the same time that it flouts it. Hite comes back to this argument in a more recent essay where she reads *Absalom, Absalom!* with *Gravity's Rainbow* (2002, 59–60).

CHAPTER 1: TIME, REPRESENTATION, AND POSTMODERN MEMORY

1. Nabokov scholarship has identified Proustian elements in early Nabokov and in late novels like *Ada*, in his fiction as well as in his memoirs, literary criticism, and interviews (see, for example, Sicker 1987). It has dealt especially with themes such as voluntary and involuntary memory, duration, the blending of multiple temporal strata, "the magical sense of time" and "nostalgia" (Sicker 1987, 253), the structure of the ego, sensation, recollection and fabulation, love and loss.

2. I wish to stress briefly the basic distinction between temporality and chronology, and refer, for an extensive approach to this issue, to Gareth H. Steel's *Chronology and Time in À la recherche du temps perdu*. The "architecture of time" in Proust and Nabokov, to use Richard Macksey's formula (1962), or, narrative chronology is not my focus here. I am interested in the opposition between "empiric" and "absolute" ("aesthetic") time rather than in "temporal patterns." These constitute the object of numerous readings informed by narrative poetics, such as John Houston Porter's "Temporal Patterns in À *la recherche du temps perdu*" or Gérard Genette's influential *Narrative Discourse*.

3. *Speak, Memory* addresses the Hegelian logic of *Aufhebung* in a reference to "Hegel's triadic series (so popular in old Russia)." Hegel's thesis-antithesis-synthe-

sis sequence, Nabokov writes, "expresse[s] merely the essential spirality of all things in their relation to time." In hindsight, the narrator views his "own life" as "a colored spiral in a small ball of glass" (1966, 275).

4. In *La Doctrine de la réalité chez Proust*, Alain De Lattre calls this type of time *le temps pur*, "pure time" (1978, 200–214).

5. As Julia Kristeva points out in *Proust and the Sense of Time*, for all its concreteness, Proustian sensation is a fragment of "pure" time (1993, 53).

6. This is Proust's "original vision," extensively discussed by critics. What I want to look at in this chapter is primarily the dynamic of writing, time, and the "timeless" "authenticity of experience," to quote Daniela De Agostini (1984, 202).

7. Time, Jaime Torres Bodet argues, is the actual protagonist of *Remembrance*, but also its "enemy." Moreover, the purpose of Proust's whole work "consists in defeating time" (Bodet 1967, 61–85). By and large, Nabokov's autobiography makes a similar attempt.

8. See Martin-Deslias's essay "Le mythe du temps" (n.d., 28–29).

9. See Jacques-Yves Tadié's *Proust et le roman. Essai sur les formes du roman dans À la recherche du temps perdu*, especially "Chapitre X. Le Temps" (293–319).

10. John Burt Foster insists that Nabokov's early "breakthrough into the autobiographical does not exclude certain fictional elements" (1993, 35). Nabokov's work is marked by an increasing "fictionalization" and "manipulation" (126) of the materials supplied by the writer's memory.

11. Critics have repeatedly explored Proust's world of signs and the interpretation of these signs taking place within Proust's fictional world. See, for instance, Deleuze's *Proust and Signs* and Hayden White's article "The Rhetoric of Interpretation."

12. *The Gift*, the last novel Nabokov wrote in Russian, offers both a sample and a theory of "novelistic," fictive biography, of its writing and reading. The theory can be applied to Nabokov's "revisited" autobiography itself. It is also noteworthy that in *The Gift*, a piece dealing with time and the obsession of writing, Koncheyev, a sort of alter ego of the protagonist, expresses his belief that "there is no time" (1993, 342).

13. "Nabokov," Page Stegner argues, "would undoubtedly agree with many of his characters that the pains of a finite consciousness in an infinite world, the suffering produced by brutal mindlessness, and the conventional patterns of timeless beauty are escapable only through art. Indeed, . . . it is this escape—the finding of one's immortal soul through artistic creation—that is the central concern of all Nabokov's fiction" (1967, 133).

14. Hans Robert Jauß convincingly described, before *La Nouvelle Critique*'s exquisite analyses of the *Recherche*, the connections between time and textual elaborations, more specifically, between *die Suche nach der verlorenen Zeit*, "the pursuit of lost time" and [*der*] *Weg zur Kunstwerk*, "the way to the work." See his *Zeit und Erinnerung in Marcel Prousts À la recherche du temps perdu. Ein Beitrag zur Theorie des Romans* (1970, 194).

15. It is worth mentioning that Proust's narrator goes through a similar experience in *Swann's Way*. He is fascinated by the "stray drop[s], lingering in the hollow of a leaf, . . . run[ning] down and hang[ing] glistening from the point of it until suddenly they splashed on to our upturned faces from the top of the branch" (1982, 1:164). The episode illustrates the theme of writing. It is under the porch of Saint-André-des-Champs that the narrator takes shelter—a "written" shelter, "record[ing] certain anecdotes of Aristotle and Virgil" (164). Later on, he resumes his usual walks "after long ours spent over a book" (169) and, again, following a

break caused by rain. His ardent desire mingles erotic and aesthetic yearnings during these wanderings. Finally, in the same settings and during a similar walk, Proust's narrator catches a glimpse of the steeples of Martinville and, unable to resist the urge of "compos[ing] a little fragment" (197–98), creates his own analogon—and precursor—of Nabokov's poem.

16. David Shields maintains that "some of the most powerful moments in *Speak, Memory* occur when Nabokov bumps up against the time-wall between the present and the past" (1987, 51).

17. Robert Alter notices that the "transcendence of time" is also a most salient aspect of *Ada* (Alter 1987, 175).

18. Robert Grossmith looks closely at Nabokov's "heart and heartbeat as images of chronological time and its succession or measurement." He points out the recurrence of these "non-time" metaphors in texts such as *The Defense, Glory, Bend Sinister, The Eye, Ada, Lolita, Look at the Harlequins!,* and *Speak, Memory* (Grossmith 1986, 38–43).

19. See Alexandrov, *Nabokov's Otherworld* (1991, 46). The critic relates the narrator's escape from "time's prison," and thus the "paradoxical nature of time in Nabokov's view" (1991, 25), to Proust. He suggests that Nabokov's references to the famous episode of the *madeleine* as an example of "epiphany," on the one hand, and the writer's own "cosmic synchronization" image, on the other, are linked. The latter occurs, as Alexandrov proves, in key passages of different Nabokovian works.

20. The inventive, fictionalizing thrust of recollection is obvious in *Speak, Memory.* Critics have noted, in fact, Nabokov's "fictional remembrance." John Burt Foster discusses the phenomenon of "anticipatory memory" with reference to the "things past" that can occur or reoccur in the future and thus highlight the projective, "creative" aspect of memory. See Foster's article "Nabokov before Proust: The Paradox of Anticipatory Memory."

21. Writing, creation in general appear in Nabokov as "wrestling with time." See Virgil Nemoianu's discussion of this aspect in Nabokov's and Mircea Eliade's works (Nemoianu 1980).

22. See Jean-Pierre Richard's fundamental work *Proust et le monde sensible.*

23. John Burt Foster, in *Nabokov's Art of Memory and European Modernism* (205), and Robert Alter, in "Nabokov and Memory" (620–29), examine this motif in Proust and Nabokov. Howard Moss has also attempted an extended analysis of this Proustian theme in *The Magic Lantern of Marcel Proust.*

24. The magic lantern can be viewed as a textual metaphor, bearing out the "analogy between building identity and building a text" (Schloss 1982, 225). Nabokov fancies the architecture of the self as a structure of distinct biographical layers, which parallels the sequence of the slides projected on the wall. Similarly, autobiographical discourse "shows" these slides one by one. At the same time, this "poignant and exigent attempt to resists the flow of time" (Green 1981, 22) weaves fictional and actual images together. Projection does not just retrieve past reality mimetically. It recreates reality, rendering it an inextricable combination of past and present events, truth and fabulation, as Nabokov himself insists in his commentary on related aspects in Proust (1980, 249).

25. See John Leonard's comments on National Public Radio reproduced in a blurb for Hoffman's book (1990). Sarah Phillips Casteel names Malamud, to whose book, *The Assistant,* Hoffman herself refers in *Lost in Translation* (127), V. S. Naipaul's *Enigma of Arrival,* Bellow's *Herzog,* and Bharati Mukherjee (Casteel 2001, 295–97) as possible models. In her turn, Danuta Zadworna Fjellestad remarks that "*Lost*

in Translation resembles such tales of exile as Maxine Hong Kingston's *The Woman Warrior* or Ihab Hassan's *Out of Egypt*" (Fjellestad 1995, 143). Kellman mentions, among others, Joseph Conrad (Kellman 1998, 153), perhaps the most famous Polish writer who made a name for himself in English, and Jerzy Kosinski, the latter having left Poland two years before Hoffman (154). Both are no longer children when they switch to English. In fact, Kosinski arrives in the U.S. when he is twenty-four, and, as Kellman reminds us, some have argued that *The Painted Bird*, published in 1965, was originally written in Polish. At any rate, given the mosaic of Hoffman's linguistic, ethnic, and cultural identity, critics have proposed a host of contexts and traditions for *Lost in Translation*: Jewish-American writing broadly conceived, with an additional focus on autobiography (see Krupnick 1993); Polish-American and, in particular, "American Women Writers of Polish Descent" (to quote the title of Thomas S. Gladsky and Rita Holmes Gladsky's anthology) where the Jewish background is also underscored (see Gitenstein 1997); post-Nabokovian East European writers with recognized works both in their native language and English or other languages (see Poles like Gombrowicz and Milosz, then Brodsky, Kundera, and others); assimilation/counterassimilation narrative with an emphasis, on the one hand, on immigration, multiculturalism, the critique of the melting-pot story, and, on the other hand, on gender and postmodern identity (Kingston, Mukherjee, Anzaldúa).

26. In the introduction to her 1993 book, *Exit into History*, Hoffman declares that Eastern Europe "remained for me an idealized landscape of the mind. Because I had loved and lost it, because I had been cut off from it summarily and, it seemed, irrevocably, it stayed arrested in my imagination as a land of childhood sensuality, lyricism, vividness, and human warmth" (ix). Unlike the time travel of *Lost in Translation*, *Exit into History* sets out to recover an Eastern Europe (Hungary, Romania, Bulgaria, and former Czechoslovakia besides Poland) "without my childhood fantasies and projections" and before it "disappear[s]" (x). For *Exit into History* is not only about postcommunist changes in Eastern Europe but also about its incipient globalization.

27. In *Telling Lies in Modern American Autobiography*, Timothy Dow Adams defines autobiography as an unavoidable mix of design, truth, and lies (plain or less so, deliberate or euphemistic, etc.) (1990, 14–16). Otherwise, Hoffman herself stresses that "memoirs allow recourse to certain techniques of fiction—compression, selection, shifting." "The main task of a memoir," she adds, "is finding a shape for the narrative without imposing a false one on the life" (1994, 67).

28. See Proefriedt's articles "The Education of Mary Antin" and "The Education of Eva Hoffman."

29. Hoffman refers to the "story" of language in her piece "*Lost in Translation* Five Years Later" (1994, 67).

30. See Eakin on "The Referential Aesthetic of Autobiography" in *Touching the World* (1992, 29).

31. See Kristeva's observations on *l'être parlant* and *l'ordre du discours*, quoted by Scarpetta in the "Archéologie de l'enracinement" chapter of *Éloge du cosmopolitisme* (1981, 81–82).

32. On Hoffman's postmodern self and "style," which critics discuss in conjunction with her "poststructuralist" model of language, also see Karpinski (1996, 2), Friedrich (1999, 161), Kellman (1998, 152), and Fjellestad (1995, 142–43).

33. Many critics have pinpointed the "binary logic" of modern rationality. Martin Albrow joins them (1997, 35) but only to insist that the "global age" takes us past this binarism.

34. In *Imaginary Homelands*, Rushdie also points out that the writer "who is out of the country and even out of language" experiences exile and "loss" more intensely than others. On the other hand, "this may enable him to speak properly and concretely on a subject of universal significance and appeal" (1991, 12). See Besemeres for an application of Rushdie's insight to *Lost in Translation* (1998, 329).

35. Marjorie Perloff makes the important point that "*narrative* (but not fiction) is an integral feature of the talk poem" in Antin, comparing his typical "story" to Cage's *koan* (Perloff 1981, 330). Here, I trade upon the distinction Antin draws between narrative and story.

36. "The history of genre theory," Gérard Genette contends, "is shaped throughout by these fascinating schemes that both inform and skew the oftentimes heterogenous reality of the literary field and claim to discover a natural 'system' while, in fact, they lay out an artificial symmetry consisting of illusory categories" (1979, 49). See David Antin, "The Stranger at the Door" (1989, 233–35) for a similar position on "genre membership" (235).

37. In "the river," Antin tells us that, failing to persuade his New Directions publishers not to promote his work as poetry, he tried to convince "them to put [him] in the prose section as well" (1993b, 125). On the other hand, Antin "insists that [his talk-poems] are not prose, which is a much more frozen thing" (Hornick 1979, 8). In the talk-poem "is this the right place," Antin also submits that "writing is a form of fossilized talking which gets put inside of a can called book . . . or maybe we should say a frozen food container called a book" (1976, 45–46).

38. In her distinguished book on Wittgenstein and the twentieth-century poetic avant-garde, Marjorie Perloff lists Antin's work among the "growing body" of contemporary "Wittgensteiniana" (1996, 6).

39. We are witnessing, Jerome Rothenberg writes in his essay-manifesto on the "poetics of performance," "an unquestionable and far-reaching breakdown of boundaries and genres: between 'art' and 'life' (Cage, Kaprow), between various conventionally defined arts (intermedia and performance art, concrete poetry), and between arts and non-arts (*musique concrete*, found art, etc.)" (1994, 640). See Perloff 1981, 288–339, for an analysis of John Cage's and David Antin's "poetry of performance." Also see Lazer's essay on Rothenberg and Antin (Lazer 1995).

40. Here is Antin's response to a question about the distinction between "writing and thinking": "I'm not interested in any forms where distinctions between 'fictionality' and 'factuality' can be clearly formulated. . . . 'Fiction' is a label that positions all the works grouped under it too straightforwardly in the domain of the imaginary and the untrue, or at least contrafactual, and takes away its stakes as human experience. I don't want anybody to be sure whether what I say is a lie or a truth, whether I remembered it, heard it, imagined it, dreamt it, or invented it" (1996, 41).

41. See Antin's conversation with Hazel Smith and Roger Dean, "Talking and Thinking" (1), for a discussion of Antin's work as "improvised poetry."

42. In his review of Perloff's *Wittgenstein's Ladder*, Antin teases out the "narrative implications" of the Wittgensteinian reflections on the "idea of personal identity" (1998, 149) from *The Blue Book*. He notices the impact of such implications both on what the philosopher has to say and on the saying or telling itself, on "the process of narrativization" uncovered in *The Blue Book*. Specifically, Antin notes that Wittgenstein asks how many persons we are dealing with in a "man whose memory on the odd days of his life consists only of his experiences of the odd days, while his memory on the even days consists only of his experiences of the even days, and asks if we have here one person or two" (149). Of course, this situation could be

complicated ad infinitum—each day corresponding to a different person—but the argument remains essentially the same: first, identity is *narrated,* determined by narrative; and second, one's sense of a *coherent* identity, the "story," depends on how one deals with narrative "tests," with crises and moments of potential transformation.

43. Resulting from the logic of "exemplifying" discourse is a real problem for Antin's critics. As Charles Altieri comments on Antin's "postmodern" metaphor of "tuning," there is at times hardly any need to "explain" Antin's ideas since the author does the explaining himself in his talk pieces (Altieri 1986, 13). This also places them in the tradition of the "meditative poem" (Garber 1987, 220).

44. Walter Ong follows, on this score, Eric A. Havelock's works on Homer and Plato.

45. Memory, Antin states in an interview with one of his critics, "is central to all human concepts of the real, including science, history, and personal identity. It is an effort to create a continuum which makes self possible" (qtd. in Hornick 1979, 7).

46. See Scholes and Kellogg's critique of the "common misconception" regarding the "corruption" of the original story through its oral delivery (1966, 23).

47. As Antin describes the relation between oral and textual rendition in his work, "these talks are not 'prose' which is as i see it a kind of 'concrete poetry with justified margins' while these texts are the notations or scores of oral poems with margins consequently unjustified" (1976, i).

Chapter 2: Naming, Representing: Postmodern Onomastics

1. Lévinas finds this form of responsibility in Jewish tradition. "Habitation justified by movement toward the other is essentially Jewish," he avers in *Proper Names* (1996, 45). Specifically, he distinguishes this movement in writers like Paul Celan and their handling of names to "found" things poetically. "Things will indeed appear," Lévinas writes, "the said of this poetic saying, but in the movement that carries them toward the other, as figures of this movement. 'All things, all beings, as they journey toward the other, will be figures, for the poem, of that other. . . . Around me who calls out and *gives it a name* [my italics] it can gather.' The centrifugal movement of the *for the other*—might it be the mobile axis of being? Or its rupture? Or its meaning? The fact of speaking to the other—the poem—precedes all thematization; it is in that act that qualities gather themselves into things. But the poem thus leaves the real its 'otherness,' which pure imagination tears away from it; the poem 'lets otherness's ownmost also speak: the time of the other" (43–44).

2. The *Mann ist Mann* Brechtian passage reproduced earlier is also quoted in Moi's *Sexual/Textual Politics* (2001, 160).

3. I elaborate on these intertextual connections in Auster in great detail in *Rewriting* (2001, especially 77–82).

4. The parallels between Rushdie's *Fury* and DeLillo's *Mao II* would be worth pursuing. In both, the artist's disappearance is a major theme. DeLillo's Bill Gray and Rushdie's Malik Solanka do their best to vanish in America, "to which" Professor Solanka "had come to erase himself" (2001, 44). That does not work as they are dragged back into the media spotlight but is about to happen when terrorists/

rebels take them hostage abroad (in Lebanon, in *Mao II*, or in an imaginary South Pacific country, in Rushdie's book).

5. These are original publication years for Auster's novels.

6. I should mention that Auster—the real one—gives Quinn's name to several characters in *The Locked Room*, *Mr. Vertigo*, *In the Country of Last Things*, and elsewhere, making him a conspicuous Austerian/authorial index.

7. Kafka's "hungry artistry" (Sussman 1997, 284), his motif of tragic-absurd transformation are key to Auster's own "existential art."

8. See Maltby's essay "Romantic Metaphysics" as well as his book *The Visionary Moment* (2002, 73–84).

9. Another remarkable name novel, David Malouf's 1993 postcolonial classic, *Remembering Babylon*, plays abundantly upon Babel and Babylon as symbolic places of linguistic diversification and confusion (Brittan 2002, 1167). This confusion surfaces in our inability to get through to others, to (re)present our ideas or ourselves to them. Significantly, not only is "Jimmy" or "Gemmy" (Malouf 1993, 10) unable to say his own name, to use English coherently following the years among the aborigines, but he also stutters, even as he declares (while de facto annulling) his identity: "I am a B-b-british object" (3).

10. Davis writes, "for Morrison power is largely the power to name, to define reality and perception" (qtd. in Plasa 1998, 150, note 7).

11. See Robert Stepto's interview with Morrison, "Intimate Things in Place: A Conversation with Toni Morrison" (qtd. in Mackethan 1986–1987, 207).

12. For the crucial relation between name and identity in *Song of Solomon*, *Tar Baby*, and other novels by Morrison also see Stein (1980), Fishman (1984), Rabinowitz (1983), and Valerie Smith (1993). As for a larger discussion of the issue of naming in African American literature, see Lucinda H. Mackethan's useful bibliographical references (1986–1987), which include essays by Ralph Ellison, Lloyd W. Brown, Michael Cooke, Kimberley W. Benston, Margaret M. Dunn, and Ann R. Morris.

CHAPTER 3: REMEMBERING THE POSTHUMAN: INTIMATIONS OF HETEROGENEITY

1. See Fuery and Mansfield (2000, especially 1–36) for an overview of "posthuman" scholarship and its impact on the human sciences.

2. "[T]he 'post' of 'posthuman,'" Halberstam and Livingston specify, "interests us not really insofar as it posits some subsequent developmental state, but as it collapses into *sub-*, *infra-*, *trans-*, *pre-*, *anti-*" (1995, viii).

3. Badmington (2000) offers a useful survey of the posthuman problematic in fields as diverse as philosophy, theology, poststructuralism, postmodernism, and cinema.

4. Chambers makes an interesting argument on the impact of the "postcolonial" on universalism, the universal notion of humanism, and the humanities (2001, 3, 22, 26–27). For Chambers, posthumanism is essentially a critical stance or awareness. It means noticing Western humanism's limits and thus "register[ing] [the] limits that are inscribed in the locality of the body, of the history, the power and the knowledge" (26).

5. Lisa D. Campolo is one of the critics who have stressed that "the relationship between deconstruction and ethics is necessarily uneasy." "Ethics, if conventionally

understood," she explains, "is a matter of how we 'ought' to conduct ourselves in the world. Ethical thought entails the development of normative strategies directed toward the achievement or approximation of a moral ideal. This moral ideal usually presupposes the ultimate propriety of a pure human essence. It thus marks ethics as fundamentally humanistic, in the sense of being concerned that we realize our worth in our human essence and that we not step outside this essence and become 'inhumane.' Humanistic values, however, are grounded in what Derrida called the framework of logocentric metaphysics, which deconstruction insistently calls into question" (1985, 429).

6. In the famous "Letter on Humanism" written in reply to Jean Baufret's request that he determine the relation of ontology to ethics, Heidegger talks about morals as a discourse already embedded in the ontological analysis he developed in *Being and Time*. Therefore, as Robert Bernasconi contends, "supplementing" ontology (a sui generis "original ethics" in Heidegger) with an overt, "derivative" ethics is neither ethically necessary nor logically feasible (1987, 123).

7. Reacting to what he deems a "wrong" understanding of deconstruction, Christopher Norris argues that an "ethical dimension" lies at the core of Derrida's work inasmuch as this work "press[es] . . . the aporias to the limits of conceptual explanation" (1987, 194). The conclusion concurs with the argument J. Hillis Miller makes in his analysis of the "ethics of reading" in response to those denouncing deconstruction's "immorality" (1987, 9).

8. In his article "The Ethics of Deconstruction," Mark Edmundson maintains that "the self . . . which has been conventionally conceived of as potentially stable and potentially unified, is here called into doubt." "For," he goes on, "if the activity of reading, or of being in the world, is constituted by the play of differences, then what is called the self is similarly in flux. To assume that the self can become sufficiently composed and coherent to make absolute, binding pronouncements on things as they are is again to falsify the radically temporal and uncertain experience of being" (1988, 628).

9. In *Gravity's Rainbow*, Europe is the prime technological site. However, technology reveals its profoundly colonizing essence in Africa, whence the Schwarzkommando come. More generally, technology colonizes the human body regardless of racial or geographic origin.

10. Pynchon's insights into the sexual bearings of technological embodiment have been confirmed by gender studies. Mary Ann Doane, for example, states that "when technology intersects with the body in the realm of representation, the question of sexual difference is inevitably involved" (1990, 163). It is also noteworthy that, as a sign of "manhood," the engendered representation of the technological in Pynchon is often at odds with modernist texts' tendency to "equate machines with women" (Springer 1991, 305, in a comment on Andreas Huyssen's interpretation of Fritz Lang's *Metropolis*).

11. See Moravec (1988) for an analysis of the "postbiological world."

12. According to Lyotard, the body as "hardware" is a symptom of the "inhuman" age (1991, 13).

13. In his introduction to *Thomas Pynchon's* Gravity's Rainbow (1986, 3–9), Harold Bloom proposes a compelling reading of "The Story of Byron the Bulb" (in *Gravity's Rainbow*, 1973, 647–55).

14. Doane discusses similar aspects regarding technophilia and the representation of the feminine in film (1990, 166).

15. "Science tells us," Nabokov's Charles Kinbote says in *Pale Fire*, "that the Earth would not merely fall apart, but vanish like a ghost, if Electricity were suddenly removed from the world" (1989, 193).

16. Hugo Caviola maps out Pynchon's "Zone" in his essay on the "perception and presentation of space in German and American postmodernism." He challenges Brian McHale's view of the Zone as "tropological" (McHale 1987, 140), "deconstructive geography" (Caviola 1991, 110), emphasizing its "(re)constructive" dimension instead. In other words, the Swiss critic stresses the "thematization" of the reading process in *Gravity's Rainbow*. "Unlike McHale," Caviola writes, "I perceive the postmodernist Zone as a textual vacuum which makes the reader's interpretative activity a function of the text's meaning" (110). My own reading of the Zone focuses on its "t(r)opology," on its functioning as an ethical *trope* and textual *topos* simultaneously.

17. Douglas Fowler observes that, as a symbol of an absolute alteration of Nature, plastic and "plasticity [are] linked to Nazism" (1980, 149).

18. The corporate subject—Pynchon's "aggregate They" (Hume 1987, 58–59)—is another "technological" upshot. Here, the self dissolves into a "transsubjective" apparatus welding together humans and machines and serving Technology's goals.

19. Eddins (1990) has written a whole book on Pynchon's gnosticism.

20. For an erudite study of Rilke's influence on *Gravity's Rainbow*, see Hohmann (1986).

21. The difference between V-2 and Enola Gay is rather insignificant in Pynchon.

22. Peter Schwenger (1990) surveys recent "nuclear criticism" that takes up the analogy between textual dynamics and atomic *dunamis*. Also see Tobin Siebers's conclusions on "the ethics of nuclear criticism" (1988, 220–40).

23. Among other works on the topic, I would single out Lois Parkinson Zamora's *Writing the Apocalypse: Historical Vision in Contemporary U.S. and Latin American Fiction*.

24. Derrida reminds us in *Raising the Tone of Philosophy* (1993, 118) that etymologically apocalypse points to disclosure, unveiling. This makes apocalyptic technology a somewhat tautological phrase since the apocalypse marks the technological moment per se. If the apocalypse brings forth a supreme revelation, this is technology's, its self-disclosure through "Zonal" writing. In another sense, the tautology lies in technology's inherently lethal, destructive effects.

25. The French philosopher analyzes the relation between representation and "missile" in "Envoi," an essay from *Psyché. Inventions de l'autre* (109–43). Also see Alan Bass's glossary to his translation of Derrida's *Carte postale* for clarifications of the complex meaning of *envoi* and *destin* (*destinée*) (Derrida 1997b, xix–xxi).

26. Pursuing the ethics of technology in Derrida and Heidegger, Lisa D. Campolo addresses Heidegger's attempt to redefine technicians as poets and thinkers, "guardians of Truth" (*a-letheia*), that is, "technicians in an original and unheard-of sense, who must question, wait, and care" (Campolo 1985, 447). As *poiesis*, *techne* belongs to the ethical realm of care. As such, it waters down, if not completely sheds, its "nihilism." See, for the relation between technology and nihilism, Fandozzi (1982, especially 71–129). Also see Bernstein (1992) for an interpretation of *ethos* in Heidegger's conference on technology.

27. My conclusion differs from that of critics like Mark Richard Siegel (1978, 123) insofar as this chapter underscores technology's aggressiveness and "vampiric" domination of the human. The logic of this domination is rooted in the "autopoietic nexus of the machine" (Guattari 1993, 15). According to this logic, the human turns into a tool of technological "autopoiesis," self-generation.

28. See Hans Jonas's ethical observations in his chapter on "Man as an Object of Technology" (1984, 17–21).

29. Kranzberg, and Nef, Vanderkop, and Wiseman characteristically use the phrase "pervasive technology" in the titles of their anthologies *Ethics in the Age of Pervasive Technology* and *Ethics and Technology: Ethical Choices in the Age of Pervasive Technology*, respectively. On the social effects of this pervasiveness, see Frank (1987).

30. Geoffrey Green (1987) shows extensively how Roth "metamorphoses" Kafka. I would add that Roth's relation to Kafka reaches far beyond *The Breast*, as the writer acknowledges in his essays and suggests in works such as *The Dying Animal, The Prague Orgy*, and elsewhere in the Zuckerman series. Let me also note that, besides Roth, several other contemporary American writers have exploited this sort of relationship with "The Metamorphosis" in particular and Kafka's work in general. A few names come to mind: Guy Davenport, Auster, Updike (see his recent story, "Metamorphosis," from the 2000 collection, *Licks of Love*), Raymond Federman, and even William S. Wilson, despite the title of his 1977 short story anthology, *Why I Don't Write Like Franz Kafka*. On Wilson and Kafka, see Chénetier 1994, 175–177. Marc Estrin's *Insect Dreams: The Half Life of Gregor Samsa* (2002) is also worth mentioning here.

31. Bruce Clarke (1995) pursues "the subject of metamorphosis" from the ancient Greeks to Shakespeare, Milton, Coleridge, and contemporary writers like Bulgakov, Calvino, and García Márquez. Since metamorphosis ties into the double motif (Bravo 1992), most surveys of metamorphosis, transformation, and change also discuss the "identity search" theme (Massey 1976, 17), the self, its other, and the resulting doppelgängers from Ovid and Homer to Gogol, Chamisso, Flaubert, and other moderns (Massey 1976). See Skulsky for the various "fantasies of transformation" (1981, 24) that emphasizes moral-psychological aspects.

32. "Inscribing and incorporating practices" (Hayles 1993b, 156) set in train an ongoing modification of body boundaries. The distinction between these types of practices is important as it shows the body's different responses to sociocultural pressures. Following Maurice Merleau-Ponty's *Phenomenology of Perception* and Paul Connerton's *How Societies Remember*, Hayles defines an inscribing practice as "an action that is encoded into bodily memory until it becomes habitual" (1993b, 157). Learning to type, for example, is such a practice.

33. In this regard, Leyner joins more established—and slightly more "serious"—writers such as Don DeLillo (*Great Jones Street, Mao II*, and *White Noise* are prime examples).

34. See again Hayles (1993b, 165) for an account of textuality's "loss of materiality."

35. Following Adorno, Ben Agger focuses in *Fast Capitalism* on the "tendency for the signifying nature of writing to degrade where the exterior worlds of money, science, edifice, and figure become 'texts,' thus compelling adjustment and precluding the possibility of new versions standing at one remove from the world they address" (1989, 3).

36. Pierce has done a useful overview of the superman theme in science fiction (1987, 25–48).

37. "I am slashing a path through the rank vegetation of American popular culture with the warped machete of my mind," says Leyner's protagonist in *Tooth Imprints on a Corn Dog* (1995, 145).

38. See Richard L. Ochberg's essay "The Male Career Code and the Ideology of Role" in Harry Brod's anthology (1987, 173–91). Also see David H. J. Morgan (1992, 99–119) for an analysis of unemployment viewed as a "challenge to masculinity." It is relevant, in this view, that Leyner plays the absolute employer in *Et Tu, Babe*. His compulsory self-promotion may parody the male complex of unemployment internalized as lack of manhood.

39. "I often feel like a surgeon trapped in a writer's body," the narrator of *Tooth Imprints on a Corn Dog* tells us (1995, 2). Leyner's 1995 book features a whole obsession with surgery as writing and (self-)rewriting. "I am a writer and aesthetician by trade, but an internist and surgeon by avocation," Leyner says (113). See also pp. 15, 116, 126, 146, 173, 210, 211 for relevant references to surgery, excision, dermatology, vasectomy, and other "aesthetic" alterations of the body.

40. "Leyner Headquarters" is another parody of celebrity lifestyle. In *I Smell Esther Williams* Leyner talks about "study[ing] Clint Eastwood at the Clint Eastwood Institute in Clint Eastwood, California" (1983, 74).

41. In *My Cousin, My Gastroenterologist* Leyner's hyperbolization of the male body takes up a more poetic form (1990, 89). There are whole passages that can be read as "endocrinological" allegories. The aggressively sexual "cosmic body" is one of the book's themes.

CHAPTER 4: "THE COLLAPSE OF DISTANCE"

1. Regarding the concept of "the dominant," McHale acknowledges his debt to Russian Formalists such as Jurij Tynianov and Roman Jakobson (McHale 1987, 6).

2. "Prophet of the postmodern world" (Lotringer 1992, 38) or not, Baudrillard uses the concept of postmodernism sparely. In general, the term strikes him as a symptom of "intellectual fashion" (1993, 158). When told by Mike Gane that "many people think of [him] as the high priest of postmodernism," Baudrillard replies that "this reference to priesthood is out of place. . . . The first thing to say is that before one can talk about anyone being a high priest, one should ask whether postmodernism, the postmodern, has a meaning. It doesn't as far as I am concerned. It's an expression, a word which people use but which explains nothing. It's not even a concept. It's nothing at all. It's because it's impossible to define what's going on now, grand theories are over and done with, as Lyotard says. That is, there is a sort of void, a vacuum. It's because there is nothing really to express that an empty term has been chosen to designate what is really empty. So in a sense there is no such thing as postmodernism. If you interpret it this way, it is obvious that I do not represent this emptiness. . . . It doesn't have anything to do with me, and I am not the only one in this situation" (21–22). Gane gives us a clear account of Baudrillard's complex relation with postmodernism in *Critical and Fatal Theory* (1991, 46–70).

3. Habermas delivered the speech with this title, "Die Moderne—ein unvollendetes Projekt," in 1980, when he accepted the Adorno Prize in Frankfurt. The text was immediately published in a German newspaper of wide circulation, translated into English in *New German Critique* in 1981, and included in Habermas's *Kleine Politische Schriften* series (1981). His author comes back to some of its ideas in *The Philosophical Discourse of Modernity*, published in 1985 and translated into English in 1987 (Habermas 1987).

4. See Readings's *Introducing Lyotard* (1991, 86–139) for the ethical and political dimension of Lyotard's rhetorical and aesthetic models.

5. French criticism begins questioning the notion of reality and realism more radically under the impact of structuralist poetics and primarily in publications such as *Poétique* and *Communications*. Barthes, Todorov, Genette, Ricardou, Philippe Hamon, and others had uncovered the cultural constitution of reality, the "precodification" of the referent, and other "mimetic fallacy" aspects prior to posts-

tructuralist thinkers like Foucault, Derrida, Lyotard, Deleuze, Baudrillard, or Virilio.

6. Satya P. Mohanty has voiced her suspicion about postmodern and poststructuralist concerns with "reality" on various occasions including a 1986 essay on theory's "ambiguous politics of meaning." In the 1997 book *Literary Theory and the Claims of History: Postmodernism, Objectivity, Multicultural Politics*, she formulates the objectivist position of a "postpositivist realism" (xii–xiii) as a "reasonable alternative" (18) to the politically impotent formalism allegedly at play in the postmodern inability to account for reference, reality, and other nonlinguistic, social fields. In my turn, I find unconvincing the distinction implied here (linguistic vs. nonlinguistic), as well as the whole opening rereading of de Man, where the case against his reference theory is mounted. See Caruth's article on de Man and "The Claims of Reference" for an interesting discussion of de Manian "reference" as effect of language resistance (1995, 103). In a note, I should add, Caruth refers in passing to Mohanty's 1986 essay. See, too, the whole book edited by Caruth and Esch (1995), which features an excellent section on "Reference, Materiality, and History" in poststructuralist thought (11–210).

7. In *The Differend*, Lyotard fleshes out his theory of reality as "différend" (1988, see especially "The Referent, The Name" chapter, 31–58). This intervention is consistent with his earlier definition of the referent as "disputable" reality, a reality to be created by discursive means.

8. Nietzsche's famous rhetorical-genealogical analyses of truth are the early pieces such as *Über das Pathos der Wahrheit* (On the Pathos of Truth, 1872), *Rhetorik* (Introduction to Rhetoric 1872–1874), and especially *Über Wahrheit und Lüge im außermoralischen Sinne* (On Truth and Lying in an Extramoral Sense, 1873). See Nietzsche, "Friedrich Nietzsche. Rhétorique et langage," for Nancy and Lacoue-Labarthe's comprehensive translations of, and annotations to, the German philosopher's texts on rhetoric and language. Finally, Alan D. Schrift's book (1990) is a more recent study of Nietzsche's truth theory and its impact on Continental and American criticism.

9. See Roy Johnson's commentary posted on Jan. 15, 1996 on the Nabokov Listserv, Vladimir Nabokov Forum, <NABOKOV-L@UCSBVM,USCB.EDU>.

10. Matei Calinescu discusses Nabokov's fiction in terms of playful rereading (1993, 123–33).

11. Movies are an important theme and source of narrative techniques in *King, Queen, Knave, Lolita, Laughter in the Dark* (Stuart 1979, 89) and other works by Nabokov. Films' magical landscapes and the "ghostly," "spectral," "stereoscopic dreamland"—"Mademoiselle O," in Nabokov (1995, 477–78)—of Nabokovian reality are congruent fictional worlds.

12. Also see Judith Butler's comments on Fredric Jameson's distinction between pastiche and parody (1990, 138–39).

13. See again Roy Johnson (note 9 above).

14. In his book on Nabokovian parody, Dabney Stuart writes that "the best fiction," "fiction that is most consciously itself," keeps the reader "at a substantial distance from not only the characters but the book in which they appear," reminds "[him] of the nature of the experience he is involved in" (1979, 88).

15. Michael Wood contends that "the real for Nabokov is always refracted. There are no bare facts, as he puts it in his book on Gogol. The inevitable refraction is a disappointment to our dream of an uncomplicated, unmediated truth, an easily accessible real life, but there is no opposition between reality and refraction. The real is not less real because it is refracted, that is the way it comes to us" (1994, 31–32).

16. William Woodin Rowe argues that "Nabokov employs several devices that tend to create a reciprocal relationship between the real and the unreal. . . . Some of the methods seem rather scornfully to undermine 'reality' but are in fact a special brand of Romantic irony calculated to entice the reader into sympathy with various effects exposed by the author" (1971, 73). It seems obvious to me that Nabokov does undermine "reality," that the irony at stake in "The Assistant Producer" aims at "denaturalizing" the "real" by exposing the artifact and the fictional nested in it.

17. In the *Nabokov's Dozen* version (75–93), "The Assistant Producer"'s last two paragraphs are omitted. However, both versions end with the same suggestion: facts are "possibly" true as much as the Slavska was "possibly" dead by the time the German officers came to see her at the prison's hospital (Nabokov 1995, 555).

CHAPTER 5: REPRESENTATION, UNREADABILITY, INTERTEXTUALITY: READING THE POSTMODERN SUBLIME

1. For American criticism, see the collective volume edited by Hugh J. Silverman and Gary E. Aylesworth. For French and German scholarship, see *Du Sublime*, collection prefaced by Nancy (Nancy et al., 1992), as well as Christine Pries's anthology, *Das Erhabene. Zwischen Grenzerfahrung und Größenwahn*.

2. Rob Wilson discusses the sublime of contemporary art with reference to urban architecture (the Sears Towers and other "lofty" buildings) as elements of the "postmodern sublime" (1991, 197–227). He also mentions the latter's technological versions (see "the nuclear sublime" chapter, 228–63). Lyotard, Derrida (*La Vérité en peinture*), and Louis Marin ("Les fins"; "Sur une tour de Babel") analyze painting in sublime terms.

3. See primarily Lentricchia (1990) and DeLillo (1990).

4. Jameson contends that in postmodern culture the commodification of objects and the commodification of human subjects are similar. The latter "are themselves commodified and transformed into their own images" (1991, 11).

5. In his essay on "the economics of publishing," Dan Lacy talks about the writer's own transformation into "material" for the "communication industries" (1970, 408). See Charles Newman's *Post-Modern Aura* for a more recent critique of "the preemption by the media of the writer as *celebrity*" (1985, 161). For a full account of the media's role in DeLillo, see Douglass Keesey's monograph (1993).

6. See Osteen (1994, 170) for the ethics of "mastering commerce" in *Great Jones Street*.

7. Robert E. Lane views shopping in general as "an intrinsically rewarding family experience" (1984, 539). Unlike Lane, DeLillo hints at the lack of "reward" such a glorious "family event" entails. Also see Ferraro's essay "Whole Families Shopping at Night" for DeLillo on "the contemporary American family" (1991, 15).

8. See Duvall's essay (1994) for a full-fledged analysis of television in *White Noise*.

9. See Maltby's *Visionary Moment* (2002, 121–22) for "critical literacy," a notion similar to what I call "postmodern literacy." It bears repeating here the point I make in this chapter: DeLillo both identifies a literacy crisis in postmodern society and addresses this crisis in postmodern terms.

Epilogue

1. Pera's book did come out eventually, in 1999, in Ann Goldstein's excellent translation, from a rather obscure press, Foxrock. *Lo's Diary* was prefaced as per a legal agreement, and in a rather nasty tone, by Nabokov's litigious son, Dmitri.

2. Lee Siegel's *Net of Magic: Wonders and Deceptions in India* bears mentioning here because it resembles his fictions in terms of both focus (India) and structure. This is a scholarly book that weaves together personal and travel narrative in diary form, and anthropological-cultural research.

3. In a foreword footnote, Saighal gives us a list of translations of the *Kamasutra*. The list includes real texts such as Richard Burton's and F. F. Arbuthnot's but also a "Zemblan" version by one Romulus Arnor, which supposedly appeared in 1956— another Nabokovian allusion.

Works Cited

Acker, Kathy. 1986. *Don Quixote, Which Was a Dream.* New York: Grove Press.

———. 1989. *Great Expectations.* New York: Grove Weidenfeld.

———. 1997. *Bodies of Work: Essays.* London: Serpent's Tail.

Ackroyd, Peter. 1992. *English Music.* New York: Ballantine Books.

Adams, Henry. 1999. *The Education of Henry Adams.* Edited with an introduction and notes by Ira B. Nadel. Oxford: Oxford University Press.

Adams, Timothy Dow. 1990. *Telling Lies in Modern American Autobiography.* Chapel Hill: University of North Carolina Press.

Agger, Ben. 1989. *Fast Capitalism: A Critical Theory of Significance.* Urbana: University of Illinois Press.

Aizenberg, Edna, ed. 1990. *Borges and His Successors: The Borgesian Impact on Literature and the Arts.* Columbia: University of Missouri Press.

Albrow, Martin. 1997. *The Global Age: State and Society Beyond Modernity.* Stanford, CA: Stanford University Press.

Alexandrov, Vladimir E. 1991. *Nabokov's Otherworld.* Princeton, NJ: Princeton University Press.

———, ed. 1995. *The Garland Companion to Vladimir Nabokov.* New York: Garland.

Alpert, Barry. 1995. "Postmodern Oral Poetry: Buckminster Fuller, John Cage, and David Antin." In *Early Postmodernism: Foundational Essays,* edited by Paul A. Bové, 188–206. Durham, NC: Duke University Press.

Alter, Robert. 1987. "*Ada,* or the Perils of Paradise." In *Vladimir Nabokov,* edited and with an introduction by Harold Bloom, 175–90. New York: Chelsea House.

———. 1991. "Nabokov and Memory." *Partisan Review* 4 (Spring): 620–29.

Altieri, Charles. 1986. "The Postmodernism of David Antin's *tuning.*" *College English* 48 (1): 9–26.

Antin, David. 1976. *talking at the boundaries.* New York: New Directions.

———. 1989. "The Stranger at the Door." In *Postmodern Genres,* edited by Marjorie Perloff, 229–47. Norman: University of Oklahoma Press.

———. 1991. "Thinking about Novels." *Review of Contemporary Fiction* 11 (2): 210–16.

———. 1993a. "Talking and Thinking: David Antin in Conversation with Hazel Smith and Roger Dean." *Postmodern Culture* 3 (3). http://www.muse.jhu.edu/journals/postmodern_culture/v003/3.3smith.html.

———. 1993b. *what it means to be avant-garde.* New York: New Directions.

———. 1996. "Matches in a Dark Space. An Interview with David Antin." By Larry McCaffery. In Larry McCaffery, *Some Other Frequency: Interviews with Innovative American Authors,* 36–58. Philadelphia: University of Pennsylvania Press.

———. 1998. "Wittgenstein Among the Poets." Review of Marjorie Perloff's *Wittgenstein's Ladder: Poetic Language and the Strangeness of the Ordinary*. *Modernism/Modernity* 5 (1): 149–66.

Antin, Mary. 1946. *The Promised Land*. Boston: Houghton Mifflin.

Apter, Emily. 2001a. "The Human and the Humanities." *October* 96 (Spring): 71–85.

———. 2001b. "On Translation in a Global Market." *Public Culture* 13 (1): 1–12.

Auster, Paul. 1989. *Moon Palace*. New York: Viking.

———. 1990. *The New York Trilogy: City of Glass. Ghosts. The Locked Room*. New York: Penguin.

———. 1993. *The Art of Hunger: Essays, Prefaces, Interviews, and* The Red Notebook. New York: Penguin.

———. 1997. *Hand to Mouth: A Chronicle of Early Failure*. New York: Henry Holt and Company.

Badmington, Neil. 2000. *Posthumanism*. New York: Palgrave.

Bal, Mieke, Jonathan Crewe, and Leo Spitzer, eds. 1993. *Acts of Memory: Cultural Recall in the Present*. Hanover, NH: University Press of New England.

Barth, John. 1984. *The Friday Book: Essays and Other Nonfiction*. New York: G. P. Putnam's Sons.

Barthes, Roland. 1981. *Camera Lucida: Reflexions on Photography*. Translated by Richard Howard. New York: Hill and Wang.

———. 2000. "The Death of the Author." In Lodge and Wood 2000, 146–50.

Baudrillard, Jean. 1983a. "The Ecstasy of Communication." In *The Anti-Aesthetic*, edited by Hal Foster, 126–34. Port Townsend, WA: Bay Press.

———. 1983b. *Simulations*. Translated by Paul Foss, Paul Patton, and Philip Beitchman. New York: Semiotext(e).

———. 1987a. *Forget Foucault*. Translated by Nicole Dufresne. New York: Semiotext(e).

———. 1987b. *L'Autre par lui-même. Habilitation*. Paris: Galilée.

———. 1988. *De la séduction*. Paris: Denoël.

———. 1993. *Baudrillard Live: Sellected Interviews*. Edited by Mike Gane. London: Routledge.

Bauman, Zygmunt. 1993. *Postmodern Ethics*. Oxford: Blackwell.

Beardsworth, Richard. 1992. "On the Critical 'Post': Lyotard's Agitated Judgement." In *Judging Lyotard*, edited by Andrew Benjamin, 43–80. London: Routledge.

Beckett, Samuel. 1965. *Three Novels by Samuel Beckett: Molloy. Malone Dies. The Unnamable*. New York: Grove Press.

Benhabib, Seyla. 1984. "Epistemologies of Postmodernism: A Rejoinder to Jean-François Lyotard." *New German Critique* 33 (Fall): 103–26.

Bernasconi, Robert. 1987. "Deconstruction and the Possibility of Ethics." In *Deconstruction and Philosophy: The Texts of Jacques Derrida*, edited by John Sallis, 122–39. Chicago: University of Chicago Press.

Bernstein, Richard J. 1992. "Heidegger's Silence?: *Ethos* and Technology." In *The Ethical-Political Horizons of Modernity/Postmodernity*, 79–141. Cambridge, MA: MIT Press.

Bérubé, Michael. 1994. *Public Access: Literary Theory and American Cultural Politics.* London: Verso.

Besemeres, Mary. 1998. "Language and Self in Cross-Cultural Autobiography: Eva Hoffman's *Lost in Translation.*" *Canadian Slavonic Papers / Revue canadienne des slavistes* 40 (3–4): 327–44.

Bloom, Harold. 1975. *Kabbalah and Criticism.* New York: Seabury Press.

———, ed. 1986. *Thomas Pynchon's "Gravity's Rainbow."* Edited and with an introduction by Harold Bloom. New York: Chelsea House.

Blumenthal, Ralph. 1998a. "Nabokov Son Files Suit to Block a Retold *Lolita.*" *New York Times,* October 10, 1998, B9.

———. 1998b. "Disputed *Lolita* Spinoff Is Dropped by Publisher." *New York Times,* November 7, 1998, B7.

Bodet, Jaime Torres. 1967. "La lucha contra el tiempo." In *Tiempo y memoria en la obra de Proust,* 61–85. Mexico: Editorial Porrua.

Booth, Wayne C. 1988. *The Company We Keep: An Ethics of Fiction.* Berkeley and Los Angeles: University of California Press..

Borges, Jorge Luis. 1998. *Collected Fictions.* Translated by Andrew Hurley. New York: Penguin.

Bravo, Nicole Fernandez. 1992. "Doubles and Counterparts." In *Companion to Literary Myths, Heroes and Archetypes,* edited by Pierre Brunel and translated by Wendy Allatson, Judith Hayward, and Trista Selous, 343–82. London: Routledge.

Brison, Susan J. 1993. "Trauma Narratives and the Remaking of the Self." In Bal, Crewe, and Spitzer 1993, 39–54.

Brittan, Alice. 2002. "B-b-british Objects: Possession, Naming, and Translation in David Malouf's *Remembering Babylon.*" *PMLA* 117 (5): 1158–71.

Brod, Harry, ed. 1987. *The Making of Masculinities.* Boston: Allen & Unwin.

Bruce, Iris. 1996. "Elements of Jewish Folklore in Kafka's *Metamorphosis.*" In *Franz Kafka*: The Metamorphosis. *Translation, Background and Contexts, Criticism,* translated and edited by Stanley Corngold, 107–25. New York: W. W. Norton.

Bukatman, Scott. 1993. *Terminal Identity: The Virtual Subject in Postmodern Science Fiction.* Durham, NC: Duke University Press.

Burke, Kenneth. 1967. *The Philosophy of Literary Form: Studies in Symbolic Action,* 2nd ed. Baton Rouge: Louisiana State University Press.

Butler, Judith. 1990. *Gender Trouble: Feminism and the Subversion of Identity.* New York: Routledge.

Butler, Rex. 1999. *Jean Baudrillard: The Defence of the Real.* London: Sage.

Caldwell, Christopher. 2004. "Who Invented *Lolita?* The Paternity of the Famous Nymphet Is Put in Question." *New York Times Magazine,* May 23, 2004, 11–12.

Calinescu, Matei. 1993. *Rereading.* New Haven: Yale University Press.

Calvino, Italo. 1968. *Cosmicomics.* Translated by William Weaver. San Diego: Harcourt Brace.

Campolo, Lisa D. 1985. "Derrida and Heidegger: The Critique of Technology and the Call to Care." *Journal of the American Academy of Religion* 53 (3): 429–48.

Cantor, Paul A. 1991. "'Adolf, We Hardly Knew You.'" In Lentricchia 1991, 39–62.

Carmean, Karen. 1993. *Toni Morrison's World of Fiction.* Troy, NY: Whitston Publishing.

Carter, Angela. 1994. *The Infernal Desire Machines of Doctor Hoffman.* New York: Penguin.

Caruth, Cathy. 1995. "The Claims to Reference." In Caruth and Esch 1995, 92–105.

Caruth, Cathy, and Deborah Esch, eds. 1995. *Critical Encounters: Reference and Responsibility in Deconstructive Writing.* New Brunswick, NJ: Rutgers University Press.

Casteel, Sarah Phillips. 2001. "Eva Hoffman's Double Immigration: Canada as the Site of Exile in *Lost in Translation.*" *Biography* 24 (1): 288–301.

Caviola, Hugo. 1991. *In the Zone: Perception and Presentation of Space in German and American Postmodernism.* Basel: Birkhäuser.

Chambers, Iain. 2001. *Culture after Humanism: History, Culture, Subjectivity.* London: Routledge.

Chénetier, Marc. 1994. *Sgraffites, encres & sanguines. Neuf études sur les figures de l'écriture dans la fiction américaine contemporaine.* Paris: Presses de l'École Normale Supérieure.

Clarke, Bruce. 1995. *Allegories of Writing: The Subject of Metamorphosis.* Albany: SUNY Press.

Cohn, Dorrit. 1999. *The Distinction of Fiction.* Baltimore: Johns Hopkins University Press.

Conroy, Mark. 1994. "From Tombstone to Tabloid: Authority Figured in *White Noise.*" *Critique* 35 (2): 97–110.

Couturier, Maurice. 1993. *Nabokov ou la tyrannie de l'auteur.* Paris: Seuil.

Cowart, David. 2002. *Don DeLillo: The Physics of Language.* Athens: University of Georgia Press.

Culler, Jonathan. 1979. "Structuralism and Grammatology." *boundary 2* 8 (1): 75–85.

Dällenbach, Lucien. 1977. *Le récit spéculaire. Essay sur la mise en abyme.* Paris: Seuil.

De Agostini, Daniela. 1984. "L'Écriture du rêve dans *À la recherche du temps perdu.*" *Cahiers Marcel Proust.* Nouvelle série, 12. Études proustiennes, 5: 184–211.

De Lattre, Alain. 1978. *La Doctrine de la réalité chez Proust.* Paris: José Corti.

Deleuze, Gilles. 1974. *Proust and Signs.* Translated by Richard Howard. New York: George Braziller.

Deleuze, Gilles, and Félix Guattari. 1994. *A Thousand Plateaus.* Translated by Brian Massumi. Minneapolis: University of Minnesota Press.

DeLillo, Don. 1973. *Great Jones Street.* Boston: Houghton Mifflin.

———. 1978. *Running Dog.* New York: Alfred A. Knopf.

———. 1980. *Ratner's Star.* New York: Random House.

———. 1986. *White Noise.* New York: Penguin.

———. 1989. *Libra.* New York: Penguin.

———. 1990. "'An Outsider in This Society': Interview with Don DeLillo." By Anthony DeCurtis. *South Atlantic Quarterly* 89 (2): 281–304.

———. 1991. *Mao II.* New York: Viking.

———. 2003a. *Cosmopolis.* New York: Scribner.

———. 2003b. "'Don DeLillo: retour vers le futur.' Propos recueillis par Minh Tran Huy." *Magazine littéraire* 425 (November): 80–81.

De Man, Paul. 1979. *Allegories of Reading: Figural Language in Rousseau, Nietzsche, Rilke, and Proust.* New Haven: Yale University Press.

———. 1984. "Phenomenality and Materiality in Kant." In *Hermeneutics: Questions and Prospects,* edited by Gary Shapiro and Antony Sica, 121–44. Amherst: University of Massachusetts Press.

———. 1987. "Hegel on the Sublime." In *Displacement: Derrida and After,* edited and with an introduction by Mark Krupnick, 139–53. Bloomington: Indiana University Press.

Derrida, Jacques. 1972a. *La Dissémination.* Paris: Seuil.

———. 1972b. *Marges de la philosophie.* Paris: Minuit.

———. 1976. *Of Grammatology.* Translated and with an introduction by Gayatri Chakravorty Spivak. Baltimore: Johns Hopkins University Press.

———. 1978. *La Vérité en peinture.* Paris: Flammarion.

———. 1979. *L'Écriture et la différence.* Paris: Seuil.

———. 1984. "No Apocalypse, Not Now (Full Speed Ahead, Seven Missiles, Seven Missives)." Translated by Caterine Porter and Philip Lewis. *Diacritics* 14 (2): 20–31.

———. 1985. *Otobiographies: The Teaching of Nietzsche and the Politics of the Proper Name.* Translated by Avital Ronell. *The Ear of the Other: Otobiography, Transference, Translation.* Texts and Discussions with Jacques Derrida. English edition edited by Christie McDonald. Translation by Peggy Kamuf of the French edition edited by Claude Levesque and Christie McDonald. Lincoln: University of Nebraska Press.

———. 1987. *Psyché. Inventions de l'autre.* Paris: Galilée.

———. 1992. " 'Eating Well,' or the Calculation of the Subject: An Interview with Jacques Derrida." In *Who Comes after the Subject?,* edited by E. Cadava, Peter Connor, and Jean-Luc Nancy, 96–119. New York: Routledge.

———. 1993. *Raising the Tone of Philosophy: Late Essays by Immanuel Kant, Transformative Critique by Jacques Derrida.* Edited by Peter Fenves. Baltimore: Johns Hopkins University Press.

———. 1994. *Specters of Marx: The State of Debt, the Work of Mourning, & the New International.* Translated by Peggy Kamuf. Introduction by Bernd Magnus and Stephen Cullenberg. New York: Routledge.

———. 1995. *On the Name.* Translated and edited by Thomas Dutoit. Stanford, CA: Stanford University Press.

———. 1997a. *Politics of Friendship.* Translated by George Collins. London: Verso.

———. 1997b. *The Post Card: From Socrates to Freud and Beyond.* Translated with an introduction and additional notes by Alan Bass. Chicago: University of Chicago Press.

———. 2001. "Deconstruction and Actuality." In *Postmodern Debates,* edited by Simon Malpas, 75–78. New York: Palgrave.

Doane, Mary Ann. 1990. "Technophilia: Technology, Representation, and the Feminine." In *Body/Politics: Women and the Discourses of Science,* edited by Mary Jacobus, Evelyn Fox Keller, and Sally Shuttleworth, 163–76. New York: Routledge.

Doctorow, E. L. 1971. *The Book of Daniel.* New York: Random House.

Doležel, Lubomír. 1998. *Heterocosmica: Fiction and Possible Worlds.* Baltimore: Johns Hopkins University Press.

Duvall, John N. 1994. "The (Super)Marketplace of Images: Television as Unmediated Mediation in DeLillo's *White Noise*." *Arizona Quarterly* 50 (3): 127–53.

Eakin, Paul John. 1992. *Touching the World: Reference in Autobiography*. Princeton, NJ: Princeton University Press.

Eddins, Dwight. 1990. *The Gnostic Pynchon*. Bloomington: Indiana University Press.

Edmundson, Mark. 1988. "The Ethics of Deconstruction." *Michigan Quarterly Review* 27 (4): 622–44.

Escarpit, Robert. 1971. *Sociology of Literature*. Translated by Ernest Pick. 2nd ed. With a new introduction by Malcolm Bradbury and Bryan Wilson. London: Frank Cass.

Fabre, Genevieve. 1988. "Genealogical Archaeology or the Quest for Legacy in Toni Morrison's *Song of Solomon*." In *Critical Essays on Toni Morrison*, edited by Nellie Y. McKay, 105–14. Boston: G. K. Hall.

Fandozzi, Phillip R. 1982. *Nihilism and Technology: A Heideggerian Investigation*. Washington, DC: University Press of America.

Faulkner, William. 1990. *Light in August*. New York: Random House.

Fernbach, Amanda. 2002. *Fantasies of Fetishism: From Decadence to the Post-Human*. New Brunswick, NJ: Rutgers University Press.

Ferraro, Thomas J. 1991. "Whole Families Shopping at Night." In Lentricchia 1991, 15–38.

Fforde, Jasper. 2003. *The Eyre Affair*. New York: Penguin.

Fishman, Charles. 1984. "Naming Names: Three Recent Novels by Women Writers." *Names* (1): 33–44.

Fjellestad, Danuta Zadworna. 1995. "'The Insertion of the Self into the Space of Borderless Possibility': Eva Hoffman's Exiled Body." MELUS 20 (2): 132–47.

Foster, John Burt. 1989. "Nabokov Before Proust: The Paradox of Anticipatory Memory." *Slavic and East European Journal* 33 (1): 78–95.

———. 1993. *Nabokov's Art of Memory and European Modernism*. Princeton, NJ: Princeton University Press.

Foucault, Michel. 1984. *The Foucault Reader*. Edited by Paul Rabinow. New York: Pantheon Books.

———. 1988. *Technologies of the Self: A Seminar with Michel Foucault*. Edited by Luther H. Martin, Huck Gutman, and Patrick H. Hutton. Amherst: University of Massachusetts Press.

———. 1993. *Language, Counter-Memory, Practice: Selected Essays and Interviews*. Edited with an introduction by Donald. F. Bouchard. Translated by Donald F. Bouchard and Sherry Simon. Ithaca, NY: Cornell University Press.

———. 1994. *The Order of Things: An Archaeology of the Human Sciences*. A Translation of *Les Mots and les choses*. New York: Random House.

Fowler, Douglas. 1980. *A Reader's Guide to* Gravity's Rainbow. Ann Arbor, MI: Ardis.

Frank, Jerome D. 1987. "Galloping Technology: A New Social Disease." In *Contemporary Moral Controversies in Technology*, edited by Pablo A. Iannone, 17–26. New York. Oxford: Oxford University Press.

Friedrich, Marianne M. 1999. "Reconstructing Paradise: Eva Hoffman's *Lost in Translation*." *Yiddish* 11 (3–4): 159–65.

Frow, John. 1990. "The Last Things Before the Last: Notes on *White Noise*." *South Atlantic Quarterly* 89 (2): 413–29.

Fuery, Patrick, and Nick Mansfield. 2000. *Cultural Studies and Critical Theory.* Oxford: Oxford University Press.

Gane, Mike. 1991. *Critical and Fatal Theory.* London: Routledge.

Garber, Frederick. 1987. "The Talk Poems of David Antin." *North Dakota Quarterly* 55 (4): 217–38.

Gasché, Rodolphe. 1990. "On Mere Sight: A Response to Paul de Man." In Silverman and Aylesworth 1990, 109–15.

Geertz, Clifford. 2000. *Local Knowledge: Further Essays in Interpretive Anthropology.* New York: Basic Books.

Genette, Gérard. 1976. *Mimologiques. Voyage en Cratylie.* Paris: Seuil.

———. 1979. *Introduction à l'architexte.* Paris: Seuil.

———. 1980. *Narrative Discourse.* Translated by Jane E. Lewin. Ithaca: Cornell University Press.

Gibson, William. 1984. *Neuromancer.* New York: Ace Books.

Gitenstein, Barbara R. 1997. "Eva Hoffman: Conflicts and Continuities of the Self." In *Something of My Very Own to Say: American Women Writers of Polish Descent,* edited by Thomas S. Gladsky and Rita Holmes Gladsky, 261–75. New York: Columbia University Press.

Goffman, Erving. 1986. *Frame Analysis: An Essay on the Organization of Experience.* With a new foreword by Bennett M. Berger. Boston: Northeastern University Press.

Goodwin, James. 1993. *Autobiography: The Self Made Text.* New York: Twayne.

Grabes, Herbert. 1985. "The Parodistic Erasure of the Boundary between Fiction and Reality in Nabokov's English Novels." *Canadian-American Slavic Studies* 19 (3): 268–81.

Graham, Elaine L. 2002. *Representations of the Post/Human: Monsters, Aliens and Others in Popular Culture.* New Brunswick, NJ: Rutgers University Press.

Gray, Chris Hables. 2001. *Cyborg Citizen: Politics in the Posthuman Age.* New York: Routledge.

Green, Geoffrey. 1981. "The Speech of Memory in Nabokov's Fiction." *Vladimir Nabokov Research Newsletter* 6 (Spring): 21–23.

———. 1987. "Metamorphosing Kafka: The Example of Philip Roth." In *The Dove and the Mole: Kafka's Journey into Darkness and Creativity,* edited by Ronald Gottesman and Moshe Lazar, 35–46. Malibu, CA: Undena.

Greenblatt, Stephen. "The circulation of social energy." In Lodge and Wood 2000, 495–511.

Grimes, William. 1992. "The Ridiculous Vision of Mark Leyner." *New York Times Magazine,* September 13, 1992, 34–35, 51, 64–66.

Grossmith, Robert. 1986. "Nabokov's Horological Hearts." *The Nabokovian* 16 (Spring): 38–43.

Guattari, Félix. 1993. "Machinic Heterogenesis." In *Rethinking Technologies,* edited by Verena Andermatt Conley on behalf of the Miami Theory Collective, 13–27. Minneapolis: University of Minnesota Press.

Gunn, Giles. 2001. *Beyond Solidarity: Pragmatism and Difference in a Globalized World.* Chicago: University of Chicago Press.

Gunn, Janet Varner. 1982. *Autobiography: Towards a Poetics of Experience.* Philadelphia: University of Pennsylvania Press.

Habermas, Jürgen. 1987. *The Philosophical Discourse of Modernity: Twelve Lectures.* Translated by Frederick Lawrence. Cambridge, MA: MIT Press.

Halberstam, Judith, and Ira Livingston, eds. 1995. *Posthuman Bodies.* Bloomington: Indiana University Press.

Haraway, Donna. 1990. "A Manifesto for Cyborgs: Science, Technology, and Socialist Feminism in the 1980s." In *Feminism/Postmodernism*, edited by L. J. Nicholson, 190–233. New York: Routledge.

Hayles, N. Katherine. 1993a. "The Life Cycle of Cyborgs: Writing the Posthuman." In *A Question of Identity: Women, Science, and Literature*, edited by Marina Benjamin, 152–72. New Brunswick, NJ: Rutgers University Press.

———. 1993b. "The Materiality of Informatics." *Configurations* 1 (1): 147–70. http://muse.jhu.edu/journals/configurations/toc/con1.1.html.

———. 1999. *How We Became Posthuman: Virtual Bodies in Cybernetics, Literature, and Informatics.* Chicago: University of Chicago Press.

Heartney, Eleanor. 1997. *Critical Condition: American Culture at the Crossroads.* Cambridge: Cambridge University Press.

Heidegger, Martin. 1962. *Die Technik und die Kehre.* Pfulligen: Günter Neske.

———. 1975. *Poetry, Language, Thought.* Translated and with an introduction by Albert Hofstadter. New York: Harper & Row.

———. 1977. *Basic Writings from "Being and Time" (1927) to "The Task of Thinking" (1964).* Edited, with general introduction and introduction to each selection by David Farrell Krell. New York: Harper and Row.

Herman, David. 2002. *Story Logic: Problems and Possibilities of Narrative.* Lincoln: University of Nebraska Press.

Hirsch, Marianne. 1993. "Projected Memory: Holocaust Photographs in Personal and Public Fantasy." In Bal, Crewe, and Spitzer 1993, 3–23.

Hite, Molly. 1983. *Ideas of Order in the Novels of Thomas Pynchon.* Columbus: Ohio State University Press.

———. 1989. *The Other Side of the Story: Structures and Strategies of Contemporary Feminist Narrative.* Ithaca: Cornell University Press.

———. 2002. "Modernist Design, Postmodernist Paranoia: Reading *Absalom, Absalom!* with *Gravity's Rainbow.*" In *Faulkner and Postmodernism*, edited by John N. Duvall and Ann J. Abadie, 57–80. Jackson: University Press of Mississippi.

Hoffman, Eva. 1990. *Lost in Translation: A Life in a New Language.* New York: Penguin.

———. 1993. *Exit into History: A Journey Through the New Eastern Europe.* New York: Viking.

———. 1994. "*Lost in Translation* Five Years Later." *2B* 2 (3–4): 67.

Hohmann, Charles. 1986. *Thomas Pynchon's "Gravity's Rainbow": A Study of Its Conceptual Structure and of Rilke's Influence.* New York: Peter Lang.

Hollinger, Veronica. 1990. "Cybernetic Deconstructions: Cyberpunk and Postmodernism." *Mosaic* 23 (2): 29–44.

Horkheimer, Max, and Theodor W. Adorno. 1982. *Dialectic of Enlightenment.* Translated by John Cumming. New York: Continuum.

Hornick, Lita. 1979. *David Antin / Debunker of the "Real."* Putnam Valley, NY: Swollen Magpie Press.

Hume, Kathryn. 1987. *Pynchon's Mythography: An Approach to "Gravity's Rainbow."* Carbondale: Southern Illinois University Press.

Irigaray, Luce. 2000. "The bodily encounter with the mother." In Lodge and Wood 2000, 414–23.

Jakobson, Roman. 2000. "Linguistics and poetics." In Lodge and Wood 2000, 31–55.

James, Williams. 1978. *"Pragmatism" and "The Meaning of Truth."* Introduction by A. J. Ayer. Cambridge, MA: Harvard University Press.

Jameson, Fredric. 1984. "The Politics of Theory: Ideological Positions in the Postmodern Debate." *New German Critique* 33 (Fall): 53–65.

———. 1991. *Postmodernism, or, The Cultural Logic of Late Capitalism.* Durham, NC: Duke University Press.

Jauß, Hans Robert. 1970. *Zeit und Erinnerung in Marcel Prousts À la recherche du temps perdu. Ein Beitrag zur Theorie des Romans.* Heidelberg: Carl Winter.

Johnston, John. 1998. *Information Multiplicity: American Fiction in the Age of Media Saturation.* Baltimore: Johns Hopkins University Press.

Jonas, Hans. 1984. *The Imperative of Responsibility: In Search of an Ethics for the Technological Age.* Translated by Hans Jonas with the collaboration of David Herr. Chicago: University of Chicago Press.

Kaplan, Justin, and Anne Bernays. 1997. *The Language of Names: What We Call Ourselves and Why It Matters.* New York: Simon and Schuster.

Karpinski, Eva C. 1996. "Negotiating the Self: Eva Hoffman's *Lost in Translation* and the Question of Immigrant Autobiography." *Canadian Ethnic Studies* 28 (1): 127–35.

Kearney, Richard. 1993. "Derrida's Ethical Re-Turn." In *Working through Derrida,* edited by Gary B. Madison, 28–50. Evanston, IL: Northwestern University Press.

Keesey, Douglass. 1993. *Don DeLillo.* New York: Maxwell Macmillan.

Kellman, Steven G. 1998. "Lost in the Promised Land: Eva Hoffman Revises Mary Antin." *Prooftexts: A Journal of Jewish Literary History* 18 (2): 149–59.

King, Noel. 1991. "Reading *White Noise:* floating remarks." *Critical Quarterly* 33 (3): 66–83.

Kranzberg, Melvin, ed. 1980. *Ethics in an Age of Pervasive Technology.* Boulder, CO: Westview Press.

Kristeva, Julia. 1993. *Proust and the Sense of Time.* Translated and with an introduction by Stephen Bann. New York: Columbia University Press.

Kroker, Arthur, and Marilouise Kroker. 1987. *Body Invaders: Panic Sex in America.* New York: St. Martin's Press.

Krupnick, Mark. 1993. "Assimilation in Recent American Jewish Autobiographies." *Contemporary Literature* 34 (3): 451–74.

Kundera, Milan. 2000. *Ignorance.* Translated from the French by Linda Asher. New York: HarperCollins.

Lacan, Jacques. 2000. "The insistence of the letter in the unconscious." In Lodge and Wood 2000, 62–87.

Laclau, Ernesto. 1989. Preface to *The Sublime Object of Ideology,* by Slavoj Žižek, ix–xv. London: Verso.

Lacoue-Labarthe, Philippe. 1971. "Le détour (Nietzsche et la rhétorique)." *Poétique* 5: 53–76.

————. 1991. "Sublime Truth (Part I)." *Cultural Critique* 18 (Spring): 5–31.

————. 1991–1992. "Sublime Truth (Part II)." *Cultural Critique* 20 (Winter): 207–29.

Lacy, Dan. 1970. "The Economics of Publishing, or Adam Smith and Literature." In *The Sociology of Art and Literature. A Reader,* edited by Milton C. Albrecht, James H. Barnett, and Mason Griff, 407–25. New York: Praeger Publishers.

Lane, Robert E. 1984. "The Road Not Taken: Friendship, Consumerism, and Happiness." *Critical Review* 8 (4): 521–54.

Lazer, Hank. 1995. "Thinking Made in the Mouth: The Cultural Poetics of David Antin and Jerome Rothenberg." In *Picturing Cultural Values in Postmodern America,* edited by William G. Doty, 101–39. Tuscaloosa: University of Alabama Press.

LeClair, Tom. 1987. *In the Loop: Don DeLillo and the Systems Novel.* Urbana: University of Illinois Press.

Lejeune, Philippe. 1989. *On Autobiography.* Edited and with a foreword by Paul John Eakin. Translated by Katherine Leary. Minneapolis: University of Minnesota Press.

Lentricchia, Frank. 1990. "*Libra* as Postmodern Critique." *South Atlantic Quarterly* 89 (2): 432–53.

————, ed. 1991. *New Essays on "White Noise."* Cambridge: Cambridge University Press.

Lévinas, Emmanuel. 1996. *Proper Names.* Translated by Michael B. Smith. Stanford, CA: Stanford University Press.

Leyner, Mark. 1983. *I Smell Esther Williams and Other Stories.* New York: Fiction Collective.

————. 1990. *My Cousin, My Gastroenterologist.* New York: Harmony Books.

————. 1992. *Et Tu, Babe.* New York: Harmony Books.

————. 1995. *Tooth Imprints on a Corn Dog.* New York: Harmony Books.

Lodge, David, ed., with Nigel Wood. 2000. *Modern Criticism and Theory: A Reader.* 2nd ed., revised and expanded by Nigel Wood. Harlow, UK: Longman.

Lotringer, Sylvère. 1992. "Hyperreal." In *Jean Baudrillard: The Disappearance of Art and Politics,* edited by William Stearns and William Chaloupka, 38–42. New York: St. Martin's Press.

Luckhurst, Roger. 1991. "Border Policing: Postmodernism and Science Fiction." *Science Fiction Studies* 55, no. 18, part 3 (November): 358–66.

Lyotard, Jean-François. 1984. *The Postmodern Condition: A Report on Knowledge.* Translated by Geoff Bennington and Brian Massumi. Foreword by Fredric Jameson. Minneapolis: University of Minnesota Press.

————. 1986. *Le Postmoderne expliqé aux enfants. Correspondence 1982–1985.* Paris: Galilée.

————. 1988. *The Differend: Phrases in Dispute.* Translated by Georges Van Den Abbeele. Minneapolis: University of Minnesota Press.

————. 1991. *The Inhuman: Reflections on Time.* Translated by Geoffrey Bennington and Rachel Bowlby. Stanford, CA: Stanford University Press.

————. 1993. *The Postmodern Explained: Correspondence 1982–1985.* Translation edited by Julian Pefanis and Morgan Thomas. Translation by Don Barry, Bernadette Maher, Virginia Spate, and Morgan Thomas. Afterword by Wlad Godzich. Minneapolis: University of Minnesota Press.

Mackethan, Lucinda H. 1986–1987. "Names to Bear Witness. The Theme and Tradition of Naming in Toni Morrison's *Song of Solomon.*" *CEA Critic* 49, vol. 2–4 (Winter 1986–Summer 1987): 199–207.

Macksey, Richard. 1962. "The Architecture of Time: Dialectics and Structure." In *Proust: A Collection of Critical Essays,* edited by R. N. Girard, 104–21. Englewood Cliffs, NJ: Prentice-Hall.

Malouf, David. 1993. *Remembering Babylon.* New York: Random House.

Maltby, Paul. 1996. "The Romantic Metaphysics of Don DeLillo." *Contemporary Literature* 37 (2): 258–77.

———. 2002. *The Visionary Moment: A Postmodern Critique.* Albany: SUNY Press.

Margolin, Uri. 2002. "Naming and Believing: Practices of the Proper Name in Narrative Fiction." *Narrative* 10 (2): 107–27.

Marin, Louis. 1981. "Les fins de l'interprétation ou les traversées du regard dans le sublime d'une tempête." In *Les fins de l'homme. À partir du travail de Jacques Derrida,* edited by Philippe Lacoue-Labarthe and Jean-Luc Nancy, 317–44. Paris: Galilée.

———. 1992. "Sur une tour de Babel dans un tableau de Poussin." In Nancy et al. 1992, 237–58.

Mark, Thomas J. 1987. *Ethics and Technology.* Lanham, MD: University Press of America.

Martin-Deslias, Noël. n.d. "Le mythe du temps." In *Idéalisme de Marcel Proust,* 19–29. Montpellier: F. Janny.

Massey, Irving. 1976. *The Gaping Pig: Literature and Metamorphosis.* Berkeley and Los Angeles: University of California Press.

McElroy, Joseph. 1977. *Plus.* New York: Alfred A. Knopf.

McHale, Brian. 1987. *Postmodernist Fiction.* New York: Methuen.

———. 1992. *Constructing Postmodernism.* London: Routledge.

McHoul, Alec, and David Wills. 1990. *Writing Pynchon: Strategies in Fictional Analysis.* Urbana: University of Illinois Press.

Merivale, Patricia. 1967. "The Flaunting of Artifice in Vladimir Nabokov and Jorge Louis Borges." In *Nabokov: The Man and His Work,* edited by L. S. Dembo, 209–24. Madison: University of Wisconsin Press.

Michael, Magali Cornier. 1994. "The Political Paradox within Don DeLillo's *Libra.*" *Critique* 35 (3): 146–56.

Miller, J. Hillis. 1987. *The Ethics of Reading: Kant, de Man, Eliot, Trollope, James, and Benjamin.* New York: Columbia University Press.

Mohanty, Satya P. 1997. *Literary Theory and the Claims of History: Postmodernism, Objectivity, Multicultural Politics.* Ithaca: Cornell University Press.

Moi, Toril. 2001. *Sexual/Textual Politics.* London: Routledge.

Moraru, Christian. 1990. *Poetica reflectarii. Incercare in arheologia mimezei.* Bucharest: Univers Press.

———. 1995. "Exploring Names: Notes on Onomastics and Fictionality in Marcel Proust's *Remembrance of Things Past.*" *Names* 43 (2): 119–30.

———. 2001. *Rewriting: Postmodern Narrative and Cultural Critique in the Age of Cloning.* Albany: SUNY Press.

Moravec, Hans. 1988. *Mind Children: The Future of Robot and Human Intelligence.* Cambridge, MA.: Harvard University Press.

Morgan, David H. J. 1992. *Discovering Men.* London: Routledge.

Morrison, Toni. 1978. *Song of Solomon.* New York: Penguin.

———. 1998. *Beloved.* New York: Alfred A. Knopf.

Moss, Howard. 1962. *The Magic Lantern of Marcel Proust.* New York: Grosset and Dunlap.

Mott, Christopher M. 1994. "*Libra* and the Subject of History." *Critique* 35 (3): 131–45.

Mowitt, John. 1992. *Text: The Genealogy of an Antidisciplinary Object.* Durham, NC: Duke University Press.

Nabokov, Vladimir. 1958. *Nabokov's Dozen: A Collection of Thirteen Stories.* Garden City, NY: Doubleday.

———. 1966. *Speak, Memory: An Autobiography Revisited.* New York: G. P. Putnam's Sons.

———. 1973. *Strong Opinions.* New York: McGraw-Hill.

———. 1980. *Lectures on Literature.* Edited by Fredson Bowers. Introduction by John Updike. New York: Harcourt Jovanovich, Bruccoli Clark.

———. 1981. *Ada or Ardor: A Family Chronicle.* New York: McGraw-Hill.

———. 1989. *Pale Fire.* New York: Vintage Books.

———. 1993. *The Gift.* Translated from the Russian by Michael Scammell with the collaboration of the author. New York: Vintage Books.

———. 1995. *The Stories of Vladimir Nabokov.* New York: Alfred A. Knopf.

Nadel, Ira B. 1999. Introduction to Henry Adams 1999, vii–xxviii.

Nancy, Jean-Luc. 1992. "L'Offrande sublime." In Nancy et al. 1992, 37–75.

Nancy, Jean-Luc et al. 1992. *Du Sublime.* Preface by Jean-Luc Nancy. Paris: Belin.

Nef, Jorge, Jokelee Vanderkop, and Henry Wiseman, eds. 1989. *Ethics and Technology: Ethical Choices in the Age of Pervasive Technology.* Toronto: Wall and Thompson.

Nemoianu, Virgil. 1980. "Wrestling with Time: Some Tendencies in Nabokov's and Eliade's Later Works." *Southeastern Europe/L'Europe de Sud-Est* 7 (1): 74–90.

Newman, Charles. 1985. *The Post-Modern Aura: The Act of Fiction in an Age of Inflation.* With a preface by Gerald Graff. Evanston, IL: Northwestern University Press.

Nietzsche, Friedrich. 1924. *The Future of Our Educational Institutions.* Vol. 2 of *The Complete Works of Friedrich Nietzsche.* Edited by Oscar Levy. Translated by J. M. Kennedy. New York: Macmillan.

———. 1971. "Friedrich Nietzsche. Rhétorique et langage. Textes traduits, présentés et annotés par Philippe Lacoue-Labarthe et Jean-Luc Nancy." *Poétique* 5: 99–142.

———. 1978. Vol. 83 of *Sämtliche Werke.* Stuttgart: Kröners Taschenausgabe.

———. 1989. "On Truth and Lying in an Extra-Moral Sense." In *Friedrich Nietzsche on Rhetoric and Language,* edited and translated with a critical introduction by Sander Gilman, Carole Blair, and David J. Parent, 246–57. New York: Oxford University Press.

Norris, Christopher. 1986. "On Derrida's 'Apocalyptic Tone': Textual Politics and the Principle of Reason." *Southern Review* 19 (1): 13–30.

———. 1987. *Derrida.* London: Fontana.

———. 1990. *What's Wrong with Postmodernism: Critical Theory and the Ends of Philosophy.* Baltimore: Johns Hopkins University Press.

O'Donnell, Patrick. 1992. "Engendering Paranoia in Contemporary Narrative." *boundary 2* 19 (1): 181–204.

Ong, Walter J. 1982. *Orality and Literacy: The Technologizing of the Word.* London: Routledge.

Osteen, Mark. 1994. "'A Moral Form to Master Commerce': The Economies of DeLillo's *Great Jones Street.*" *Critique* 35 (3): 157–72.

O'Sullivan, Gerry. 1990. "The Library Is on Fire: Intertextuality in Borges and Foucault." In Aizenberg 1990, 109–21.

Palmer, Michael D. 1989. *Names, Reference and Correctness in Plato's "Cratylus."* New York: Peter Lang.

Parker, Helen N. 1984. *Biological Themes in Modern Science Fiction.* Ann Arbor, MI: UMI Research Press.

Parker, Jan Stephen. 1991. "Vladimir Nabokov and the Short Story." *Russian Literature Triquarterly* 24: 63–72.

Pavel, Thomas. 1986. *Fictional Worlds.* Cambridge, MA: Harvard University Press.

Penley, Constance, and Andrew Ross. 1991. Introduction to *Technoculture,* edited by Constance Penley and Andrew Ross, viii–xvii. Minneapolis: University of Minnesota Press.

Perloff, Marjorie. 1981. *The Poetics of Indeterminacy: Rimbaud to Cage.* Princeton, NJ: Princeton University Press.

———. 1996. *Wittgenstein's Ladder: Poetic Language and the Strangeness of the Ordinary.* Chicago: University of Chicago Press.

Pierce, John J. 1987. *Great Themes of Science Fiction: A Study in Imagination and Evolution.* Foreword by Thomas J. Roberts. New York: Greenwood Press.

Pireddu, Nicoletta. 1992. "Il rumore dell'incertezza: sistemi chiusi e aperti in *White Noise* di Don DeLillo." *Quaderni di lingue e letterature* 17: 129–40.

Plasa, Carl, ed. 1998. *Toni Morrison: Beloved.* New York: Columbia University Press.

Porter, John Houston. 1962. "Temporal Patterns in *À la recherche du temps perdu.*" *French Studies* 16: 33–44.

Porush, David. 1985. *The Soft Machine: Cybernetic Fiction.* New York: Methuen.

Poulet, Georges. 1956. *Studies in Human Time.* Translated by Elliott Coleman. Baltimore: Johns Hopkins University Press.

Powers, Richard. 2000. *Plowing the Dark.* New York: Farrar, Straus and Giroux.

Pries, Christine. 1989. *Das Erhabene. Zwischen Grenzerfahrung und Größenwahn.* Weinheim: VCH, Acta Humaniora.

Proefriedt, William A. 1990. "The Education of Mary Antin." *Journal of Ethnic Studies* 17 (4): 81–100.

———. 1991. "The Education of Eva Hoffman." *Journal of Ethnic Studies* 18 (4): 123–35.

Proust, Marcel. 1982. *Remembrance of Things Past.* The definitive French Pléiade edition translated by C. K. Scott Moncrieff and Terence Kilmartin. 3 vols. New York: Vintage Books.

Pynchon, Thomas. 1973. *Gravity's Rainbow.* New York: Viking.

———. 1999. *The Crying of Lot 49.* New York: HarperCollins.

Rabaté, Jean-Michel. 1984. *James Joyce. Portrait de l'auteur en autre lecteur.* Petit-Roeulx: CISTRE.

———. 1996. *The Ghosts of Modernity.* Gainesville: University Press of Florida.

Rabinowitz, Paula. 1983. "Naming, Magic, and Documentary: The Subversion of the Narrative in *Song of Solomon, Ceremony,* and *China Men.*" In *Feminist Re-Visions. What Has Been and Might Be,* edited by Vivian Patraka and Louise A. Tilly, 26–42. Ann Arbor: University of Michigan Press.

Rapaport, Herman. 1990. "Borges, De Man, and the Deconstruction of Reading." In Aizenberg 1990, 139–54.

Readings, Bill. 1991. *Introducing Lyotard: Art and Politics.* London: Routledge.

Richard, Jean-Pierre. 1974. *Proust et le monde sensible.* Paris: Seuil.

Ricoeur, Paul. 1984. *Time and Narrative. Vol. I.* Translated by Kathleen McLaughlin and David Pellauer. Chicago: University of Chicago Press.

Rosenberg, Ruth. n.d. "'And the Children May Know Their Names': Toni Morrison's *Song of Solomon.*" *Literary Onomastic Studies* 8: 195–217.

Ross, Andrew. 1989. "Baudrillard's Bad Attitude." In *Seduction and Theory: Readings of Gender, Representation, and Rhetoric,* edited by Diane Hunter, 214–25. Urbana: University of Illinois Press.

Roth, Philip. 1972. *The Breast.* New York: Holt, Rineheart and Winston.

Rothenberg, Jerome. 1994. "New Models, New Visions: Some Notes Toward a Poetics of Performance." In *Postmodern American Poetry: A Norton Anthology,* edited by Paul Hoover, 640–44. New York: W. W. Norton.

Rowe, William Woodin. 1971. *Nabokov's Deceptive World.* New York: New York University Press.

Rushdie, Salman. 1991. *Imaginary Homelands: Essays and Criticism 1981–1991.* London: Granta and Viking.

———. 2001. *Fury.* New York: Random House.

Ruthrof, Horst. 1990. "Narrative and the Digital: On the Syntax of the Postmodern." *AUMLA: Journal of the Australian Universities Language and Literature Association* 74 (November): 185–200.

Ryan, Marie-Laure. 1997. "Postmoderism and the Doctrine of Panfictionality." *Narrative* 5 (2): 165–87.

Said, Edward. 1994. *Orientalism.* New York: Random House.

Sayre, Henry M. 1982. "David Antin and the Oral Poetics Movement." *Contemporary Literature* 23 (4): 428–50.

Scarboro, Ann Armstrong. 1994. Afterword to *I, Tituba, Black Witch of Salem,* by Maryse Condé translated by Richard Philcox, foreword by Angela Y. Davis, afterword by Ann Armstrong Scarboro, 187–225. New York: Ballantine Books.

Scarpetta, Guy. 1981. *Éloge du cosmopolitisme.* Paris: Bernard Grasset.

———. 1985. *L'Impureté.* Paris: Bernard Grasset.

———. 1988. *L'Artifice.* Paris: Bernard Grasset.

Schloss Carol. 1982. "*Speak, Memory*: The Aristocracy of Art." In *Nabokov's Fifth Arc: Nabokov and Others on His Life's Work,* edited by J. E. Rivers and Charles Nicol, 224–29. Austin: University of Texas Press.

Scholes, Robert. 1979. *Fabulation and Metafiction.* Urbana: University of Illinois Press.

Scholes, Robert, and Robert Kellogg. 1966. *The Nature of Narrative.* London: Oxford University Press.

Schrift, Alan D. 1990. *Nietzsche and the Question of Interpretation: Between Hermeneutics and Deconstruction.* New York: Routledge.

Schwab, Gabriele. 1994. *Subjects without Selves: Transitional Texts in Modern Fiction.* Cambridge, MA: Harvard University Press.

Schwartz, Hillel. 1996. *The Culture of the Copy: Striking Likenesses, Unreasonable Facsimiles.* New York: Zone Books.

Schwenger, Peter. 1990. "Nuclear Critics and the Monstrous New." *Dalhousie Review* 70 (1): 56–67.

Shaviro, Steven. 2003. *Connected, or What It Means to Live in the Network Society.* Minneapolis: University of Minnesota Press.

Shields, David. 1987. "Autobiographic Rapture and Fictive Irony in *Speak, Memory* and *The Real Life of Sebastian Knight.*" *Iowa Review* 17 (1): 44–54.

Sicker, Philip. 1987. "Practicing Nostalgia: Time and Memory in Nabokov's Early Russian Fiction." *Studies in Twentieth Century Literature* 11 (2): 253–70.

Siebers, Tobin. 1988. *The Ethics of Criticism.* Ithaca: Cornell University Press.

Siegel, Lee. 1995. *City of Dreadful Night: A Tale of Horror and the Macabre in India.* Chicago: University of Chicago Press.

————. 1999. *Love in a Dead Language.* Chicago: University of Chicago Press.

Siegel, Mark Richard. 1978. *Pynchon: Creative Paranoia in "Gravity's Rainbow."* Port Washington, NY: Kennikat Press.

Silko, Leslie Marmon. 1986. *Ceremony.* New York: Penguin.

Silverman, Hugh J. 1990. Introduction to Silverman and Aylesworth 1990, xi–xix.

Silverman, Hugh J., and Gary E. Aylesworth, eds. 1990. *The Textual Sublime: Deconstruction and Its Differences.* Stony Brook: SUNY Press.

Skulsky, Harold. 1981. *Metamorphosis: The Mind in Exile.* Cambridge, MA: Harvard University Press.

Smith, M. W. 2001. *Reading Simulacra: Fatal Strategies for Postmodernity.* Albany: SUNY Press.

Smith, Paul. 1988. *Discerning the Subject.* Foreword by John Mowitt. Minneapolis: University of Minnesota Press.

Smith, Valerie. 1993. "*Song of Solomon.* Continuities of Community." In *Toni Morrison: Critical Perspectives. Past and Present,* edited by Henry Louis Gates, Jr., and K. A. Appiah, 273–83. New York: Amistad.

Sollers, Philippe. 1968. "Écriture et révolution. Entretien de Jacques Henric avec Philippe Sollers." In Michel Foucault et al. *Théorie d'ensemble,* 67–79. Paris: Seuil.

Sontag, Susan. 1990. *On Photography.* New York: Doubleday.

Spivak, Gayatri Chakravorty. 1999. *A Critique of Postcolonial Reason: Toward a History of the Vanishing Present.* Cambridge: Harvard University Press.

Springer, Claudia. 1991. "The pleasure of the interface." *Screen* 32 (3): 303–23.

Steel, Gareth H. 1979. *Chronology and Time in "À la recherche du temps perdu."* Genève: Librairie Droz.

Stegner, Page. 1967. *Escape into Aesthetics: The Art of Vladimir Nabokov.* London: Eyre and Spottiswoode.

Stein, Karen. 1980. "'I Didn't Even Know His Name': Name and Naming in Toni Morrison's *Sula.*" *Names* 28 (3): 226–29.

Stuart, Dabney. 1979. *Nabokov: The Dimensions of Parody.* Baton Rouge: Louisiana State University Press.

Sussman, Henry. 1997. *The Aesthetic Contract: Statutes of Art and Intellectual Work in Modernity.* Stanford, CA: Stanford University Press.

Tabbi, Joseph. 1995. *Postmodern Sublime: Technology and American Writing from Mailer to Cyberpunk*. Ithaca: Cornell University Press.

———. 2002. *Cognitive Fictions*. Minneapolis: University of Minnesota Press.

Tadié, Jacques-Yves. 1986. *Proust et le roman. Essai sur les formes et techniques du roman dans À la recherche du temps perdu*. Paris: Gallimard.

Thoreau, Henry David. 1992. *Walden*. With Ralph Waldo Emerson's essay on Thoreau. Introduced by Christopher Bigsby. London: Everyman's Library.

Ulmer, Gregory. 1985. *Applied Grammatology: Post(e)-Pedagogy from Jacques Derrida to Joseph Beuys*. Baltimore: Johns Hopkins University Press.

Updike, John. 1998. *Bech at Bay: A Quasi-Novel*. New York: Alfred A. Knopf.

Varsava, Jerry A. 1990. *Contingent Meanings: Postmodern Fiction, Mimesis, and the Reader*. Tallahassee: Florida State University Press.

Walton, Kendall L. 1993. *Mimesis as Make-Believe: On the Foundations of the Representational Arts*. Cambridge, MA: Harvard University Press.

White, Hayden. 1988. "The Rhetoric of Interpretation." *Poetics Today* 9 (2): 253–74.

———. 1999. *Figural Realism: Studies in the Mimesis Effect*. Baltimore: Johns Hopkins University Press.

Wilson, Elizabeth. 1995. "The Rhetoric of Urban Space." *New Left Review* 209 (January–February): 146–60.

Wilson, Rob. 1991. *American Sublime: The Genealogy of a Poetic Genre*. Madison: University of Wisconsin Press.

Wolfe, Cary. 1995. "In Search of Post-Humanist Theory: The Second-Order Cybernetics of Maturana and Varela." *Cultural Critique* 30 (Spring): 33–70.

Wood, Douglas Kellogg. 1982. *Men Against Time: Nicolas Berdiaev, T. S. Eliot, Aldous Huxley, & C. G. Jung*. Lawrence: University of Kansas Press.

Wood, Michael. 1994. *The magician's doubts: Nabokov and the risks of fiction*. London: Chatto & Windus.

Woodmansee, Martha. 1994. "On the Author Effect: Recovering Collectivity." In *The Construction of Authorship: Textual Appropriation in Law and Literature*, edited by Martha Woodmansee and Peter Jaszi, 15–28. Durham, NC: Duke University Press.

Zamora, Lois Parkinson. 1989. *Writing the Apocalypse: Historical Vision in Contemporary U.S. and Latin American Fiction*. Cambridge: Cambridge University Press.

Žižek, Slavoj. 2001. *On Belief*. London: Routledge.

Index

Acker, Kathy, 28, 35, 36, 74, 86, 87, 97, 98, 99, 113–18, 194, 206, 232, 235 n. 1; *Bodies of Work*, 114–17; *Don Quixote, Which Was a Dream*, 117; *Empire of the Senseless*, 117; *Great Expectations*, 113, 117; *My Death My Life by Pier Paolo Pasolini*, 117

Ackroyd, Peter: *English Music*, 30

Adams, Henry, 54–71, 134; *The Education of Henry Adams*, 54–71 passim; *Mont-Saint-Michel and Chartres*, 64

Adams, Timothy Dow, 239.n27

Adorno, Theodor W., 207, 245 n. 35

agency, 36; ethical, 135; and government agencies in DeLillo, 158; and technology, 130, 131, 133, 136

Agger, Ben, 153, 217, 245 n. 35

Albrow, Martin, 73, 239 n. 33

Alexandrov, Vladimir E., 50, 238 n. 19

Alger, Horatio, 57

Alien, 145

Allen, Woody, 184

Alter, Robert, 238 nn. 17 and 23

Altieri, Charles, 241 n. 43

anagram, 228–29, 232

Antin, David, 28, 33, 53, 75–85, 232, 240 nn. 35, 36, and 37, 39–42, 241 nn. 43, 45, 47; *talking at the boundaries*, 76, 81; *what it means to be avant-garde*, 76

Antin, Mary, 54–75; *The Promised Land*, 54–75 passim; *They Who Knock at Our Gates*, 55

Anzaldúa, Gloria, 239 n. 25

Appadurai, Arjun, 226, 231

Apter, Emily, 230

Apuleius, Lucius, 149

Arabian Nights, The, 230

Arbuthnot, F. F., 249 n. 3

Aristotle, 26, 95, 131

Auerbach, Erich, 40

Aufhebung, 42, 236 n. 3

Augustine: *Confessions*, 89

Auster, Paul, 28, 34, 40, 86, 99–102, 113, 115, 158, 207, 232, 242 nn. 5, 6, 7, 245 n. 30; *The Art of Hunger: Essays, Prefaces, Interviews*, 99, 101; *The Book of Illusions*, 99, 100; *City of Glass*, 97, 100–2; *In the Country of Last Things*, 99, 242 n. 6; *Ghosts*, 97; *Hand to Mouth: A Chronicle of Early Failure*, 30, 87, 99; *The Locked Room*, 97, 100, 242 n. 6; *Moon Palace*, 99, 100; *The New York Trilogy*, 97, 99, 100; *Oracle Night*, 99, 100; *Timbuktu*, 99; *Mr. Vertigo*, 99, 242 n. 6

author: authorial index, in Auster, 242 n. 6; and authoring, 15; and authority, 90; and authorship, 15, 208; in Barthes, 16, 126; Beckettian model of, in DeLillo, 213, 219, 223; and consumption of (*see under* consumption); death of, in DeLillo, 210–12; figure of, commodified, 151–56, 212–15; figure of postmodern author in *Libra*, 222; and Foucault, 15, 16, 18; and indebtedness (*see under* indebtedness; *see also under* intertextuality and memorious discourse); in Leyner, 151–56 passim; in modernism versus postmodernism, 15–16, 19; and memorious, 24; and New Historicism, 18; and origin/originality/origination, 15–16, 18, 126; and posthuman, 152; and postmodernism, 17, 19, 24; and "presence," 126; and representation, 15; and reprise (*see under* reprise); romantic myth of, 219; and sexuality (*see under* sexuality and masculinity); and text as intertext, 18, 102; autobiography (*see under* genre, intertextuality, and memorious discourse)

avant-garde, 168, 174

avant-pop, 40, 127, 145, 150, 151, 156, 173

avant-pop, 127; and body/embodiment (*see under* body); and cyberculture, 127; and cybernetics, 127; and cyberpunk, 127; ethics, 131; and film, 127, 242 n. 3; and gender/engendering, 145–62 passim; and human, 127, 158–59 (*see also under* human); and humanities, 146, 149, 242 n. 1; and hypermasculinity in Leyner, 152–55 (*see also under* masculinity); intertextual/memorious, 36, 128–29, 142, 145; and ontology, 37, 162; and philosophy, 242 n. 3; and popular culture (*see* popular culture); and postbiological, 146; and "postdiscourse," 150; versus posthumanist, 127–28; and postmodernism/postmodernity, 125–62 passim, 242 n. 3; and postorganic, 146; and poststructuralism, 242 n. 3; in Pynchon, 129–44; re(-)presentation of, 128; and science fiction, 127, 145, 150, 153, 245 n. 36; and subject/subjectivity (*see under* subject/subjectivity); and superhuman, in Leyner, 152–55; and technology, 131–57; and theology, 242 n. 3
posthumanism, 125–62 passim: and authorship, 18; and body (*see under* body); and celebrity culture, 152–56; and ethics, 29, 143; evolution of, 145; and *Gravity's Rainbow*, 35; and human/humanism, 36, 105, 125–62 passim, 242 n. 4 (*see also* human and humanism/humanist); and modernity, 127; and names in DeLillo, 35; and posthuman (*see under* posthuman); and posthumanist, 29, 125–62 passim; and postmodernism/postmodernity, 125–62 passim; and rehumanization, 145, 156; and subject (*see under* subject); and technology, 131–56
(post)literacy (*see under* postmodern)
postmemoir or postmodern memoir, 28–30, 56–57, 235 n. 5; and apocryphal memoir, 29–30; and memorious memoir, 31, 33, 46; and "memorial" versus "memorious," 31, 52; and postmemory (*see under* memory)
postmodern: epoch, 74; landscape, 161; and modern (*see under* postmodern-

ism); perception, 51; (post)literacy, 38, 197, 205-23 passim, 248 n. 9; and representation (*see under* representation); turn, 40–41, 52–53, 192
postmodernism: and anonymity (*see under* onomastics); and Antin, 80, 241 n. 43; and appropriation, 17, 19, 21, 53, 113, 114, 117; and author (*see* author); and body (*see under* body); and bricolage (*see* bricolage); and critique, 36, 37, 158, 162, 164, 213, 215, 223, 248 n. 9 (*see also under* memorious discourse, reading, and representation); and cultural memory (*see* memorious discourse); and cyberpunk (*see under* cyberpunk); defined as memorious discourse (*see under* memorious discourse); double bind of, 36, 172; epistemology of, 108, 125; and ethics, 129, 233; and fictionality, 235 n. 7; and global/globalization (*see under* global/globalization); and history, 9, 37, 64, 233; and human (*see under* human); and identity, 97, 102, 239 n. 25; and intertextuality (*see* intertextuality); and invention, 172; and *le récit spéculaire*, 235 n. 1; Lyotard's, 169–72; and mimesis as imitation (*see under* mimesis); and modernism/modernity, 165, 167, 169–70, 181, 233; ontology/reality in, 29, 37–38, 129, 156–81, 187, 193, 195, 247 n. 6; and origin (*see under* origin); and originality (*see under* origin); and pastiche (*see* pastiche); and plagiarism (*see* plagiarism); and politics, 9, 19, 26, 37–38, 116, 166–80 passim, 195–96, 233, 247 n. 6; and posthuman/posthumanism (*see under* posthuman and posthumanism); and pragmatism (*see* pragmatism); and reading (*see under* reading); and spectrality, 235 n. 4; and recycling, 196; and relation/relatedness/relationality, 9, 21, 22, 26, 93, 116–17, 134, 142, 164–65, 193, 199–200, 208, 211, 219, 223, 230 (*see also* intertextuality); and representation (*see under* representation); and reprise (*see* reprise); and recycling, 16; retro drive of, 196; and self/selfhood (*see under* self/self-